READING LGBTQ+
CHILDREN'S PICTURE BOOKS

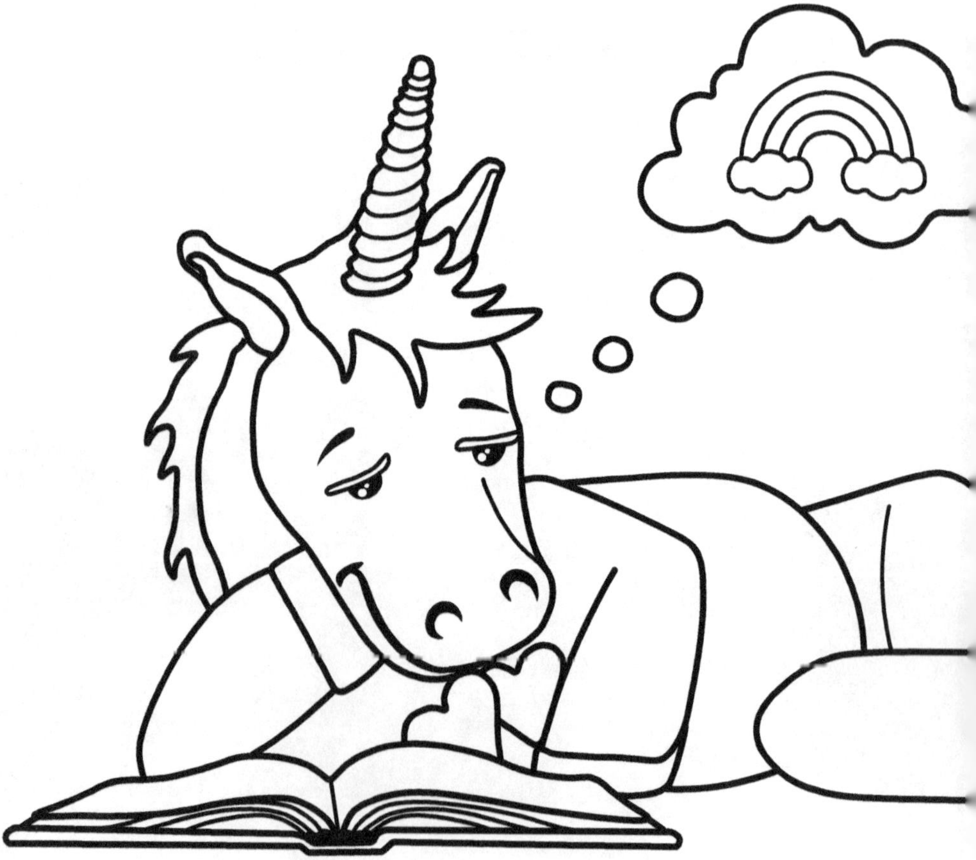

Children's Literature Association Series

READING LGBTQ+ CHILDREN'S PICTURE BOOKS

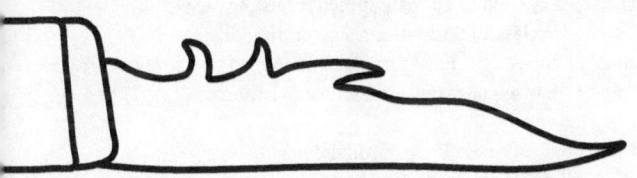

EDITED BY
JENNIFER MILLER
AND **SARA AUSTIN**

UNIVERSITY PRESS OF MISSISSIPPI
JACKSON

The University Press of Mississippi is the scholarly publishing agency of the Mississippi Institutions of Higher Learning: Alcorn State University, Delta State University, Jackson State University, Mississippi State University, Mississippi University for Women, Mississippi Valley State University, University of Mississippi, and University of Southern Mississippi.

www.upress.state.ms.us

The University Press of Mississippi is a member of the Association of University Presses.

Any discriminatory or derogatory language or hate speech regarding race, ethnicity, religion, sex, gender, class, national origin, age, or disability that has been retained or appears in elided form is in no way an endorsement of the use of such language outside a scholarly context.

Copyright © 2025 by University Press of Mississippi
All rights reserved
Manufactured in the United States of America
∞

Library of Congress Control Number: 2024043166

Hardback ISBN 9781496854902
Paperback ISBN 9781496854957
Epub single ISBN 9781496854919
Epub institutional ISBN 9781496854926
PDF single ISBN 9781496854933
PDF institutional ISBN 9781496854940

British Library Cataloging-in-Publication Data available

CONTENTS

CHAPTER 1: Reading LGBTQ+ Children's Picture Books:
An Introduction..3
Jennifer Miller

**PART 1: REPRESENTING LGBTQ+ FAMILIES IN
NORTH AMERICAN PICTURE BOOKS**

CHAPTER 2: From Roommates to Spouses: Shifting Representations
of Marriage Equality in US Picture Books from 1995 to 2020...........19
Jason Vanfosson

CHAPTER 3: "That's Not a Family": Microaggressions, Resilience,
and Agency in Depictions of Same-Sex-Parented Families.............37
Dana Rudolph

CHAPTER 4: Representation Matters Now More Than Ever:
Transgender and Nonbinary Parents in Children's Picture Books.......56
Rob Bittner

PART 2: REAL(ISTIC) REPRESENTATIONS OF GIaNTs IN PICTURE BOOKS

CHAPTER 5: Exceptional, Bullied, or Normal in the End:
Representation of GIaNTs (Gender Independent,
Nonbinary, and Trans) in Picture Books..........................79
j wallace skelton

CHAPTER 6: *Be Who You Are!*, *I Am Jazz*, *I'm Not a Girl*,
and *Sam!* Picturing Trans Childhoods..................96
Sara Austin

PART 3: MAPPING REPRESENTATIONS IN EUROPEAN PICTURE BOOKS

CHAPTER 7: The Road to Hell: Scandinavian LGBTQ+ Picturebooks....... 117
B. J. Woodstein

CHAPTER 8: Il y a plein de façons de composer une famille:
Some Recent French-Language LGBTQ+ Picture Books............... 135
Tim Morris

PART 4: QUEER(ING) CULTURE

CHAPTER 9: Many Dances, Many Regalias:
Supporting the Two-Spirit Child in *47,000 Beads*................... 153
Kaylee Jangula Mootz

CHAPTER 10: Queering Christmas: An Autoethnographic
Author Interview about Publishing *The Christmas Truck* 172
J. Bradley Blankenship

CHAPTER 11: *The Hips on the Drag Queen Go Swish, Swish, Swish*:
Playing Around with Gender and Celebrating Difference............ 189
J. River Vooris

PART 5: WORLD MAKING IN LGBTQ+ CHILDREN'S PICTURE BOOKS

CHAPTER 12: Apples Begone: Queer and Trans
of Color Aesthetics of Joy in ABC Books 207
Isabel Millán

CHAPTER 13: Children's Imagination and the Desire
for Something Different: Nonhuman Subjects in LGBTQ+
Children's Literature and the Possibility of More Just Futures 222
Caitlin Howlett

PART 6: LGBTQ+ NONFICTION CHILDREN'S PICTURE BOOKS

CHAPTER 14: AIDS and the Antisocial Subject in Queer Biographical Picture Books: A Case Study on Keith Haring 239
Gabriel Duckels

CHAPTER 15: Now vs. Then, Here vs. There: Queer Identity and Community in Picture-Book Biographies 255
Jennifer Miller

ACKNOWLEDGMENTS 277

ABOUT THE CONTRIBUTORS 279

INDEX 283

READING LGBTQ+ CHILDREN'S PICTURE BOOKS

CHAPTER 1

READING LGBTQ+ CHILDREN'S PICTURE BOOKS
An Introduction

Jennifer Miller

I'm a sucker for a good origin story, a tale of becoming that lingers on process, showing work that would otherwise be obscured behind the final product. So in addition to a methods section discussing *how* contributors produced their scholarship, this introduction also includes an origin story discussing *why* the collection was created and identifying the conditions of its emergence. After all, a constellation of opportunities and constraints inevitably shaped both the process and the product. As a result, the material conditions of knowledge production are elucidated throughout this introduction, mirroring discussions of the material production of lesbian, gay, bisexual, trans, queer, plus (LGBTQ+) picture books that are the focus of many essays in the collection.

Until quite recently, little scholarship about LGBTQ+ picture books existed despite the hundreds of titles available for study. However, since the 2010s, literary scholars have begun directing their analytical prowess at explicit LGBTQ+ representations in children's picture books. Just over a decade ago, significant scholarship began to appear, including work collected in Kenneth B. Kidd and Michelle Ann Abate's *Over the Rainbow: Queer Children's and Young Adult Literature* (2011), Jaime Campbell Naidoo's *Rainbow Family Collections: Selecting and Using Children's Books with Lesbian, Gay, Bisexual, Transgender, and Queer Content* (2012), and B. J. Epstein's *Are the Kids All Right? Representations of LGBTQ Characters in Children's and Young Adult Literature* (2013).[1] Kidd and Abate collected previously published scholarship about LGBTQ+ picture books and young adult novels, while Naidoo's project is bibliographic and includes brief summaries and evaluations of LGBTQ+

picture books. Epstein's early work is more analytical and considers the social-cultural work that picture books can do. Epstein, now known as Woodstein, continues to produce groundbreaking scholarship about LGBTQ+ children's picture books, including her recent coedited collection *International LGBTQ+ Literature for Children and Young Adults* (Epstein and Chapman; 2021) as well as a chapter in this collection. Both Naidoo and Woodstein see LGBTQ+ picture books as well as other cultural texts as playing a significant role in how children perceive themselves, each other, and the world.

Whereas Naidoo and Woodstein take an optimistic look at what LGBTQ+ picture books can do, much work in the early 2010s and the little that existed before that dismiss explicit LGBTQ+ representations as homonormative, didactic, and antiqueer. For instance, both Nathan Taylor's 2012 article "U.S. Children's Picture Books and the Homonormative Subject" and Jasmine Z. Lester's 2014 article "Homonormativity in Children's Literature: An Intersectional Analysis of Queer-Themed Picture Books" argue that explicit representations of LGBTQ+ characters are homonormative. Melynda Huskey's 2002 publication "Queering the Picture Book" is a forerunner of Taylor and Lester's critiques. Huskey describes LGBTQ+ picture books as politically ineffective. In fact, she argues that queerness is most present in books where explicit homosexuality is absent.

In line with this thinking, much of the existing work at the intersection of LGBTQ+ studies and picture books explores popular texts that lack explicitly queer representations. For example, many of the contributions in Kidd and Abate's collection queer popular children's literature or analyze lesbian and gay young adult fiction. A couple of notable exceptions identify and explore explicit representations, including Robert McRuer's "Reading and Writing 'Immunity': Children and the Anti-Body" and Elizabeth A. Ford's "H/Z: Why Lesléa Newman Makes Heather into Zoe." Additionally, Jody Norton's fascinating article "Transchildren and the Discipline of Children's Literature" is reprinted in the collection. With some important exceptions, the queerness Huskey and several authors in Kidd and Abate's collection reference is void of LGBTQ+ embodied experience, cultural specificity, and queer community.

Scant academic consideration doesn't mean that parents, bloggers, librarians, teachers, and other stakeholders haven't been thinking about, talking about, and writing about LGBTQ+ picture books. They have! Because of this, scholarship by picture-book creators, publishers, and bloggers who have celebrated and developed the field of LGBTQ+ picture books outside of academia is foregrounded in this collection alongside work by traditional scholars.

IN THE BEGINNING (AND MIDDLE AND END)

I spent 2020–21 revising my 2022 book *The Transformative Potential of LGBTQ+ Children's Picture Books* (Miller) while working as an English lecturer at the University of Texas at Arlington. The revision process involved responding to reader reports generated by experts in the field of children's literature. The reports were very enthusiastic—in fact, they demonstrated a desire for *more* genealogical, interpretive, and comparative work than I could accomplish in a single text. This prompted me to contact my editor at the University Press of Mississippi (UPM), Katie Keene, to suggest developing an edited collection of original scholarship about LGBTQ+ children's picture books. Katie was very supportive and brought the idea to UPM's editorial board. The board was similarly interested in publishing more work in the field of LGBTQ+ children's picture books.

While beginning to revise my manuscript, I also started the preliminary work of identifying possible contributors to an edited collection of LGBTQ+ picture books. I wrote a call for papers and circulated it on H-Net as well as in relevant social media groups. Additionally, I contacted academics, bloggers, creators, and scholars whose work in the fields of LGBTQ+ children's and young adult literature I admire. As such, this collection deliberately expands possibilities for acknowledging critical queer knowledge production beyond academia. Indeed, from the beginning, I worked to include cultural creators and critics with a variety of access points to the field of LGBTQ+ picture books as well as personal and political investments in the existence and shape of the field. For instance, Dana Rudolph has blogged about LGBTQ+ family life and culture since 2005. She is well positioned to provide nuanced overviews and readings of the field, including shifts in representations, which she does in her contribution to this collection. Additionally, picture-book author J. Bradley Blankenship provides fascinating insights into the process of creating and publishing picture books through an autoethnography formatted as an author interview. Further expanding these access points, j wallace skelton, cofounder of Flamingo Rampant Press, reflects on advocating for trans-inclusive children's books in public elementary schools. Other scholar-creators include Isabel Millán, who recently published the first bilingual Spanish-English picture book to depict two young girls in love. This book, *Chabelita's Heart* (2022), was published by Reflection Press, which also published the first bilingual Spanish-English picture book to depict two young boys in love, *Cuando Amamos Cantamos/When We Love Someone We Sing to*

Them (2018). I'm thrilled to offer a collection that includes contributors with such diverse access points to and experiences of LGBTQ+ picture books.

My decision to solicit contributions from variously positioned stakeholders was paired with a desire to include contributors with different gender and sexual as well as racial and ethnic identities. I also hoped to include more scholarship by marginalized scholars, particularly emerging scholars, and I was able to speak with some amazing graduate students, who were not quite able to commit to this project. My discussions with "the ones who got away" made me think about how little support graduate students researching and writing about LGBTQ+ picture books likely have since so few scholars working in the field hold university positions. Of course, this isn't to say that no one holding a tenure-track line researches in the field but rather simply that most of us don't. This led me to wonder what supporting scholarship untethered from academia might look like. As tenure-track positions dwindle, it seems about time to ask that question. I find that parallels between the lack of institutional support for LGBTQ+ picture books and scholarship about it reflect a continued commitment to regimes of heteronormativity that push queer culture and scholarship to the periphery—a token presence in dominant institutions, if that. But as I hope to demonstrate with this collection, we don't need academia to produce scholarship about LGBTQ+ children's picture books. In fact, in 2022, I left my precarious non-tenure-track position as an English lecturer at the University of Texas at Arlington and am now a high school English teacher in Texas. Because of changes to my professional life, I asked the brilliant Sara Austin to join me as a coeditor, which she graciously agreed to do. Without her support, expertise, and work ethic, this project would not have been completed.

As discussed above, contributors to this collection come from within, outside, and at the periphery of academia. Furthermore, those within academia have multiple academic homes—most notably, gender studies, education, and English. Contributors use a variety of research methods, disciplinary approaches, and interpretive frameworks to produce their scholarship about LGBTQ+ picture books. Many scholars have taken a genealogical approach. Overall, contributors agree that LGBTQ+ picture books are a queer-world-making project that can support young readers as they (1) negotiate the existing social world and develop resilience, (2) develop and articulate self-understanding, (3) imagine and enact self-advocacy and allyship, and (4) imagine unmitigated joy in difference and the possibilities of community without commensurability. This scholarship moves beyond considerations of specific books as "good" or "bad," "positive" or "negative," and toward considering the affective and social work they can accomplish, allowing us to think differently about the self, the other, and the world.

CHAPTER SUMMARIES

Part 1: Representing LGBTQ+ Families in North American Picture Books

Part 1 includes three chapters, all of which place the picture books analyzed within a larger, social, cultural, and political matrix that both enables and constrains representations and representational content. Furthermore, each author considers the work that cultural texts, such as picture books, may accomplish—for instance, modeling modes of agency, acceptance, and queerness. Two of the chapters—Jason Vanfosson's "From Roommates to Spouses: Shifting Representations of Marriage Equality in US Picture Books from 1995 to 2020" and Dana Rudolph's "'That's Not a Family': Microaggressions, Resilience, and Agency in Depictions of Same-Sex-Parented Families"—identify 2015 as the year representations of LGBTQ+ family life in picture books published in North America began to change, although each author focuses on different themes and texts. Vanfosson's contribution centers on representations of marriage. His close readings of picture books before and after 2015 demonstrate that the language used to describe same-sex couples, their unions, intimacy, and other content shifted significantly after marriage equality was secured in the United States. Rudolph's contribution focuses on picture books that represent children of same-sex parents negotiating microaggressions. Her thoughtful analysis demonstrates that representations of children parented by same-sex couples changed significantly after 2015. Rudolph shows that children were more likely to be represented as resilient social agents when confronted with microaggressions after the 2015 legalization of marriage equality. Additionally, Rudolph's research shows that the types of microaggressions shifted. Both chapters convincingly argue that LGBTQ+ picture books respond to social-political shifts, which I suggest makes LGBTQ+ youth literature a fascinating historical archive cataloging changing realities and, perhaps, even subtly shaping them since they are used, as Rudolph argues, as tools of resilience and, as contributor Rob Bittner suggests, as pedagogical aids that encourage social justice. Bittner's "Representation Matters Now More Than Ever: Transgender and Nonbinary Parents in Children's Picture Books" is, as the title suggests, a multifaceted exploration of representations of trans parents in picture books. Bittner explores many aspects of the texts he identifies—most notably, shifts in language available to authors to describe trans experiences. He takes a genealogical approach to build a convincing argument about shifts in language over time as well as the pedagogical motivations and possibilities embedded in the texts he discusses.

Part 2: Real(istic) Representations of GIaNTs in Picture Books

Part 2 focuses on representations of GIaNTs (gender independent, nonbinary, and trans) in picture books. In chapter 5, j wallace skelton explains,

> My four-year-old taught me that we need to pay more attention to the stories in the books to really see what kind of messages these books were sharing. My child wanted, in the words of Lavern Cox, "possibility models," and they wanted to imagine something beyond merely surviving or enduring bullying (@Lavernecox). My acronym "GIaNT" is a response to their need for possibilities. I use "GIaNT" to refer to gender-independent, nonbinary, and trans children as an intentional way of taking up space as GIaNT children have been made to be small for too long. It's part of my commitment to not just think about their identities but also honor, uphold, and celebrate them.
>
> My four-year-old's dissatisfaction launched me into analyzing picture books with GIaNT main characters, published in English between 1936 and 2015. I found 144 of them....
>
> ...This chapter puts trans theory to the task of analyzing these books. Trans theory demands that we "theorize transsexual and transgender experience on its own terms." (Rubin 279)

skelton's work explores erasure as a central concept by considering how, in the few texts that do center GIaNTs, other forms of identity erasure are prevalent, including the erasure of GIaNT children of different racial and ethnic groups as well as GIaNT children with disabilities.

Chapter 6, "*Be Who You Are!*, *I Am Jazz*, *I'm Not a Girl*, and *Sam!* Picturing Trans Childhoods" by Sara Austin, explores biographical texts about transgender youth. Austin suggests, "Readers can look for the real-world activism and experiences these picture-book protagonists are engaging in and see models and possibilities for transgender existence." The books Austin explores represent queer resilience and work normalizing transgender youth experience. Furthermore, by showing "systemic antitransgender bias in terms that young children can understand," these texts introduce representations of reality that encourage critical consciousness of social injustices and provide strategies of resistance.

Part 3: Mapping Representations in European Picture Books

Part 3 is certainly not an exhaustive catalog of European LGBTQ+ picture books, but I wanted to include explorations of LGBTQ+ representations in picture books beyond the United States to allow for cross-cultural consideration. Like contributions in the first part of the collection, B. J. Woodstein's chapter, "The Road to Hell: Scandinavian LGBTQ+ Picture Books," explores the relationship between political context and cultural content. Woodstein has produced extensive work about North American LGBTQ+ picture books, where, as seen in much of this collection, LGBTQ+ identities and experiences are often represented as problems to be solved. She anticipated Scandinavia's progressive political climate would encourage representations of unproblematized queer identities, but counter to her hypothesis, she identified a cultural lag between legal and political contexts and children's literature. Like several authors in the collection, Woodstein includes information about publishers to reflect on the gatekeeping context inhibiting queer representations in children's culture.

Her findings about Scandinavian picture books reflect those of scholars researching American children's culture. However, unlike American picture books, there are many family forms explored beyond gay and lesbian echoes of the heterosexual nuclear-family unit. Several of the books she identifies depict nonnuclear arrangements, including children parented by a gay couple and a lesbian couple as well as a same-sex parenting unit composed of two friends who are not romantically or sexually involved. Additionally, like Rudolph, Woodstein notes that books fail to explore multiple intersecting identities and represent cultural specificity. In Woodstein's archive, almost all characters are white, whereas Rudolph notes that when racially and ethnically diverse characters are present in LGBTQ+ picture books, cultural specificity is rarely, if ever, explored.

Tim Morris laments conducting his search of French picture books from a computer in the United States—an approach he adopted due to constraints imposed by COVID—instead of perusing bookshelves in France. Yet even from his computer, Morris was able to identify fascinating content. In chapter 8, he notes that much picture-book content reflects that found in US and Scandinavian texts, but there are notable exceptions. French picture books are far more likely to embrace negative affect—the bad feelings that can envelop queer experiences—which US and Scandinavian picture books, even when they gesture toward this emotional reality, refuse to dwell on. Along with negative affect, Morris has uncovered queer childhood crushes in France! We have so very few of these in US literature.

Part 4: Queer(ing) Culture

In chapter 9, Kaylee Jangula Mootz notes that the picture book *47,000 Beads* emphasizes gender as tied to one's role in the community rather than connected to the sexed body. The book also "answers the call of so many Two-Spirit authors, artists, and activists to create Two-Spirit stories that act as a road map for young Native people to follow," Mootz explains. These stories offer a path to embrace both gender identity and cultural or communal connection. In *47,000 Beads*, Peyton explains that she does not want to wear her jingle dress and that there are no dances "for kids like me" (Adeyoha and Adeyoha 8), and Eyota understands that Peyton is likely Two-Spirit and needs someone to guide her. With the help of Eyota, a Two-Spirit elder named L, and the rest of her family and community, Peyton begins to understand that she can be true to herself and that she has a place in the community regardless of what type of dance or what gender she feels fits her best.

Chapter 10, "Queering Christmas: An Autoethnographic Author Interview about Publishing *The Christmas Truck*" by J. Bradley Blankenship, is a deeply insightful autoethnography formatted as an author interview that provides critical insights into the publication process as well as the complex motivations for producing LGBTQ+ picture books. Blankenship details his own experience attempting to publish an LGBTQ+ picture book, including rejections based on assumed pushback from audiences not ready for a Christmas story about a family parented by gay dads. As mentioned, many contributors acknowledge the gatekeeping function of publishers and the challenges of publishing queer content, but Blankenship is uniquely positioned to discuss his firsthand experience with the process. In fact, Blankenship's autoethnography helps us understand why so many LGBTQ+ picture books are self-published. It's also fascinating to have access to Blankenship's reflections on intentionally blurring boundaries around race and gender identity while working with an illustrator, as well as other areas in which he worked to aesthetically queer the page, including the subtle yet deliberate inclusion of queer cultural references.

His intentions point toward new avenues for literary scholarship. Through his descriptions of how reading his book has inspired queer Christmas traditions, such as yearly readings at a Chicago-based feminist bookstore paired with a wishing tree to collect diverse book donations, Blankenship's contribution also shows the work queer picture books do in the world.

In chapter 11, "*The Hips on the Drag Queen Go Swish, Swish, Swish*: Playing Around with Gender and Celebrating Difference," J. River Vooris explains that "the books teach children about breaking free of the gender binary and the importance of self-love and self-expression," yet "the representations of drag in many of these books are disconnected from the lesbian, gay, bisexual, trans, queer, plus (LGBTQ+) community and do not address the historical connections between drag and the LGBTQ+ rights movement.... Historically, drag queens and children have been placed in opposition to each other, particularly in a culture that presumes that gay identities are adult identities (Stockton) and that adult sexualities are dangerous to children (Rivers; Halberstam; Talburt)." Exposure to drag allows children to imagine a world where diverse gender expressions are celebrated.

Part 5: World Making in LGBTQ+ Children's Picture Books

Chapter 12, "Apples Begone: Queer and Trans of Color Aesthetics of Joy in ABC Books" by Isabel Millán, posits the question, "How do authors mobilize queer and trans of color ABC books to reimagine their own communities—both within and off the page?" Millán is invested in reading abecedaries by queer and trans of color authors for the politics of justice and joy they envision for their readers. This chapter asks us not to dismiss ABC books when considering the children's literary canon of LGBTQ+-themed picture books. Although some queer ABC books may include characters of color, this subgenre is overwhelmingly white and cisgender. Responding to the call for more diverse books, ABC or alphabet books such as *M Is for Mustache: A Pride ABC Book* (2015) and *They, She, He: Easy as ABC* (2019) provide an idealized world where queer and trans children of color and their communities can experience love and joy while living their authentic selves. Millán contends that the books she explores model an idealized reality where various modalities of difference are celebrated. Millán lingers over representations of queer communities of color and the types of relationality and sociality that emerge in these images. Throughout, Millán convincingly claims that ABC books can help readers imagine a world of radical inclusivity. For Millán, the abecedaries explored in the chapter help readers, young and old, imagine and desire a world without "the injustices or prejudices that exist" systemic to the one we inherited.

It will become clear to readers that many contributors to the collection are critical of animal characters in LGBTQ+ picture books. Woodstein, for one, offers a particularly compelling critique. However, chapter 13, "Children's Imagination and the Desire for Something Different: Nonhuman Subjects in LGBTQ+ Children's Literature and the Possibility of More Just Futures" by Caitlin Howlett, suggests reading animal characters through a speculative framework might "cultivate curiosity, questioning, and imagination of a radical kind." The nonhuman characters Howlett considers inhabit an "imaginary world that does not abide by the rules of identity, through which many of us are still so restricted and confined." While recognizing the histories of dehumanization that render social-justice-oriented readings of nonhuman characters problematic, Howlett contends that the speculative and transformative potential of nonhuman characters should not be dismissed because of this history. Instead, if read through a speculative or imaginative lens that considers "absorption, transportation, estrangement, opening, and multispecies responsibilities," nonhuman characters have the ability to "open us up to new forms of resistance that might then inspire us to act and exist in new ways." Howlett offers compelling readings of the picture books discussed, framed through a speculative lens that encourages readers to rethink social relations through queer ethics modeled in the texts. Howlett's speculative readings of the text provide fascinating insights that refuse interpretive foreclosure, remaining open to imagining the world differently.

Part 6: LGBTQ+ Nonfiction Children's Picture Books

Chapter 14, "AIDS and the Antisocial Subject in Queer Biographical Picture Books: A Case Study on Keith Haring" by Gabriel Duckels, explores two interrelated questions: "How can the life stories of queer historical figures who are at once deeply political and highly sexual be constructed in texts for children?" and "How do these representational practices change or challenge the meanings of 'queerness' that young people are permitted to access within a dramatically expanded scene of youth-oriented queer visibility?" Duckels builds a nuanced argument about adult sexuality and childhood that refuses to construct them as oppositional, suggesting instead that both share an investment in pleasure. His chapter can be productively paired with Vooris's for a provocative take on the collapse of children's and queer cultures.

In the final chapter, "Now vs. Then, Here vs. There: Queer Identity and Community in Picture-Book Biographies," I update my recent publication *The Transformative Potential of LGBTQ+ Children's Picture Books*, which surveys the LGBTQ+-picture-book scene through 2018 and considers the transformative work that nonfiction can do. Specifically, I look at how contemporary queer picture-book biographies use time and space to differentiate between a homophobic rural past and a queer urban present. I discuss what these picture books do well and my concerns regarding the lack of community in certain books and the tendency to make homophobia seem like an issue of the past. I provide close readings of the words and images of these books, outlining possible pedagogical issues, as well as a chart for quick reference.

APPROACHING *READING LGBTQ+ CHILDREN'S PICTURE BOOKS*

The books chronicled and analyzed in these chapters represent a historical archive, showing and shaping queer experience in the material world. These books, at times, reveal the limits of our ability to imagine justice queerly (Duckels), although, perhaps, they also demonstrate our hope for justice beyond our current experience and social conceptions. Fascinating connections can be made across the contributions. Scholars have often been drawn to approaching picture books thematically and exploring representations genealogically to better grasp the evolution of specific representations and representational practices. Scholars have also recognized the importance of publishing context, often tracing distinctions among texts that are self-published, published by small, mission-oriented presses, and published by traditional presses. Finally, many contributors place the picture books they explore within a larger social-political matrix to consider how subfields of LGBTQ+ children's picture books have responded to social-political transformations.

As such, many contributors imply a claim that I explicate in my 2022 publication *The Transformative Potential of LGBTQ+ Children's Picture Books*—namely, LGBTQ+ picture books make up a fascinating historical archive that maps shifts in sociocultural understandings of gender and sexual identity as well as adult-child relationships. These chapters, as well as the books they discuss, work at queering concepts, from Christmas to childhood, that have often been conceptualized as antithetical to queer desire or identity. For instance, Duckels notes that Keith Haring's life and legacy elucidate the queerness of children and childhood while juvenilizing queerness and highlighting the play and pleasure associated with both childhood and queer desire.

Clearly, there are many, many ways one could cluster the brilliant contributions that comprise this collection. I want to note other shared investments, themes, and observations by showing my scrap work, or the other versions of this text that could have existed. Many authors note that queer culture is becoming far more available to youth (Vooris, Duckels, and Miller), but this is not an unmitigated success—sanitation remains the cost, as does increased public scrutiny from the Right, resulting in book bans and library closures.

Several scholars, including Bittner, Austin, Vooris, Duckels, and Miller, also consider the importance of naming queer expressions and identifications. In other words, how authors render queer identities visible matters. Although naming identities may seem antithetical to the blurring of boundaries that Blankenship associates with queer theory, it is significant for children to be able to articulate a self-understanding and connect to a larger community. In fact, many—particularly Vooris, Duckels, and Miller—note the absence of connection to a larger LGBTQ+ community in LGBTQ+ picture books. These scholars lament the absence of such community representation and point out how important that connection might be for children who currently feel isolated by their own gender, sexual identity, or familial difference.

Any or all of these throughlines could produce generative organizing principles for the chapters in this collection. When I imagine how this book might be used in a classroom or research setting, I encourage readers to rearrange the chapters in a way that provides the most useful structure for that project. If the chapters here and the project of collecting them has reaffirmed anything about knowledge production, it is that structural limitations—be they chapter order, university department, or job title—are artificial. Queer scholarship, therefore, encourages us to break down these barriers, to play with them, and to rearrange both the academy and ourselves into new and better versions and possibilities, allowing for the creation of a more just and vibrant future.

NOTE

1. B. J. Epstein is now known as B. J. Woodstein. Throughout this volume, these differing names are used depending on the context, such as which name a given publication was published under.

WORKS CITED

Adeyoha, Angel, and Koja Adeyoha. *47,000 Beads*. Illustrated by Holly McGillis, Flamingo Rampant, 2017.

Epstein, B. J. *Are the Kids All Right? Representations of LGBTQ Characters in Children's and Young Adult Literature*. HammerOn Press, 2013.

Epstein, B. J., and Elizabeth L. Chapman, editors. *International LGBTQ+ Literature for Children and Young Adults*. Anthem, 2021.

Ford, Elizabeth A. "H/Z: Why Lesléa Newman Makes Heather into Zoe." *Children's Literature Association Quarterly*, vol. 23, no. 3, 1998, pp. 128–33.

Halberstam, Jack. *The Queer Art of Failure*. Duke UP, 2011.

Huskey, Melynda. "Queering the Picture Book." *The Lion and the Unicorn*, vol. 26, no. 1, 2002, pp. 66–77. *Project Muse*, https://doi.org/10.1353/uni.2002.0005.

Kidd, Kenneth B., and Michelle Ann Abate. *Over the Rainbow: Queer Children's and Young Adult Literature*. U of Michigan P, 2011.

@Lavernecox. "@MTVact I prefer 'possibility model.' Some of my p. models: Leontyne Price and Eartha Kitt to name a few. #AskLaverne." *Twitter*, 14 Oct. 2014, 12:13 p.m., https://x.com/Lavernecox/status/522072765336416256?s=20.

Lester, Jasmine Z. "Homonormativity in Children's Literature: An Intersectional Analysis of Queer-Themed Picture Books." *Journal of LGBT Youth*, vol. 11, no. 3, July 2014, pp. 244–75. *ERIC*, https://doi.org/10.1080/19361653.2013.879465.

McRuer, Robert. "Reading and Writing 'Immunity': Children and the Anti-Body." *Children's Literature Association Quarterly*, vol. 23, no. 3, 1998, pp. 134–42.

Miller, Jennifer. *The Transformative Potential of LGBTQ+ Children's Picture Books*. UP of Mississippi, 2022.

Naidoo, Jamie Campbell. *Rainbow Family Collections: Selecting and Using Children's Books with Lesbian, Gay, Bisexual, Transgender, and Queer Content*. Libraries Unlimited, 2012. *Open WorldCat*, http://public.eblib.com/choice/publicfullrecord.aspx?p=894796.

Norton, Jody. "Transchildren and the Discipline of Children's Literature." *The Lion and the Unicorn*, vol. 23, no. 3, 1999, pp. 415–36.

Rivers, Daniel. "'In the Best Interests of the Child': Lesbian and Gay Parenting Custody Cases, 1967–1985." *Journal of Social History*, vol. 43, no. 4, 2010, pp. 917–43.

Rubin, Henry S. "Phenomenology as Method in Trans Studies." *GLQ*, vol. 4, no. 2, 1998, pp. 263–81. *Project Muse*, https://doi.org/10.1215/10642684-4-2-263.

Stockton, Kathryn Bond. *The Queer Child, or Growing Sideways in the Twentieth Century*. Duke UP, 2009.

Talburt, Susan. Introduction. *Youth and Sexualities*, edited by Eric Rofes and Mary Louise Rasmussen, Palgrave Macmillan, 2004, pp. 1–13.

Taylor, Nathan. "U.S. Children's Picture Books and the Homonormative Subject." *Journal of LGBT Youth*, vol. 9, no. 2, 2012, pp. 136–52.

PART 1

REPRESENTING LGBTQ+ FAMILIES IN NORTH AMERICAN PICTURE BOOKS

CHAPTER 2

FROM ROOMMATES TO SPOUSES
Shifting Representations of Marriage Equality in US Picture Books from 1995 to 2020

Jason Vanfosson

On June 26, 2015, the US Supreme Court handed down their ruling in the *Obergefell v. Hodges* case that authorized legal marriages between same-sex partners in all fifty states. Lesbian, gay, bisexual, trans, queer, plus (LGBTQ+) activists have advocated for marriage equality for queer communities for several years before this ruling, going as far back as 1970 when two men in Minnesota applied for a marriage license.[1] In fact, prior to the ruling, several states permitted civil unions and marriages for same-sex couples so that these couples might receive the same state benefits offered to other married couples. As a result of *Goodridge v. Department of Public Health* in 2004, Massachusetts became the first state to legalize marriages for same-sex couples.

Marriage equality has remained a contested, public debate but has also been a debate within queer communities. I will not replicate the public arguments for and against marriage equality here. These discussions have been well documented in other, accessible studies, but I do want to highlight this dispute within the context of queer histories. Kathleen Hull explicates a tension about marriage equality within queer discourses:

> Gays and lesbians have been debating the desirability and importance of same-sex marriage for years, and this intracommunity debate reflects deeper tensions and oppositions within gay and lesbian communities, conflicts over the political and cultural goals of the gay and lesbian movement and over the tactics used to accomplish those goals. In particular, the marriage question reveals a fault line among gay and lesbian activists and commentators, a divide between

those who embrace a rights-oriented approach to social change, viewing assimilation as the ultimate goal of gay and lesbian activism, and those who advocate a liberationist or "queer" ethic focused on deconstructing fixed sexual categories and transforming dominant cultural understandings of intimacy, sexuality, family and the state. (78–79)

Hull makes clear the motives in the debate for and against marriage equality within the larger queer liberation movement by emphasizing the conflict between assimilationist approaches and liberation-based approaches to gender identity and sexual orientation. The assimilationist practices and rhetorics give rise to "heteronormativity," a term popularized by Michael Warner in 1991 and defined as "the presumption and privileging of gender conformity, heterosexuality, and nuclear families over all other 'deviant' forms of gender expression, sexuality, and families" (Pollitt et al. 522). Heteronormativity, then, allows queer people to conform to the existing heterosexual models and systems that have otherwise oppressed individuals who identify as LGBTQ+ and participates in the continual oppression of others by replicating and reinforcing the systems of oppression rooted in heterosexism, such as marriage.

Resistance to marriage equality from queer activists also came from a differing agenda. Warner explains that, historically, marriage equality was "never a broad-based movement among gay and lesbian activists" (*Trouble* 85). Instead, he further highlights, "No one was more surprised by the rise of the gay marriage issue than many veterans of earlier forms of gay activism. To them, marriage seems both less urgent and less agreed upon than such items as HIV and health care, AIDS prevention, the repeal of sodomy laws, antigay violence, job discrimination, immigration, media coverage, military antigay policy, sex inequality, and the saturation of everyday life by heterosexual privilege" (84). Warner's statement elucidates that marriage equality, while important, has sometimes overshadowed more urgent fights for LGBTQ+ rights in the United States. Warner does not note, though, the ways that marriage equality can ultimately better some of these issues. For instance, marriage equality provides legal protections for spousal healthcare and access that are important in the fight for HIV/AIDS prevention and treatment.

These dialogues about marriage equality extend to the larger field of youth literature as well. Representations of marriages between same-sex couples in youth literature have shifted substantially since the marriage-equality ruling in 2015. In this chapter, I trace the development of marriage equality in picture books from 1995 to 2020 that were created and published in the United

States to understand the cultural messages young people receive about marriages between same-sex couples. These books can succinctly be classified as those published before 2015 and those published after 2015, when the ruling in *Obergefell v. Hodges* made marriage equality a legal right. Even though the depictions of marriage equality change during this time, all the depictions—except one—reinforce a heteronormative narrative of marriage that continues to exclude certain populations within the queer community and continues to question the place of marriage equality in larger queer-activist projects.

Traditional presses only published four picture books depicting same-sex marriage before the marriage-equality ruling in 2015: *Daddy's Wedding* (1996) by Michael Willhoite; *Uncle Bobby's Wedding* (2008) by Sarah S. Brannen; *Operation Marriage* (2011) by Cynthia Chin-Lee; and *Donovan's Big Day* (2011) by Lesléa Newman.[2] A few self-published authors also created picture books that address marriage for same-sex couples, such as Eric Ross's *My Uncle's Wedding* (2011), but these titles fall beyond the scope of this chapter since part of my analysis understands how publishers—ranging from independent presses to larger, mainstream publishing houses—reflect dominant ideas of marriage equality in the United States before and after the *Obergefell v. Hodges* ruling. Self-published books, however, can provide an important counternarrative by offering readers different models of marriage between same-sex couples that mainstream publishers could not or would not release for fear of disappointing sales or controversy.

The four books released before 2015 come from both specialized presses and imprints of major publishing houses. All these texts, though, focalize the story of marriage equality through a young person's perspective. *Daddy's Wedding*, *Operation Marriage*, and *Donovan's Big Day* feature the parents of a young person marrying a same-sex partner, while *Uncle Bobby's Wedding* centralizes the narration through a niece of the groom. These books share overwhelming similarities, and they all showcase the ways that queer stories of marriage equality circulated prior to the 2015 ruling.

Alyson Wonderland, a defunct imprint of Alyson Books that focused on producing LGBTQ+-inclusive picture books and the original publisher of the now-celebrated queer picture book *Heather Has Two Mommies* (1989) by Newman, published the first book for young readers to address marriage for same-sex couples. In 1996, Alyson Wonderland released *Daddy's Wedding* by Willhoite—a follow-up to Willhoite's controversial 1990 picture book *Daddy's Roommate*. In *Daddy's Wedding*, Willhoite tells the story of Nick, a child of divorce who learns that his father, Daniel, is going to marry Frank, who Willhoite previously introduced as Daniel's "roommate."

This initial representation of marriage for same-sex partners presents many challenges for a picture-book creator in 1996 because no laws or policies permitted two men to marry. Willhoite takes time to explain this point in the book and indicates that same-sex couples can instead have a commitment ceremony. After Daniel shares the nuptial news, Nick asks, "Can men get married to each other?" (Willhoite, *Daddy's Roommate* 7). Frank, not Daniel, responds, "We call it a commitment ceremony, Nick.... That's *like* a wedding" (8; emphasis added). Importantly, Frank sidesteps the question and does not directly answer if two men can or cannot marry one another. Instead, he provides an alternative name to a ceremony with which Nick is already familiar. Rather than having a "wedding," Daniel and Frank will have a "commitment ceremony." Despite this distinction early in the text, Willhoite continues to use the term "wedding" throughout the rest of the picture book. Frank's explanation is the only time in the book that the words "commitment ceremony" even appear. In titling the book *Daddy's Wedding* and only referring to the ceremony as a "wedding," Willhoite heteronormalizes the queer relationship between Daniel and Frank by relying on the exclusive heterosexual institution of marriage, even as the two men do not and cannot receive the same rights, benefits, and privileges associated with marriage for opposite-sex couples.

Another complication arises in *Daddy's Wedding* with the terms used to describe Daniel and Frank's relationship. Even though *Daddy's Wedding* serves as a companion book to *Daddy's Roommate*, it can be read independently, which provides an interpretive challenge. On the first page of the text, Willhoite illustrates a typical heterosexual, nuclear family. Nick's mother places a yellow tablecloth over a picnic table. A blonde man stands at a charcoal grill with a spatula and looks at Nick, who stands next to him holding a platter of raw chicken. From the text on the page, Nick identifies this blond man as his stepfather, Steven (Willhoite, *Daddy's Wedding* 1). This page establishes that Nick is familiar with wedding ceremonies and changing family dynamics as he has a mother, a stepfather, and a biological father. Yet throughout the text, Willhoite makes no attempt to define the relationship between Daniel and Frank as anything other than roommates. When Nick introduces the reader to the couple, he simply explains, "Daddy and his roommate Frank were the last to arrive" (4). Reading this text independently of *Daddy's Roommate* in which Willhoite defines gay as "one more kind of love," then, would indicate that Daniel and Frank marry as cohabitants of a space rather than as a queer couple (26). In her analysis of *Daddy's Roommate*, B. J. Epstein explains that "a euphemism may be employed in order to avoid referring to something openly because it is shameful or unacceptable. The euphemism 'roommate' might, therefore, suggest shame and taboo" (126). The insistence to continue using euphemisms in *Daddy's Wedding* continues this potential for "shame and taboo" even within the heteronormative institution of marriage. While, in some ways, this avoidance of defining marriage between same-sex partners refuses heteronormative language and frameworks, such as marrying for love or referencing "husband" and other hetero-patriarchal terms, it also positions queer relationships as inferior to heterosexual relationships by representing the marriage as one of roommates.

Even though Willhoite opts to refer textually to these men as "roommates"—albeit a common nomenclature for cohabiting, same-sex partners since before the 1990s—he illustrates Daniel and Frank in ways that represent the intimacy they share (Pleck 12). Specifically, Willhoite shows the two men kissing at the conclusion of their commitment ceremony, which obviously indicates a relationship more intimate than roommates. While Willhoite created the first picture book to represent marriage for a same-sex couple, there was not another picture book depicting a marriage ceremony in which the same-sex newlyweds kiss in an illustration until Jessica Love's *Julián at the Wedding*, published in 2020.[3] The tensions between the words and the illustrations of the picture book offer more interpretative possibilities for young readers who might encounter the book to understand LGBTQ+ marriage equality. Still, there remains the issue that the relationship is never defined in the book and, read independently from *Daddy's Roommate*, implies that marriages for same-sex couples are between platonic roommates.

Twelve years after Willhoite published *Daddy's Wedding*, G. P. Putnam's Sons published the second picture book addressing marriage equality. In 2008, Sarah Brannen released *Uncle Bobby's Wedding* about two male guinea pigs who decide to marry and start their own family. During a family picnic, Uncle Bobby announces that he is going to marry Jamie. All the guinea pig family members support the two except for Uncle Bobby's niece Chloe, who explains, "I don't understand! How can Uncle Bobby get married?" (Brannen [2008] 7). Chloe's confusion does not come from a place of homophobia in which she does not understand the potential of two male guinea pigs deciding to marry, but rather she says, "I don't want him to get married" because he "is my special uncle" (8). In this way, Brannen's book is less focused on the issue of marriage equality and more concerned with the way an uncle's marriage impacts the niece.

The normalization of marriage equality within Brannen's book, however, is facilitated by her use of guinea pigs instead of humans. In chapter 13 of this volume, Caitlin Howlett discusses the ways that authors use nonhuman subjects to explore issues relevant to queer lives yet also points out that "there is a long history of equating queerness in any form with the less than human, if not inhuman altogether" in picture books that address topics and themes related to LGBTQ+ experiences and representations (Howlett 223). Brannen's text, then, dehumanizes and relegates queer representation to the realm of animals. Interestingly, Brannen clearly acknowledges that this book should function as an anthropomorphic tale since she dedicates the book "to my family, and to all *people* who love each other" (emphasis added). The use of the term "people" on the dedication page—and the specific focus on *all* people who are in love—suggests that Brannen asks the reader to interpret *Uncle Bobby's Wedding* as an allegorical tale that uses guinea pigs as stand-ins for humans. Nonetheless, Brannen's depiction of marriage equality as exclusively among the realm of guinea pigs serves to dehumanize queer experiences and lives by denying human representations of marriage between same-sex couples at a time when marriage equality was starting to become legal in individual states, such as Massachusetts and Connecticut.

In 2011, Cynthia Chin-Lee's *Operation Marriage* appeared with illustrations by Lea Lyon. This book provides a new perspective of marriage-equality picture books by depicting the challenging political and social realities that nuclear, queer families face. The book is copublished by PM Press, which "is an independent radical publisher of books and media to educate, entertain, and inspire" ("About"), and Read and Teach, "a peace and social justice learning company dedicated to transforming the world through teachable moments" ("Welcome to Reach"). Even though marriage equality was slowly gaining acceptance nationally, at the time of publication of *Operation Marriage*, only "Connecticut, Iowa, New York, Massachusetts, New Hampshire, and Vermont perform[ed] same-sex marriages" (Chin-Lee 32). As more states began to afford legal marriages to same-sex couples and as national debates about marriage equality became more prominent, picture books depicting marriage equality began to include the complicated political and legal ramifications of marriage equality.

Chin-Lee tells the story of two lesbian partners, Kathy and Lee, who had a commitment ceremony prior to adopting their two children, Nicky and Alex. Based on a true story, Alex is teased at school by her best friend, Zach, whose homophobic father tells him that Alex's parents are not really married and that he can no longer be friends with her. Since the story occurs sometime between July and November 2008 in California, marriages for same-sex couples were a legal option in the state. This time was also when Proposition 8 was on the state ballot, which would again make marriage equality illegal in California.

The story centers on Alex and Nicky pressuring their moms to marry legally, which they ultimately do before Proposition 8 passes. Their marriage remained legal, even as other couples could no longer legally marry in the state.

Operation Marriage moves beyond other picture books before marriage equality by emphasizing the political and cultural implications of marriage equality in the lived experiences of queer couples. Whereas *Daddy's Wedding* equates a commitment ceremony to a wedding, Chin-Lee makes the distinction clearer. Mama Kathy and Mama Lee uphold a narrative that they are indeed married even though that marriage was not formally recognized by the state of California or the United States. Nicky begins to insist that his moms get married, to which Mama Kathy simply declares, "But Mama Lee and I are married" (Chin-Lee 7). As Nicky further questions his mom, Mama Kathy explains, "We had a commitment ceremony, but we couldn't get a marriage license back then.... [W]e've done everything possible to have the same rights as married people. You know that I've adopted both of you" (7). Mama Kathy differentiates the legal affordances offered to married couples—including expanded rights for adoptive families—and implies that commitment ceremonies are not unlike weddings in the performance, but marriages with marriage licenses offer additional rights and privileges that performative commitment ceremonies do not. Hull makes this discernment clearer in her 2006 study *Same-Sex Marriage: The Cultural Politics of Love and Law*:

> Marriage is increasingly available to American gay and lesbian couples in *cultural* terms, but remains mostly inaccessible in *legal* terms. Same-sex couples can use a range of cultural practices to define their relationships as marriages: public or private commitment rituals (which sometimes include the participation of religious officials), exchange of rings, use of marriage-related terminology to refer to their partners and their relationships. But same-sex couples are much more limited in their ability to access the legal dimension of marriage. (2)

Hull's explanation highlights the distinction that Chin-Lee attempts to delineate in *Operation Marriage*: even though same-sex couples can perform marriage ceremonies that are rooted in replicating heteronormativity (such as the rituals, rings, and lexicon Hull mentions), the legal affordances remain unavailable to these couples. Chin-Lee's book then emphasizes the way that, in 2011, the United States remained a heterosexist society that denied legal rights to couples in same-sex relationships.

In the same year that Chin-Lee published *Operation Marriage*, Lesléa Newman wrote and Mike Dutton illustrated *Donovan's Big Day* (2011) about a young boy's experience on the day that his two moms marry. Even though the book does not depart from many of the same tropes found in *Daddy's Wedding* and *Operation Marriage*, *Donovan's Big Day* indicates a major shift in the publishing industry's willingness to address marriage equality. Tricycle Press, which is an imprint of Random House, published the book in 2011—the same year that a Gallup poll indicated that 53 percent of Americans were in favor of marriage equality ("First Time"). This poll marked the first time that over half of the population approved of marriage equality for same-sex couples and reveals the growing acceptance of marriage equality in the United States, including in the children's publishing industry.

Even though *Donovan's Big Day* tells the story of a young boy preparing to participate in a ceremony, the book never names the ceremony or act. Throughout the text, Newman writes of "a very BIG day" that finds Donovan with "a very BIG job to do" (Newman, *Donovan's Big Day* 2; emphasis original). While Newman references the heteronormative institutions of marriage throughout—such as wearing a suit (9), walking down the aisle (20), and exchanging rings (22)—the terms "commitment ceremony" and "wedding" that Willhoite, Brannen, and Chin-Lee use remain absent in this text. In this way, I agree with a *Publisher's Weekly* review that criticized the book by asserting that "it's less about gay marriage than a child's wedding preparations—no matter who's getting hitched" (Review 130). Newman normalizes a wedding or commitment ceremony for same-sex couples, but her depiction ultimately refuses to engage the cultural and legal implications that Hull identifies in her study. Whereas *Daddy's Roommate* and *Operation Marriage* directly address the inequality of performative marriage between same-sex couples by showcasing the cultural and legal distinctions, *Donovan's Big Day* presents the marriage between two women as the smallest part of Donovan's day and only features the same-sex couple—and subsequently any allusion to the fact that the couple is a same-sex couple—in the final two spreads of the picture book. *Donovan's Big Day* avoids engaging rhetorics of queerness or the social, cultural, and legal implications of marriage for same-sex couples in 2011.

These four picture books were published between the years 1996 and 2015, yet the representation of marriage equality in books for young readers would soon expand exponentially. After the ruling of *Obergefell v. Hodges* in 2015, picture books depicting LGBTQ+ marriage equality became much more common and explicit starting in 2016. These depictions range from genderqueer and inclusive portrayals to politically charged books that call out specific politicians who actively seek to repeal and undermine the Supreme Court ruling. Noticeably, animals feature prominently in these texts, which indicates a hesitancy by publishers to humanize marriage equality despite the mostly positive representations. As publishers offer more examples of marriage equality of humans in picture books, affection and intimacy remain largely absent from the text and illustrations. Nonetheless, picture books published after 2015 that do feature human characters overwhelmingly represent interracial couples or exclusively nonwhite couples, which signifies a shift toward more inclusive picture books that acknowledge the intersections of race and queer identity, as well as honoring racial marriage equality won in the Supreme Court's case of *Loving v. Virginia* in 1967.

Balzer and Bray, an imprint of HarperCollins, released the first picture book to address marriage equality after it became legal in the United States. Written by J. J. Austrian and illustrated by Mike Curato, *Worm Loves Worm* (2016) follows two seemingly nongendered worms who decide to marry. As the opening spread succinctly explains, "Worm loves Worm. 'Let's be married,' says Worm to Worm" (Austrian 3). The following story focuses on the worms preparing for a wedding ceremony and the other insects who insist on following marrying conventions, even as Worm and Worm only wish to marry. The story concludes with the worms finally celebrating their love in a wedding ceremony of their own style.

Worm Loves Worm complicates the previous heteronormative marriage ceremonies found in picture books before 2015 by representing the tensions of marital and gender expectations commonly found in wedding ceremonies. As the worms move throughout the story, they are met with typical wedding traditions, such as an officiant, a wedding party, rings, cake, and, of course, a bride and a groom. Austrian and Curato never indicate the gender of either worm but rather refer to them as Worm and illustrate them neutrally as two brown worms. Still, when the time comes to get married, the bees, who are now the "bride's bees," ask, "But which one of you is the bride?" (Austrian 19). The response here initially places this as a wedding between a couple of same-sex worms since Austrian writes, "'I can be the bride,' says Worm. 'I can, too,' says Worm" (20). This exchange in which both worms volunteer to perform the role of bride indicates, at first, that it is two female-presenting worms that will wed. Significantly, though, the worms both articulate that they *can* be the bride to signify the ability to present or express a feminine gender. The worms can negotiate their gender presentations and focus on the marriage and love themselves rather than the gender pairing between the two. On this spread, Curato illustrates one of the worms in a white bridal gown who watches as Spider places a veil on the other. The veil and dress read as distinctively bridal and work to further the narrative that these are two female worms about to wed.

After the page turn, however, the narrative continues to complicate ideas of gender when Beetle simply asks, "But one of you has got to be the groom, or how can I be best beetle?" (Austrian 21). The worms respond in the same way they did to the bride question by both saying, "I can be the groom" (21). Here is the pivotal moment in which the creators reject a heteronormative framework of marriage and use gender to queer the marriage itself. Rather than having one worm relinquish the female-identifying characters to perform the role of the groom, both worms embody the bride and groom. The worm donning a veil now also wears a black bowtie and black, suit-like sleeve. Meanwhile, the worm dressed in a white gown accessorizes with a black top hat. The worms represent the groom and the bride in a way that breaks down the gender binary by placing markers of masculine and feminine gender expression on the worms' bodies. Importantly, the worms never state how they identify in terms of gender, but they do create and express their gender in queer ways that refuse male-female binaries and heteronormativity.

This refusal of heteronormativity becomes even more clear when right before the wedding, Cricket, the officiant, declares that having two worms expressing both masculine and feminine gender identities "isn't how it's always been done" (Austrian 24). This line—a common refrain from Cricket throughout the text—has a different meaning here because it directly correlates to a heteronormative understanding of marriage that relies on masculine and feminine pairings. In many moments throughout the book, Cricket expresses his disdain for the queer ways that the worms decide to marry and thus reinforces narratives of heteronormativity by historicizing the institution of marriage with this one line. Specifically, Cricket cites an officiant, rings, and a groom-bride pairing as "how it's always been done" (11). Collectively, these aspects of marriage are identifiable as traditional practices that align distinctly with a heterosexual marriage ceremony. Whenever Cricket references how weddings have historically been performed, the worms always address the issue and resist giving into Cricket's objections. For example, when Cricket notes that they need an officiant, Cricket volunteers. When Cricket points out that the worms need rings, the worms explain there are no fingers on which to wear them. Appeasing Cricket, the worms decide to "wear them like belts" (12). Even the exchange of rings become symbolically queer as the worms find innovative ways to reinscribe the exchange as belts instead of jewelry. In the next objection, Cricket explains that they need a bride and a groom, but the worms simply refuse and declare, "Then we'll just change how it's done" (24). In many ways, this line epitomizes the pervasive queerness in this book because it refutes the heteronormativity of a wedding ceremony *and* refutes the prescribed gender expectations surrounding weddings. By refusing to conform to gender expectations—or, more accurately, embracing gender expansiveness—the worms offer a new model of marriage equality that not only refutes heteronormativity but also complicates the ideals of gender expression through embodying both genders at the wedding ceremony.

Though *Worm Loves Worm* provides the first representation of marriage equality after *Obergefell v. Hodges*, more books would soon follow but take a different tone as the US political climate shifted as the result of Donald J. Trump winning the 2016 presidential election with Mike Pence as his vice president. In March 2018, just fourteen months after Trump and Pence were sworn into office, Pence's wife and daughter, Karen Pence and Charlotte Pence, respectively, collaborated on a picture book about the Pence family rabbit: *Marlon Bundo's a Day in the Life of the Vice President*. Just one day prior to the release, however, comedian John Oliver used his platform to create and promote another book about the bunny. Written by Jill Twiss—Oliver's senior writer for his weekly talk show—and illustrated by E. G. Keller, *A Day in the Life of Marlon Bundo* imagines a world in which the rabbit meets another male-identified rabbit named Wesley. The two fall in love within the day and soon marry—despite a stink bug resembling Mike Pence insisting that two boy bunnies cannot marry.

Charlotte and Karen Pence's book about Marlon Bundo seemingly keeps politics out of the narrative of the story. The reader watches Bundo hop alongside the vice president as he visits several offices and locations throughout his day-to-day agenda. The book ends, though, with Pence, known as Grandpa throughout the book, reading the Bible and praying at the close of the day. Significantly, Pence has used the rhetoric of religion as a way to promote anti-LGBTQ+ policy. For example, Pence employed religious ideology to sign the Religious Freedom Restoration Act (RFRA) as governor of Indiana on March 26, 2015, which, as Robert Katz observes, "Many [opponents] expressed concern over the Act's potential impact on local laws designed to protect LGBT individuals from discrimination" (37). Katz further explains that the RFRA offers a legal loophole for organizations and businesses to discriminate against LGBTQ+ folks based on religious beliefs (38). Even in a book about the former vice president's rabbit, the rhetoric of religion that Pence has used to forward anti-LGBTQ+ policy remains an essential part of Pence's narrative.

On the other hand, Twiss and Keller's *A Day in the Life of Marlon Bundo* critiques and, in some ways, parodies *A Day in the Life of the Vice President* and Pence's stance on LGBTQ+ rights. Twiss immediately distinguishes Marlon Bundo as anti-Pence. Marlon describes the vice president's residence as "stuffy" and explains, "This isn't going to be about [Pence], because he isn't very fun. This story is about me, because I'm very, very fun" (Twiss 3–4). By positioning the fun-loving Bundo against Pence, Twiss creates a book in which Pence's wrath of oppression cannot be escaped by anyone, including his own gay rabbit.

After Marlon and Wesley decide to "get married and hop together Forever" (Twiss 16), the couple announces to the local animals and insects their plans. Everyone—the bugs, the badger, the turtle, the hedgehog, and the dog—is excited and cheers for the engaged bunnies except Stink Bug, who forcefully declares from a pulpit, "You can't get married!" (19). In the following spread, Stink Bug elaborates, "I Am the Stinkiest and I Am In Charge. Boy Bunnies Marry Girl Bunnies. Girl Bunnies Marry Boy Bunnies. This is the Way It Has Always Been. You. Are. Different. Different Is Bad" (22). In this parody, Stink Bug is clearly meant to represent Mike Pence. After all, on July 18, 2006, in a congressional speech, Pence argued for a constitutional amendment that would legally define marriage between a man and a woman. He even asserted that "throughout history, societal collapse was always brought about following an advent of the deterioration of marriage and family" (M. Pence H5302). Stink Bug, then, espouses the same sentiments as Pence himself by defining marriage as between a man and a woman and referencing historical precedent that excludes marriage between same-sex partners. The end of Stink Bug's speech, too, has important implications as the message of "Different Is Bad" directly addresses queerness more broadly. Using Michael Warner's definition of "queer" as "a term defined against 'normal'" authorizes reading this scene as antiqueer because anything that is not "normal" according to Stink Bug is decidedly queer and consequently inferior ("Introduction" 16).

Keller's illustrations reinforce these parallels between Pence and Stink Bug by relying on visual signifiers. The other animals are featured in bright colors and are typically surrounded by white space, but Keller employs a grotesque green and orange mix that contrasts the otherwise colorful and bright animals. When Stink Bug first appears on the page, he stands atop a podium with a stink bug seal that is not unlike the seal seen at official White House events. To make the comparison even more apparent, Keller also gives Stink Bug a white, comb-over hairstyle that matches Pence's hair. None of the other animals have any natural human features added, such as hair, which highlights the visual iconography that Keller relies on to cement the parallels between Stink Bug and Pence. Finally, Stink Bug also has a red necktie and white shirt collar around his neck that replicates the red tie that Pence dons in his official White House portrait (Cullen). The visual signifiers and anti-marriage-equality rhetoric collectively construct and critique Pence by making him a disgusting bug that is unanimously voted out of his "in-charge" position and removed from the book by screaming wildlife so the bunnies can marry and celebrate their love.

While *Worm Loves Worm* and *A Day in the Life of Marlon Bundo* feature wedding ceremonies after marriage equality in the United States, these books still use allegorical storytelling that tells of worms and bunnies marrying rather than humans. Daniel Haack, however, provides two picture books that end with a same-sex marriage. *Prince and Knight* (2018) and *Maiden and Princess* (2019) use structures commonly associated with the fairy tale genre to depict marriages that result in the common happily-ever-after conclusions.

In *Prince and Knight*, which was published less than three months after the Bundo books, a king and queen realize that their son will soon ascend to the throne and, as such, must be married to take over the kingdom. While many women attempt to court the prince, a dragon attacks the kingdom, so the prince goes to battle. There, he meets a knight, and they fall in love and get married. Even though this is the first picture book to feature human characters in a wedding for a same-sex couple after the *Obergefell v. Hodges* ruling, the book does not represent the ceremony in the text or illustrations. Instead, Haack concludes the book with, "And on the two men's wedding day, the air filled with cheer and laughter, for the prince and his shining knight would live happily ever after" (33). Even though Haack avoids discussing the wedding ceremony at all, this instance is the first time that a US author uses the term "wedding" independently of "commitment ceremony" for human characters. This shift is likely the result of the legal rights garnered for same-sex couples after 2015 since authors no longer needed to distinguish between cultural and legal definitions of marriage. Stevie Lewis, the illustrator, also evades depicting the wedding ceremony by rendering the couple closely dancing on the facing page while the women who previously tried to court the prince, the prince's and the knight's parents, and some villagers gaze upon the newlyweds. The refusal to portray the ceremony in a textual or visual way highlights the continued hesitancy by publishers to represent marriage equality in mainstream books for young readers.

The next year, Haack coauthored *Maiden and Princess* with Isabel Galupo to tell a similar story, but this time, the book focuses on two female characters marrying at the end. In this story, a king and queen search for a bride for their son by throwing a ball. The maiden attends at the insistence of her mother, who knowingly coaxes her by explaining, "The prince might not be right, but you could meet the one" (Haack and Galupo 10). The mother encourages the potential of a same-sex pairing since the ball is presumably attended by women hoping to catch the prince's eye. She also avoids gendering the maiden's potential partner but rather allows for the queer possibility of a same-sex union by using the genderless phrase "the one." At the ball, everyone (including the king and queen) tries to pair the prince with the maiden since they know each other so well from battling together. However, the maiden ends up needing a break from this heterosexual pressure and ends up speaking with the princess, who she falls in love with. They spend their days together and eventually marry and receive the requisite happy ending.

Like in *Prince and Knight*, the wedding again happens off the page in *Maiden and Princess*. In this book, the wedding is only alluded to textually and never visually. Haack and Galupo write in the final spread of the book, "When the day finally came to prove their love was true, the maiden and the princess happily said, 'I do'" (33). On the facing page, the maiden and the princess soar together over the land on the back of the maiden's pet dragon. While there are thirteen indistinguishable silhouettes in the bottom corner of page 33 waving at the maiden and princess, the illustrator, Becca Human, emphasizes the couple leaving the kingdom instead of a ceremony or even a celebration, like in *Prince and Knight*.

Still, *Maiden and Princess* makes much progress in the canon of marriage-equality representations. Even though the wedding is off the page, this is the first picture book to feature a same-sex kiss that also addresses marriage equality since *Daddy's Wedding* in 1995. After the maiden and princess develop their attraction to one another, they share in a dance together. The narrator of the book relates, "They held each other close as they spun across the floor. And when they shared a kiss? Their hearts began to soar" (Haack and Galupo 29). Not only does Haack and Galupo reference the kiss, Human illustrates the two as kissing in a spotlight on the dance floor. They are in a circle of onlookers—including the prince and knight from Haack's earlier book—who gaze excitedly at the romantic and intimate moment between the two women. By representing this kiss, Human departs from a tradition of showing same-sex humans in picture books as not physical or affectionate with one another beyond a hug or holding hands.

Collectively, *Prince and Knight* and *Maiden and Princess* offer these initial, human depictions of marriages between two same-sex humans in a post-marriage-equality United States. Haack and Galupo rely on fairy tale motifs to create this human possibility that focalizes marriages between same-sex couples, as opposed to previous books that focalize the story through animals or adjacent children. By engaging traditional and popular fairy tale conventions that often end with a marriage—such as "Cinderella," "Sleeping Beauty," and "Beauty and the Beast"—Haack and Galupo design a narrative possibility in which the main characters themselves are married. It is noteworthy that in modeling these stories after common fairy tales, the authors use elements of fantasy that implicitly place marriage equality as something otherworldly and part of the fantastic. While I am certainly not advocating for representations of young children taking vows of marriage, queer youth deserve representation that is both realistic and not focalized through a young child trying to understand and come to terms with the queerness of marriage equality as previously represented. These renderings suggest that even though marriage equality offers same-sex couples the right to marry, the acceptance of marriages for same-sex couples remains something unseen as the books never depict these marriages. Still, Haack's judicious use of the fairy tale motifs offers young readers a way to reimagine the compulsory heterosexuality prevalent in most fairy tales and their mainstream adaptations.

Building on the representations found in Haack and Galupo's books, Sarah S. Brannen republished her 2008 book *Uncle Bobby's Wedding* in 2020 with new illustrations and a slightly revised text. The publisher also moved from Putnam to Little Bee Books, where it was published in partnership with the Gay and Lesbian Alliance against Defamation (GLAAD), which has a stated commitment to "integrating and elevating positive LGBTQ representation in children's literature" ("GLAAD"). Brannen's book particularly demonstrates one of the key developments of marriage-equality representations in picture books. In the 2008 edition, Brannen illustrates the characters as anthropomorphic guinea pigs, whereas the 2020 edition includes new human illustrations by Lucia Soto. In an interview with Dana Rudolph for her blog, *Mombian*, Brannen explains, "The new editor wanted to publish the book with new illustrations, showing people instead of animals. I had chosen animals originally to make the story universal, but I really wrote it about people. Maybe animals made the story more accessible in 2008, but in 2020, it seems appropriate to let my characters inhabit their true form" ("New Edition"). Despite Brannen's claim that the animals allow the story to be more "universal" and "accessible," *Uncle Bobby's Wedding* is the only picture book that includes a same-sex wedding before 2015 using animals instead of human characters.

The 2020 edition of this book, then, is the first picture book to depict textually *and* visually a human wedding after marriage equality in the United States. As such, this book reflects larger cultural acceptance of same-sex marriages; however, like all the books depicting marriage equality prior to this one, Brannen still uses a heteronormative framework to describe marriage equality to young people. This book, more than the others, deploys a didactic tone to explain marriage—whether of same-sex couples or not. For example, Chloe's mom explains that "when grown-up people love each other that much, sometimes they get married" (Brannen [2020] 9). When Chloe asks Uncle Bobby why he insists on getting married, he shares, "Jamie and I want to live together and have our own family" (11). The mother's response interestingly roots marriage in adult love, whereas Uncle Bobby focuses on replicating heteronormative ideas of cohabitation, family, and reproduction. Uncle Bobby's justification to Chloe about his upcoming marriage suggests that marriage is the only way that he can share a home with Jamie and the only acceptable avenue to a family, which Chloe interprets as wanting children and Uncle Bobby confirms (11). This response, of course, negates numerous family structures that are not built on cohabitation, marriage, or reproduction and serves to replicate heterosexual institutions and frameworks within a same-sex relationship and a young person's understanding of the relationship.

The depictions of marriage equality in picture books since 1995 have reflected the major cultural and legal attitudes toward marriage between same-sex couples. All the human representations after 2015 feature interracial, same-sex couples, thereby showcasing the intersections of racial marriage equality and LGBTQ+ marriage equality. Nonetheless, more depictions advocating for more expansive understandings of marriage are needed. In addition to the overwhelming heteronormative representations found in the books considered in this chapter, these picture books exclusively focus on lesbian and gay couples and do not discuss the ways marriage operates differently for bisexual, trans, and queer people. For example, none of the published works currently address the trans experience and the ways that trans people can still be denied rights—such as healthcare and adoption rights—in spite of their marital status. Even though marriage equality has expanded the legal and cultural ideas of marriage, the institution of marriage remains accessible only to those in a couple relationship. Any other model of relationship, such as polyamory, continues to be excluded from legal protections and rights. As marriage equality has offered more acceptance for marriages for interracial couples and same-sex couples, we must continue to consider the implications of celebrating heterosexual institutions within queer communities while also remaining vigilant of the many continued fights for civil rights the LGBTQ+ community faces.

NOTES

1. For clarity, I use the term "marriage equality" to specifically reference LGBTQ+ marriage equality. When necessary to distinguish between racial marriage equality and LGBTQ+ marriage equality, I use the appropriate terms. I also follow the Gay and Lesbian Alliance against Defamation's recommendation, which suggests "preferred terminology includes marriage equality and marriage for same-sex couples. Note, the terms 'gay marriage' and 'same-sex marriage' should be avoided, as they can suggest marriage for same-sex couples is somehow different than other marriages" ("In Focus").

2. In 2002, Tricycle Press published an English translation of *King and King*, by Linda de Haan and Stern Nijland, in which Prince Bertie and Prince Lee fall in love and get married at the end of the story. This book, however, does not meet the criteria for the text set of this essay since it was originally written and published in the Netherlands in 2000 and this chapter centers specifically on US created texts and contexts.

3. Daniel Haack and Isabel Galupo's *Maiden and Princess*, published in 2019, includes an illustration of the titular characters kissing after first meeting but not during any marriage ceremony or afterward.

WORKS CITED

"About." *PM Press*, https://blog.pmpress.org/about/. Accessed 19 June 2021.
Austrian, J. J. *Worm Loves Worm*. Illustrated by Mike Curato, Balzer and Bray, 2016.
Brannen, Sarah S. *Uncle Bobby's Wedding*. Illustrated by Brannen, G. P. Putnam's Sons, 2008.
Brannen, Sarah S. *Uncle Bobby's Wedding*. Illustrated by Lucia Soto, Little Bee Books, 2020.
Chin-Lee, Cynthia. *Operation Marriage*. Illustrated by Lea Lyon, Read and Teach / PM Press, 2011.
Cullen, Myles D. *Mike Pence: Official White House Portrait*. 24 Oct. 2017. *The White House*, https://trumpwhitehouse.archives.gov/people/mike-pence/.
Epstein, B. J. *Are the Kids All Right? Representations of LGBTQ Characters in Children's and Young Adult Literature*. HammerOn Press, 2015.
"For First Time, Majority of Americans Favor Legal Gay Marriage." *Gallup*, 20 May 2011, https://news.gallup.com/poll/147662/First-Time-Majority-Americans-Favor-Legal-Gay-Marriage.aspx.
"GLAAD and Bonnier Publishing USA Announce Children's Book Publishing Partnership." *GLAAD*, 17 May 2018, https://www.glaad.org/releases/glaad-and-bonnier-publishing-usa-announce-children%E2%80%99s-book-publishing-partnership.
Haack, Daniel. *Prince and Knight*. Illustrated by Stevie Lewis, Little Bee Books, 2018.
Haack, Daniel, and Isabel Galupo. *Maiden and Princess*. Illustrated by Becca Human, Little Bee Books, 2019.
Hull, Kathleen. *Same-Sex Marriage: The Cultural Politics of Love and Law*. Cambridge UP, 2006.
"In Focus: Family and Parenting." *GLAAD Media Reference Guide*, 11th edition, *GLAAD*, 27 Feb. 2024, https://glaad.org/reference/family.
Katz, Robert. "Indiana's Flawed Religious Freedom Law." *Indiana Law Review*, vol. 49, no. 1, Dec. 2015, pp. 37–56. *EBSCOhost*, https://doi.org/10.18060/4806.0060.
Love, Jessica. *Julián at the Wedding*. Candlewick, 2020.
"New Edition of LGBTQ Picture Book '*Uncle Bobby's Wedding*' Is Brighter, Bolder, and More Human." *Mombian*, 12 May 2020, https://mombian.com/2020/05/12/new-edition-of-lgbtq-picture-book-uncle-bobbys-wedding-is-brighter-bolder-and-more-human/.

Newman, Lesléa. *Donovan's Big Day*. Illustrated by Mike Dutton, Tricycle Press, 2011.

Newman, Lesléa. *Heather Has Two Mommies*. Illustrated by Diana Souza, In Other Words, 1989.

Pence, Charlotte. *Marlon Bundo's a Day in the Life of the Vice President*. Illustrated by Karen Pence, Regnery Kids, 2018.

Pence, Mike. *Congressional Record, V. 152, Pt. 11, July 13, 2006, to July 24, 2006*. US Government Printing Office, 2010.

Pleck, Elizabeth H. *Not Just Roommates: Cohabitation after the Sexual Revolution*. U of Chicago P, 2012.

Pollitt, Amanda M., et al. "Heteronormativity in the Lives of Lesbian, Gay, Bisexual, and Queer Young People." *Journal of Homosexuality*, vol. 68, no. 3, Feb. 2021, pp. 522–44. https://doi.org/10.1080/00918369.2019.1656032.

Review of *Donovan's Big Day*, by Lesléa Newman, illustrated by Mike Dutton. *Publisher's Weekly*, 21 Feb. 2011, p. 130.

Ross, Eric. *My Uncle's Wedding*. Illustrated by Tracy K. Greene, CreateSpace, 2011.

Twiss, Jill. *A Day in the Life of Marlon Bundo*. Illustrated by E. G. Keller, Chronicle Books, 2018.

Warner, Michael. "Introduction: Fear of a Queer Planet." *Social Text*, no. 29, 1991, pp. 3–17. *JSTOR*, https://www.jstor.org/stable/466295.

Warner, Michael. *The Trouble with Normal: Sex, Politics, and the Ethics of Queer Life*. Harvard UP, 2000.

"Welcome to Reach and Teach." *Reach and Teach*, 26 Mar. 2020, https://shop.reachandteach.com/welcome-reach-and-teach.

Willhoite, Michael. *Daddy's Roommate*. Illustrated by Willhoite, Alyson Wonderland, 1990.

Willhoite, Michael. *Daddy's Wedding*. Illustrated by Willhoite, Alyson Wonderland, 1996.

CHAPTER 3

"THAT'S NOT A FAMILY"
Microaggressions, Resilience, and Agency in Depictions of Same-Sex-Parented Families

Dana Rudolph

Since the early 1980s, one of the most common plotlines of picture books featuring children with same-sex parents has involved a child experiencing microaggressions about their family or feeling that it was in some way different.[1] "Microaggressions" are "brief and commonplace daily verbal, behavioral, or environmental indignities, whether intentional or unintentional" that communicate "hostile, derogatory, or negative" messages to a marginalized group (Sue et al. 271). Originally a concept used to describe a form of racial discrimination, microaggressions can also be based on sexual orientation or transgender identity (Nadal et al.).

At least eleven books have used such a theme, and they seem very similar at first. Nine involve incidents at a school. Nine protagonists are girls. Seven involve children with only moms. Six show a child drawing a picture of their family as a way of responding to microaggressions. Yet a closer look reveals not only different types of microaggressions but also different ways the children show resilience (defined as "good outcomes in spite of serious threats to adaptation or development" [Masten 228]) and differences in how much agency they demonstrate.

Social science research confirms that real children with same-sex parents may experience microaggressions and stigma about their families, so it stands to reason that these books serve as important models of resilience while also validating children being raised by parents (Farr et al. 93; Litovich and Langhout 430; Gartrell et al., "Mothers" 546). Real-life microaggressions may involve overt teasing, derogatory comments, or discrimination but can also include the assumption of a heterosexual norm (for example, when peers ask a child with two dads, "Where's your mom?"), public outing of details about a child's family, having others question the legitimacy of their family, or being asked lots of questions about same-sex parent families (Farr et al. 93). All these types of microaggressions appear in the eleven books discussed in this chapter. The books thus reflect the types of incidents that children with same-sex parents may actually encounter.

Social science research also shows that children with same-sex parents often demonstrate resilience when confronted with microaggressions (Farr et al. 94–96; Gartrell et al., "Mothers" 546–47; Gartrell et al., "10-Year-Old Children" 522; Goldberg et al., "Talking about Family," 111). There is evidence that resilience among children with same-sex parents is not necessarily gained after negative experiences; it can be built beforehand by internalizing positive messages about their families (Farr et al. 96). These realities are reflected in the picture books explored here, which I suggest may serve as tools for resilience in same-sex-parented families.

My analysis of these books reveals a gradual but nonlinear chronological shift toward greater initial resilience and increased agency by the protagonists, with the greatest shift around 2015, the time that the battle for marriage equality was culminating in the United States. There is also a shift in the microaggressions depicted. Prior to 2015, children were more likely to experience microaggressions expressing disbelief that families like theirs could exist. After this time, microaggressions have tended to involve misunderstandings of how a same-sex-parented family works or institutional assumptions of heterosexuality but not the families' existence and legitimacy.

These shifts reflect the growing visibility and acceptance of same-sex parents and their children in the media, law, and everyday life, which were given significant momentum by the marriage-equality movement that placed the well-being of children at its heart. Concerted attempts to secure marriage equality began in the 1990s ("Winning the Freedom"). In 2004, Massachusetts became the first state to enact it (after the 2003 Massachusetts Supreme Judicial Court ruling in *Goodridge v. Department of Public Health*). Four of the seven plaintiff couples in *Goodridge*—including the lead couple—were parents, and the ruling emphasized the impact of marriage on children, noting, "For those who choose to marry, and for their children, marriage provides an abundance of legal, financial, and social benefits" (Massachusetts State Supreme Judicial Court 312–14). In the wake of the decision, one study found that nearly 70 percent of Massachusetts same-sex couples surveyed "felt more accepted by their communities" after marriage (Ramos et al. 1); another study of lesbian, gay, bisexual, and queer individuals in Massachusetts found that two-thirds of respondents felt that simply having *access* to legal marriage brought with it "acceptance and social inclusion" whether or not they were actually married (Ocobock 375). The mere possibility of marital recognition for same-sex couples, I believe, helped other people understand that same-sex relationships were very much like their own, which helped bolster acceptance.

After 2004, some states followed Massachusetts in enacting marriage equality, while others passed laws against it. The next decade also saw numerous other advances toward the acceptance and equality of same-sex parents and their children. In 2013, the US Supreme Court ruling in *United States v. Windsor* tore down part of the Defense of Marriage Act (DOMA) and extended federal protections to same-sex married couples. In *Windsor*, too, one of the key arguments was that children with same-sex parents were as well adjusted as any others but suffered from stigma because their parents could not marry. This child-centered approach was a response to opponents' argument that children do best when raised by one mother and one father (NeJaime 1236). The ruling notes, "[DOMA] humiliates tens of thousands of children now being raised by same-sex couples . . . [and] makes it even more difficult for the children to understand the integrity and closeness of their own family and its concord with other families in their community and in their daily lives" (United States Supreme Court, *Windsor* 23). Variations of that argument were then used to win almost every other federal decision on marriage equality through late 2014, except for the one in the Sixth Circuit, which ruled against marriage equality and thus precipitated its hearing before the Supreme Court in *Obergefell v. Hodges*. That case, in which most of the plaintiffs were parents, was heard by the court in April 2015.

When US Supreme Court justice Anthony Kennedy wrote the majority opinion in *Obergefell* in June 2015, legalizing marriage equality nationwide, he noted, "Without the recognition, stability, and predictability marriage offers, children suffer the stigma of knowing their families are somehow lesser" (United States Supreme Court, *Obergefell* 3). While marriage equality did not remove all inequalities for same-sex couples and their children, it has helped lift some of this stigma.

Framing my reading of lesbian, gay, bisexual, trans, queer, plus (LGBTQ+) picture books through the history of marriage equality as well as social science research about microaggressions, agency, and resilience demonstrates how culture texts like picture books reflect and respond to larger social contexts. Additionally, my chapter shows that picture books not only reflect childhood agency and resilience, but they also model it. As such, these texts can be used to help children with same-sex parents feel part of a community of queer families, build confidence, and identify concrete strategies that help them negotiate stigma.

EARLY BOOKS

In the two earliest books depicting children of same-sex parents experiencing microaggressions—*Lots of Mommies* (1983) by Jane Severance and *Heather Has Two Mommies* (1989) by Lesléa Newman—neither protagonist begins with many tools for resilience. *Lots of Mommies* focuses on a girl being raised jointly by four women. While none are definitively queer, queerness seems likely in this all-women, coparenting household. Their daughter, Emily, is initially nervous on her first day of school but soon begins a conversation with some other children. When they start discussing their family members, a boy asks her, "What do you have?" (Severance 18). She wonders, "Was there a word for what she had?" (18). She and her parents have clearly not spoken about this. When she says she has "lots of mommies," the other children say, "That's dumb," and call her a liar (20). They cannot even imagine a family with more than one mom.

Emily "felt like crying" and tries to find the teacher, who has met two of her moms, but the teacher is busy with other students (Severance 20). Emily does not have a response except to leave the scene. She goes to play on the jungle gym alone and finds comfort in knowing that she has met families of different types, even though she was unable to express this. She then falls and hurts her arm. The teacher comes over and asks if her mother is still around but does not, as Emily had hoped, understand that she has more than one mother. Despite having met two of the moms, the teacher does not acknowledge more than one as a parent.

It is only when all four mothers arrive that the children realize Emily told the truth about her family. When three of her moms must return to work and the other asks if she wants her to stay, Emily responds, "No, I'm okay now" (Severance 34). She could be talking about her arm, her sense of being accepted, or both. The text is perhaps intentionally ambiguous so as not to fully confront the initial challenge to Emily's family form. In this early book, Emily is a passive observer who looks on as the other children learn a lesson. She doesn't seek adult assistance or even fully articulate the issue to herself.

Heather Has Two Mommies has gone through several editions since it was first published in 1989. In this chapter, I focus on the original edition and the significantly revised 2015 edition. The 1990 edition was a republication of the original; the 2000 edition is substantially the same, although a section on how Heather's parents met and started their family was cut and the overall text shortened. The 1989 version involves a first-day situation, like *Lots of Mommies*, though for a playgroup, not school. Heather cries a little when her moms drop her off at the caregiver's house but soon settles in. When the caregiver reads the children a story about a boy whose father is a veterinarian, two of the boys in the group mention their own fathers.

This leads to the pivotal moment. "'I don't have a daddy,' Heather says. She'd never thought about it before. Did everyone except Heather have a daddy? Heather feels sad and begins to cry" (Newman, *Heather* [1989] 21). Like Emily, she's pained to the point of tears. There is no real microaggression here (although this changes in the 2015 version, as I discuss below), but Heather has never before felt that her family lacked something, and the thought causes her distress.

Heather, who is still not in school and thus younger than Emily, does not even get the chance to ask for help. The playgroup facilitator immediately steps in to reassure her she's not the only one without a daddy. She then has the students draw and display pictures of their variously structured families. Heather happily shows her picture to her moms when they come to pick her up. She has learned to take pride in her family after realizing its difference but still needed the teacher to initiate the lesson. Both she and Emily ultimately learn resilience but do not display much agency in addressing their situations.

GAINING CONFIDENCE

The next three books show children all actively seeking and receiving help from their parents in the face of microaggressions and demonstrating more agency while still facing significant invalidations of their families.

In *Asha's Mums* (1990) by Rosamund Elwin and Michele Paulse, the protagonist is slightly older (her class is going on a field trip to the Science Centre) and starts with a little more knowledge and confidence about her family, which she maintains even in the face of more active discrimination and microaggressions.

When Asha's teacher refuses to accept her field trip permission form because it has two mums' names on it, Asha tells her mums, who say they will talk with the teacher. As in *Lots of Mommies*, the existence of queer families is not believed. Asha does not cry, however, like Emily and Heather, and knows to ask her mothers for help. Additionally, the next day at school, even before her mums speak with the teacher, Asha draws a picture of her mums, her brother, and herself walking to the Science Centre and talks about her drawing to the class. She herself came up with this response to the teacher's doubt, in contrast to Heather, whose family drawing was prompted by the teacher. This could be a factor of age but also feels like progress in representation to see a picture-book protagonist advocating for her same-sex-parented family. The first-person narrative also reinforces the sense of Asha's agency.

Unlike Heather and Emily, Asha speaks up to defend and explain her family. When another child, Coreen, asks why she has two mummies, Asha first replies, "Because I do" (Elwin and Paulse 11). When others chime in, variously saying Asha can and can't have two mums, Coreen explains that her parents say, "You can't have two mothers living together. My dad says it's bad" (14). It's unclear what Coreen herself thinks. Asha tells Coreen, "My mummies said we're a family because we live together and love each other" (14). Asha and her mums have already spoken about what it means to be a family (in contrast to Emily and Heather), and Asha is confident enough to express this even in the face of a direct invalidation. One boy asks the teacher if having two mummies is wrong, and she hesitates but is interrupted by the students before she can answer.

When Asha's moms say they spoke with the teacher, Asha wants to know if she can go on the field trip and if the teacher believes she has two moms. Upon hearing that she can go, Asha starts to run off. One mum asks if she wants to know the answer to her other question. "I did but not right then," Asha says (Elwin and Paulse 18). We never learn the answer, which may feel like a loose end, but it also indicates that Asha already has the resilience she needs, no matter what the teacher thinks. The focus for her is the field trip, not spreading a message about family diversity. As in this fictionalized depiction of a two-mom family, social science research has found that children may cut off conversations about their families when they are either uncomfortable with such personal discussions in public or just tired of them (Mitchell 404; Litovich and Langhout 427). This self-care is another form of resilience modeled in the book.

On the day of the trip, Asha excitedly gets ready. The other children ask each of her mums in turn, "Which mummy are you?" and laugh in amusement, not derision, when they each respond, "Mummy number one" (Elwin and Paulse 20). Like Emily's classmates, they cannot dispute what is before their eyes, but Asha's defense of her family may have swayed them as well.

Molly's Family (2004) by Nancy Garden shows us a child who, like Emily and Heather, is still learning resiliency but, unlike the protagonists so far, finds a broader base of adult support from both her teacher and her parents. It starts with Molly, a kindergartener, drawing a picture in class for the school's open house. She chooses to draw her family: Mommy, Mama Lu, and Sam, her puppy. In *Heather Has Two Mommies* and *Asha's Mums* (and several books below), a family drawing is used as a way for the protagonists to reinforce to themselves or others that their families are legitimate; here, it also triggers another child's doubt, as a boy named Tommy tells Molly, "That's not a family" (Garden 7). She insists, "It is so. . . . It's my family" (7). When Tommy asks, "Where's your daddy?" Molly says she doesn't have one but adds, "I have Mommy and Mama Lu and Sam" (9). Tommy tells the class that "there's no such thing" as such a family (9). Like the children in *Lots of Mommies*, *Asha's Mums*, and (below) *Love Is Love*, he cannot believe that such families exist. Other children speak up with their varied family configurations.

Although Molly asserts her family's validity in a way that Emily and Heather could not, she now, like them, "tried not to cry" (Garden 10). She is not upset, like Heather was, at the idea of not having a father (perhaps because, as a kindergartener, she is a little older) but seems not to have had the tools to prepare her for the repeated invalidations of her family. Unlike the slightly older Asha, though, she does not yet have a general definition of "family"; she just knows what hers is.

The first help she receives is from the teacher but not because she asks. Tommy is the one who approaches the teacher, asking her to affirm his view of Molly's family. The teacher, however, after confirming that Mama Lu is neither Molly's aunt nor a visitor, tells Molly, "It looks to me as if you can have a mommy and a mama" (Garden 12). The teacher does not, like Heather's playgroup facilitator, make this into a class lesson about families (and clearly has not met Mama Lu) but is more helpful than either Emily's or Asha's teacher.

The teacher's helpfulness (in a school setting, a more public forum than Heather's playgroup) is perhaps a sign of the growing public awareness and acceptance of same-sex couples and their children at the time of the book's publication. After getting support from her teacher, Molly goes home and initiates a conversation with Mommy and Mama Lu, asking if they are her real mommy and mama. She communicates Tommy's concerns. Her parents reassure her that they are her real parents, explain how they started their family, and stress, "There are lots of different kinds of families" (Garden 17). For the first time in these books, we see same-sex parents actively giving their child tools for resilience, perhaps indicating a perceived need for modeling such discussions.

Molly is still worried about displaying her picture, though the teacher encourages her. She thinks about the other children's families and realizes that families do come in all types, then remembers her parents' explanation and feels "warm inside." Molly chooses to bring her picture the next day, demonstrating her agency, and the teacher shares it with the class. No one questions her family further. She has found her resilience by putting all the pieces of the puzzle together: the examples of other families (as Heather also has) as well as her parents' information and the support of her teacher.

In *Antonio's Card/La Tarjeta de Antonio* (2005), a bilingual story by Rigoberto González, we also see a child working through new information from his parents to develop resilience against microaggressions. Antonio lives with Mami (English "mommy") and Leslie, his mother's partner. As we learn later, his father left when he was a baby; Leslie joined their household at some point afterward. When Leslie, an overall-clad artist, meets him after school, some of the children say she "looks like a guy" and "like a rodeo clown" (González 6). While the insults target Leslie's gender expression, they also indicate that the children don't see her as fitting a known parental role. Antonio is hurt and embarrassed.

When his class makes Mother's Day cards, he draws one for both women but does not want anyone to know about Leslie. He "hunches over" the paper so no one can see as he draws the three of them and the word "FAMILY" (González 15). Again, we see a child using a drawing to visually reinforce their family's legitimacy, but this time, the child is proving it only to themselves, afraid others will still not accept them.

He later tells Mami about the teasing and suggests that Leslie not meet him after school. Mami helps him realize that the way Leslie dresses and walks is just the way she is and that everyone is different. She encourages him to make his own decision about what to do, giving him agency rather than taking action herself.

When Leslie meets him the next day, he rushes her off to her art studio rather than wait at the school for Mami to pick them up. She shows him a painting she is making Mami as a Mother's Day present, and Antonio realizes he is lucky to have Leslie in his family. He tells her he has a surprise for her at the school Mother's Day display.

Antonio is already able to spell well and is thus older than most if not all of the protagonists above (except perhaps Asha). Despite this, Leslie came into his life after his birth, and Antonio is clearly still developing resilience about his new family structure. Like Molly, he processes the information he has been given as he comes to his own decision, demonstrating his agency despite needing a nudge from his mother.

EMPOWERED KIDS

A revised edition of *Heather* was published in 2015, about a week before the next book to tackle microaggressions about a child with same-sex parents was released—*Stella Brings the Family* (2015) by Miriam B. Schiffer. One of the notable changes in the new edition of *Heather* is that her mommies now wear wedding rings, a clear sign of marriage equality's impact on representation in picture books. In this edition, Heather is slightly older and off to her first day of school (presumably preschool), not just a playgroup. She is also more confident. While the text tells us that, as in 1989, she still cries ("but only a little") when she is dropped off, the picture no longer shows her looking sad but smiling (Newman, *Heather* [2015] 14).

During story time, the other children now mention their fathers *and* mothers. When one boy says his daddy is a doctor, Heather says her mommy is too—she is a more engaged participant than before. The boy then asks what her daddy does, and Heather "looks around the circle and wonders, *Am I the only one here who doesn't have a daddy?*" (Newman, *Heather* [2015] 19). The boy's assumption of her family structure is now a heterosexist microaggression, albeit an unintentional one. Unlike in the earlier edition, however, Heather doesn't feel sad or cry but merely wonders if there are others with similar family structures. Simply having a family that is different is no longer a cause for tears. Her change in response could be because she is a little older, but as Molly shows (and as Riley will show us below), even children in school may shed tears or be close to tears. Age may thus not account for the whole change. With proudly married moms, though, Heather's resilience in 2015 could be seen as reflecting a greater sense of confidence and acceptance within the overall LGBTQ+ community.

In *Stella*, the protagonist shows even greater agency and confidence. Stella, who has two dads, doesn't know who to bring as a guest to her class's Mother's Day celebration. A classmate asks what's wrong, and she explains. The other children, upon hearing she has no mother, are then puzzled about who does various caretaking tasks in her family. She explains that each dad does some and other relatives help too. One child suggests she brings all of them. Stella thinks about this and works hard on her invitation, which includes a drawing of her family, continuing the importance of visual depiction we have seen in previous books and emphasizing that her family is as deserving of an invitation as any. At the party, she sees that other children have various family structures. Her dads interact with the class, and everyone has a good time.

At the end, Stella tells her teacher not to worry about Father's Day, when she won't bring as many people—"just two" (Schiffer 23).

Stella moves us to a scenario where the main microaggression is systemic rather than individual: the teacher has not thought about incorporating all families into the Mother's Day celebration. The children here do not invalidate the protagonist's family structure or doubt its existence, as in most of the stories above; this again indicates a shift in perception of same-sex-parented families. The children's many questions about how Stella's family operates are themselves a form of microaggression but a less harsh one based on the persistent assumption of heterosexuality. Nevertheless, the story suggests a need for institutional change to keep up with shifting societal norms.

Stella herself seems more resilient than the earlier protagonists. We don't know her exact age, but the class story time on a rug indicates a lower elementary grade. Stella is, however, able to talk confidently about her family. She knows "she would be the only one without a mother" but, unlike Heather in 1989, does not cry when she thinks about her family's difference (Schiffer 4). She does not herself come up with the solution to her problem, but the fact that one of her peers does so reflects societal progress toward LGBTQ+ inclusion, and it is Stella who ultimately makes the decision to follow up on the suggestion. No adult input is given or needed.

We see a similar kid-driven solution in *The Zero Dads Club* (2015) by Angel Adeyoha. In it, two elementary school students, Akilah and Kai, are discussing their class Father's Day project, painting pictures of neckties. Neither Akilah nor Kai has a dad, however. Akilah thinks the project is unfair and that they should protest for the cancellation of Father's Day. Kai suggests instead doing their own projects and creating a special "Moms Only Club" since Akilah has two moms and Kai one (Adeyoha 7). The teacher lets them advertise the club and special project. Soon, though, other children come over who have neither moms nor dads but live with other relatives. One suggests changing the name to "the Zero Dads Club" (13). They all make cards depicting their families and take turns talking about them to the club. Drawing here becomes a tool for reaffirming the worth of their families. In the end, the children are excited about sharing the cards with their recipients and about "their new club of friends" (28).

As in *Stella*, the problem is an institutional microaggression, not an individual one. No one is doubting the validity of any family, which feels like progress, but the class activity nevertheless excludes children without dads. *The Zero Dads Club* also shows us not just one but many children impacted by the microaggression, an acknowledgment of a whole community of families with same-sex parents (and other diverse family types). This sense of community is further developed in the next book here, as we shall see.

The growing victories of marriage equality—and the well-being of children with same-sex parents—were in the media a lot while *Stella, Heather* (2015), and *The Zero Dads Club* were being created. Support for marriage equality had risen from 31 percent in 2004 to 61 percent in 2015, while opposition fell almost exactly in reverse, from 60 percent to 31 percent (Doherty et al. 2). The era between *Antonio's Card* and *Stella* was also marked by several other major advances toward LGBTQ+ visibility and equality. It makes sense that the protagonists of picture books published after these events reflect a greater confidence and agency, even if some challenges have remained. Importantly, two texts published in 2015 shift the focus from individuals who do not believe in the possibility of same-sex-parented families to social institutions and practices that reveal a lag in their ability to include them.

BEYOND SAMENESS

This attitude carries forward into the next two books, which also explore new aspects of microaggressions and resilience. Michael Genhart's *Love Is Love* (2017) is narrated by an unnamed boy who is explaining to a friend that he has a problem: some kids were saying that his shirt with a rainbow-colored heart was "gay" (4). He thinks it's because he has two dads. He doesn't like when kids use the term "gay" derogatorily or say his family is not a real one. Here, we see the old microaggression of children disbelieving that this type of family can exist, but we also encounter a specific insult (calling things "gay" as a general slur) that first became common in the 1990s and has continued since (Conan).

We then see images of happy people around the world wearing similar rainbow shirts as the boy ponders that being different might be scary to some people but that his dads really love each other and him. He also tells us he knows "lots of other gay people," including his teacher and others in his community, and that there are "lots of famous gay people" too (Genhart 15–16). He says that his dads have told him being gay is nothing to be ashamed of, though some people think so. The family gathers to fly kites with other people wearing rainbow-heart shirts (presumably other LGBTQ+ families) as the protagonist explains that the love in their family is what matters.

The protagonist of *Love Is Love* has already spoken with his dads about family diversity, homophobia, and even gay culture and can convey these lessons to others. Although he begins by saying that "I've got a problem," by the end, he is telling us, "When some kids say 'Your dads are gay!' I'll just say, 'Yes, they are!'" and "When some kids say 'You're not a real family!' I'll just say 'Yes, we are!'" (Genhart 21). He may have a problem, but he already has the solution. In fact, the problematic situation is only mentioned as a past event. It feels much less immediate than in the pre-2015 books, continuing the shift, which we first detected in *Stella*, away from a focus on the microaggressions themselves and toward the strength of the protagonist.

Marriage equality plays a role here as well. On one page, the boy shows us a wedding photo of his dads next to a wedding photo of his friend's mom and dad and explains that their love is not any different. The boy has also absorbed and is sharing this message of equality.

My Footprints (2019) by Bao Phi brings another new element to the treatment of microaggressions and resilience—intersectional identities. Although there are racially and ethnically diverse characters in the other books discussed, no other text considers how these identities affect the protagonist. This story centers on a Vietnamese American girl (whom the book's target age range places in early elementary school), Thuy, in the aftermath of being teased by classmates about having two moms, bothered for being a girl, and told to "go back where I come from" (Phi 16). She expresses her feelings and desires by imitating wild creatures, such as a bird that can fly away and a deer who looked "out of place," although "its family must have been close" (5). Her moms help her pretend further, suggesting real and mythological creatures from their own cultural identities (Vietnamese American and South Asian Hindu) that can stand up to the bullying. When the moms ask Thuy her favorite, she makes up one with black hair and eyes (like her) that is "both a boy and a girl" and whose skin keeps changing colors, "not to hide, but because it always wants to be different shades of pretty—and it never hurts or makes fun of anyone" (22). The three of them make the footprints of the empowering creature in the snow together.

Thuy initiates the therapeutic animal imitations herself, reinforcing her own resilience after being harassed. Her moms follow her lead but also help her to see how identities can be a source of strength. In the end, though, Thuy's favorite animal is her own creation, a symbol of her resilience. As in *Love Is Love*, we only hear about the microaggressions in retrospect and the focus is no longer on the problem per se but rather on the protagonist's resilience.

My Footprints is the only book here that mentions microaggressions based on racial or ethnic identity, although the majority have protagonists of color. (Emily is Asian, with one Asian mom, one Black, and two white;

Asha and her family are Black; Antonio and Mami are Latinx; Akilah and Kai are Black; Riley is Black, with one Black and one white dad; Elvi is dark-skinned with one light-skinned and one dark-skinned mom; the other families are all white.) Given that same-sex parents and their children are more likely to be people of color than different-sex parents and their children (Gates 1) and that children of color may also be stigmatized because of their racial/ethnic identities, treating anti-LGBTQ+ microaggressions and stigma in isolation may not reflect the real experiences of many children with same-sex parents.

Why the previous books treated them separately may be explained by an observation from Sandra Patton-Imani in a recent book on lesbian motherhood. She says that the emphasis on the fundamental sameness of all families in books like *Heather* and *Molly's Family* "is consistent with the colorblind, neoliberal framing of race in this era; difference is repackaged as sameness to resolve tensions between divergent definitions of family legitimacy" (Patton-Imani 205–6). With the legitimizing stamp of marriage equality also resolving some of this tension, I believe picture books could be freer to celebrate family differences as well as sameness. While earlier books showed families and individuals of color, their identities *as* families of color were not stressed. *My Footprints*, however, shows each parent using her specific cultural tradition to help build Thuy's resilience.

Love Is Love also challenges the idea of sameness but in a different way. Although the equality of all families is noted, the emphasis is on what is distinct and valuable about the LGBTQ+ community. It is the first of the books here to use a term ("gay") for a parent's sexual identity rather than just talking about family diversity. (Other picture books not discussed here do so but not in the context of addressing a microaggression.) It is also the first of these books to offer a vision of the wider LGBTQ+ community as a tool for building resilience against stigma, which may reflect the community's post-marriage-equality confidence. (While secondary characters in both *Heather* and *Stella* had same-sex parents, there is no sense that these families are part of a larger LGBTQ+ culture.)

Many real lesbian and gay parents, however, engage in a variety of socialization practices with their children in order to convey values and customs that help instill pride in their families and help prepare them to face potential stigma (Oakley et al. 56). These include participating in LGBTQ+ parent groups, talking about LGBTQ+ history and culture, and attending Pride parades and other LGBTQ+ events (Gipson 123; Goldberg et al., "Lesbian," 283–84; Mitchell 404). Picture books have picked up these themes, and ones about LGBTQ+ history, famous LGBTQ+ people, and the celebration of Pride have greatly increased in number since the mid-2010s, the peak years of the marriage-equality battle. It is not surprising, then, that one of the books discussed here also took up the theme of queer community at that time.

As marriage equality took hold too, even some proponents feared that it could lead to assimilation into the mainstream and a decline of LGBTQ+ culture (Ocobock 369). Showing same-sex parents engaged with the broader LGBTQ+ community also offers a vision for how family life need not stand in opposition to LGBTQ+ cultural engagement.

UNSURE AGAIN

Papa, Daddy, and Riley (2020) by Seamus Kirst, however, feels in many ways like a throwback. The story is very similar to *Molly's Family*, with a child who can articulate some positive things about her family but encounters difficulties when faced with invalidating microaggressions. It is another first-day-of-school tale, told from the first-person perspective of Riley, who has two dads. Her friend Olive questions which dad is her "*dad* dad" and asks where her mom is (Kirst 7). Riley responds that they both are her dads and that her "belly mommy" doesn't live with them (9).

Olive continues to question, and Riley wonders if she needs to pick just one. She thinks about how she shares characteristics of her "belly mommy" and each of her dads and likes to do different things with each dad. When her dads pick her up, she's "upset" and "wails" that she loves them both (Kirst 19). The next spread has the words "I don't want to have to choose!" across one full page and an image of her with her hands over her face on the other (20–21). She has no tools for handling this. While her dads have told her about her origins as an adopted child, they have not spoken about her family's two-dad structure vis-à-vis other families.

Daddy now assures her she doesn't have to choose and explains that families have different forms. Papa adds that neither of them gave birth to her, "But we carried you in our hearts" (Kirst 22). When Riley asks what makes a family, Daddy replies, "Love" (22). Riley responds that she loves them both, so they are both her dads.

While Riley's consternation may evoke *Lots of Mommies* and *Molly's Family*, the microaggressions she experiences are somewhat different. No one is telling Riley that her family is not a real one or that there is no such thing as a family like hers. Instead, Olive asks, "Which dad is the *real* dad?" (Kirst 9). Patton-Imani is again helpful here, citing a real-life instance of a child asking this question (though about moms) and noting that even children who understand that some families have two moms (or, by extension, two dads) may still struggle against a learned social narrative that says people can have only one. This "[precludes] the complete and unqualified acceptance of both of them on equal terms" and may lead to questions like, "Who's the real mom?" (Patton-Imani 207). Olive faces this struggle as she asks Riley about her dads—and even Riley falls prey to this narrative before her dads explain otherwise. Marriage equality may have helped legitimize families with same-sex parents, making it less likely (though far from impossible) that someone would say "That's not a family," but for some, there may still be a learning curve to full understanding in the face of societal assumptions.

KID IN CONTROL

Who's Your Real Mum? (2020) by Bernadette Green tackles head-on the question of which is the "real" parent and gives all the agency to the child protagonist. A boy named Nicholas asks the titular question of a girl named Elvi, who replies, "They're both my mum" (Green 1–2). Nicholas argues, "Only the one who had you in her tummy can be your real mum" (3). Elvi gives him a clue: "She's wearing jeans" (4). Nicholas observes that they both are. "She's got dark hair," Elvi adds (5). They both do, Nicholas responds. Elvi's clues get increasingly elaborate and whimsical. Her real mum "can do a handstand on one finger," is "a pirate in disguise," and "speaks fluent gorilla" (8–14). Eventually, Elvi shifts from silliness to instruction. Her real mum, she says, is the one who holds her when she's scared and kisses her goodnight. They both do, Nicholas says. "Exactly!" Elvi replies (30).

Elvi's age is unspecified, but the book's target audience places her in the early elementary grades. She is nevertheless supremely confident in her family structure and pokes gentle fun at Nicholas for not (yet) having the same inclusive perspective about family.

Stella, Elvi, Akilah and Kai, and the boy in *Love Is Love* all address microaggressions without any adult assistance (although the latter refers to previous conversations with his parents). The focus is on how the protagonists use the information, not on how they gain it, implying a more advanced state of understanding that suits the societal shift.

CONCLUSION

Same-sex parents have long used children's books about families like theirs and about family diversity more broadly to help children develop language for understanding and talking about their families (Gianino et al. 221; Goldberg et al., "Lesbian" 284). Such books do not necessarily need to revolve around microaggressions, however. Indeed, some research indicates that lesbian and gay parents of young children are more likely to focus on "positive aspects of family diversity" rather than stress differences or the potential for stigma (Goldberg et al., "Lesbian" 290). Even two authors here, Newman and Garden, have expressed the desire to move away from an issue-driven focus and did so in later works (Rudolph, "Same-Sex Weddings"; Smith). Others have urged the same with respect to children's books focusing on other marginalized identities (Alam; Doshi; McQuinn; Tate; Welch). While some less issue-driven books about same-sex-parented families have long existed, the relative paucity of LGBTQ+-inclusive picture books as a whole until about 2017 (Rudolph, "2021 Rainbow Book List") has meant that books about microaggressions are often among those recommended.

The longevity of the microaggression theme also indicates that some continue to find it valuable. Microaggressions still exist, and books that offer specific models of response and resilience building may assist both children and adults. At the same time, authors and publishers (as well as parents and teachers) should not make books centering microaggressions the only tales they tell about families with same-sex parents (or about LGBTQ+ people more broadly). Our lives encompass more than that, and books should reflect that breadth. Some authors and publishers have responded to this call, particularly in the past few years. Nevertheless, as we have seen, books about microaggressions can and have changed to reflect the changing climate of LGBTQ+ equality and acceptance, and we should expect that they will continue to evolve and to remain one of many tools for resilience.

NOTE

1. I use "same-sex parents" to be inclusive of families that may include bisexual members as well as lesbian and gay ones. While "same sex" excludes single queer parents, no single parents are shown in any of the books here, so the term is appropriate in this context. When my sources specify identities, I follow their usage in citing them.

WORKS CITED

Adeyoha, Angel. *The Zero Dads Club*. Illustrated by Aubrey Williams, Flamingo Rampant, 2015.
Alam, Rumaan. "We Don't Only Need More Diverse Books. We Need More Diverse Books Like *The Snowy Day*." *Slate Magazine*, 2 Aug. 2016, https://slate.com/culture/2016/08/ezra-jack-keats-the-snowy-day-is-a-model-for-treating-black-characters-in-childrens-books.html.
Conan, Neal. "Why Is It OK to Say 'That's So Gay?'" *NPR*, 25 June 2009, https://www.npr.org/templates/story/story.php?storyId=105909348.
Doherty, Carroll, et al. "Majority of Public Favors Same-Sex Marriage, but Divisions Persist." *Pew Research Center*, 14 May 2019, https://www.pewresearch.org/politics/2019/05/14/majority-of-public-favors-same-sex-marriage-but-divisions-persist/.
Doshi, Payal. "The Importance of Joyful Stories in Diverse Children's Books." *We Need Diverse Books*, 14 June 2021, https://diversebooks.org/the-importance-of-joyful-stories-in-diverse-childrens-books/.
Elwin, Rosamund, and Michele Paulse. *Asha's Mums*. Illustrated by Dawn Lee, Women's Press, 1990.
Farr, Rachel H., et al. "Microaggressions, Feelings of Difference, and Resilience among Adopted Children with Sexual Minority Parents." *Journal of Youth and Adolescence*, vol. 45, no. 1, Jan. 2016, pp. 85–104. *Springer Link*, https://doi.org/10.1007/s10964-015-0353-6.
Garden, Nancy. *Molly's Family*. Illustrated by Sharon Wooding, Farrar Straus Giroux, 2004.
Gartrell, Nanette, et al. "The National Lesbian Family Study: 3. Interviews with Mothers of Five-Year-Olds." *American Journal of Orthopsychiatry*, vol. 70, no. 4, 2000, pp. 542–48. *Crossref*, https://doi.org/10.1037/h0087823.
Gartrell, Nanette, et al. "The National Lesbian Family Study: 4. Interviews with the 10-Year-Old Children." *American Journal of Orthopsychiatry*, vol. 75, no. 4, Oct. 2005, pp. 518–24. *PubMed*, https://doi.org/10.1037/0002-9432.75.4.518.
Gates, Gary J. "LGBT Parenting in the United States." *Williams Institute*, Feb. 2013, https://williamsinstitute.law.ucla.edu/publications/lgbt-parenting-us/.
Genhart, Michael. *Love Is Love*. Illustrated by Ken Min, Little Pickle Press, 2018.
Gianino, Mark, et al. "Family Outings: Disclosure Practices among Adopted Youth with Gay and Lesbian Parents." *Adoption Quarterly*, vol. 12, no. 3–4, 2009, pp. 205–28.
Gipson, Cynthia Kay. *Parenting Practices of Lesbian Mothers: An Examination of the Socialization of Children in Planned Lesbian-Headed Families*. 2008. U of Texas at Austin, PhD dissertation. *ProQuest*, http://search.proquest.com/docview/194009841/abstract/A330D31C695642BAPQ/1.
Goldberg, Abbie E., et al. "Lesbian, Gay, and Heterosexual Adoptive Parents' Socialization Approaches to Children's Minority Statuses." *Counseling Psychologist*, vol. 44, no. 2, Feb. 2016, pp. 267–99. *SAGE Journals*, https://doi.org/10.1177/0011000015628055.
Goldberg, Abbie E., et al. "Talking about Family: Disclosure Practices of Adults Raised by Lesbian, Gay, and Bisexual Parents." *Journal of Family Issues*, vol. 28, no. 1, Jan. 2007, pp. 100–131. *Crossref*, https://doi.org/10.1177/0192513X06293606.
González, Rigoberto. *Antonio's Card / La tarjeta de Antonio*. Illustrated by Cecilia Concepción Alvarez, Children's Book Press, 2005.
Green, Bernadette. *Who's Your Real Mom?* Illustrated by Anna Zobel, Scribble, 2020.
Kirst, Seamus. *Papa, Daddy, and Riley*. Illustrated by Devon Holzwarth, Magination Press, 2020.
Litovich, Marianna L., and Regina Day Langhout. "Framing Heterosexism in Lesbian Families: A Preliminary Examination of Resilient Coping." *Journal of Community and Applied Social Psychology*, vol. 14, no. 6, John Wiley, Nov. 2004, pp. 411–35. *EBSCOhost*, https://doi.org/10.1002/casp.780.

Massachusetts State Supreme Judicial Court. *Goodridge v. Department of Public Health*. Massachusetts Reports, vol. 440, 18 Nov. 2003, pp. 309–95. *FindLaw*, https://caselaw.findlaw.com/ma-supreme-judicial-court/1447056.html.

Masten, Ann S. "Ordinary Magic: Resilience Processes in Development." *American Psychologist*, vol. 56, no. 3, Mar. 2001, pp. 227–38. *EBSCOhost*, https://doi.org/10.1037/0003-066X.56.3.227.

McQuinn, Anna. "Reflecting Realities." *Anna McQuinn*, http://www.annamcquinn.com/article--reflecting-realities.html. Accessed 22 Sept. 2021.

Mitchell, Valory. "The Birds, the Bees . . . and the Sperm Banks: How Lesbian Mothers Talk with Their Children about Sex and Reproduction." *American Journal of Orthopsychiatry*, vol. 68, no. 3, 1998, pp. 400–409. *Wiley Online Library*, https://doi.org/10.1037/h0080349.

Nadal, Kevin L., et al. "Sexual Orientation Microaggressions: 'Death by a Thousand Cuts' for Lesbian, Gay, and Bisexual Youth." *Journal of LGBT Youth*, vol. 8, no. 3, July 2011, pp. 234–59. *EBSCOhost*, https://doi.org/10.1080/19361653.2011.584204.

NeJaime, Douglas. "Marriage Equality and the New Parenthood." *Harvard Law Review*, vol. 129, no. 5, Mar. 2016, pp. 1185–266.

Newman, Lesléa. *Donovan's Big Day*. Illustrated by Mike Dutton, Tricycle Press, 2011.

Newman, Lesléa. *Heather Has Two Mommies*. Illustrated by Diana Souza, In Other Words, 1989.

Newman, Lesléa. *Heather Has Two Mommies*. Illustrated by Laura Cornell, Candlewick Press, 2015.

Oakley, Marykate, et al. "Same-Sex Parent Socialization: Understanding Gay and Lesbian Parenting Practices as Cultural Socialization." *Journal of GLBT Family Studies*, vol. 13, no. 1, Jan. 2017, pp. 56–75. *EBSCOhost*, https://doi.org/10.1080/1550428X.2016.1158685.

Ocobock, Abigail. "Status or Access? The Impact of Marriage on Lesbian, Gay, Bisexual, and Queer Community Change." *Journal of Marriage and Family*, vol. 80, no. 2, 2018, pp. 367–82. *Wiley Online Library*, https://doi.org/10.1111/jomf.12468.

Patton-Imani, Sandra. *Queering Family Trees: Race, Reproductive Justice, and Lesbian Motherhood*. New York UP, 2020.

Phi, Bao. *My Footprints*. Illustrated by Basia Tran, Capstone Editions, 2020.

Ramos, Christopher, et al. "The Effects of Marriage Equality in Massachusetts: A Survey of the Experiences and Impact of Marriage on Same-Sex Couples." *Williams Institute*, May 2009, https://escholarship.org/uc/item/9dx6v3kj.

Rudolph, Dana. "Same-Sex Weddings Inspire Pioneering Author's New Picture Book." *Mombian*, 23 May 2011, https://www.mombian.com/2011/05/23/same-sex-weddings-inspire-pioneering-authors-new-picture-book/.

Rudolph, Dana. "2021 Rainbow Book List Shows Record Increase in LGBTQ Kids' Books." *Mombian*, 10 Feb. 2021, https://mombian.com/2021/02/10/2021-rainbow-book-list-shows-record-increase-in-lgbtq-kids-books/.

Schiffer, Miriam B. *Stella Brings the Family*. Illustrated by Holly Clifton-Brown, Chronicle Books, 2015.

Severance, Jane. *Lots of Mommies*. Illustrated by Jan Jones, Lollipop Power, 1983.

Smith, Cynthia Leitich. "Behind the Story: Nancy Garden on *Molly's Family*." *Cynthia Leitich Smith*, 30 Apr. 2015, https://cynthialeitichsmith.com/lit-resources/read/authors/stories-behind/storygarden/.

Sue, Derald Wing, et al. "Racial Microaggressions in Everyday Life: Implications for Clinical Practice." *American Psychologist*, vol. 62, no. 4, May 2007, pp. 271–86. *EBSCOhost*, https://doi.org/10.1037/0003-066X.62.4.271.

Tate, Emily. "The Evolving Role of Race in Children's Lit, From 'Harry Potter' to 'The Hate U Give.'" *EdSurge*, 5 Mar. 2019, https://www.edsurge.com/news/2019-03-05-the-evolving-role-of-race-in-children-s-lit-from-harry-potter-to-the-hate-u-give.

United States Supreme Court. *Obergefell v. Hodges. United States Reports.* Opinions, vol. 576, docket 14-556, 26 June 2015, pp. 644ff. *Justia,* https://supreme.justia.com/cases/federal/us/576/644.

United States Supreme Court. *United States v. Windsor. United States Reports.* Opinions, vol. 570, docket 12-307, 26 June 2013, pp. 744ff. *Justia,* https://supreme.justia.com/cases/federal/us/570/744.

Welch, Brynn. "Missing Adventures: Diversity and Children's Literature." *YouTube,* uploaded by TEDxEHC, 28 Apr. 2016, https://www.youtube.com/watch?v=Yq2opVinciA.

"Winning the Freedom to Marry Nationwide: The Inside Story of a Transformative Campaign." *Freedom to Marry,* http://www.freedomtomarry.org/pages/how-it-happened. Accessed 26 Sept. 2021.

CHAPTER 4

REPRESENTATION MATTERS NOW MORE THAN EVER

Transgender and Nonbinary Parents in Children's Picture Books

Rob Bittner

In 2016, Jennifer Ingrey, Christine Stamper, and I conducted a survey of books for young readers that feature queer and trans characters, including picture books. The literary landscape was somewhat limited in terms of actual queer and trans children in picture books, and while there is still very limited representation of queer children, the number of trans and gender-nonconforming children in picture books has grown exponentially since that survey was conducted. Before discussing more specific histories of these texts, however, I would like to make a note regarding terminology. Using the term "queer" in relation to children outside of an academic context has a history of causing feelings of panic among some adults who see it as an attempt to sexualize young people (Bruhm and Hurley). Existing scholarship also vacillates between the use of "trans" and "queer" to discuss identities related to children. Therefore, I use both terms when engaging with picture books that feature trans and queer children in the first section of this chapter before focusing on trans adults (regardless of sexuality). However, it is also important to understand that "queer" can and has been used as a term to encompass both gender and sexuality, and thus the queer child can be any child who is transgressing gender and sexual norms in some way, whether leading into queer or trans adulthood or not. I rely on the use of "trans" and "nonbinary" specifically in relation to adult characters within children's literature, though, as these are the terms that are often used either within the texts, the back matter, or the publisher's synopsis of the books. Now, back to the history of children's literature with trans and queer representation.

The history of lesbian, gay, bisexual, trans, queer, plus (LGBTQ+) picture books is relatively short, even including books that are not explicitly queer but that incorporate aspects of gender nonconformity. The 1970s saw several picture books enter the children's literature market, exploring gender's and society's reliance on heteronormative gender roles and expression. *William's Doll* (1972) by Charlotte Zolotow was one of the first children's books to explicitly attempt a disruption of societal expectations around childhood and gender, particularly gendered toys, clothes, and activities. A few years later came *X: A Fabulous Child's Story* (1978) by Lois Gould and *Oliver Button Is a Sissy* (1979) by Tomie dePaola. All three of these books found ways to challenge reliance on gender stereotypes in childhood as a way of directing children toward a "proper" (cis)gendered path to adulthood. Predictably, reception to these texts was mixed at the time, though all three are now often cited in fields such as library studies and education as examples of progressive texts that allow children to see the possibilities of gender-role reversal and existing outside the bounds of (gender-conforming) adult expectations. It would be another few decades, however, before picture books explicitly engaging with transgender characters would appear in the realm of children's literature. Some of these early works include *10,000 Dresses* (2008) by Marcus Ewert and *I Am Jazz* (2014) by Jessica Herthel and Jazz Jennings, among others. As can be noted by the publication dates, the emergence of transgender children in picture books was relatively recent, although, since these titles appeared, there has been steadily growing trans representation, including books like *When Aidan Became a Brother* (2019) by Kyle Lukoff, which was written by a transgender author and featured a nonwhite protagonist. Much of this shift over the years has been due to overall social and cultural changes around the world in response to transgender activism and individuals coming out earlier in life.

Unfortunately, in recent years, there has been a concerted effort by small but vocal groups throughout North America and around the world to remove access to children's books that contain any reference to gender or sexuality in any form.[1] While activism has led to an increase in representation in literature, this also means that there are more books featuring LGBTQ+ characters to ban than ever before. It is not just a fight over books, though. As Kyle Lukoff notes, "This is very much about the rights of LGBTQ people and people of color to exist and to thrive in a society with full power and equality, if not equity" ("Banned in the USA"). I point this out not to be discouraging but rather to further emphasize the necessity and importance of the books being explored throughout the remainder of this chapter. With shouts of "groomer" and "pedophile" following many queer and trans adults and especially parents

TITLE	DATE	PUBLISHER	AUTHOR	ILLUSTRATOR
Carly: She's Still My Daddy	2004	Transgender Network of PFLAG	Mary Boenke	Dolores Dudley
My Mommy Is a Boy	2011	Self-published (Lulu.com)	Jason Martinez	Karen Winchester
My New Mommy	2012	Spun Silver Productions	Lilly Mossiano	Sage Mossiano
My New Daddy	2012	Spun Silver Productions	Lilly Mossiano	Sage Mossiano
Rachel's Christmas Boat	2017	Flamingo Rampant	Sophie LaBelle	Sophie LaBelle
My Maddy	2020	Magination Press	Gayle E. Pitman	Violet Tobacco

Table 4.1. Picture books about trans parents and transition

and those working with children, it is essential that nuanced depictions of trans and nonconforming adults continue to be published, studied, and shared with as large an audience as possible.

The overarching purpose of this chapter is to continue the examination of trans and gender-nonconforming representation in picture books but, this time, in relation to adults and parents rather than child characters. In order to do so, I will be utilizing a combination of theoretical lenses, including "a pedagogy of possibility that is rooted in gender equity and social justice" (Bittner et al. 949). This approach to children's texts allows for the possibility of multiple readings and looks to the historical, social, and political contexts in which the books are created, distributed, and read. The possibilities for each of these texts are open-ended, and no single reading will likely be the same. A young person reading *10,000 Dresses* when it first came out might find it inspiring and aspirational because of the less trans-accepting social and political context. Today, with more options available, readers may see *10,000 Dresses* as dated and overly simplistic, failing to truly disrupt heteronormative reliance on binaries and assumptions around gender expression and gendered accessories.

Similarly, the books I discuss throughout this chapter (see table 4.1) can be understood both as products of their time and stepping stones toward greater possibilities for representation of trans adults and rainbow families in picture books.[2] It is true that in addition to the six primary texts that I will be discussing in depth, there are a few picture books that include trans-parent families or trans adults, though the narratives are not focused on exploring those characters in detail. These picture books (see table 4.2) show possibilities for literature incorporating trans-parent families into the larger rainbow-families category, but they are not focused on examining questions and experiences specific to those families and parent-child relationships. Therefore, I will be focusing on the texts in table 4.1 for the majority of this chapter.

TITLE	DATE	PUBLISHER	AUTHOR	ILLUSTRATOR
The Zero Dads Club	2017	Flamingo Rampant	Angel Adeyoha	Aubrey Williams
Families Are like Ice Cream Flavors	2018	Self-published (CreateSpace)	E. L. George	
Vincent the Vixen	2018	Jessica Kingsley Publishers	Alice Reeves	Phoebe Kirk
Bridge of Flowers	2019	Flamingo Rampant	Leah Lakshmi Piepzna-Samarasinha	Syrus Marcus Ware

Table 4.2. Picture books with trans-adult representation

CONTEXTUALIZING THE PRIMARY TEXTS

As a field, children's publishing is relatively responsive to sociocultural shifts, particularly in terms of what is of interest to parents, children, and their lived experiences. As more children are recognized as transgender and nonbinary and as rainbow families become less stigmatized within various societies and cultures, children's publishing has become more open to the possibilities for stories that represent the experiences of these children and their families. It was not long after marriage equality started to become more mainstream and accepted throughout North America and around the world that children's books began to move beyond representation of children with same-sex parents to children witnessing or being a part of weddings between gay and lesbian couples, such as in *Uncle Bobby's Wedding* (2008) by Sarah S. Brannen and *Donovan's Big Day* (2011) by Lesléa Newman. When marriage equality was made a federal right through the 2015 Supreme Court case in the United States, it was less than a year before Richard Peck's children's novel *The Best Man* (2016) came out. Similarly, after what Katy Steinmetz termed the "transgender tipping point" in her 2014 *Time* article, transgender representation in picture books began to increase at a much faster rate. Prior to 2014, there were only a few picture books with explicitly transgender-child characters, but later trans and gender-nonconforming children became much more prevalent within children's literature publishing.

Since 2014, there have been years with multiple trans-representative picture books published, mirroring other forms of representation that have increased in number after significant moments in history. Although the numbers are increasing, the accessibility of these texts is still very limited due to publication through independent and niche publishers as well as the use of self-publishing. These publication methods can seriously limit access since bookstores and libraries are dependent on mainstream book reviews and publisher marketing strategies to find and acquire many of their titles. As can

TITLE	AVAILABILITY (WORLDCAT AND VOILA)
Carly: She's Still My Daddy	6 libraries (USA); 2 libraries (AUS)
My Mommy Is a Boy	3 libraries (USA); 1 library (CAN)
My New Mommy	5 libraries (USA); 2 libraries (AUS); 1 library (CAD)
My New Daddy	4 libraries (USA); 2 libraries (AUS); 1 library (CAD)
Rachel's Christmas Boat	7 libraries (USA); 2 libraries (AUS); 3 libraries (CAD)
My Maddy	199 libraries (USA); 8 libraries (AUS); 2 libraries (NZ); 4 libraries (CAD)

Table 4.3. Approximations of availability

be seen in table 4.3, aside from *My Maddy*, most titles discussed in this project have very limited availability (at least in library systems), which indicates an overall likelihood that the texts are not known to many families, educators, or librarians who lack significant knowledge of the LGBTQ+ literary landscape.

Within the history of LGBTQ+ children's stories, the majority of existing texts can be split into two streams: those stories about children with gay or lesbian parents and those about transgender and gender-nonconforming children. There are very few existing children's books that look to the experiences of transgender and/or nonbinary parents or to the experiences of children whose parents may be in the process of social or medical transition. Furthermore, as Carla A. Pfeffer and Kierra B. Jones note, "An unfortunately common occurrence across research literature is to lump trans-parent families into analyses of LGBTQ-parent families. While this may be helpful in distinguishing the issues that 'nontraditional' families face, as a group, certain experiences and challenges may be unique to trans individuals and their families. Thus, this literature may inadvertently minimize or erase trans and trans family experience" (202). This chapter explores existing texts, as of 2021, that contain representations of transgender and nonbinary parents, examining the use of language and terminology, the roles of the children and adults in the various narratives, and similarities in plot structure. I will be asking several questions to guide this examination, including: Are these useful narrative constructs for children to understand trans and nonbinary identities, or are they reductive and/or problematic in the long term? This and other questions can help create a productive discussion of possibilities for understanding current representation and looking toward future representation in children's literature. Beyond the narratives, language, and representation, I am also interested in who is publishing the texts, their general availability, and how they are being reviewed and marketed. What does it say to trans-parent families that the bulk of existing picture books are self-published or published mainly by niche publishers? These indicators reveal an intended audience and also highlight how mainstream publishing continues to be lacking in inclusive representation.

When studying picture books within an academic context, it can be tempting to use theory in a particular way to interpret literature or to come up with expectations for how literature *should* represent something, but it can be much more difficult to accept the messiness of lived experience and people being imperfect, both inside the narratives and in the process of creating the literature in the first place. But creating literature with a purpose can still provide pedagogical possibilities while also helping to guide and educate children and families on certain concepts, including reinforcement of respectful and inclusive language by children toward trans adults and parents. This language, however, is difficult to pin down and is likely to shift over time in ways that may be difficult for people to keep up with, even if they are trans themselves. As such, the analytical component of this project consists of a more flexible approach, namely a descriptive, open-ended mapping of representation and representational practices that can help to reveal more personal and social dimensions of gender as they appear in the chosen picture books.

SHIFTING LANGUAGE AND TERMINOLOGY

An integral part of understanding representation and connections to social constructs of gender is language and terminology. Using the mapping approach noted previously, I noticed a steady shift in language from the earlier texts to the most recent—an almost steady progression that reflects the language of activism and academics (see table 4.4). The approach of mapping representation and in particular the progression of language allows me to analyze the language without any need to evaluate the language as necessarily right or wrong but rather as indicative of a particular context in which the text was written and published. Understanding that some of the outdated terminology—"transsexual," "male-to-female," "female-to-male"—is being used in good faith by trans authors within the texts allows me to focus less on the terms themselves and more on the ways in which each text offers pedagogical possibilities for examining or explaining gender and language to child readers and the adults who read to them.

The language used for subject headings for each of the picture books explored in this chapter, for instance, change from year to year, as do the ways in which pronouns and other gendered language are approached within

TITLE	COMMON SUBJECT HEADINGS
Carly: She's Still My Daddy	Transsexual parents—Juvenile fiction Transsexuals—Juvenile fiction Sex change—Juvenile fiction
My Mommy Is a Boy	Female-to-male transsexuals—Juvenile fiction Female-to-male transsexuals
My New Mommy	Children of transgender parents—Juvenile literature Transgender parents—Juvenile literature Transgender people—Juvenile literature
My New Daddy	Children of transgender parents—Juvenile literature Transgender parents—Juvenile literature Transgender people—Juvenile literature
Rachel's Christmas Boat	Children of transgender parents—Juvenile literature Transgender parents—Juvenile literature Gender identity—Juvenile literature
The Zero Dads Club	Fatherless families—Juvenile fiction Fatherless families
Families Are like Ice Cream Flavors	Families—Juvenile literature Families
Vincent the Vixen	Sociology; Gender identity—Juvenile fiction Gender identity Juvenile nonfiction (?)
Bridge of Flowers	Families—Juvenile fiction Households—Juvenile fiction Bridges—Juvenile fiction
My Maddy	Parent and child—Juvenile fiction Gender identity—Juvenile fiction Children of transgender parents—Juvenile fiction Gender-nonconforming people—Juvenile fiction

Table 4.4. Subject headings

each narrative. This can create confusion for adult readers who are not trans themselves or who are unfamiliar with the history of trans activism and the evolution of gender studies within the academic realm, even while children find themselves able to adapt relatively easily when given explanations and an opportunity to process. In a post on her blog, Julia Serano writes on what she terms the "activist language merry-go-round," in which some people can feel the need to change language in response to social stigma. As a result of this stigma, she notes, "many activists feel compelled to focus on changing language (i.e., swapping out "bad" words with new words that feel more neutral or empowering)" (Serano). This can particularly be seen in the evolution of subject headings (see table 4.4) and the terminology used within LGBTQ+ literature for children. In many ways, this project has the potential to fall victim to just such a binary understanding of each examined text as either "good" or "bad," "right" or "wrong." It is my hope, however, that by mapping representation and language in these texts rather than attempting to evaluate them through a particular temporally situated lens, it is possible to see the educational potential that exists within individual texts and the larger body of existing literature.

EXPLAINING GENDER TO CHILDREN

While, in the previous section, I noted that language around trans identities is not necessarily good or bad but rather is dependent upon historical context, wrapped up in activist language and social stigma, as we continue to develop new and more inclusive understandings of trans identities, what is considered "acceptable" by trans people from various generations continues to shift. As such, each generation of children will learn new language and new ways of being inclusive and accepting of trans people within society at large. This section and the accompanying examples can be understood as a particular moment in history, as an example of the possibilities for helping children learn to be respectful and inclusive using the language and terminology available in a particular moment in time. While these examples may not hold true indefinitely as language continues to evolve, they do reveal a foundation, at least, from which conversations around language and terminology can continue to evolve along with the literature that will be available for parents to read to their children or for teachers to use within classroom and library spaces. Children's literature can be used to help children understand and accept gender and sexual diversity but only if there is enough varied representation to show a whole spectrum of trans and queer experiences.

In her article on teaching children to use inclusive language, Lora Grady interviews parents about how they approach the use of inclusive and respectful language related to trans kids and adults. One parent, Lorie English, shared her experiences with her son, Ben, and her daughter, Jack:

> English explained Jack's transition to her son, Ben, now five, in simple terms: "Jack believes she is a girl, so Jack is going to be your sister." As soon as they started using she/her pronouns at home, Ben caught on right away. Other than some questions about anatomy . . . the explanation was "literally that simple." Now, Ben introduces Jack as his sister and will correct others when they make mistakes with Jack's pronouns. (Grady)

Similarly, Amber Leventry, when exploring how to talk to children about gender, completed interviews with parents in order to assess how children respond to discussions of gender and language in various contexts, including highlighting the dynamics between a nonbinary parent and their child: "Casey Brown came out as nonbinary when their daughter was six.... Using a big piece of paper, Brown and their daughter wrote down gendered and neutral words. Their daughter understood that the 'girl' words felt good to describe herself, and that helped her to understand that Brown felt best being described with the words in the neutral column." The picture books being discussed here have, for the most part, been created by people who desire to provide an opportunity to help children learn and understand various concepts around gender, particularly in relation to parent-child dynamics.

Since this is the case, the pedagogical possibilities for the texts are numerous, though, as seen in a number of cases, these possibilities become limited by mixed messages. The use of varied pronouns and the reinforcement of gender stereotypes and gendered language not only create potential confusion but also limit the possibility of helping children break the cycle of binaries and binary language that many of these authors rely on. And while it is not in itself problematic for trans individuals to identify within a binary, if the only representation that exists relies on binaries, it can make it more difficult to use existing literature to help children understand the complexities (and existence) of, for example, nonbinary and genderqueer identities. The process used by both adults in the scenarios above shows that there is potential for learning opportunities through the incorporation of discussions around respect and self-confidence; in both cases, the adults showed that the use of certain terms and pronouns made people happier and more confident. Though these examples will likely end up becoming outdated or perhaps might even be considered problematic by others in the future, these scenarios, at their core, show how exploring language with children can lead to better understandings of acceptance, inclusivity, and respect, particularly with regard to trans and queer people.

EXISTING LITERATURE

The number of picture books that currently exist with transgender adults and parents is limited. *Carly: She's Still My Daddy* (2004) by Mary Boenke is one of the first to examine a child's response to a parent's transition, though it was never meant to be a widely circulated piece of literature, having been created as more of a zine by the transgender network PFLAG to help explain certain issues around gender transition to children.[3] *Carly* was originally published as a computer printout with black-and-white illustrations, like a zine, for families to explain the process of transition to a child audience. While useful within PFLAG at the time it was created, it is now a text that remains firmly fixed within a particular timeframe and purpose and is not easily accessible or entirely useful for a contemporary audience after seventeen years of change in social, political, and academic understanding of transgender people and history.

Carly begins, as all the following picture books do, with a child narrator introducing themselves and giving readers an introduction to their trans parent: "My daddy is turning into a WOMAN! I can't believe it!" (Boenke 3). These lines are accompanied by an illustration of a young boy, Tommy, sitting on some stairs in front of a house, a thought bubble of question marks over his head, his chin resting in his hands. This text uses terms and definitions that currently would be disputed or updated for greater inclusivity and acceptance of nonbinary individuals. For instance, Tommy notes, "Daddy started talking to a COUNSELOR who helped him figure out that he was TRANSGENDERED.[4] (That's the word for people who look like boys, but know, inside, they are really girls, or the other way around)" (5). This description not only uses (what is now considered) problematic language but also is quite narrow and limiting, conforming to a binary understanding of gender and failing to acknowledge the existence of nonconforming genders and gender expressions. However, what this text does that others—until *My Maddy* (2020)—do not is introduce other terms and language around gender expression and other identities, such as the concept of intersex individuals (7).

Boenke's text, even with some introduction to concepts considered radical in their time, conforms to gendered language and particular gender roles. For instance, Tommy notes, "My daddy's best friend told me he used to be a woman and now he's a man. He has a beard and *a man's voice*" (Boenke 8; emphasis added). Later in the narrative, Tommy also states that Carly—the title he has chosen over "mom" or "dad"—has "started going to work *dressed as a women* [sic]" (15; emphasis added). These examples, along with other instances throughout the text, point back to mainstream and "traditional" expectations around what people should wear, how they should sound and act, and how they should express their genders depending on whether they are seen as male or female and whether they conform to that expectation. As the first book on this topic for children, *Carly* created something of a template for future picture books on the subject to follow, from the child narrator's self-introduction to the explanation of what their parent looked like and acted like "before" to how they act and look during and after social and physical transitions to a happy ending that reinforces the relief and happiness of the trans parent now that their gender expression and their gender both match. This is, as one would expect considering a child audience, rather simplistic as a narrative structure and one that unfortunately reinforces certain mainstream expectations around gender, binaries, and the process of transition, but it also opens the world of children's literature to the possibility of giving children a starting point from which to engage in respectful questioning and dialogue when faced with a parent's transition.

My Mommy Is a Boy (2011), like *Carly*, was self-published—though, in this case, using an online platform—and was also created by author Jason Martinez to explain the process of transitioning to his daughter. Although both books were likely helpful at the time, as will be discussed in more detail later, they create some unfortunate confusion through the use of conflicting gendered language and terminology. While, theoretically, this does mirror the confusion experienced by children and parents during the process of social and physical transition, if the purpose of these texts is to help clarify and reduce confusion, that goal may not be fully achieved. Here is one example from the text: "Some people call my mom, 'He,' some call her, 'She.' It doesn't bother her but she likes, 'He' better" (Martinez 5). The accompanying image shows Amaya, the protagonist, laying on a carpeted floor with sheets of paper in front of her, the words "he" and "she" scribbled on them, while her parent watches from an armchair. Within this single page are a number of conflicting approaches to pronouns and gender, with Amaya discussing her parent using both he/him and she/her pronouns. Additionally, throughout the book, Amaya refers to things through a binary gendered lens, such as "Mommy likes to wear boy's clothes and cut her hair really short," and "She also changed her name to a boy's name" (4, 8). This type of conflation of hair styles and clothing choices with specific genders reinforces for the child reader—and adult readers—that there is a binary choice of how to express gender and that there is no real impact on a child-parent relationship if pronouns and name changes are ignored or considered optional for children. It can take time to change these habits, depending on the child's age, but *My Mommy Is a Boy* seems to be more concerned with reinforcing gender stereotypes than looking at respectful language. Although the book may be attempting to mirror the messier ways of thinking and interacting that happen in reality, fiction also allows authors to present different, perhaps even less confusing, ways of approaching subjects for young readers. In this case, the vacillating pronoun usage and reliance on gendered language can end up causing even further confusion for a young reader rather than clarification.

As Jennifer Miller notes in her online review of *My Mommy Is a Boy*, "The confusion his daughter may have experienced, confusion [Martinez] tried to convey, doesn't translate well to helping other children understand the gender transition of a parent." Martinez's use of she/her pronouns along with the continued use of "mommy" throughout the text even though the parent is a trans man creates a continued sense of instability around gendered language and terminology that fails to clarify much of the transition process for young readers. The books noted in table 4.1 are those that focus on physical and social transition of a parent as the main narrative arc (with the exception of *My Maddy*, which asks readers to simply accept that the protagonist's parent is nonbinary from the beginning).

This same style of storytelling—with a child looking back at how a parent "used to be"—is also evident in *My New Mommy* (2012) and *My New Daddy* (2012). Written by Lilly Mossiano and illustrated by her wife, Sage Mossiano, the two books were also created for a specific educational purpose and as a form of advocacy attempting to destigmatize trans-parent families. A note at the end of *My New Mommy* explains, "Being transgender in today's society can be challenging. Without a lot of education or tolerance being taught, gender nonconforming individuals often find themselves in uncomfortable and dangerous situations" (Mossiano). Both of these books use a child narrator to look back at what their parent used to be like in terms of physical attributes and other forms of gender expression, including gender roles to some extent. As with the first two books discussed, these two have a very specific purpose for being published: "This book explains, in simple terms, male to female transition. Though the retitling of a parent is something that is as private a decision as transition itself, the use of 'daddy' and 'mommy' here are more strictly to explain the mental acceptance of Violet, our little narrator, then to indicate the need for such a title change" (*My New Mommy*). With both of Mossiano's books, the use of pronouns and gender-role titles is more consistent than in Martinez's book, showing a more stable and steady progression for the child narrators, highlighting their ability to change how they see their parent in terms of gender and role. Mossiano, however, also relies on certain stereotypical gender attributes, such as clothing and hair length/style, to show a physical transition, which can be an impediment to understanding the fluidity of gender and the existence of trans parents who are nonbinary.

My New Mommy begins with the following: "Hi, my name is Violet, and this is what my daddy used to look like" (Mossiano). The accompanying illustration shows Violet standing in a yard with her parent standing in a pile of leaves, waving at the reader. The parent has short brown hair and a scruffy beard and is wearing jeans and a T-shirt. As the book progresses, Violet's parent shows signs of transition: "He used to have a beard. Then, one day, he shaved it off," and "He used to have short hair. Then over time, he let it grow out." Halfway through, Violet tells the reader, "My daddy sat down with me and explained to me that nature made a mistake and he should have been born a girl like me." This seems to be an attempt at a simplistic explanation for the sake of a child reader, which is not in itself a problem, but the use of the born-in-the-wrong-body trope has become somewhat problematic as a metaphor. The UK-based Mermaids group exists to support gender-diverse children and young people, and they recently posted a response to the phrase "born in the wrong body." A patron of Mermaids, Munroe Bergdorf, writes, "I know why I used to use [the phrase]; because other people struggled to understand, but looking back I know it did me harm. Saying you have the wrong body feels like a kind of self-abuse" ("Do You Use the Phrase"). It is not "wrong" to say it if it is how a person feels about themselves, but like so many issues around representation, it is not about the existence of a trope but rather the continued use of a single trope with no variation. While children may not care much about these distinctions and complexities, it seems a missed opportunity to utilize the educational element of these texts and show that there are more nuanced ways of understanding transness. The born-in-the-wrong-body trope continues to this day, including in the more recent picture book *Rachel's Christmas Boat* (2017) by Sophie Labelle.

In Labelle's picture book, Lulu is enjoying the final weeks before Christmas. She loves to make gifts for people, and this year, she has made a toy sailboat for her dad. But two weeks before Christmas, Lulu's parents sit her down for a talk. It turns out that her "dad found out she liked the name Rachel better than her old name, and that being a lady was much more true to her heart than being a man" (Labelle 5). Unlike the previous four titles, which are set in the present looking back at the adult's transition, *Rachel's Christmas Boat* is happening in the present, allowing readers to experience the news and parts of the transition along with Lulu. Her response is immediately accepting: "So dad is a woman? Cool!" (5). This serves as a slight change from the responses of the child protagonists in earlier narratives, which all indicate a longer period of acceptance and understanding. This narrative allows children to witness Lulu's acceptance of her parent's gender, while the accompanying illustrations show the happiness her parents feel because of her response, thereby reinforcing the positive aspects of accepting and supporting a trans person's gender and gender expression. The core of this story revolves around not Lulu's acceptance and support—that happens quickly and easily—but rather her sudden realization that now she has to change the name that she painted on the boat she made for Christmas and also her fear that Santa won't find out in time to change Rachel's name on her other gifts. The main component that follows from earlier texts is that Rachel still gives Lulu the option of calling her "dad," which could potentially lead to similar confusion as in the other texts.

Each of these previous texts, either self-published or published by niche publishers, is attempting to act as both an educational resource for transparent families and a point of entry into the world of children's publishing to shed light on an area of trans representation that is all too often ignored within mainstream publishing. Both a positive and a negative aspect of publishing a book without a mainstream publisher for backing is marketing. While concerns about what is "marketable" might keep mainstream publishers from purchasing works such as those discussed above, those same concerns are sometimes used productively to help encourage authors and illustrators to respond to larger sociopolitical shifts that might otherwise be missed. An example of a text that manages to avoid many of the complications and potentially confusing treatments of terminology and language is Gayle E. Pitman's *My Maddy* (2020), which is also the only example of a nonbinary parent out of all the examples noted in this chapter.

My Maddy follows an unnamed young girl and their parent, who is neither male nor female, through routine daily activities. The child calls their parent Maddy. This can be seen by readers as either a name or a title—a combination of "mommy" and "daddy"—and provides the child audience with possible new language to use for parents who are neither male nor female. Interestingly, coming sixteen years after *Carly*, Pitman's book also explores what it means to be intersex.[5] Since Maddy is not transitioning throughout the narrative—taking a break from the traditional narrative structure that Boenke spawned—the focus of the book is rather on breaking down boundaries and expectations around gender roles and gender expression and finding ways to discuss the concept of gender with children without relying on or reinforcing binary stereotypes. In this way, *My Maddy* serves as a counterpoint to the previous texts about trans parents and as an exemplary text in its own right. This is also the only book from a mainstream publisher, written by a long-time author and illustrated by a veteran artist. It is also the only book reviewed by professional review journals, thus helping it to find a home on more library shelves and in more bookstores than any of the other texts about this subject.

Pitman's book also allows for the possibility of shedding gendered titles for a parent altogether, choosing to have the narrator call their parent Maddy rather than "mom" or "dad" or variations thereof. In some ways, this mirrors Boenke's text where Tommy chooses to use a name other than "mom" or "dad" to refer to his trans parent. Research on trans-parent families suggests that it is sometimes a very useful option to opt out of gendered terminology, even if this means combining or playing with existing language: some children opt to use a name other than "mom" or "dad" to refer to their parent, such as a gender-neutral pronoun (like "they") or an agreed-upon nickname for the trans parent (Dierckx et al. 407; see also Dierckx and Platero; Hines). Utilizing this strategy can help children and adults to move beyond a reliance on binaries. As Jody Norton writes, "Children's literature continues to operate on the basis of an outmoded binary paradigm of gender, in part because psychiatry, the social sciences, legal theory, education, and the humanities continue to function, for the most part, as though it had not already been clearly demonstrated that there are neither two sexes and two genders, nor two sex/genders" (295). *My Maddy*, therefore, allows parents, educators, and children to see possibilities beyond male/female genders and binary gender expression and gender roles and highlights opportunities for exploring what it means to be a nonbinary parent outside of the familiar transition narrative.

Many of these books contain elements of what might be considered "good" or "bad" by some, depending on the context and positionality of the reader(s), but it is clear that each narrative was created with a purpose—to generate a space for interrogation of social and political expectations on gender, transition, parenting, and childhood. This is done in slightly different ways within each picture book, using a variety of illustration styles, publishing methods, and uses of certain terminology, but they still, with the exception of *My Maddy*, continue to rely on a narrative that follows the process of transition within a very normative context: white, middle class, and with adherence to certain normative aspects of gender and expression.

CONCLUSIONS

Much like the early days of other LGBTQ+ narratives in children's literature, the early days of trans-parent narratives have relied on individuals pushing boundaries and attempting to show that change and acceptance is possible in the mainstream. But self-publishing and niche publishing often fail to find a large audience due to a lack of resources (as seen in table 4.3). Library acquisitions staff often rely on larger review publications, such as *Booklist*, *The Horn Book*, *School Library Journal*, *Publishers Weekly*, *Kirkus Reviews*, and *Shelf Awareness*, to make decisions on books to purchase for their collections. Niche publishing and self-publishing, though, can allow for more freedom for authors and illustrators to include more inclusive representation. As noted earlier, however, the history of trans-parent representation is rather white and normative in picture books in which the focus is adult transition. There is more positive and inclusive representation of disabled and nonwhite adult characters in those books that explore multiple families and those in which trans parents are not the focus, showing that there are possibilities for more inclusive representation in the future and hopefully more so in books that focus on trans-parent families.

As with so much literature about topics not considered to be mainstream enough, many start out self-published or published by small, niche publishers—one need only look to the original publication of *Heather Has Two Mommies* (1989) by Lesléa Newman, for instance—but it is either the case that these books are eventually picked up by a larger publisher (as in Newman's case) or that new books on similar topics are later seen as marketable by the big publishing houses.[6] This can be seen through the progression of picture books about transgender adults and parents, starting with a book printed and folded like a zine, moving to niche publishers, such as Flamingo Rampant (which at the time of writing this chapter, has made a deal with a midsize publishing house in Canada for distribution to increase visibility and accessibility), and finally to *My Maddy* (2020) published by Magination Press, a mainstream publishing division of the American Psychological Association specializing in LGBTQ+ stories. This progression, along with shifting terminology used in associated subject headings and within the narratives themselves, is also encouraging as it shows that there is a certain amount of willingness among authors and publishers, as well as librarians and educators, to adapt to sociocultural shifts.

The purpose of this chapter has been to understand the possibilities for reading picture books with trans adults and trans parents, to see the ways in which these texts are products of their time as well as how the entire body of existing literature has evolved over time. Parents, librarians, and educators, with an understanding of this overview, can use the possible readings and examinations of each text in order to find ways of engaging with children, whether their own or those in classrooms and libraries, to help them better comprehend concepts related to gender, gender expression, and language use around pronouns and terminology. These texts, along with other more

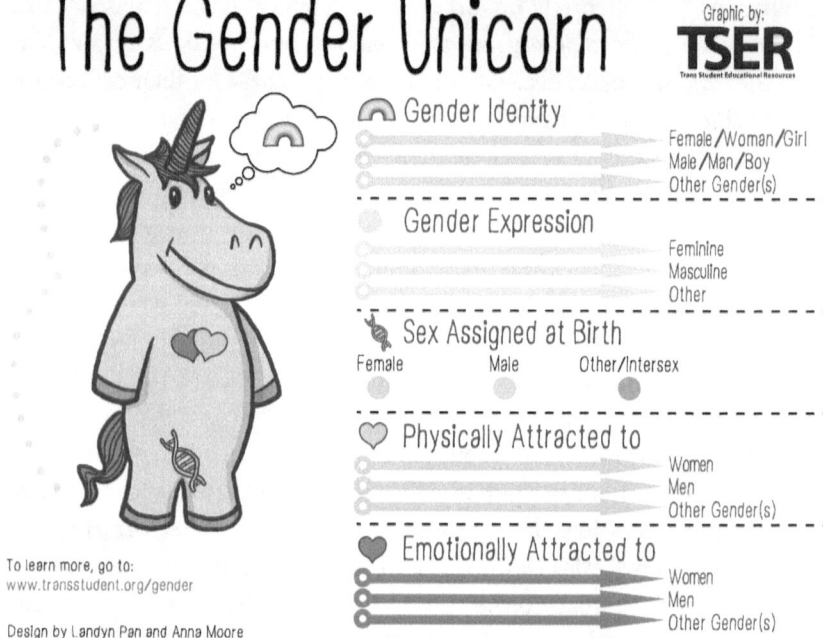

Figure 4.1. The "Gender Unicorn" is a tool for helping people understand the components of gender, expression, and sexuality. *Source*: "Gender Unicorn."

current resources such as the Gender Unicorn (see figure 4.1), can give children a glimpse into the many possible ways of existing in the world as a trans person. And trans-parent families can use this combination of resources to help engage with their own children and others in productive ways to make a more understanding and empathetic future for trans people in all stages of life. Picture books, like all literature, have the potential to help people see themselves and others in new ways, to visualize new perspectives and create awareness of the nuanced and complex approaches to gender, family, and relationships (Bishop). And what could be more important at this moment in time when trans and queer people are the subjects of physical, emotional, and political violence in the name of "protecting" children?

NOTES

1. A story in the *Washington Post* reports that the majority of all book challenges in America—from a sample of 986 recorded challenges from 2021 to 2022—were filed by only eleven people (Natanson).

2. The books I discuss do not make up a comprehensive list, but they do constitute most of the existing literature that respectfully explores trans adults and trans parents. *My Dad Wears*

Pirate Shoes: A Young Boy's Struggle over His Transgender Father (2012) by Gae Hall is about a cross-dressing parent who eventually comes out as trans, but it is framed as deviant and harmful behavior that pits the child against his trans parent, and such books are not productive texts within the context of this chapter. I do believe it is important to bring awareness to its existence, however, if those reading this chapter come across it at any point.

Also, a word on terminology: "rainbow families" can be understood as those with lesbian, gay, bisexual, transgender, or queer people or individuals who have a child or children or who are hoping for or expecting a child.

3. PFLAG originally stood for Parents and Friends of Lesbians and Gays and, later, Parents, Families and Friends of Lesbians and Gays, but it is no longer an acronym, just the name of the organization.

4. According to the *GLAAD Media Reference Guide*, "The adjective *transgender* should never have an extraneous '-ed' tacked onto the end. An '-ed' suffix adds unnecessary length to the word and can cause tense confusion and grammatical errors. It also brings transgender into alignment with lesbian, gay, bisexual, and queer. You would not say that Elton John is 'gayed' or Ellen DeGeneres is 'lesbianed,' therefore you would not say Chaz Bono is 'transgendered'" ("Glossary of Terms").

5. According to InterACT (Advocates for Intersex Youth), "Intersex is an umbrella term for differences in sex traits or reproductive anatomy. Intersex people are born with these differences or develop them in childhood. There are many possible differences in genitalia, hormones, internal anatomy, or chromosomes, compared to the usual two ways that human bodies develop" ("What Is the Definition"). Additionally, "Some intersex traits are noticed at birth. Others don't show up until puberty or later in life. Intersex people often face shame—or are forced or coerced into changing their bodies, usually at a very young age. Most surgeries to change intersex traits happen in infancy."

6. In an interview with Shannon Maughan, Newman notes, "We stuffed and licked envelopes and used mailing lists from the readings I had for my books for adults. We raised $4000, mostly in $10 donations. We promised people a book or their money back if it didn't get published. A year later 4,000 copies were printed and about half were spoken for."

WORKS CITED

"Banned in the USA Q&A: Kyle Lukoff on the 'Desperate Importance' of Fighting Book Bans." *PEN America: The Freedom to Write*, 21 Sept. 2022, https://pen.org/kyle-lukoff-on-the-desperate-importance-of-fighting-book-bans/.

Bishop, Rudine Sims. "Mirrors, Windows, and Sliding Glass Doors." *Perspectives: Choosing and Using Books for the Classroom*, vol. 6, no. 3, pp. ix–xi.

Bittner, Robert, et al. "Queer and Trans-Themed Books for Young Readers: A Critical Review." *Discourse: Studies in the Cultural Politics of Education*, vol. 37, no. 6, 2016, pp. 948–64.

Boenke, Mary. *Carly: She's Still My Daddy*. Illustrated by Dolores Dudley, Transgender Network of Parents, Families and Friends of Lesbians and Gays, 2004.

Brannen, Sarah S. *Uncle Bobby's Wedding*. Illustrated by Brannen, G. P. Putnam's Sons, 2008.

Bruhm, Stephen, and Natasha Hurley, editors. *Curiouser: On the Queerness of Children*. U of Minnesota P, 2004.

dePaola, Tomie. *Oliver Button Is a Sissy*. Illustrated by dePaola, Houghton Mifflin Harcourt, 1979.

Dierckx, Myrte, et al. "Resilience in Families in Transition: What Happens When a Parent Is Transgender?" *Family Relations: Interdisciplinary Journal of Applied Family Science*, vol. 66, no. 3, 2017, pp. 399–411.

Dierckx, Myrte, and R. Lucas Platero. "The Meaning of Trans* in a Family Context." *Critical Social Policy*, vol. 38, no. 1, 2018, pp. 78–98.

"Do You Use the Phrase: 'Born in the Wrong Body'?" *Mermaids*, 25 Sept. 2020, https://mermaidsuk.org.uk/news/do-you-still-use-the-phrase-born-in-the-wrong-body/.

Ewert, Marcus. *10,000 Dresses*. Illustrated by Rex Ray, Triangle Square, 2008.

"The Gender Unicorn." *Trans Student Educational Resources*, 2015, www.transstudent.org/gender.

"Glossary of Terms: Transgender." *GLAAD Media Reference Guide*, 11th edition, *GLAAD*, https://glaad.org/reference/trans-terms/. Accessed 22 Feb. 2024.

Gould, Lois. *X: A Fabulous Child's Story*. Illustrated by Jacqueline Chwast, Daughters Publishing, 1978.

Grady, Lora. "How to Teach Your Kids to Use Inclusive Language." *Parents Canada*, 20 June 2020, https://www.parentscanada.com/family-life/how-to-teach-your-kids-to-use-inclusive-language/.

Hall, Gae. *My Dad Wears Pirate Shoes: A Young Boy's Struggle over His Transgender Father*. Illustrated by Melanie Carter, CreateSpace, 2012.

Herthel, Jessica, and Jazz Jennings. *I Am Jazz*. Illustrated by Shelah McNicholas, Dial Books, 2014.

Hines, Sally. "Intimate Transitions: Transgender Practices of Partnering and Parenting." *Sociology*, vol. 40, no. 2, 2006, pp. 353–71.

Labelle, Sophie. *Rachel's Christmas Boat*. Illustrated by Labelle, Flamingo Rampant, 2017.

Leventry, Amber. "Explaining Nonbinary: How to Talk to Kids about Gender." *Parents*, 11 Mar. 2020, https://www.parents.com/kids/how-to-talk-to-kids-about-gender/.

Lukoff, Kyle. *When Aidan Became a Brother*. Illustrated by Kaylani Juanita, Lee and Low, 2019.

Martinez, Jason. *My Mommy Is a Boy*. Illustrated by Karen Winchester, 2013.

Maughan, Shannon. "A Second Life for '*Heather Has Two Mommies*.'" *Publisher's Weekly*, 16 Mar. 2015, www.publishersweekly.com/pw/by-topic/childrens/childrens-book-news/article/65886-a-second-life-for-heather-has-two-mommies.html.

Miller, Jennifer. Review of *My Mommy is a Boy* by Jason Martinez. *Raise Them Righteous*, 29 Sept. 2019, https://raisethemrighteous.com/2019/09/29/jason-martinezs-my-mommy-is-a-boy-2013/.

Mossiano, Lilly. *My New Daddy*. Illustrated by Sage Mossiano, Spun Silver Productions, 2012.

Mossiano, Lilly. *My New Mommy*. Illustrated by Sage Mossiano, Spun Silver Productions, 2012.

Natanson, Hannah. "Objection to Sexual, LGBTQ Content Propels Spike in Book Challenges." *Washington Post*, 23 May 2023, https://www.washingtonpost.com/education/2023/05/23/lgbtq-book-ban-challengers/.

Newman, Lesléa. *Donovan's Big Day*. Illustrated by Mike Dutton, Tricycle Press, 2011.

Newman, Lesléa. *Heather Has Two Mommies*. Illustrated by Diana Souza, Alyson Books, 1989.

Norton, Jody. "Transchildren and the Discipline of Children's Literature." *Over the Rainbow: Queer Children's and Young Adult Literature*, edited by Michelle Ann Abate and Kenneth Kidd, U of Michigan P, 2011, pp. 293–313.

Peck, Richard. *The Best Man*. Dial, 2016.

Pfeffer, Carla A., and Kierra B. Jones. "Transgender-Parent Families." *LGBTQ-Parent Families: Innovations in Research and Implications for Practice*, edited by Abbie Goldberg and Katherine Allen, Springer, 2020, pp. 199–214.

Pitman, Gayle E. *My Maddy*. Illustrated by Violet Tobacco, Magination Press, 2020.

Serano, Julia. "On the 'Activist Language Merry-go-round,' Stephen Pinker's 'Euphemism Treadmill,' and 'Political Correctness' More Generally." *Whipping Girl*, 2 June 2014, http://juliaserano.blogspot.com/2014/06/on-activist-language-merry-go-round.html.

Steinmetz, Katy. "The Transgender Tipping Point." *Time*, 29 May 2014, https://time.com/135480/transgender-tipping-point/.

"What Is the Definition of Intersex?" *InterACT*, 26 Jan. 2021, https://interactadvocates.org/faq/, Accessed 17 May 2021.

Zolotow, Charlotte. *William's Doll*. Illustrated by William Pène du Bois, HarperCollins, 1972.

PART 2
REAL(ISTIC) REPRESENTATIONS OF GIaNTs IN PICTURE BOOKS

CHAPTER 5

EXCEPTIONAL, BULLIED, OR NORMAL IN THE END
Representation of GIaNTs (Gender Independent, Nonbinary, and Trans) in Picture Books

j wallace skelton

In 2005, when I first began engaging schools in the work of anticipating, welcoming, and celebrating children of all gender identities, teachers would tell me that they could not talk about trans identities in class "because there aren't any books!" This was not true then and is even less true now, but books with GIaNT (gender-independent, nonbinary, and trans) characters were seldom in school libraries, taught in teacher education programs, or in the Scholastic Book Fair. What teachers meant was "I don't know of any books yet." They often wanted the books, but they didn't know where or how to find them. Their experience with picture books for GIaNT children was one of absence and erasure.

At the time, I was a member of a school board's Equity Team, responsible for work connected to sexual orientation and gender identity, in 102 schools. I was often asked for book recommendations. I discovered that when I gave teachers a couple of book suggestions, this was often met with resistance, including statements like "This isn't right for my age group" or "This book does not match the trans child in my class." My next strategy was to purchase every book I came across with GIaNT characters, and I accumulated two large suitcases full of them. I would arrive at a school, set up a beautiful display of books, and invite teachers to select books that were right, in their professional opinions, for their students. Teachers then felt as though there were plenty to choose from, which meant GIaNT characters in picture books seemed more normative, GIaNT children became more normative, and teachers felt empowered to make their own choices and talk with their students. I felt pretty good about this.

Then, one evening, my then-nonbinary four-year-old asked me to read them some of the many books that had newly arrived at our home. They wanted new stories, stories about nonbinary kids like them. So we snuggled in and started. In each of the books that evening, the GIaNT child was bullied and harassed. Sometimes, it was by their parents; sometimes, it was by their teachers; often, it was by their peers. My child told me that they didn't want any more "bully books" and asked me to read them something else.

My four-year-old taught me that we need to pay more attention to the stories in the books to really see what kind of messages these books were sharing. My child wanted, in the words of Lavern Cox, "possibility models," and they wanted to imagine something beyond merely surviving or enduring bullying (@Lavernecox). My acronym "GIaNT" is a response to their need for possibilities. I use "GIaNT" to refer to gender-independent, nonbinary, and trans children as an intentional way of taking up space as GIaNT children have been made to be small for too long. It's part of my commitment to not just think about their identities but also honor, uphold, and celebrate them.

My four-year-old's dissatisfaction launched me into analyzing picture books with GIaNT main characters, published in English between 1936 and 2015. I found 144 of them. My four-year-old was right—many of the books contained themes that reinforced negative messages about GIaNT children; the books either (1) required GIaNT characters to do something exceptional to be accepted, (2) are focused on bullying, or (3) contained redemptive stories where the GIaNT child (or their behavior) was accepted only because, in the end, it served to reinforce heteropatriarchy and the gender binary.

This chapter is not simply a look at picture books with GIaNT characters. This chapter puts trans theory to the task of analyzing these books. Trans theory demands that we "theorize transsexual and transgender experience on its own terms" (Rubin 279). Trans theory enables us to look at these books not from the lens of how they might educate cis peers but for the ways they center the GIaNT children themselves, their existence, their needs and desires and the ways they grant them access to language, history, and stories about themselves. Trans theory necessitates us moving beyond the question, "Are there any books?" and demands we write and purchase books by and for GIaNT people with stories that are not corrective or punishing but rather where we get to flourish.

CREATING A LIST OF BOOKS FOR ANALYSIS

My first inclusion criterion for books is that they are be picture books intended for children and published in English (original or translation) between 1936 and 2015. Self-published books are included if they are available in print. Second, one of the main characters must either identify as GIaNT or is explicitly identified as breaking gendered expectations through their words, actions, clothing, or desires. My third criterion is that I am able to assess the book myself—the physical book, an electronic copy, pdf, or photographs are all fine, but I do not rely on others' descriptions.

I compared my lists to those previously identified by scholars, including Jamie Cambell Naidoo's, B. J. Epstein's, Nancy Silverrod's, and Patricia Sarles's, as a way of validating my research and ensuring I was not missing titles. My analysis includes 144 books with GIaNT characters, as compared to Naidoo's forty-nine, Silverrod's sixty, and Sarles's seventy-one. Of course, I had the advantage of being able to access their work.

The list I created includes forty-five titles where boys break gender stereotypes, forty-nine where girls break gender stereotypes, sixteen that allow children to project their own understandings of gender (often via analogy), and thirty-seven with characters that are explicitly GIaNT. Some books appear on more than one sublist.

WHAT'S WRONG WITH ERASURE?

When the teachers described in my introduction stated, "There aren't any books!" they were both describing and engaging in erasure (Namaste). Erasure names the way that GIaNT characters are excluded from much of children's literature. We're just not there. Academic papers with titles like "Missing Persons' Report! Where Are the Transgender Characters in Children's Picture Books?," by A. L. Sullivan and L. L. Urraro, document our absence. Mainstream awards in children's literature, such as the Newbery Medal or the Caldecott Medal, practice erasure and have never once been awarded to a book about GIANT children. Both the Newbery and Caldecott Medals are prestigious. Given annually by the American Library Association, the Newbery has recognized children's authors since 1921, and the Caldecott has recognized illustrators since 1937. Neither one of them have ever recognized a book that centers on a GIaNT child. Erasure tells GIaNT children that they do not exist, that their lives are not possible. This absence of books creates "testimonial injustice" where GIaNT children are deprived of access to words and stories about their own identities and, because of this absence, may face disbelief when they talk about their identities (Steele and Nicholson 4). Young children seldom make the purchasing decisions for schools and libraries; this is a harm perpetuated by adults and that adults need to fix. When we don't, it puts the responsibility on children to ask for these books, risking them being seen as demanding, as exceptions, as the problem.

Erasure is experienced by most GIaNT children, and then specific GIaNT children experience erasure even within books intended to celebrate GIaNT children. In particular, Black, Indigenous, and people of color (BIPOC) experience erasure, as do disabled people.

ERASURE OF BIPOC GIaNT CHILDREN

Christine Jenkins performed a race and class analysis of young adult novels with lesbian, gay, bisexual, trans, queer, plus (LGBTQ+) characters. She analyzed sixty books published between 1969 and 1992 and found, "according to both the earlier and the more recent novels, most gay/lesbian people are white and middle class. Only three of the sixty books portray people of colour as gay or lesbian, all of the African-American" (Jenkins 149).[1] In my own analysis of books including GIaNT children (see the section "Books Surveyed" in the list of works cited), there is a similar overrepresentation of white middle class males. In the books I have identified as displaying the theme of "boys can break gender stereotypes," 89 percent of the main characters are white, meaning there are only three books with protagonists of color. In a further sixteen books (37 percent), conversations of race were avoided by having animal or monster main characters. Skin color, however, is not the only way to signal race, and the animals often have names of Anglophone, European background, participate in cultural activities that signal whiteness, live in homes that resemble homes of white suburban middle America, or otherwise signal whiteness through their clothes, music, etc. So even when the animals are not themselves actually white, they have sufficient cultural markers that they are coded white, allowing white children to see themselves and relegating BIPOC children to the experience of erasure. The animals never engage in conversations that might indicate being newcomers; they never talk about immigrating, having relatives in another country, finding it hard to find familiar foods, or speaking a different language at home than they do elsewhere. In this way, books using animals, monsters, or amorphous blobs become a way of sidestepping conversations about race—the authors can claim to have written books that are not centered on white individuals while having sufficient signifiers of whiteness such that they attract and soothe the white gaze and erase BIPOC people entirely.

Among the books with human main characters on the list in which boys can break gender stereotypes, 89 percent of the main characters are white, meaning there are only three books with protagonists of color. This is the same percentage of books about people of color that the Cooperative Children's Book Centre (CCBC) found in all children's books published in 2014 ("Books"). In keeping with Jenkins's research findings, all the protagonists of color are Black, thus limiting diversity to only two of many possibilities.

In *Histories of the Transgender Child* (2018), Jules Gill-Peterson carefully documents the activism of actual trans children of color in the United States since before the rise of the gender clinic. She argues that trans children of color have always existed and that their demands for appropriate care and treatment have shaped the standards of care that trans people experience today. Gill-Peterson resists erasure. Excitingly, we are beginning to see picture books that do similar work, and books such as *Sylvia and Marsha Start a Revolution! The Story of the Trans Women of Color Who Made LGBTQ+ History* by Joy Michael Ellison provides GIaNT children of color with possibility models.

ERASURE OF DISABLED GIaNT CHILDREN

Of 144 titles in the section "Books Surveyed" in the list of works cited, only eleven include some representation of a person with a disability. The person with a disability is named in only two of these texts, and only in one are they the central character. The person with a disability only speaks in three of the books, making them less like characters and more like an attempt by the author and/or illustrator to indicate they are inclusive. Disabled GIaNT children not only frequently experience erasure, even when they are present, they also are often silenced.

While, as per Jenkins's work above, children's literature uses Blackness to signify people of color (POC), people with disabilities are flattened and signified by a "person using a wheelchair." The symbolic way this operates often feels like the chair is there to show us that the book is diverse, not because the person using the chair is part of the story or doing something interesting.

It's about the chair, not the person. In both cases, these visual symbols are not intended for the people they represent but for people who are not members of the group. In fact, the people they depict are likely to experience this as tokenistic, while the richer and broader category that they claim to represent goes without further exploration or representation. In "Contrived or Inspired: Ability/Disability in the Children's Picture Books," Z. Sonia Worotynec explains that the circle-of-inclusion checklist has three main criteria and details some common failures in well-meaning books: "The main categories of the Circle of Inclusion checklist call for books to show children with disabilities as leaders, problem-solvers and role models."

Applying this test, only three available picture books would pass: *The Zero Dads Club* by Angel Adeyoha, *Is That for a Boy or a Girl?* by S. Bear Bergman, and *Frida* by Jonathan Winters—in other words, three out of 144 books, or 2 percent. The character with a disability is only named in two of the books. It seems relevant to note that Adeyoha is a person with a disability, and the eponymous Frida is a person with a disability. It seems a terrible failure of imagination that only a person with a disability or a person writing a biography about a person with a disability can portray the lives of named people with disabilities in a meaningful way.

GIaNT children need books that anticipate them. They need books where they, and not their gender identity, are central characters. They need books that center their experiences and their understanding of the world. GIaNT children need books that show them in their intersectional glory, that acknowledge their race and ethnicity, their faith, their disabilities, their neurodivergence, their class, and their geography. All GIaNT children need an end to the erasure; when purchasing books, look for books that address these intersections and the needs of people who face greater systemic barriers.

WHAT'S WRONG WITH BEING EXCEPTIONAL?

Of the books I examined that feature children who were assigned male at birth and display feminine behavior, 25 percent are stories of these characters achieving acceptance through exceptionality. The characters may save a life, win a talent show, or perform feats of superhuman strength, but the message is that who you are is worthy of bullying and ridicule—until or unless you complete a truly heroic feat.

The first form this damaging trope takes is that a boy can be feminine as long as he is also a hero and saves a life or the lives of others. Here, a boy's gender-exceptional behavior is accepted by the community only *after* he has demonstrated that it is an asset to someone else. Examples include *Derek: The Knitting Dinosaur* (1990) by Mary Blackwood, with a protagonist who knits warm clothing for other dinosaurs to keep them warm and allows them to survive the mass extinction of the Ice Age, and *The Sissy Duckling* (2002) by Harvey Fierstein, in which Elmer, the sissy duckling, saves his father from certain death by creating a warm home and feeding him through the winter after he is shot by a hunter. This trope is concerning because it implies that to be feminine, boys must also contribute to their families or communities in ways that are well beyond the capabilities of most children. These books also feature bullying—all of them include the main character being bullied or excluded before the heroic act and the bullying stopping after. This also positions it as the responsibility of the child being bullied to address the problem and easily leads to the idea that if you cannot do anything sufficiently heroic to stop experiencing bullying, you deserve what you get. For cis children, the books normalize bullying children who transgress gender roles and sets a standard that the bullying only needs to stop if the GIaNT child does something truly exceptional. This is particularly concerning as *The Sissy Duckling* often shows up on lists of teacher resources as a recommended title ("2SLGBTQ+"; "Recommendations"). It remains in print and is one of the more available titles in schools.

Connected to this, although not quite as unattainable, is the trope that a boy can be feminine as long as he is also a winner of a public contest. While this is somewhat more possible, it still contains the message that you don't deserve to be accepted or valued for who you are, but if you are publicly successful, maybe you will be accepted. Well known in this category is *Oliver Button Is a Sissy* (1999) by Tomie dePaola, in which Oliver Button wins a talent competition, and then is accepted by his peers. These books position behavior outside of gender expectations as suspect and as needing to be compensated for before a child (or dog) is considered good enough to be treated on par with the others.

The final variation trope is that it is acceptable for a boy to engage in feminine behavior as long as he also performs a superhuman feat. In this variation of the hero trope, the task must be seen as outside the capability of all other characters and will win their admiration. Curiously, the two books with this form of the trope also have boy characters who are naturally pink, which also suggests that it is important that this feminine trait is not the fault of the main child—it is not their choice but something that is outside of their control and outside of the realm of possibility for actual children. Instead of saving a life or lives, the protagonists accomplish other seemingly inconceivable feats. In *Pink!* (2009), the penguin Patrick swims for a week by himself all the way to Africa to meet flamingos and then swims back (Rickards). The protagonist in *The Boy with Pink Hair* (2011) creates a giant, pink feast for all his classmates and their families when the school's stove breaks (Hilton).

In these books, acceptance is conditional, dependent on the exceptionality of the GIaNT, and bullying is not addressed. It would allow an actual GIaNT child to hear that their failure to be heroic is responsible for any negativity they encounter, and for others, it normalizes bullying and harassment. In none of the books is the bullying addressed; after the great feat, the GIaNT character is always so glad to be accepted that there is no discussion or consequence for the hurtful behaviors. Of all the books I analyzed, boy characters who enjoyed or engaged in feminine activities were most likely to be punished. GIaNT children need books that value them as they are; these books center the views and needs of the cis others, with the GIaNT child's value dependent on their ability to provide exceptional service to others.

WHAT'S WRONG WITH BULLY BOOKS?

The books my child first objected to include *Jacob's New Dress* (2014) by Sarah Hoffman and Ian Hoffman and *Morris Micklewhite and the Tangerine Dress* (2014) by Christine Baldacchino, which send the clear message that wearing a dress is a wrong thing for a boy to do. Jacob's parents explicitly try to teach him that he can only wear dresses at home (Hoffman and Hoffman). Morris is so shamed by his peers for his interest in wearing a tangerine dress that he pretends to be sick so he can stay home (Baldacchino). While *Morris Micklewhite and the Tangerine Dress* gets recommended as a book that shows a boy wearing a dress (something I feel enthusiasm for), it also spends half the book showing ways in which Morris is bullied: he is called names and excluded, children attempt to rip his dress off him, and he's told he is not a boy. The only adult intervention is that his mother loves him. The children engaging in the hurtful behavior are never addressed; there are never any consequences. Morris ends the bullying by creating a marvelous painting and being a very appealing and fun play partner. While I want books that value the problem solving of children, when books present ending bullying as the sole responsibility of the child being targeted, they contribute to a sense of isolation and hopelessness.

Many of the books that claim to dismantle gender stereotypes begin by reinforcing them and often contain the subtle message "You can be who you are, but you should expect to be punished for it." If used in a classroom setting, there is plenty to reinforce the negative stereotypes that other children may have about GIaNT children. The more normatively gendered children depicted in the books might occasionally receive a friendly talking to by the teacher about the importance of accepting others and/or not making fun of what someone else likes, but none of the books depict more serious consequences for the students engaged in bullying behavior.[2] In none of the books do we see a child who has engaged in bullying addressed individually—the teacher always speaks to the whole class, which "teaches" that either the bullying is done on behalf of the whole class or that teachers will not make you face individual consequences for acts of gender-based violence. An incautiously chosen selection from some other lists could easily result in children internalizing the message that the expected or correct course of action is to bully or harass trans or gender-independent children.

It's significant to me that bullying is present in only 20 percent of the books I consider that were published outside of mainstream publishing, but present in 63 percent of the books from mainstream presses. It means that there are positive stories available but often not from mainstream presses, often not with distribution, and often not from book sellers with agreements with major school boards.

WHAT'S WRONG WITH USING GIaNT CHILDREN TO REINFORCE HETEROPATRIARCHY AND THE GENDER BINARY?

In these books, it's okay to break gender stereotypes as long as, ultimately, it will reinforce an appropriately masculine identity or role. This takes two forms: one that points to future heteronormative parenting and one that points to athletic prowess. Boys can love dolls as long as they are doing it to practice the skills they will need to be good fathers, as seen in *William's Doll* (1972) by Charlotte Zolotow, or a boy dog can be "proper, precious and pink" as long as they grow up, mate with a female, and produce puppies, such as in *Gaston* (2014) by Kelly Dipucchio (21). The boy's or dog's appropriate heterosexual reproductive futurity reassures their parents. This reflects the adult anxiety that gender variance in children is a protogay expression and offers reassurance that this is not necessarily so; puppies or grandchildren can still be in your future. These books stand out as discussion of reproduction or "fathering children" is unusual in picture books. *William's Doll*, *Gaston*, and *Boys Don't Knit* (1990) by Janice Schoop, and *Mister Seahorse* (2004) by Eric Carle, all contain this theme. As a professional working to support children of all gender identities, all the research points to the importance of loving, supporting, and believing in the child now—not worrying about an eventual future. These books contain the message that who you are is unacceptable, but with time, you'll straighten out.

The other variation of this is that feminine-coded activities, such as ballet, can be engaged in as long as the real purpose is to improve an appropriately masculine skill. Max's interest in ballet leads to improvements in his baseball playing in *Max* (1976) by Rachel Isadora. Steven discovers that the ballet classes he has been secretly attending have improved his ability to jump while playing basketball in *Jump!* (1992) by Michelle Magorian. Tucker's interest in ballet improves his football skills in *The Only Boy in Ballet Class* (2007) by Denise Gruska. The pleasure of dancing is insufficient and must be justified by improving an appropriate masculine-coded activity. This is harmful in several ways in that it both dismisses boys who want to dance for the love of dancing and reinforces that masculine-coded activities are preferable to feminine-coded ones.

Only 23 percent of the books on my list completely avoid the negative/undermining tropes discussed above. Of those ten books—*Jesse's Dream Skirt* (1979) by Bruce Mack; *Strega Nona's Magic Lessons* (1982) by Tomie dePaola; *An Enchanted Hair Tale* (1987) by Alexis De Veaux; *What Mommies Do Best* (1998) by Laura Numeroff; *Different Dragon* (2006) by Jennifer Bryan; *Time to Get Up, Time to Go* (2006) by David Milgram; *It's a George Thing!* (2008) by David Bedford; *Play Free* (2012) by McNall Mason and Max Suarez; *Made by Raffi* (2014) by Craig Pomranz; and *The Newspaper Pirates* (2015) by j wallace skelton—seven are out of print, two are self-published or made through small presses and not available through mainstream distributors, and only one is a commercial book still in print. This makes these books harder to find and harder to buy.

THE BOOKS GIANT CHILDREN NEED

Rudine Sims Bishop developed the language of windows and mirrors to talk about the need for racial diversity in children's literature. She talks about the importance of children being able to see themselves, of having their lives reflected to them (mirror), and of books offering views into the lives of others (windows), an ability to see their reality, empathize with the characters, and sometimes step through and escape into the world in a book (sliding glass door). It is a beautiful way to think about what books can offer children and has helped me understand why there cannot be a single perfect book about gender diversity for children that will meet all needs. Because both windows and mirrors require specificity, a single book cannot provide the depth and engagement with all identities and cultures. Children, classrooms, and libraries need collections of books, not a single approved title. In this chapter, I have mostly written about books in which the main character was assigned male at birth, which could be seen as a capitulation to the overall maleness of children's literature. Instead, I am positioning this as focusing on the GIaNT identities that experience the greatest amount of violence and harassment—and the most virulent violence and harassment. To truly focus on those who are most at risk, though, we cannot just pay attention to gender expression. In Canada (Jaffray), the United States (Grant et al.; *Epidemic of Violence*; *Black LGBTQ People*), and internationally (Transgender Europe and Balzar), transphobic violence most often targets young, low-income, trans people who are racialized, Indigenous, and/or Black. With that in mind, it feels necessary to attend to other ways picture books with GIaNT characters uphold the kyriarchy—the intersecting and overlapping power structure that privileges some and subjugates many (Schüssler).

Finally, coming back to testimonial injustice, it's important to note who is writing these books. Most of the books I have collected have been written by cis people; rarely do GIaNT people get to tell our own stories. We don't often get to hear our stories through our own experiences. An exciting exception to this is Jessica Herthel and Jazz Jennings's *I Am Jazz* (2014). Jazz Jennings's book is the first commercially published book to be written by an openly trans child. In it, Jazz addresses the reader in the first person and shares her experiences, hobbies, and interests.

As readers and book buyers, if we want to create testimonial justice for GIaNT children, we need to make choices that center GIaNT children's experiences and affirm their self-knowledge. GIaNT children need books that:

- Center the experience of GIaNT children.
- Affirm GIaNT identities, demonstrating valuing characters' self-knowledge.
- Avoid the tropes of:
  - requiring a GIaNT to be heroic to be accepted;

- bullying that dominates the story and goes unaddressed by authority figures;
- justifying the child's gender-unexpected behavior as supporting a masculine goal; and
- justifying the child's gender-unexpected behavior as preparing them for later expected heterosexual parenting roles.
* Are written by someone who is a GIaNT.
* Acknowledge the multiple intersecting identities GIaNT people may hold. In particular, GIaNT children need to see books by and about BIPOC people and by and about people with disabilities.

There is tremendous affirming and social justice possibilities for picture books featuring GIaNT children and, still, work to be done.

NOTES

1. Jenkins uses "LGBTQ" and "gay/lesbian" interchangeably in her research. I do not believe that these two terms mean the same thing, although lesbian and gay people often use "LGBTQ" or something similar as an attempt to signify that they are inclusive of other nonheterosexual identities while simultaneously excluding those same identities. In Jenkins's work and elsewhere, it would be far more equitable to recognize the exclusion and thus name the erasure. Without separately analyzing the books she studied, it is impossible to say what identities she actually looked for.

2. My practice is to talk about an individual's behavior rather than to allow their behavior to define who someone is. I encourage educators in schools to do this too. If you tell the child that they are a bully, you are defining their identity and creating a role for them to live into. If you identify their behavior as "bullying behavior," you address their actions and create greater possibilities for them to create a more positive identity, which they can then conform their behavior to.

WORKS CITED

Books Surveyed

Note: A book's inclusion on this list indicates they met the inclusion criteria and does not indicate an endorsement. The inclusion criteria are as follows:

* They are picture books published in English (original or translation) between 1936 and 2015 and are intended for children. Self-published books are included as long as they are available in print by some means.
* One of the main characters either identifies as GIaNT or is explicitly identified as breaking gendered expectations through their words, actions, clothing, or desires.
* I am able to assess the book myself—the physical book, an electronic copy, pdf, or photographs are all fine, but I do not rely on others' descriptions.

Adeyoha, Angel. *The Zero Dads Club*. Illustrated by Aubrey Williams, Flamingo Rampant, 2015.
Aphrodite, Layde. *Hello, It's Only Me! The Diary of a Transgendered Kid*. Illustrated by Janae Brewer-Robinson, Jordan Brewer, and Idasia-Brewer, CreateSpace, 2012.
Axel, Brett. *Goblin Heart: A Fairy Tale*. Illustrated by Terra Bidlespacher, East Waterfront, 2012.
Baker-Street, Margaret. *Michael and Me*. Xlibris Corporation, 2014.
Baldacchino, Christine. *Morris Micklewhite and the Tangerine Dress*. Illustrated by Isabelle Malenfant, Groundwood Books, 2014.
Bansch, Helga. *Odd Bird Out*. Illustrated by Bansch, 21st Century / Gecko Press, 2011.
Bedford, David. *It's a George Thing!* Illustrated by Russell Julian, Egmont, 2008.
Bergman, S. Bear. *The Adventures of Tulip, the Birthday Wish Fairy*. Illustrated by Suzy Malik, Flamingo Rampant, 2012.
Bergman, S. Bear. *Backwards Day*. Illustrated by K. D. Diamond, Flamingo Rampant, 2012.
Bergman, S. Bear. *Is That for a Boy or a Girl?* Illustrated by Rachel Dougherty, Flamingo Rampant, 2015.
Bhatia, Niki. *Pink Is Just a Color and So Is Blue*. CreateSpace, 2012.
Blackwood, Mary. *Derek: The Knitting Dinosaur*. Illustrated by Kerry Argent, Carolrhoda Books, 1990.
Boenke, Mary. *Carly: She's Still My Daddy*. Illustrated by Dolores Dudley, Transgender Network of PFLAG, 2004.
Bone, Jeffrey. *Not Every Princess*. Illustrated by Lisa Bone, American Psychological Association, 2014.
Bradley, Kimberly. *Ballerino Nate*. Illustrated by R. W. Alley, Dial, 2006.
Broadhead, Talcott. *Meet Polkadot*. Illustrated by Dean Spade, Danger Dot, 2013.
Bryan, Jennifer. *Different Dragon*. Illustrated by Danamarle Hosler, Two Lives, 2006.
Bunnell, Jacinta, and Julie Novak. *Girls Are Not Chicks Coloring Book*. Illustrated by Bunnell and Novak, Soft Skull Press, 2009.
Bunnell, Jacinta. *Sometimes the Spoon Runs Away with Another Spoon Coloring Book*. Illustrated by Nathaniel Kusinitz, PM Press, 2010.
Bunting, Eve. *Cheyenne Again*. Illustrated by Irving Toddy, Clarion Books, 1993.
Carle, Eric. *Mister Seahorse*. Illustrated by Carle, Philomel Books, 2004.
Carr, Jennifer. *Be Who You Are!* Illustrated by Ben Rumback, AuthorHouse, 2010.
Chen, Chih-Yuan. *Gugi Gugi*. Kane/Miller, 2003.
Cheng, Andrea. *When Bees Fly Home*. Illustrated by Jolie McFadden, Tilbury House, 2002.
Codell, Esme Raji. *The Basket Ball*. Illustrated by Jennifer Plecas, Abrams Books, 2011.
Cole, Babette. *Princess Smartypants*. Illustrated by Cole, Puffin, 2004.
Costa, Monique. *When Leonard Lost His Spots: A Transparent Tail*. Illustrated by Marina Shupik, Dodi Press, 2012.
Cristaldi, Kathryn. *Baseball Ballerina*. Illustrated by Abby Carter, Random House, 1992.
dePaola, Tomie. *Oliver Button Is a Sissy*. Illustrated by dePaola, Harcourt Brace, 1999.
dePaola, Tomie. *Strega Nona's Magic Lessons*. Illustrated by dePaola, Houghton Mifflin Harcourt, 1982.
De Veaux, Alexis. *An Enchanted Hair Tale*. Illustrated by Cheryl Hanna, Harper Trophy, 1987.
Dipucchio, Kelly. *Gaston*. Illustrated by Christian Robinson, Atheneum Books, 2014.
Ewert, Marcus. *10,000 Dresses*. Illustrated by Rex Ray, Seven Stories Press, 2008.
Fabrikant, Amy. *When Kayla Was Kyle*. Illustrated by Jennifer Levine, Avid Readers, 2013.
Falconer, Ian. *Olivia and the Fairy Princesses*. Illustrated by Falconer, Atheneum Books, 2012.
Fierstein, Harvey. *The Sissy Duckling*. Illustrated by Henry Cole, Simon and Schuster, 2002.
Fox, Mem. *Tough Boris*. Illustrated by Kathryn Brown, Houghton Mifflin Harcourt, 2001.
Funke, Cornelia. *Pirate Girl*. Illustrated by Kerstin Meyer, Chicken House, 2005.

Funke, Cornelia. *The Princess Knight*. Illustrated by Kerstin Meyer, Chicken House, 2004.
Funke, Cornelia. *Princess Pigsty*. Illustrated by Kerstin Meyer, Chicken House, 2007.
Geeslin, Campbell. *Elena's Serenade*. Illustrated by Anna Juan, Atheneum Books, 2004.
Gilori, Debbi. *No Matter What*. Illustrated by Gilori, Harcourt Brace, 1999.
Gonzalez, Maya Christina. *Call Me Tree*. Illustrated by Gonzalez, Children's Book Press, 2014.
Gonzalez, Maya Christina. *Gender Now Coloring Book*. Illustrated by Gonzalez, Reflection Press, 2010.
Gould, Louis. *X: A Fabulous Child's Story*. Illustrated by Jacqueline Chwast, Daughters, 1978.
Green, Michelle Y. *A Strong Right Arm: The Story of Mamie "Peanut" Johnson*. Illustrated by Kadir Nelson, Dial Books, 2002.
Greenberg, Melanie Hope. *Mermaids on Parade*. Illustrated by Greenberg, G. P. Putnam's Sons, 2008.
Gruska, Denise. *The Only Boy in Ballet Class*. Illustrated by Amy Wummer, Gibbs Smith, 2007.
Hall, Gae. *My Dad Wears Pirate Shoes: A Young Boy's Struggle over His Transgender Father*. Illustrated by Melanie Carter, Expose the Lie, 2013.
Hall, Michael. *Red: A Crayon's Story*. Illustrated by Hall, Greenwillow Books, 2015.
Hernandez, Catherine. *M Is for Mustache*. Illustrated by Marisa Firebaugh, Flamingo Rampant, 2015.
Herthel, Jessica, and Jazz Jennings. *I Am Jazz*. Illustrated by Shelagh McNicholas, Dial, 2014.
Hill-Meyer, Tobi. *A Princess of Great Daring*. Illustrated by Eleanor Toczynski, Flamingo Rampant, 2015.
Hilton, Perez. *The Boy with Pink Hair*. Illustrated by Jen Hill, Celebra Children's Books, 2011.
Hoffman, Mary Frances. *Amazing Grace*. Illustrated by Caroline Binch, Lincoln, 1991.
Hoffman, Sarah, and Ian Hoffman. *Jacob's New Dress*. Illustrated by Chris Chase, Albert Whitman, 2014.
Homan, Dianne. *In Christina's Toolbox*. Illustrated by Mary Heine, Lollipop Power, 1981.
Hopkinson, Deborah. *Knit Your Bit: A World War I Story*. Illustrated by Steven Guarnaccia, G. P. Putnam's Sons, 2013.
Howe, James. *Pinky and Rex*. Illustrated by Melissa Sweet, Atheneum Books, 1990.
Isaacs, Anne. *Swamp Angel*. Illustrated by Paul O. Zelinsky, Puffin, 1994.
Isadora, Rachel. *Max*. Illustrated by Isadora, Macmillan, 1976.
Jiang, Wei, and Cheng Au Jiang. *The Legend of Mu Lan: A Heroine of Ancient China*. Illustrated by Jiang and Jiang, Victory Press, 1992.
Jimenez, Karleen Pendleton. *Are You a Boy or a Girl?* Green Dragon Press, 2000.
Johnson, Angela. *Just Like Josh Gibson*. Illustrated by Beth Peck, Simon and Schuster, 2004.
Johnson, Phyllis Hacken. *The Boy Toy*. Illustrated by Lena Shiffman, Lollipop Power, 1988.
Judes, Marie-Odile. *Max, the Stubborn Little Wolf*. Illustrated by Bourre Martine, HarperCollins, 2001.
Kay, Verla. *Rough, Tough Charley*. Illustrated by Adam Gustavsom, Tricycle Press, 2007.
Kelly, E., and E. Webster. *The Little Boy*. Lulu, 2008.
Kemp, Anna. *Dogs Don't Do Ballet*. Illustrated by Sara Ogilvie, Simon and Schuster, 2010.
Kiernan-Johnson, Eileen. *Roland Humphrey Is Wearing a WHAT?* Illustrated by Katrina Revenaugh, Huntley Rahara Press, 2012.
Kilodavis, Cheryl. *My Princess Boy*. Illustrated by Suzanne DeSimone, Simon and Schuster, 2009.
King, Thomas. *A Coyote Columbus Story*. Illustrated by William Kent Monkman, Groundwood Books, 1992.
Kroll, Virginia. *A Carp for Kimiko*. Illustrated by Katherine Roundtree, Charlesbridge, 1993.
Labelle, Sophie-Genevieve. *Penguins Won't Judge / Colouring Book*. Illustrated by Labelle, 2013.

Labelle, Sophie-Genevieve. *Surprise Box. One of a Kind Colouring Book*, vol. 1, illustrated by Labelle, 2013.
Lam, Jessica. *The Adventures of Tina & Jordan*. Illustrated by Christopher Lam, Xlibris, 2013.
Landström, Lena, and Olof Landström. *Pom and Pim*. Illustrated by Olof Landström, Gecko Press, 2014.
Lee, Jeanne M. *The Song of Mu Lan*. Illustrated by Lee, Front Street, 1995.
Leone, Katie. *But, I'm Not a Boy!* Illustrated by Alison Pfeifer, CreateSpace, 2014.
Levy, Elizabeth. *Nice Little Girls*. Illustrated by Mordicai Gerstein, Delacorte Press, 1974.
MacDonald, Ross. *Another Perfect Day*. Illustrated by MacDonald, Roaring Brook Press, 2002.
Mack, Bruce. *Jesse's Dream Skirt*. Illustrated by Marian Bichanan, Lollipop Power, 1979.
Mackall, Dandi Daley. *A Girl Named Dan*. Illustrated by Renée Graef, Sleeping Bear Press, 2011.
Maclear, Kyo. *Spork*. Illustrated by Isabelle Arsenault, Kids Can Press, 2010.
Magorian, Michelle. *Jump!* Illustrated by Jan Ormerod, Walker Books, 1992.
Martin, Bill, Jr., and John Archambault. *White Dynamite and Curly Kidd*. Illustrated by Ted Rand, Henry Holt, 1989.
Martinez, Jason. *My Mommy Is a Boy*. Illustrated by Karen Winchester, 2010.
Mason, McNall, and Max Suarez. *Play Free*. Illustrated by Mason and Suarez, MaxNmeStudio, 2012.
McAllister, Angela. *Yuck! That's Not a Monster*. Illustrated by Alison Edgson, Good Books, 2010.
McCully, Emily Arnold. *Beautiful Warrior: The Legend of the Nun's Kung Fu*. Illustrated by McCully, Arthur A. Levine Books, 1998.
McCully, Emily Arnold. *The Pirate Queen*. Illustrated by McCully, G. P. Putnam's Sons, 1995.
McMath, Sonorra. *My Mom's a Stud*. Illustrated by Mujale Chisebuka, 2013.
Milgram, David. *Time to Get Up, Time to Go*. Illustrated by Milgram, Clarion Books, 2006.
Moss, Marissa. *Mighty Jackie: The Strikeout Queen*. Illustrated by C. F. Payne, Simon and Schuster, 2004.
Moss, Marissa. *Nurse, Soldier, Spy: The Story of Sarah Edmonds, a Civil War Hero*. Illustrated by John Hendrix, Abrams, 2011.
Munro, Leaf. *The Story of Ferdinand*. Illustrated by Robert Lawson, Viking Juvenile, 1936.
Munsch, Robert. *The Paperbag Princess*. Illustrated by Michael Martchenko, Annick Press, 1992.
Newman, Lesléa. *The Boy Who Cried Fabulous*. Illustrated by Peter Ferguson, Tricycle Press, 2007.
Newman, Lesléa. *A Fire Engine for Ruthie*. Illustrated by Cyd Moore, Clarion Books, 2004.
Numeroff, Laura. *What Mommies Do Best*. Illustrated by Lynn Munsinger, Simon and Schuster, 1998.
Ogburn, Jacqueline K. *A Cowboy Named Ernestine*. Illustrated by Nicole Rubel, Dial, 2001.
Parr, Todd. *It's Okay to Be Different*. Illustrated by Parr, Little, Brown Books, 2001.
Pattison, Darcy. *19 Girls and Me*. Illustrated by Steven Salerno, Philomel Books, 2006.
Phillips, Lynn, *Exactly Like Me*. Lollipop Power, 1972.
Pinkney, Andrea Davis. *Alvin Ailey*. Illustrated by Brian Pinkey, Hyperion Books, 1993.
Plourde, Lynn. *School Picture Day*. Illustrated by Thor Wickstrom, Dutton, 2002.
Pomranz, Craig. *Made by Raffi*. Illustrated by Margaret Chamberlain, Frances Lincoln, 2014.
Puttock, Simon. *Earth to Stella*. Illustrated by Philip Hopman, Clarion Books, 2006.
Rickards, Lynne. *Pink!* Illustrated by Margaret Chamberlain, Birlinn, 2009.
Roth, Susan L. *Hard Hat Area*. Illustrated by Roth, Bloomsbury, 2004.
Rothblatt, Phyllis. *All I Want to Be Is Me*. Illustrated by Rothblatt, CreateSpace, 2011.
Scamell, Ragnhild. *Toby's Doll House*. Illustrated by Adrian Reynolds, Levinson, 1998.
Schlein, Miriam. *The Girl Who Would Rather Climb Trees*. Illustrated by Judith Gwyn Brown, Harcourt, 1976.

Schoop, Janice. *Boys Don't Knit*. Illustrated by Laura Beingessner, Three O'Clock Press, 1990.
Silverberg, Cory. *What Makes a Baby*. Illustrated by Fiona Smyth, Triangle Square, 2012.
Sinclair, Adrian Prawns. *He, Her, Him, Free, Fer, Frim*. Illustrated by Sylvie Ls, Microcosm, 2007.
Skeers, Linda. *Tutus Aren't My Style*. Illustrated by Anne Wilsdorf, Dial, 2010.
skelton, j wallace. *The Newspaper Pirates*. Illustrated by Ketch Wehr, Flamingo Rampant, 2015.
Solomon, Sharon. *Cathy Williams, Buffalo Soldier*. Illustrated by Doreen Lorenzetti, Pelican, 2010.
Stamm, Claus. *Three Strong Women: A Tall Tale from Japan*. Illustrated by Sandra Tseng, Viking, 1962.
Stiller, Laurie. *Princess Max*. Illustrated by Gregory Rogers, Random House, 2002.
Tétro, Marc. *A Barbecue for Charlotte*. McArthur, 2005.
U'Ren, Andrea. *Mary Smith*. Illustrated by U'Ren, Farrar, Straus and Giroux, 2003.
U'Ren, Andrea. *Pugdog*. Illustrated by U'Ren, Farrar, Straus and Giroux, 2001.
van der Beek, Deborah. *Melinda and the Class Photograph*. Illustrated by van der Beek, Piccadilly Press, 1991.
van Emst, Charlotte. *Herbie Dances*. Hutchinson, 1988.
Vernick, Audrey. *She Loved Baseball: The Effa Manley Story*. Illustrated by Don Tate, HarperCollins, 2010.
Warner, Jody Nyasha. *Bouncy and the Any Kind at All Fish*. Illustrated by Irene Angelopoulos and Christopher Felske, Centre ontarien de prévention des agressions, 2014.
Warner, Jody Nyasha. *Specs and the Best Part*. Illustrated by Irene Angelopoulos and Christopher Felske, Centre ontarien de prévention des agressions, 2014.
Warner, Jody Nyasha. *Toof and That Blanket*. Illustrated by Irene Angelopoulos and Christopher Felske, Centre ontarien de prévention des agressions, 2014.
Willhoite, Michael. *Uncle What-Is-It Is Coming to Visit!* Illustrated by Willhoite, Alyson Wonderland, 1993.
Willis, Jeanne. *I Want to Be a Cowgirl*. Illustrated by Tony Ross, Andersen Press, 2001.
Wilson, Jacqueline. *My Brother Bernadette*. Illustrated by David Roberts, Egmont, 2001.
Winters, Jonathan. *Frida*. Illustrated by Ana Juan, Arthur A. Levine Books, 2002.
Winthrop, Elizabeth. *Dumpy La Rue*. Illustrated by Betsy Lewin, Henry Holt, 2001.
Winthrop, Elizabeth. *Tough Eddie*. Illustrated by Lillian Hoban, Dutton, 1985.
Wong, Wallace. *When Kathy Is Keith*. Xlibris, 2011.
Wurst, Thomas. *Pearl's Christmas Present*. Illustrated by Wurst, Community Press, 2007.
Wyeth, Sharon Dennis. *Tomboy Trouble*. Illustrated by Lynne Woodcock Cravath, Random House, 1998.
Zolotow, Charlotte. *William's Doll*. Illustrated by William Pene du Bois, Viking, 1972.

Other

"Books by and/or about Black, Indigenous, and People of Color (All Years)." *Cooperative Children's Book Centre*, 4 May 2023, https://ccbc.education.wisc.edu/literature-resources/ccbc-diversity-statistics/books-by-about-poc-fnn/.
Bishop, Rudine Sims. "Mirrors, Windows, and Sliding Glass Doors." *Perspectives*, vol. 1, no. 3, 1990, pp. ix–xi.
Black LGBTQ People and Compounding Discrimination. Human Rights Campaign Foundation, 2020.
Ellison, Joy Michael. *Sylvia and Marsha Start a Revolution! The Story of the Trans Women of Color Who Made LGBTQ+ History*. Illustrated by Teshika Silver, Jessica Kingsley, 2020.

An Epidemic of Violence: Fatal Violence against Transgender and Gender Non-Conforming People in the United States in 2020. Human Rights Campaign Foundation, 2020.
Epstein, B. J. *Are the Kids All Right? Representations of LGBTQ Characters in Children's and Young Adult Literature*. HammerOn Press, 2013.
Gill-Peterson, Jules. *Histories of the Transgender Child*. U of Minnesota P, 2018.
Grant, J. Mottet, et al. *Injustice at Every Turn: A Report of the National Transgender Discrimination Survey*. National Center for Transgender Equality and National Gay and Lesbian Task Force, 2011.
Jaffray, Brianna. "Experiences of Violent Victimization and Unwanted Sexual Behaviours among Gay, Lesbian, Bisexual and Other Sexual Minority People, and the Transgender Population, in Canada, 2018." *Statistics Canada*, 9 Sept. 2020, https://www150.statcan.gc.ca/n1/pub/85-002-x/2020001/article/00009-eng.htm.
Jenkins, Christine. "Young Adult Novels with Gay/Lesbian Characters and Themes, 1969–92: A Historical Reading of Content, Gender and Narrative Distance." *Over the Rainbow: Queer Children's and Young Adult Literature*, edited by Michelle Ann Abate and Kenneth Kidd, U of Michigan P, 2011, pp. 147–63.
@Lavernecox. "@MTVact I prefer 'possibility model.' Some of my p. models: Leontyne Price and Eartha Kitt to name a few. #AskLaverne." *Twitter*, 14 Oct. 2014, 12:13 p.m., https://twitter.com/lavernecox/status/522072765336416256.
Naidoo, Jamie Campbell. *Rainbow Family Collections: Selecting and Using Children's Books with Lesbian, Gay, Bisexual, Transgender and Queer Content*. Libraries Unlimited, 2012.
Namaste, Viviane K. *Invisible Lives: The Erasure of Transsexual and Transgendered People*. U of Chicago P, 2000.
"Recommendations for Diverse Children's Books to Support LGBTQ+ and Gender Inclusive Schools." *Welcoming Schools: A Project of the Human Rights Campaign Foundation*, https://welcomingschools.org/resources/books. Accessed 6 Mar. 2024.
Rubin, Henry S. "Phenomenology as Method in Trans Studies." *GLQ*, vol. 4, no. 2, 1998, pp. 263–81. *Project Muse*, https://doi.org/10.1215/10642684-4-2-263.
Sarles, Patricia. "Heather Has a Donor: 30 Years of International Lesbian-Themed Children's Picture Books about Donor Insemination, 1989–2019." *International LGBTQ+ Literature for Children and Young Adults*, edited by B. J. Epstein and Elizabeth L. Chapman, Anthem Press, 2021, pp. 147–80.
Schüssler, Fiorenza E. *But She Said: Feminist Practices of Biblical Interpretation*. Beacon Press, 1992.
Silverrod, Nancy. *Soldier Girls and Dancing Boys: Gender Transgression in Books for Children, Teens, and Caring Adults*. San Francisco Public Library, 2013.
Sullivan, Ashley Lauren, and Laurie Lynne Urraro. "'Missing Persons' Report! Where Are the Transgender Characters in Children's Picture Books?" *Occasional Paper Series*, vol. 37, 2017, pp. 1–24. https://educate.bankstreet.edu/occasional-paper-series/vol2017/iss37/4.
Transgender Europe and Carsten Balzar. "TMM Update Trans Day of Remembrance 2020." *Transrespect versus Transphobia Worldwide*, 2020, https://transrespect.org/en/tmm-update-tdor-2020/.
"2SLGBTQ+." *Elementary Teachers' Federation of Ontario*, www.etfo.ca/socialjusticeunion/2slgbtq. Accessed 6 Mar. 2024.
Worotynec, Z. Sonia. "Contrived or Inspired: Ability/Disability in the Children's Picture Books." *Disability Studies Quarterly*, vol. 24, no. 1, Dec. 2004, https://doi.org/10.18061/dsq.v24i1.871.

CHAPTER 6

BE WHO YOU ARE!, *I AM JAZZ*, *I'M NOT A GIRL*, AND *SAM!*
Picturing Trans Childhoods

Sara Austin

Nonfiction picture books featuring transgender children are a relatively recent phenomenon. Previous children's books featuring gender-nonconforming characters include Lois Gould and Jacqueline Chwast's *X: A Fabulous Child's Story* (1978), about a child raised without gender, and Marcus Ewert and Rex Ray's *10,000 Dresses* (2008), featuring a protagonist who identifies as a girl but is referred to as a boy by her family. Despite their gender-nonconforming main characters and clear messages of inclusion, neither of these books directly identify their protagonists as transgender. Since 2010, however, a new genre of biographical picture books about transgender children is emerging.

This shift to biographical picture books marks a clear break with the past treatment of gender-nonconforming children's literature since these children now exist as living examples both inside and outside of the text. Readers can look for the real-world activism and experiences these picture-book protagonists are engaging in and see models and possibilities for transgender existence. This connection to real lived experience also creates tension between the utopic impulses of children's literature and the specter of systemic antitrans bias that lurks just outside the picture books' focus. Since these books are about real children, they can end with hope, but they cannot reassure parents or children that there will be a happily ever after for their characters or readers. The first four of these books published in English—Jennifer Carr's *Be Who You Are!* (2010), Jessica Herthel, Jazz Jennings, and Shelagh McNicholas's *I Am Jazz* (2014), Dani Gabriel and Robert Liu-Trujillo's *Sam!* (2019), and Maddox Lyons, Jessica Verdi, and Dana Simpson's *I'm Not a Girl* (2020)—clearly define the boundaries and characteristics of the genre.[1]

A genre profile of biographical transgender picture books should include the elements that are common across all existing texts and are therefore likely to be included in subsequent examples. Fortuitously, the four existing books represent two stories of transgender girls and two stories of transgender boys, making an even distribution of analysis possible.[2] Two of the books, one about a girl and one about a boy, are also told in first person, while two books are in third person. One factor that complicates the genre outline for these books is their respective publishers, who differ in size and budget. *Be Who You Are!* was published through AuthorHouse, a print-on-demand self-publishing company. *Sam!* was published with Penny Candy Books, a small press founded in 2016. In contrast, *I'm Not a Girl* was produced by Roaring Brook Press, a subsidiary of Macmillan, and *I Am Jazz* was produced by Dial, a subsidiary of Penguin. Both Macmillan and Penguin are part of the "Big Four" publishing houses, generating around 80 percent of all revenue for books produced in English in 2016 (McIlroy). This difference in publisher size and revenue means that considerably more resources may have been available for *I'm Not a Girl* and *I Am Jazz* than the other two examples, and these resources may have affected the books' construction. For this reason, I identify certain features directly related to the books' materiality, such as endpapers, as genre markers despite their being absent in one example.

Reading educational, parenting, and literary theory discourses next to one another reveals a bind for lesbian, gay, bisexual, trans, queer, plus (LGBTQ+) children's literature. Scholars of children's literature point to the limitations of text in depicting dynamic queer lives, especially when faced with social fears concerning queer contamination of children. For example, Melynda Huskey calls the groundbreaking LGBTQ+ picture book *Heather Has Two Mommies* "undelightful," noting lots of heavy text and poor illustrations (66). Huskey notes the threat of "contamination" lingers in LGBTQ+ children's books, and so "queerness, with all its playful associations, is replaced by earnest homosexuality and political gayness" to remove any desire to be like the queer characters or, indeed, to read the book at all (68). In order to represent lived experiences and support real parents and children, these books cannot push too stringently against existing constructions of gender. Ann Travers points out that white parents can use racial privilege along with cultural scripts of motherhood to effectively advocate for transgender children but that this strategy requires leaning into cultural expectations of race and gender (150).

Queer and trans studies theorists, including Cris Mayo and Harper Benjamin Keenan, argue that to make meaningful contributions to political discourses, these books must be overtly political and call into question cultural constraints and assumptions based in binary gender. As Huskey notes, however, if these books become too earnest or political, they must remove queer desire so that they are not labeled as inappropriate. Yet removing desire risks erasing queer sexual subjectivity and losing the attention of the child audience by making the books tedious.

Andrea Long Chu and Emmett Harsin Drager take up these contradictory positions in their polemic "After Trans Studies." Drager comments at one point in the article, "If your body modification looks too much like the original 'transsexual medical genre,' your queer cred is toast.... How can the *exact same* procedures sometimes symbolize, for queer theory, the Ghost of Genders Past and other times be the very foundation for new materialist theories of mutability, becoming, and enmeshment?" (Chu and Drager 111; emphasis original). What frustrates Chu and Drager is the tension between lived transgender experiences that often mimic cisgender experience, what Chu describes as "a cunt, a man, a house, and *a normal fucking life*," and the politics of transgender theory that require subverting binary gender with antinormative queerness (108; emphasis original). Instead, Chu and Drager call for "a methodology that would start from the premise that everyone's gender is a political disaster and refuse to fix it" (112).

I argue that biographical picture books of transgender children take up Chu and Drager's call by valuing a livable trans experience. The backmatter also makes clear that these books imagine an audience of other transgender children and that their purpose is to help normalize social transitioning while coaching parents on first steps. At the same time, these books demonstrate to parents how to mobilize existing social expectations of gender to create narratives of "naturalness" surrounding transgender children and how to advocate for social transition as a happily ever after solution. These books also work within existing inclusion models of children's literature in education, presenting transgender childhood as a consumable narrative experience to cisgender children, who may learn to accept the transgender child. These books also teach queer resilience, acknowledging that transgender children may be misgendered accidentally or on purpose but brushing past these moments in order to focus on ideas of "specialness" and the acceptance of the majority of family and peers. Finally, these books end before puberty, circumventing any discussions of medical intervention and using cultural notions of innocence to protect transgender children.

Despite the complicated position of innocence within childhood studies, as Marah Gubar observes in her *Keywords for Children's Literature* entry, "Demonizing the concept of innocence obscures its history as a driver of incremental progress toward more humane treatment of vulnerable groups" (108).[3] In this chapter, I discuss each of these picture books in detail, describing the genre patterns they establish and how those patterns fit into or challenge existing discourses of transgender identity and allyship within education, parenting, and literary theory. Finally, I argue that genre conventions—such as color-coded endpapers, social transition narratives, and a focus on prepubescent children—demonstrate how current cultural norms surrounding gender, sexuality, and childhood can be mobilized to protect transgender children. For this reason, changes to the cultural precarity of transgender people will beget genre changes to the picture books as these elements will no longer be necessary to assure cisgender readers that transgender children deserve access to the same rights and protections of childhood.

Each of these picture books use words and images to tell the story of one particular transgender child. In each story, the child knows that their gender does not match what their parents and teachers tell them it is. These children also express discomfort with clothes or activities that do not align with their gender identity. The protagonists Hannah, Sam, Jazz, and Hope each tell their parents that they are transgender. The family accepts the main character, perhaps visits a family therapist, and then begins the process of social transition. The plots of the books are remarkably similar, differing only in specific details that are unique to the child and family's experience. *Be Who You Are!* has the most comprehensive description of social transitioning, while *I Am Jazz* spends the most time with its child protagonist posttransition; *I'm Not a Girl* spends the most time with its child character pretransition, and *Sam!* is the only book both to depict its character as nonwhite and in which the title character's gender presentation does not change throughout social transition. All the books feature half- or full-page color illustrations and limited text, making them accessible for reading aloud to children who are not yet literate themselves.

EDUCATION AND ANXIETY

Each of the biographical picture books discussed here begins with the main character or the narrator explaining that the child in the book knows their gender identity and has, in some cases, spent years asserting to friends and family that "I'm not a girl" (Lyons and Verdi 6) or "I'm a girl inside" (Carr 3). Yet communicating that identity to adults, such as parents or teachers, is a source of anxiety. These books often depict dinner-table discussions (Carr 9; Gabriel 32; Lyons and Verdi 26) in which the child struggles to explain gender identity to parents as a first step toward social transition. Despite the discussions being universally positive, school remains a source of conflict in the books. Teachers often enforce natal-sex conformity either through sex-segregated bathrooms or sports teams. In *Be Who You Are!*, the teacher even tells the child character, "You're a boy Nick. Draw a boy" (Carr 4). While adults and peers at school can be "confused" by transgender children (Herthel and Jennings 19), the main characters persist in communicating gender identity and social transitioning.

Theorists argue that gender is continually interpreted as a social category through the use of visual symbols. In their often-cited 1987 article "Doing Gender," for example, Candace West and Don H. Zimmerman observe that "genitalia are conventionally hidden from public inspection," and so essential sex characteristics have very little to do with the "identification of sex category in everyday life" (132). Instead, secondary signifiers, such as dress and behavior, stand in for sex characteristics in social interactions that determine gender. In this way, visual markers of gender, such as hair and clothing, as well as behavioral markers, such as play, determine social identifications of gender and, by extension, sex. This reliance on visual cues makes picture books an ideal means to convey social transition because they demonstrate the connection between the appearance of gender and the way that a person is treated by society as a gendered body.

The child characters in these books use self-portraits to communicate gender identity in much the same way that these picture books use text and images to relate stories of transgender children to the reader. Most of these books include a page showing the reader a gender-affirming self-portrait of the main character. Jazz draws herself in boys' clothing crying or under a rain cloud but happy and in the sunshine in girls' clothing (Herthel and Jennings 7–8). Nick gets in trouble at school for drawing herself as a girl in a pink dress and then draws a similar portrait later in the book and is affirmed by her parents (Carr 4–5, 16–17).[4] Hannah draws himself early in the story, and then after he learns the word "transgender," he draws himself again to help explain his gender identity to his parents (Lyons and Verdi 7, 25).[5] The main characters may also use toys and clothing to assert gender identity. Jazz wears princess and mermaid costumes (Herthel and Jennings 11–12), Nick prefers a princess costume and a blonde wig (Carr 7), and Hannah hates the pink, ruffled pirate costume and the pink coat his mother chooses for him (Lyons and Verdi 6, 10). Selecting clothing and toys is one way that these children can affirm their gender identities, and so clothing and hairstyle become very important to many of these characters as primary visual methods of performing gender identity and initiating social transition.

This emphasis on visual cues to communicate gender, however, can also create tension between what the images in the books depict and what the text says. This tension is perhaps most evident in depictions of social institutions, such as school. In *I Am Jazz*, the text describes systemic antitransgender bias in terms that young children can understand. The book explains that social transitioning caused teachers to be "confused" and try to force Jazz into using the boys' bathroom and playing on the boys' sports teams. Adult readers will likely recognize these issues as recurring attacks on transgender people's rights to exist safely in public spaces. Yet the images accompanying these pages show Jazz talking to friends while her mother talks to teachers and Jazz sitting alone on a bench with a soccer ball (Herthel and Jennings 19–20). While it is clear in the second image that Jazz is sad, these images do not depict the scope or severity of such issues. These are merely episodes in which a few people need to be educated into acceptance. On the next page, Jazz is playing soccer with her friends; the moment of systemic oppression passed (21).

Similarly, when the text says that kids tease Jazz and "call me a boy name, or ignore me all together," the picture is of three children in the background laughing (Herthel and Jennings 22). Jazz is in the foreground, and in a thought bubble above her head, she is hugging a friend and smiling. Their relative positioning on the page not only makes Jazz larger and closer to the reader than the bullies but also makes her imagined friend tower over them. The reader's eye is drawn first to Jazz in the center, then to the friends in the upper left of the image, and finally to the bullies in the upper right. The composition of the image makes the bullies seem less powerful or important than either Jazz or her support system. In this way, though the text acknowledges, in some small ways, the systemic bias that transgender children may face, that bias is limited to school and peer interactions (rather than political or medical ones) and is downplayed by the accompanying images.

This tension between what the books say and what they show is indicative of the books' split didactic function. For readers who are transgender children, the text discusses real-life problems that the biographical subjects faced while also emphasizing the role of queer resilience through supportive relationships. For cisgender-child readers, the books teach acceptance. The bullies in *Jazz* are small and unimportant, not an enviable position for the reader. Jazz is the focus of the narrative—the storyteller and empathetic character. When the bullies make her feel "crummy," cisgender readers should reject their behavior (Herthel and Jennings 22). Educational criticism focuses on the possible didactic use of these picture books as inclusion literature, without acknowledging the transgender-child audience. Educational discourse observes that when used intentionally, queer and gender-nonconforming characters might "foster reading practices that open up imaginary possibilities for embracing the affirmation of nonnormative and more expansive forms of desire and gender expression" (Martino and Cumming-Potvin 809). Research supports transgender-inclusive pedagogies as a means of expanding acceptance of gender diversity in childhood. Kristina Olson and Selin Gülgöz's study finds that compared to gender-typical children, transgender children and their siblings are less likely to stereotype according to gender and more likely to tolerate gender nonconformity. Olson and Gülgöz attribute this difference to parental influence, suggesting that gender-variant-inclusive pedagogies are effective.

Trans pedagogy combats dominant models of identity and belonging as markers of the very constructs and power dynamics that it seeks to undermine. Trans pedagogy values "potential connections across, within, and beyond genders" (Mayo 534) because there is "no universal definition or experience of transness," and so trans studies must resist "false universality," otherwise it "runs the risk of building a new script" (Keenan 551). Educators, such as Harper Keenan, focus on transgender identity as "limitless possibilities of bodily expression [that] stand in opposition to notions of finite sexual orientation categories or binary gender" (539). Keenan argues that "we need pedagogies that concentrate more of our efforts on inviting people to be with each other in our full humanity. We need pedagogies that deeply examine how our current gender system confines us all and how that interacts with other systems, like race, class, and ability" (553). Here, Keenan outlines a philosophical approach to reading and teaching more than proposing specific content for a book or collection of books.

Despite this impulse to expand social definitions of gender performance, educators face several challenges, including access to quality books and the pedagogical knowledge to use them effectively. Robert Bittner et al. propose "reading practices that imagine possibilities for new gendered subjectivities through de-subjugating practices" (950). They note that books aimed at young children are often more concerned with the daily struggles of lived transgender experience than they are in breaking down cultural models of gender. They describe the main character in *I Am Jazz*, for example, as "recognizable because she presents as a normal girl, just with a little problem of not being born as one" (953). While this perception of gender may not challenge binary cultural assumptions, that does not make it invalid for Jazz or children like her. These books then, provide a "pedagogical service overall, educating readers about some possible ways of living as a trans or genderqueer young person" even as they refuse to engage in a larger political project of breaking down binary gender (961). While the books themselves may provide practical and livable examples and the choice to include them in classroom readings has liberatory potential, not all children have access to books that contain gender and sexual difference.[6]

As these picture books demonstrate, marginalization of LGBTQ+ bodies and stories can be a hurdle in educational spaces. Perhaps because there are so few transgender authors currently published in children's literature, many books with LGBTQ+ content suggest that gay and transgender youth are broken and that something has caused the "problem" of queer identity (Epstein). Even if the books themselves are queer affirming, libraries may shelve books with LGBTQ+ themes alongside books about parenting children with long-term illnesses or with titles focusing on "broken homes" (Naidoo 71). It is often incumbent, then, on teachers to not only research what books to buy but also keep them in personal or classroom libraries in order to avoid associations with bodily or familial "wrongness." In order to be effective, these studies argue, teachers must also have access to a variety of books with multiple examples of queer identity and experience and make arrangements to build children's vocabularies of acceptance—all while navigating possible hostility from parents, community members, or administrators.

These educational discourses also assume that the majority of children in the classroom are cisgender, and so unlike parenting discussions, education becomes an exercise in acceptance rather than survival. Perhaps this difference in stakes is why educational discussions of transgender children can more directly confront cultural regulations of binary gender performance, or perhaps it is because education is often directly responsible for enforcing social and cultural conformity, and so educational theorists must do more work to separate themselves from constructions of gender in order to effectively advocate for transgender children. Picture books that are written for the purpose of educating parents on a livable transgender experience or for showing gender-nonconforming children that they are not alone cannot simultaneously do the work of presenting a range of experiences and breaking down binary gender. These educational studies argue that any one book need not address every facet of the queer or transgender child's experience as long as educators make a commitment to diverse queer and trans pedagogies and materials.

PARENTING AND PARATEXT

Discussions of transgender children within parenting literature affirm the child's right to express their gender identity but often mitigate both the child's and parents' disruptions to established cultural codes of gender expression. These picture books reflect what pediatric psychology terms a "gender-affirmative model" of parenting, in which transgender and gender-nonconforming children "live in the gender that feels most real or comfortable to that child" and parents support "children's gender identities and expressions" despite opposition from school, church, or extended family (Kuvalanka et al. 890).

Each of these books includes a title that asserts identity either as a name (*I Am Jazz, Sam!*) for books that focus on stories after social transition or as a statement of truth concerning who the main character is "inside" (*Be Who You Are!, I'm Not a Girl*) for books that focus on stories pre–social transition. The covers are similar, presenting the child protagonist in the center but splitting along pre- and posttransition lines. Two covers (*Sam!, I Am Jazz*) depict the child, post–social transition, with images of family in the background. The other two depict the child's desire to transition. *I'm Not a Girl* shows the main character standing outside of a barber shop looking longingly inside at a boy getting a haircut. Similarly, *Be Who You Are!* shows the main character standing in front of a mirror and touching the surface. The mirror reflects the character in their posttransition gender identity.

This divide between books with pre- and post-social-transition titles and covers also marks how the books deploy names and pronouns. *I Am Jazz* and *I'm Not a Girl* are both told in first person and so do not use gendered pronouns to refer to the main characters, but *Sam!* and *Be Who You Are!* are in third person and so use gendered pronouns throughout the text. As a text with a posttransition cover, *Sam!* uses he/him pronouns throughout the book, while *Be Who You Are!* uses he/him until the moment of social transition within the text. The pre-social-transition texts also use deadnames to refer to their main characters. *Be Who You Are!* changes the name for its main character on page 25. *I'm Not a Girl* does not give a gender-affirming name for its main character since social transitioning only begins in the last three pages. In contrast, *I Am Jazz* does not deadname its main character at all, and *Sam!* only does so from the perspectives of other characters, not the narrator, and only until the moment of social transition—about halfway through the book. These two approaches to pronouns, names, and cover art suggest a split within the genre itself. Books that choose to focus on the time period pre–social transition are more likely to use deadnames and pronouns that align with natal sex, as well as choose cover art that reflects the character's struggle with gender identity, while books that focus on life after social transition are more likely to only use gender-affirming names and pronouns and picture a smiling child surrounded by family. In all these books, however, gender identity is at the center of the narrative, and the child's sense of themselves is presented as "correct."

Ironically, in advocating for the rights of transgender children, parents may not only be pressed into stereotypical presentations of gender but also rely on biological explanations for their child's gender identity. Tey Meadow observes in *Trans Kids: Being Gendered in the Twenty-First Century* that when advocating for transgender and gender-nonconforming children, parents may fall back on endocrine or physiological explanations of gender in order to justify transgender children's existence and advocate for them (193). While transgender identity suggests a separation of gender and natal sex, perhaps even a separation of gender and the sexed body, Meadow notes that chromosomal and endocrine explanations for transgender identity make it easier for some parents to accept their transgender children and to advocate for them with family or school.[7] For these parents, transgender identity is "natural" because it is part of the prenatal chromosomal environment. Thus, parents are perhaps best able to effectively advocate for their transgender children when neither the parent or the child substantially disrupts existing expectations for gender identity or presentation but merely expands the definition of "natural" alignments between gender and the sexed body.[8]

The paratextual elements of these picture books illustrate the social pressure of both parents and children to conform to gendered behaviors even while asserting transgender identity. Endpapers identify the protagonist's gender as a framing device for the narrative (Sipe and McGuire 302). *Sam!* has yellow endpapers covered in blue dinosaurs. While dinosaurs are not explicitly gendered, they appear in the background of Sam's dream of being a boy all the time, "not just inside" (Gabriel 30). The yellow-and-blue color combination, along with different dinosaur outlines, also appears on Sam's clothing in every image after his social transition, except for the final page. This combination of yellow-and-blue dinosaurs is synonymous with Sam's personality after transitioning. Similarly, Jazz identifies her favorite color as pink, and so the endpapers for her book are pink. The color-coded endpapers of pink and blue might seem coincidental if not for *I'm Not a Girl*, which uses pink endpapers for the opening of the book, then blue for the title page, pink for the creator's notes, and blue for the closing. Not only are the endpapers pink and blue, aligning with social expectations of gendered behavior, the opening of the book is also pink (when the title character is identified by family members as a girl), and the closing of the book is blue (when the character has socially transitioned). The endpapers are also blue on the pages that are closest to images of the main character. Here, colors align to, rather than question, the cultural connections between gender and behavior.

The books' end matter also asserts the gender normativity of parents, specifically framing advocacy for transgender children as an extension of maternal protection, in order to make arguing for transgender children's rights to exist in public places socially acceptable. Ann Travers explains that transgender children require their parents' help to assert gender identity since children are an especially vulnerable group from both a political and social standpoint.[9] Yet Travers notes that "much of the cultural power of movements of parents of trans kids lies in female cisgender conformity, presumed or actual heterosexuality, dominant narratives of motherhood, and middle-class whiteness" (150). In order to effectively advocate for transgender children, parents, especially mothers, may be forced to cultivate the appearance of gender conformity. All the books except for *Sam!* include resources for families, such as PFLAG or the TransKids Purple Rainbow Foundation.[10] All these books also contain an author's note that identifies one of the authors as either the child the book is about or the child's mother. *I'm Not a Girl* includes author's and illustrator's notes as well as a mother's note. In *Be Who You Are!*, the author's biography explains that the writer uses a pseudonym "to protect the safety of her family" (Carr 33). According to the biography, when Carr's daughter came out as transgender, Carr began looking for resources and founded a gender-nonconforming playgroup when no other resources were available. Carr's subsequent advocacy was born out of a desire to protect her children and other children like them.

Even in a book explicitly written for a transgender-positive audience that uses a pseudonym to protect the author's identity, cultural expectations of motherhood inform and justify the author's advocacy work on behalf of transgender children. *I'm Not a Girl* also includes a mother's note that performs similar cultural work of justifying advocacy as an extension of maternal care, and while *Sam!*'s author identifies as queer and gender fluid, they also appear in a feminine lace top for their author photo. These notes work within the book to demonstrate proximity to transgender children, to show that the authors have relevant lived experience that gives them insight into the process of coming out and social transitioning, and to reify their cultural roles as mothers.[11] In each case, white motherhood becomes the socially justifiable point of entry for LGBTQ+ child advocacy.

CHILDHOOD, GENDER, AND REPRESENTING SOCIAL TRANSITION

Parents may use existing structures of gender conformity as a tool for advocating for their transgender children, but this solution, theorists argue, can be short term and have limited scope. In the 2020 legislative session, six states sought to bar minors (even emancipated minors) from accessing hormone therapy or gender-reassignment surgery and to classify access to hormones as child abuse (Andrew). In 2023, that number rose to twenty states, with seven more considering bans ("Attacks"). Similar to Travers's warning to parents that top-down systems of rights attainment are unstable, Dean Spade argues that the rhetorics of "rights" and "visibility" often rely on white representation and so are not enough to combat contemporary power structures that threaten transgender lives and subsume trans resistance. Or, as Jennifer L. Miller explains, contemporary scholars focused on transgender children often "resist liberal accommodation models of trans inclusion and instead theorize what meaningful structural change would look like" (1). Only through dismantling the political and cultural power structures that center heterosexual and cisgender experiences to the detriment of queer lives can transgender people experience social value and care (Spade).

Transgender people must submit to diagnosis and supervision under the current system for access to medical transition through hormone therapy, surgery, or puberty blockers. As recently as the early 1980s, many doctors and psychiatrists did not agree that transgender children existed and attempted to eliminate children's gender-variant behaviors to restore "normal" behaviors and desires (Minter). More recently, the diagnostic criteria for gender dysphoria (gender identity disorder in children, or GIDC) in the *Diagnostic and Statistical Manual of Mental Disorders*, fifth edition (2013) require a gender-nonconforming child to be "distressed or impaired," but desiring gender transformation is considered in itself a form of impairment (Pyne 54). In the medicalization and "treatment" of gender-nonconforming children, families become sites of regulation and discipline, subjected to the "expert" knowledge of doctors and psychiatrists (Pyne 91–92). This medicalized system also means that transgender children face political barriers to healthcare and transition.

I argue that these picture books intentionally subvert medically centered narratives of transgender bodies by ending their stories before adolescence. In these books, social transition is the end goal and the gateway to an authentic self. There is no discussion of medical transition at all. This absence is, I argue, a genre marker in the same way that pink and blue endpapers, self-portraits, and dinner-table discussions are. The authors of these books choose to end these stories before puberty, specifically when transgender children can still claim the cultural space of childhood, free from imposition of hormones and reproductive sexual scripts. Jody Norton notes that Mark Twain's *Hellfire Hotchkiss* illustrates a problem in much queer children's literature; it does not know what to do with children who hit puberty and become sexual subjects (309). I argue that rather than a lack of attention to the child characters' futures, this narrative choice reclaims the space of childhood as a place in which transgender children can exist. By severing trans childhood from medicalization, these books also push back against the rhetorics of transition as "child abuse" or "genital mutilation" that antitrans politicians often employ to argue against gender-affirming medical access.

Social transition takes the place of the happily ever after in these picture books. In fact, it might be more accurate to describe these books as about social transition rather than about transgender children. *I'm Not a Girl* is the only book that does not directly depict transition, only dramatizing the main character's haircut on the last page of the story. The book does hint at social transition, including school photos of the main character on the title page and the recommended-resources page. The school photo on the title page is of the main character dressed in pink with long hair and a large pink bow. The school photo at the end of the text shows the character with short hair, wearing a blue shirt and smiling. As I discussed earlier, pink and blue act as gender shorthand in these books, denoting social transition. Other books spend more time explicitly discussing and depicting transition.

Sam! and *I Am Jazz* both mention that it takes peers and teachers time to adjust to using a child's new name and that sometimes this can cause anger and frustration for the character that they have to work through. Both books, however, focus on the love and acceptance of friends and family and portray the main character as happy in their new identity. In ten pages, *Sam!* moves from the dinner-table conversation to this acknowledgment of transition to Sam's parents introducing him as their son to the final closing, where Sam is happy in school. Part of the reason that the book can move so quickly is because Sam's gender presentation does not actually change throughout the book nor is his gender presentation commented on by any character, and so there is no need to demonstrate those changes for the reader. In contrast, *Jazz* begins by introducing the main character posttransition and waits ten pages before flashing back to depict the process. A younger Jazz dances around in ballet costumes and princess dresses for six pages before the family visits a doctor and Jazz transitions.

The transition process depicted in *Jazz*, like the one in *Sam!*, focuses on school and peer groups. There are six pages of Jazz interacting with peers or feeling frustrated when others do not accept her identity. The book ends as it began, with the pronouncement "I am Jazz!" Unlike Sam's case, Jazz's gender presentation does change in the book, but because the book begins and ends with Jazz posttransition and because she narrates the story, the reader can easily identify social transition with the images depicting it. The illustrations simply shift Jazz's gender presentation with the flashback sequences, and much of the social transition actually occurs outside of the reader's view, other than the issues of sports teams and bathrooms. Like with Sam, Jazz's frustrations with peers are ongoing. She says, "Even today, there are kids who tease me, or call me by a boy name, or ignore me all together" (Herthel and Jennings 22). I suggest that the books choose to illustrate these moments despite not picturing any other elements of social transition to caution parents and transgender children that these are major hurdles they will have to face, which have origins outside of the family and so cannot remain private.

While these books center social transition as a solution to the unhappiness that the child characters face living as the wrong gender, *Be Who You Are!* explains social transition as a process in much more detail than any of the other books. Transition begins on page 7 when the character asks to grow out her hair, which gets progressively longer throughout the book, marking both the passage of time and the transition process. Nick begins wearing girls' clothes on page 12, asks to be referred to as a girl on page 14, joins a transgender playgroup on page 18, and chooses the name Hope on page 25. Hope's library card appears on page 22, and she faces the reader wearing a name tag on page 25. It is on page 25 that the text refers to Hope as "she" for the first time, demonstrating the culmination of the transition process within the family. This process is what *Sam!* and *I Am Jazz* largely elide, jumping from one family conversation or doctor visit to the process of social transition with school and peers. Like *Sam!* and *I Am Jazz*, *Be Who You Are!* spends several pages explaining that it takes time for people to adjust to Hope's new name and pronouns and that some people continue to misgender Hope on purpose (Carr 27). Also like *Sam!* and *I Am Jazz*, *Be Who You Are!* emphasizes familial support as a way for the child character to navigate hostility from the outside world. The book ends with Hope being proud of who she is and with a call to the reader to be more accepting of others.

In depicting social transition as the solution, these books excise gender dysphoria and the medicalization of transgender identity from their pages. Even when the books present doctors or therapists, it is clear that the purpose of these professionals is to help parents understand transgender identity, not, at least from the reader's perspective, to diagnose or medically intervene. This decision to ignore medical intervention also diverts attention from the sexed body and from the transgender child as a sexual subject. While this elision does foreclose certain (perhaps necessary) conversations about medical transition, it also roots transgender children within cultural conventions of innocence. As I discussed at the beginning of this chapter, Marah Gubar's entry in *Keywords for Children's Literature* looks at the historical development of childhood innocence as a lack of sexual pollution or knowledge. While Gubar points to theoretical frustrations with "innocence" as a concept invented by adults and projected onto children, she also describes the real political work that innocence can do. By describing images of children in the Syrian refugee crisis, as well as the innocence of child AIDS victims, Gubar demonstrates how this cultural construction can be mobilized to build empathy for and political action on behalf of vulnerable peoples.

Chu and Drager call the current political moment the "era of the trans child" (104), and that is perhaps true in more ways than their dialogue imagines. What Drager means is that trans studies has reached a place where advocating for the existence of transgender children is feasible, even common. It is also possible, however, that these biographical picture books demonstrate a cultural moment in which mobilizing innocence on behalf of transgender children is potentially transformative, where such an argument might open up previously shuttered avenues of cultural empathy and political action in the same way that Gubar demonstrates these texts have previously done for AIDS victims. Yet, as multiple theorists have pointed out, using existing cultural conventions surrounding gender and childhood may also pose real danger. Parents can lean into expectations of "naturalness," gender stereotypes, or the expectations of white motherhood to protect their own children, but structural change may not be possible through those means. Similarly, declaring transgender children innocent may prevent those same children from claiming sexual subjectivity later in life or doom them to being culturally viewed as monstrous when they do.[12]

What the genre markers of these picture books unequivocally communicate is transgender children's and parents' understanding of the cultural scripts of gender that directly affect their lives. Using pink or blue endpapers as a visual shorthand for gender identity, depicting negative interactions with peers and at school as ongoing struggles of social transition, and refusing to engage with issues of sexuality and medical transition are all clearly politically motivated choices these books make. As they attempt to navigate an audience of transgender children who need real answers amidst a hegemonically cisgender culture in which "inclusion" is the primary approach to change, these books, perhaps independently of one another, have developed a clear system of genre markers.

While this is the existing genre landscape for such books, I anticipate two major changes in forthcoming publications. First, there will be books about pubescent and postpubescent children that deal with the medical aspects of transition or that do not rely on the happily ever after trope that these books employ. As the children depicted in these texts age and as more transgender children enter the public sphere, these books will become less tidy in their approach to transition and may begin to include not only medical aspects but also the continuous nature of gender performance. Second, as the social and cultural acceptance of transgender people increases, new books will be able to tell stories that do not center on transition as the crux of the transgender child's narrative. Transgender picture books will be limited as long as they are only able to tell one type of story. While the adaptation of real children's narratives into picture-book form is clearly a necessary element of transgender children's media, as cultural mores change, these books will be able to expand out into other aspects of transgender children's lives. This picture-book genre is both important and new, and so I look forward to watching it grow and develop as a storytelling medium alongside the cultural embrace of such stories and storytellers.

NOTES

1. I am not including fictional accounts of transgender children, such as Kyle Lukoff and Luciano Lozano's *Call Me Max* (2019), despite those books having similar themes because they are not grounded in the experiences of a particular child.

2. Even though I am able to look at these two different categories, I am not adhering to a binary understanding of gender in which trans girls and trans boys are two distinct and opposing categories.

3. Children's literature and childhood studies scholars have examined the cultural roots and consequences of childhood innocence in countless books and articles. Philippe Ariès's *Centuries of Childhood* (1960), which argues that the very social category of "children" emerged in the seventeenth century. Anne Higonnet's *Pictures of Innocence* (1998) maps the evolution of depicting childhood innocence through paintings and photography. Robin Bernstein's *Racial Innocence* (2011) discusses how Black children are denied the assumption of innocence afforded to white children throughout nineteenth- and twentieth-century America. This list is

by no means exhaustive but does demonstrate how prolific and varied scholarly discussions of childhood innocence are.

4. Because most of these books deadname their protagonists throughout, and *I'm Not a Girl*, in fact, never gives its main character a gender-affirming name, I am using those names here for consistency with the published texts. I do, however, maintain the gendered pronouns each character uses at the end of their book throughout my discussion.

5. *Sam!* is the exception here since his gender presentation does not change in the story.

6. Libraries are more likely to have LGBTQ+-themed children's books if the librarians and patrons know what to ask for, if the library is well funded, and the book is favorably reviewed (Spence). An increase in book bans and challenges in 2022 and 2023 may complicate this access.

7. Meadow recounts one instance in which "internal swelling" from celiac disease is linked to the suppression of testosterone and to gender-nonconforming behavior. Other parents described gene mutations, prenatal "hormone washes," or environmental toxins as the cause of gender-nonconforming behavior (192–93).

8. Though books about transgender children are often grouped with other gender-nonconforming or queer children's literature in both libraries and scholarship, transgender children are not necessarily genderqueer. In the books discussed in this chapter, transgender children do not question binary gender or gendered cultural scripts, but rather they assert that their gender is different from the sex assigned to them at birth. This distinction is important for understanding how the transgender children and their parents discussed here depict their stories and advocate for their rights.

9. Travers also cautions parents that government intervention is not always friendly to LGBTQ+ populations and is changeable with every election and so advocates for local, grassroots organizing efforts at inclusion rather than a top-down approach to transgender rights.

10. PFLAG, originally standing for Parents and Friends of Lesbians and Gays and, later, Parents, Families and Friends of Lesbians and Gays, is no longer an acronym but rather simply the name of the organization.

11. These notes are similar to the introductions or author's notes in the golden age of children's literature that performed proximity to childhood by explaining that the stories had been originally written for a specific child, such as a son, daughter, or family friend.

12. I am thinking here about the backlash for "pure" white female pop stars, such as Britney Spears or Miley Cyrus, when they reach adulthood.

WORKS CITED

Andrew, Scottie. "This Year, At Least Six States Are Trying to Restrict Transgender Kids from Getting Gender Reassignment Treatments." *CNN*, 22 Jan. 2020, www.cnn.com/2020/01/22/politics/transgender-healthcare-laws-minors-trnd/index.html.

Ariès, Philippe. *Centuries of Childhood: A Social History of Family Life*. Random House, 1988.

"Attacks on Gender Affirming Care by State Map." *Human Rights Campaign*, 1 June 2023, www.hrc.org/resources/attacks-on-gender-affirming-care-by-state-map.

Bernstein, Robin. *Racial Innocence*. New York UP, 2011.

Bittner, Robert, et al. "Queer and Trans-Themed Books for Young Readers: A Critical Review." *Discourse: Studies in the Cultural Politics of Education*, vol. 37, no. 6, 2016, pp. 948–64.

Carr, Jennifer. *Be Who You Are!* Illustrated by Ben Rumback, AuthorHouse, 2010.

Chu, Andrea Long, and Emmett Harsin Drager. "After Trans Studies." *Transgender Studies Quarterly*, vol. 6, no. 1, 2019, pp. 103–16.

Epstein, B. J. *Are the Kids All Right? Representations of LGBTQ Characters in Children's and Young Adult Literature.* HammerOn Press, 2013.
Ewert, Marcus. *10,000 Dresses.* Illustrated by Rex Ray, Seven Stories Press, 2008.
Gabriel, Dani. *Sam!* Illustrated by Robert Liu-Trujillo, Penny Candy Books, 2019.
Gould, Lois. *X: A Fabulous Child's Story.* Illustrated by Jacqueline Chwast, Daughters Publishing, 1978.
Gubar, Marah. "Innocence." *Keywords for Children's Literature.* Edited by Philip Nel et al., vol. 9, New York UP, 2021, pp. 105–9.
Herthel, Jessica, and Jazz Jennings. *I Am Jazz.* Illustrated by Shelagh McNicholas, Penguin, 2014.
Higonnet, Anne. *Pictures of Innocence: The History and Crisis of Ideal Childhood.* Thames and Hudson, 1998.
Huskey, Melynda. "Queering the Picture Book." *The Lion and the Unicorn,* vol. 26, no. 1, 2002, pp. 66–77. *Project Muse,* https://doi.org/10.1353/uni.2002.0005.
Keenan, Harper Benjamin. "Unscripting Curriculum: Toward a Critical Trans Pedagogy." *Harvard Educational Review,* vol. 87, no. 4, 2017, pp. 538–56.
Kuvalanka, Katherine A., et al. "Trans and Gender-Nonconforming Children and Their Caregivers: Gender Presentations, Peer Relations, and Well-being at Baseline." *Journal of Family Psychology,* vol. 31, no. 7, 2017, pp. 889–99.
Lyons, Maddox, and Jessica Verdi. *I'm Not a Girl.* Illustrated by Dana Simpson, Roaring Brook Press, 2020.
Martino, Wayne, and Wendy Cumming-Potvin. "Teaching about Sexual Minorities and 'Princess Boys': A Queer and Trans-Infused Approach to Investigating LGBTQ-Themed Texts in the Elementary School Classroom." *Discourse: Studies in the Cultural Politics of Education,* vol. 37, no. 6, 2016, pp. 807–27.
Mayo, Cris. "Queer and Trans Youth, Relational Subjectivity, and Uncertain Possibilities: Challenging Research in Complicated Contexts." *Educational Researcher,* vol. 46, no. 9, 2017, pp. 530–38.
McIlroy, Thad. "What the Big 5's Financial Reports Reveal about the State of Traditional Book Publishing." *Book Business Magazine,* 8 Aug. 2016, www.bookbusinessmag.com/post/big-5-financial-reports-reveal-state-traditional-book-publishing/.
Meadow, Tey. *Trans Kids: Being Gendered in the Twenty-First Century.* U of California P, 2018.
Miller, Jennifer L. "Queer Theory: Queer Children and Childhoods." *The Year's Work in Critical and Cultural Theory,* vol. 28, no. 1, 2020, pp. 102–23.
Minter, Shannon Price. "Supporting Transgender Children: New Legal, Social, and Medical Approaches." *Journal of Homosexuality,* vol. 59, no. 3, 2012, pp. 422–33.
Naidoo, Jamie Campbell. *Rainbow Family Collections: Selecting and Using Children's Books with Lesbian, Gay, Bisexual, Transgender and Queer Content.* Libraries Unlimited, 2012.
Norton, Jody. "Transchildren and the Discipline of Children's Literature." *Over the Rainbow: Queer Children's and Young Adult Literature,* edited by Michelle Ann Abate and Kenneth Kidd, U of Michigan P, 2011, pp. 293–313.
Olson, Kristina R., and Selin Gülgöz. "Early Findings from the Transyouth Project: Gender Development in Transgender Children." *Child Development Perspectives,* vol. 12, no. 2, 2018, pp. 93–97.
Pyne, Jake. "The Governance of Gender Non-Conforming Children: A Dangerous Enclosure." *Annual Review of Critical Psychology,* vol. 11, 2014, pp. 79–96.
Sipe, Lawrence R., and Caroline E. McGuire. "Picturebook Endpapers: Resources for Literary and Aesthetic Interpretation." *Children's Literature in Education,* vol. 37, no. 4, 2006, pp. 291–304.

Spade, Dean. *Normal Life: Administrative Violence, Critical Trans Politics, and the Limits of the Law*. South End, 2011.

Spence, Alex. "Controversial Books in the Public Library: A Comparative Survey of Holdings of Gay-Related Children's Picture Books." *Library Quarterly*, vol. 70, no. 3, 2000, pp. 335–79.

Travers, Ann. *The Trans Generation: How Trans Kids (and Their Parents) Are Creating a Gender Revolution*. NYU Press, 2019.

West, Candace, and Don H. Zimmerman. "Doing Gender." *Gender and Society*, vol. 1, no. 2, 1987, pp. 125–51.

PART 3
MAPPING REPRESENTATIONS IN EUROPEAN PICTURE BOOKS

CHAPTER 7

THE ROAD TO HELL
Scandinavian LGBTQ+ Picturebooks

B. J. Woodstein

In this chapter, I explore Swedish- and Norwegian-language picturebooks featuring LGBTQ+ characters published in Scandinavia.[1] My starting hypothesis was that Scandinavian literature would feature a wide range of characters and family setups in an accepting manner, with queerness not as the main plot but rather one characteristic out of many. In other words, I suspected that the legal rights and political situation for LGBTQ+ people in a given country would influence how people wrote about LGBTQ+ topics for children. In a region that is politically liberal, such as Scandinavia, I expected to find children's literature that featured a wide range of identities and did not problematize them. This can be considered a queer-positive approach.[2]

In previous research, I analyzed English-language picturebooks from the United States and the United Kingdom and found that many of them treat LGBTQ+ characters and topics as "issues" that need to be discussed; the works are frequently pedagogical and/or seem aimed at what I call "confirming normality," which means convincing readers that LGBTQ+ people and families are as "normal" as cisgender and heterosexual people and families (Epstein, *Are the Kids*). Given this normalizing approach, which treats LGBTQ+ people as "other," often in a negative way, I had hoped to find that works published in Sweden and Norway would be different and would not be pedagogical or normalizing. However, in more recent research analyzing Swedish young adult novels, I was surprised to find that they appear to tend to look for an explanation of why someone is LGBTQ+, suggesting that queerness is a deviation from the norm (Epstein, "Becoming versus Being").

In this chapter, I argue that most Scandinavian picturebooks featuring LGBTQ+ characters and cultures are either self-published or published by specialist publishers aimed at producing "diverse" literature, which suggests that mainstream publishers do not necessarily think it is appropriate or financially viable to include LGBTQ+ storylines; interestingly, however, despite the commitment to sexual diversity, there is little intersectionality in these works. Furthermore, the books also tend to be educational ones with apparently good intentions, often following the "confirmation of normality" or explanatory approach that I discovered in my earlier research into US and UK publications. Intriguingly, they also often feature animal characters; while it is common to feature animals in children's picturebooks, the depiction of queer people as animals may not be queer-positive, and it could also be seen as dehumanizing LGBTQ+ folks. These tropes led me to believe that Scandinavian picturebooks are not as queer-positive or norm-critical as one might anticipate and as I hypothesized. In fact, there appears to be a cultural lag between queer-affirming politics and queer-affirming representation in children's culture.

In what follows, I give some brief background, then look at four key, related findings in turn regarding the publisher, the animal characters, the pedagogical approach to the story, and the lack of diversity. My overall conclusion is that there are good intentions behind the production and publication of these books but that, unfortunately, sometimes good intentions are not quite good enough in their outcome.

BACKGROUND TO THIS PROJECT

As noted, some of my earlier research focused on English-language books, mostly from the United States and the United Kingdom, with some from Australia (e.g., Epstein, *Are the Kids*; Epstein, "Case"; and Epstein, "Eradicalisation"), and I decided to use my language competencies in order to expand this to a comparative approach. In 2016, I received a grant from the Svenska Barnboksinstitutet (Swedish Institute for Children's Books) in Stockholm to carry out research there. This enabled me access to Swedish-language picturebooks. I have subsequently been to Sweden for research at least three times. In 2020, I received a grant from the Norsk Barnebokinstitutt (Norwegian Children's Books Institute) through the Kari Skjønsbergs Fond to research in Oslo, and that is when I found the Norwegian-language books discussed here. In other words, I read books in the research libraries on those trips and also asked for recommendations at bookstores, libraries, and online. I would have gone to Scandinavia as usual at least once more, ideally to also look at books from Denmark, but unfortunately, the coronavirus pandemic made travel impossible.

It is important to recognize that Sweden is around twice the size of Norway (the Swedish population is around ten million, the Norwegian one, over five million), so it is not a surprise that I found more children's literature there generally and particularly LGBTQ+-related picturebooks. In addition, as noted, over the course of the past years, I have spent more time in Sweden, so that may have allowed me more time to find Swedish books. The result, then, is that although I tried to explore Norwegian and Swedish books equally, I acknowledge that I have more literature from Sweden.

SCANDINAVIAN LGBTQ+ RIGHTS

In endnote 3, I offer a brief overview of politics in Scandinavia, noting the liberal influence on the countries. There is an obvious connection between who people vote for and which policies people want to see enacted; perhaps, then, more liberal countries allow for more acceptance of a greater range of citizens.

While space limitations restrict how much historical information about LGBTQ+ rights I can offer here, I want to briefly mention a few relevant facts (but for more, see Epstein, "Becoming versus Being"; Warnqvist). Sweden did grant some rights and protections to LGBTQ+ people and couples earlier than many other countries (Rydström 49–58), but it is actually more challenging to become parents there than, say, the United Kingdom. For example, in Sweden, in a relationship where two women are married, the woman who does not bear the child must adopt it, whereas in the United Kingdom, that woman would automatically be legally recognized as the second parent (for more details on LGBTQ+ rights in Sweden, see "Legal Parenthood"). Similarly, it is not a simple matter for a woman to share her eggs with her partner; that is considered egg donation in Sweden (see "Assisted Reproduction"), whereas partner, or reciprocal, IVF is relatively standard in the United Kingdom.

In Norway, it appears slightly easier to get access to fertility treatment, but there, too, adoption is required in some circumstances if two LGBTQ+ people have a child together. This is particularly the case if pregnancy occurs via home insemination with a known donor ("Legal Parenthood").

So despite LGBTQ+ people having their relationships recognized in Scandinavia early on and being allowed full marriage rights sooner than in some other countries, it is not always straightforward, so to speak, for them to create their families. Given the sluggishness of regulations regarding this, it may make sense that there are fewer picturebooks about LGBTQ+ families. Much more research would need to be carried out, but something that does not easily exist in a society may not be seen as common or interesting enough to be written about, except perhaps by specialist publishers.

PUBLISHING COMPANIES

In a book that I coedited on LGBTQ+ literature for children and young adults from around the world (Epstein and Chapman), one of the major, and perhaps most striking, findings was how many of these books were published by the authors themselves (self-publishing) or otherwise by new, smaller publishers that choose to specialize in publishing LGBTQ+ or other "diverse" literature. Examples of where this happens include Italy (Forni), the Philippines (Sayuno), and generally around the world in regard to the subject of two-mother families (Sarles), among others. I have found something similar in Scandinavia.

Although I have not read every single LGBTQ+ picturebook from Norway or Sweden, so my sample is not comprehensive—and also, I must note, it is tricky to count the exact number since some are in collections—from the books I have analyzed here, only six out of thirty have been published by traditional, long-standing publishers. In other words, twenty-four, or 80 percent, of the books I found were either self-published or published by publishers dedicated to such literature.

The one specialized publisher in Norway that is relevant to this chapter is LIV Förlag, which published *Wilma har to mammaer* (Wilma has two mothers) by Lone Halvorsen and Maria Therese Olsen.[3] The same publisher also published *Cornelia flytter i fosterhjem* (Cornelia moves to a foster home) by Ritva Fyhn-Pettersen, and *Pappa sitter i fengsel* (Dad's in prison) by Elisabet Omsén, and perhaps those titles and themes provide evidence for the publisher's approach to children's literature ("Våra Böcker"). In Sweden, there are four main publishers that focus on "different" books. They are Sagolikt, Spegel, OLIKA, and Vombat, and they all appear frequently in my corpus. Sagolikt is run by an author-illustrator duo, and they wrote, illustrated, and published seven of the books here, and Sagolikt's motto is "children's books that break the norm" ("Välkommen").[4] Spegel, which means "mirror," was—it is no longer going—also run by the two people who wrote and illustrated the books. Their aim was to reflect (mirror) "children and young people whose lives do not follow the norm" ("Välkommen").[5] To that end, they had a series entitled Barn i regnbågsfamiljer (Children in rainbow families). Vombat aims to "make everyone's equality visible" ("Hem").[6] They refer to what they are doing as "norm creative," which can be said to mean challenging the norm and suggesting different ways of being.[7] Finally, OLIKA, which means "different," "challenges stereotypes with norm creativity" and "loves equality, inclusion and sustainability" ("Så jobbar OLIKA med normer").[8]

The four Swedish publishing companies and the one Norwegian one show quite clearly that these smaller publishers have the explicit aim of featuring a wider range of people and stories than more mainstream publishers. They say they want to challenge and critique the norm, be creative with the idea of the norm, and perhaps even extend what is considered the norm, but my findings suggest they actually emphasize the importance of normality. They do this, first, by relegating LGBTQ+ content to mission-oriented presses; second, through content that inadvertently represents LGBTQ+ characters as not human, distancing them from non-LGBTQ+ people; and third, by treating LGBTQ+ topics as ones that must be taught about rather than simply as part of regular life.

The majority of the LGBTQ+ picturebooks that I have found in Scandinavia are published by companies that focus on producing inclusive, diverse works; this can certainly be positive, and their intentions are clearly good, but I would suggest they fall short in some ways, such as in terms of intersectionality or due to the way they depict LGBTQ+ people and topics. If LGBTQ+ picturebooks are only published by smaller publishers, this strengthens the idea that being LGBTQ+ is "other" and possibly problematic and perhaps is not a subject worthy of inclusion by larger, more traditional publishers.[9] In addition, this links to my later discussion in this chapter about the pedagogical approach of these works; the publishing companies' intentions are educational, which gives the impression that LGBTQ+ people and topics are something that must be taught about in a particular way rather than being absorbed into society as quite ordinary or otherwise challenging society.

ANIMALS PLUS THE NORMALIZING AND EDUCATIONAL APPROACH

My analysis of the corpus found that there are several problematic representational strategies employed by creators of LGBTQ+ picturebooks. First, most LGBTQ+ characters are illustrated as animals; second, most texts invest in normalizing LGBTQ+ identities and families; and third, many address a presumably cisgender heterosexual audience and attempt to educate readers about LGBTQ+ identities.

Using animals in the illustrations as the protagonists in LGBTQ+ picturebooks is a relatively common approach, and one that other scholars have noted (DePalma; Naidoo and Zabawa). It may be that it seems less challenging to discuss queer topics through the guise of animals than humans, because (1) it makes it seem as if queerness is "natural" and "normal" and (2) it may be easier for readers, whether adults or children, to relate to the animals. And yet this emphasizes the difference and the deviation from the "mainstream" that queerness might represent, which seems to run counter to the stated aims of these works.

Sagolikt, a Swedish publisher mentioned above, has several distinct series. One series features two male giraffes, Jösta and Johan, and their adopted crocodile son, Junior. The nonbiological link the giraffes have with their son is shown in images by using a different species. Sagolikt also published *Känn med hen* (Feel with them) by Anette Skåhlberg; this will be discussed more below, but it too uses nonhuman characters—although, in this case, to explore identity beyond the gender binary. Another work, *Vem är var?* (Who is where?) by Stina Wirsén, is one of the few books in my corpus to be published by a mainstream publisher, but it also features animal characters; there is a rabbit with two mothers. The LGBTQ+ aspect is otherwise not part of the story. Additionally, in Norwegian, there is a series of picturebooks that depict two mothers and their child. Here, too, they are portrayed as animals—in this case, the spectacled bear (*brillebjørn*).

In contrast to the animals, an interesting illustration choice was made by the publisher Spegel to use the male and female symbols as characters instead, which they noted was to avoid "colors and other attributes that are often used to illustrate and describe what is manly/womanly or girlish/boyish" (Spegel Förlag).[10] My concern is that this actually strengthens the binary view of gender rather than challenging it. While this is not the same as portraying LGBTQ+ characters as animals, it is worth pointing out how it is another example of doing the opposite of humanizing LGBTQ+ people; here, people become relatively abstract symbols.

As some humans look down on animals, thinking themselves above them, it is not inconceivable that the continuing depiction of LGBTQ+ people as animals in picturebooks could be said to be negative. One could argue that queers could be said to be "like animals" and "lower than non-LGBTQ+ people" and even deserving of abuse. In my corpus, the use of animals was common; perhaps it was thought that this would make it easier for readers to relate to them, but an alternate reading is that it emphasizes the difference and the deviation from the norm that queerness might represent. And yet this seems to run counter to the stated aims of these works.

In addition to the widespread use of animals (or symbols), I also found that many of these books have a normalizing (Epstein, *Are the Kids* 39–45) and/or educational approach, by which I mean that they appear to intend to teach non-LGBTQ+ about LGBTQ+ people and to explain their families while also insisting on how normal and acceptable LGBTQ+ people are. This forces the books into an awkward middle ground, neither treating LGBTQ+ people as just like everyone else nor critiquing the norm, and thus they are more queer-negative than queer-positive.

For instance, in the Norwegian book *Wilma har to mammaer* (Wilma has two mothers), there are two different forewords, which is quite unusual for a picturebook. One of the forewords emphasizes that "these families are just like other families" (Nylund).[11] The story itself carefully explains about the egg and the sperm, the donor and the doctor, and how Wilma and her mothers are "a totally common, but slightly different family" (Halvorsen and Olsen).[12] As Patricia Sarles finds regarding similar books from around the world, the Wilma story is based on the author's own life, so perhaps that is why it is so detailed and explanatory in its approach. Interestingly, some recent research notes that Norwegian children's literature was relatively pedagogical through 2005, then began changing, and then started heading back toward the pedagogical again in the past years (Andreassen 265, 268–69).[13] If this is true, it could also be that Halvorsen and Olsen's book is part of the pedagogical turn, although the other Norwegian works do not fit this pattern.

In Sweden, works often explain where the children came from and how the families were created. This is a pedagogical approach, like that found in *Wilma*, making LGBTQ+ people and families seem different from heterosexual and/or cisgender ones, since—notwithstanding how-babies-get-made books, which are specifically about exploring pregnancy—few picturebooks feel the need to explain most families and their creation. One of the rare picturebooks to feature two fathers, as opposed to the much more common two mothers, is *Alice och papporna åker till USA* (Alice and her dads go to the USA) by Karolina Schubert. The story starts with an explanation of how her fathers adopted her in the United States—which seems unlikely, given adoption laws—instead of simply beginning with Alice and her fathers doing something unrelated to explaining their family setup. The book goes on to discuss how she sometimes thinks about why she does not have a mother, the way her friends do; however, she grew inside a woman who could not take care of her.[14]

Max och Moa har två mammor, två pappor och ett alldeles eget hus (Max and Moa have two mothers, two fathers and a house of their own), also by Schubert, again employs some of its short word count to explain how Max and Moa stay put in their house while one week, their two mothers live with them, and the next week, their two fathers do.[15] Many of the books seem to consider it necessary to describe and clarify the family before getting on with the story; other examples, all by Schubert, include *Astrid, mamma och pappa* (Astrid, mom and dad), which explains how Astrid's parents are best friends and not romantic parents and that Astrid's mother has a girlfriend; *Rufus härliga sommar* (Rufus's wonderful summer), in which the reader is told how one of Rufus's parents is neither a man or a woman and that it is important to decide one's gender for oneself; or *Maja och mammorna åker till veterinären* (Maja and her mothers go to the vet), which explains sperm donation. There are more examples, but these show what can be considered an archetypal model: explain the family and how the children were created and then move on with the plot rather awkwardly in the short remaining word count. Again, this is not common in picturebooks with non-LGBTQ+ families, and it is also not often seen in English-language LGBTQ+ picturebooks. In terms of the former, I think that since non-LGBTQ+ families are seen as the norm, there is thought to be no real need to explain how they were formed. And in regard to the latter, based on other comparative research I have carried out (Epstein, "Heaven Forbid"), I suspect this is due to the more conservative and euphemistic atmosphere that tends to prevail in English-language literature for children from the United States and the United Kingdom. Talking openly about topics such as egg and sperm might be considered inappropriate or might make adult readers uncomfortable.

Besides explaining how the children came to be and what the family setups are like, many of these books include a sentence or a section that confirms how normal and/or how special or wonderful the family is. An example is *Noras pappor ska gifta sig—med varandra!* (Nora's dads are getting married—to each other!), where Nora says it is "luxurious" to have two fathers (Schubert).[16] Oddly, a few books confirm normality through negative terms, such as by saying it is not strange to have two mothers or a different sort of family, which I would suggest actually makes a reader think that it *is* strange or abnormal.[17] It creates the idea of strangeness in the reader's mind while attempting to refute it (Epstein, *Are the Kids* 45). Showing diverse people simply living their lives would arguably do more to emphasize normality. Of course, the goal may be to emphasize the difference of queer lives, but the effect of many of these picturebooks is more homonormative than norm-critiquing.

While some books, such as those discussed above, are much more blatant in their approach, it is also a common method to show a variety of families as a way of confirming how acceptable they are. One of the few picturebooks by a well-known author-illustrator, *Min familj* (My family) by Anna-Clara Tidholm, has no plot per se but rather simply shows different types of families, normalizing them all.[18] At the end, there is space for the reader or listener to describe or draw their own family.

Another pedagogical approach is in regard to trans or nonbinary identities. Several books employ the Swedish gender-neutral pronoun "*hen*," but rather than simply doing so, they also seem to want to educate readers about it. For instance, *Känn med hen* (Feel with them) explores feelings by using five-different gender-neutral pronouns, although the characters are not human (Skåhlberg).[19] And *Kivi och monsterhund* (Kivi and the monster dog) by Jesper Lundqvist, also uses the gender-neutral pronoun "*hen*" and explains it in great detail in the paratext. For example, the author states, "Language plays a role, especially when it comes to entrenching or changing thoughts and norms. Words like '*hon*' [she] and '*han*' [he] carry many associations that are stereotypes" (Lundqvist, *Kivi och monsterhund*).[20] The book goes on to employ other, frequently neologistic gender-neutral terms for people and relationships. Lundqvist's second book about Kivi, *Kivi och den gråtande goraffen* (Kivi and the crying gorilaffe), references the debate in Swedish media that arose at that time about the use of "*hen*" and adds further pedagogical comments about when and how to use the term and how to grammatically inflect it.[21] And in yet another Kivi book, *Kivi och drakbrakaren* (Kivi and the dragon crasher), the illustrator adds a comment this time about how they "like to draw people based on their personality and characteristics, not their gender" (Lundqvist).[22] All these explanations and opinions serve to teach readers, with messages including the importance of seeing people for who they are, not for what their genitals suggest, and the need to actively change the Swedish language to make it more gender neutral. These are useful points to consider, but a question is whether a picturebook is the best place for them. In such works, the story serves the message rather than the message serving the story, which means that the characters do not feel real, and the plot is not as engaging. I would suggest that a more organic approach—with the characters and the plot coming first—would work better in terms of literary quality and would also draw in readers.

In short, there are multitudes of explanations and discussions in Scandinavian LGBTQ+ picturebooks that are simply not found in other types of picturebooks. While I certainly believe there is a need for books that explain different family setups and for books that challenge societal stereotypes and expectations, I would suggest that the number of books that are explanatory, pedagogical, and confirming of normality is excessive. It is essential to offer literature that features LGBTQ+ getting on with their lives rather than continually focusing on how they became queer, how they made their families, what words can be used to describe them, or other such educational issues. Being queer is not necessarily the most interesting thing about them, either to the characters themselves or to the people reading about them.

THE FEW EXCEPTIONS

There are relatively few exceptions in my corpus to the educational approach. One is the series *Brillebjørn* (Spectacled bear) in Norwegian, which treats young Brillebjørn's two mothers simply as a fact, which of course is what they are. The *Brillebjørn* stories often have some other message or lesson, perhaps to help child readers feel empowered through Brillebjørn's experiences, but confirming the normality of Brillebjørn's family is not one of the morals. Examples of *Brillebjørn* stories include when Brillebjørn puts out a fire that one of his mothers accidentally sets or when Brillebjørn finds his other mother's wallet, which she carelessly dropped (Jackson). The author of the series, Ida Jackson, argues that Norwegian literature is "all too heteronormative, traditional and conservative" (Nordseth).[23] Jackson claims that she knows of no other Norwegian picturebooks with two-mother families, and although she clearly missed the book about Wilma that I have discussed in this chapter, I suspect she is basically right beyond that. Jackson's "point was not that he [Brillebjørn] has two mothers, but it is important that the Brillebjørn books are available as part of the selection [of children's books]" (Nordseth).[24] In other words, Jackson is not trying to teach readers about queer family setups but rather choosing to make Brillebjørn's two mothers just one out of many aspects of his life.

A few other books likewise attempt to make the queerness not a major part of the storyline. Two books by Eva Susso—*Den magiska hajtanden* (The magical shark tooth) and *Den mystiska fyren* (The mysterious lighthouse)—are both about two sisters who visit their aunt and her partner, but the plots have nothing to do with the aunt being LGBTQ+. Amusingly, in one of the stories, the sisters, their aunt, and her partner grill vegetarian sausages (Susso, *Den magiska hajtanden*), which perhaps links to the apparent connection between vegetarians and LGBTQ+ people, as suggested by OLIKA publishing company ("Hållbarhet & klimat"), Barry Duke, and others.[25]

As a final example, *Jag vill ha baklava!* (I want baklava!) by Kalle Guettler has a (non-gender-specific) protagonist with two mothers, but the main concern of the book is about the character's desire for baklava. The book is educational about baklava (a recipe is included) and seems aimed at confirming the normality of other ethnicities. So although it is an exception in regard to normalizing queerness, it has other unfortunate elements of the pedagogical approach.

These few exceptions serve to prove the point, however: LGBTQ+ picturebooks in Scandinavia are overwhelmingly pedagogical and focused on queerness to the detriment of all other subjects and perhaps are meant to teach non-LGBTQ+ readers.

DIVERSITY, OR THE LACK THEREOF

Despite many of the publishers' stated dedication to and focus on inclusivity and diversity, I would argue that the books in my corpus are actually quite limited in their depictions. There are two-mother families and some gender-nonconforming characters but few other flavors of LGBTQ+. And the great majority of human characters appear white (and I do not want to speculate on the supposed ethnicity of animal characters).

My corpus of picturebooks do feature many LGBTQ+ parents, most often two-mother families. I would guess that the average reader or listener would assume that the women in two-mother families are lesbians/gay women, but the words in the books never confirm this; a knowing reader might wonder if any of them were bisexual or trans or otherwise queer, but without this being part of the story, it is difficult to know for sure. So although I continually reference LGBTQ+ in this chapter, it is unlikely that the books themselves feature much diversity from under the queer umbrella. There is one coparenting arrangement with two mothers and two fathers (*Max och Moa har två mammor, två pappor och ett alldeles eget hus* [Max and Moa have two mothers, two fathers and a house of their own]), a couple of two-father families, and one family with a nongendered parent (*Rufus härliga sommar* [Rufus's wonderful summer]), but otherwise, most of the children live with two mothers.

There are also some books about LGBTQ+ young people themselves, although often they are within their family setting, even if chafing against it. While it is not a surprise that picturebooks aimed at young people would mostly focus on the family, it is not inconceivable that picturebooks could depict queer children exploring their lives without parents or other adults around them.

Interestingly, one book has no children in it at all. This is a Swedish-language book from Finland, *Allan och Udo* (Allan and Udo), about an older, male couple. It is quite different from the other works explored here, not least in that it is about growing older and potentially about dementia (Linderberg). The queerness is not explained, nor is it the focus of the story, so it does not fall into the educational category.

In addition to the lack of diversity regarding the types of queerness shown, I found no real ethnic diversity. Although there may be an assumption that Scandinavia is homogenous, in fact, 20 percent of Sweden's population was born outside the country ("Hur manga"). That the only nonwhite human character I found is someone who teaches the protagonist to make the non-Scandinavian dish of baklava (in *Jag vill ha baklava!* [I want baklava!]) is concerning.

In short, I would suggest that this means that authors and publishers may feel that it is enough to feature one type of diversity—particularly two-mother families—and that it would be too complex or challenging to depict intersectionality or a range of identities. This is exactly what I found in regard to English-language LGBTQ+ literature for children and young adults (Epstein, *Are the Kids* 188–90). This shows there is much scope for additional works in the field.

CONCLUSION

I titled this chapter after the aphorism "the road to hell is paved with good intentions" because I do believe that these authors, illustrators, and publishing companies have the best of intentions when it comes to producing work that features LGBTQ+ people. Often, their stated aims are to challenge societal norms and stereotypes and to encourage a broadening of perspectives and opportunities and even a change to language itself; I would argue that this is praiseworthy and important work. However, the way in which this work is done can be quite limited and limiting.

I have discussed several main issues in regard to these works. The first is the fact that these books are nearly all published by specialized publishers, sometimes run by the authors and/or illustrators themselves. Specialized publishers are in and of themselves not problematic, but here, I believe their prominence is evidence that LGBTQ+ topics are not yet considered mainstream in Scandinavia or of interest to readers generally. When it comes to self-publishing or publishing companies run by authors and/or illustrators, there may also be issues of quality since texts may not receive the level of editing they require. I have not critiqued the language in these books in this chapter, but there are some undeniably awkward phrases or poorly written texts.

I have briefly noted how many of these works rely on animal characters and not human ones. This is not automatically a problem, but there is a potential argument about whether that dehumanizes the LGBTQ+ people or links being queer to being more like animals. It may also mean that readers might not relate to the characters.

I then explored how overwhelmingly educational most of these picturebooks are. The plots repeatedly focus on explaining LGBTQ+ people or families, confirming that they are normal and not "strange," and/or teaching people about gender stereotypes and new, gender-neutral language. This could be called an early stage in LGBTQ+ literature for young readers; later stages would assume the normality of queerness and instead focus on other plots and would be less pedagogical and/or they would be norm-critical.

Finally, I have noted that there is a surprising lack of diversity among the picturebooks. The parents in them are usually two-mother families, for example, and the human characters are nearly always able-bodied, white, young, and otherwise "norm." Of course, it is possible that a reader or listener might read something else into the illustrations in some cases, but in general, neither the words nor the images depict much intersectionality or diversity.

While space precludes me from discussing English-language picturebooks in any great detail, it is worth mentioning that all of these findings from Sweden and Norway correlate with my findings from the United States and the United Kingdom approximately ten years ago (Epstein, *Are the Kids*). I believe LGBTQ+ picturebooks in English-speaking countries have been changing over the past decade. And although many of these issues are still present, there has also been significant development. Perhaps LGBTQ+ picturebooks in Scandinavia will follow the same trajectory, and the good intentions will lead to stronger and more interesting outputs in the next few years.

NOTES

1. I write "picturebook" as one word rather than as "picture book" in order to emphasize the interwoven nature of words and images in such a text. Natalie op de Beeck writes, "The compound word *picturebook* presupposes interdependent nonverbal imagery and written language (a title at a minimum)" (20). However, I acknowledge that in this chapter, I do not give as much attention to the images as I would like to, given space constrictions.

Also, it is shorter to use the acronym LGBTQ+, which traditionally means lesbian, gay, bisexual, trans, queer, plus, but by which I mean lesbian, gay, bisexual, trans, asexual, intersex, nonbinary, polyamorous, kinky, questioning, queer, and anyone else who would like to be included. I sometimes use "queer" in this chapter as shorthand. "Rainbow" is also a term employed at times.

2. In Sweden, the Socialdemokraterna (Social Democrats), a left-wing political group, have been in power for much of the twentieth century and for some of the twenty-first, and they have instituted policies such as the welfare state. In Norway, the Venstre (Left, or Liberal) Party was influential in the twentieth century, but at the time of writing, the Arbeiderpartiet (Labour Party) has a slight majority, with the Høyre (Right) just behind. Meanwhile, in the United Kingdom over the past century, the Conservative Party has won elections eighteen times (64 percent) and the Labour Party, ten times (36 percent) (Audickas et al.). It is a bit harder to calculate this sort of data in the United States, given a rather regular swap between Democrats and Republicans there (Gelman) and the closeness of recent elections, which suggests a real divide. Still, conservative and "family-first" policies have been prominent in both the United States and the United Kingdom. Whether politics or social mores come first is a huge question, but clearly there is interinfluence and interdependence between them. In short, Scandinavia can be considered to be more liberal than the United Kingdom and the United States and, indeed, is often considered "socialist" (e.g., Norberg), and it could be argued that a more liberal culture would be more accepting of LGBTQ+ people.

3. All translations from Norwegian or Swedish are my own, unless otherwise noted. For book titles, I have translated them literally, unless there are already existing English versions. For quotes from websites, articles, or books, I have chosen to translate in a more literary way. I usually only quote a small part of the original text due to space constrictions, but I include the full section in the footnotes.

4. In Swedish, "*barnböcker som bryter normen*"; a more literary English translation would be "children's books that challenge the norm."

5. "Vår ambition är att arbeta med produktion av böcker och tillhörande material som speglar barn och ungdomar vars livssituation inte följer normen."

6. "Allas lika värde genom synliggörande."

7. "Normkreativt."

8. "Vi utmanar stereotyper med normkreativitet. Vi älskar jämlikhet, inkludering och hållbarhet."

9. There is a real need for queer literature and nonnormative perspectives, but my point here is that pedagogical approaches may do more harm than good.

10. "Vi har valt att arbeta med tecknet för man och kvinna när vi har tecknat personerna i boken. Det har vi gjort för att komma ifån färger och andra attribut som oftast används för att illustrera och beskriva vad som är manligt/kvinnligt eller flickigt/pojkigt."

11. "Disse familene er akkurat som andre familier—rett og slett unike og forskjellige fra hverandre. Allikevel er det noe som er litt spesielt med dem. De må ofte ha bistand fra noen andre før å bli gravide, og for å bringe barn til verden."

12. "En helt vanlig, men litt annerledes familie."

13. "Barnelitteraturen i Norge har i hovedtrekk utviklet seg fra å være svært pedagogisk og oppdragende første halvdel av 1900-tallet, fram til 1980- og 90-tallet da pedagogisk nærmest ble et tabubelagt uttryck i barne- og ungdomslitteratur. Tendensen har snudd noe nå i de senere år til igjen å bevege seg tilbake mot det pedagogiske, noe den lille oppmerksomheten barnelitteraturen får i form av omtaler i avisene refkleterer."

14. "Iblandt funderar Alice på varför hon inte har någon mamma som hennes kompisar har. Papporna har berättat för Alice att kvinnan som hade henne i magen och födde henne var en ung kvinna som inte kunde ta hand om Alice. Därför fick Alice pappor adoptera hene. Alice är så glad för att hon fick komma till just sina pappor i Sverige!"

15. "Max och Moa har två mammor och två pappor. Pappa Per och pappa Johan är gifta med varandra och mamma Kattis och mamma Åsa är gifta med varandra. Varannan vecka bor mammorna i huset och varannan vecka bor papporna i huset med barnen. Mammorna och

papporna tycker att det är bäst så för Max och Moa. Då slipper de packa väskor och åka mellan sina föräldrar."

16. "Lyxigt."

17. Regarding the depictions as "not strange," there are the lines "Det är inget konstigt" (Schubert) and "Emil har alltid vetat om det och tycker inte att det är något konstigt" (Schubert).

18. There are many books like this in English too; they are informative but not terribly pleasurable to read because there is no story driving the reader on.

19. This is generally considered one of the first books in Swedish to use gender-neutral pronouns. In Swedish, "*hon*" is "she" and "*han*" is "he," and this book uses the pronouns "*hen*," "*hun*," "*hin*," "*hån*," and "*hyn*." Today, "*hen*" is the primary accepted gender-neutral pronoun in Swedish.

20. The full quote is as follows: "Hen är inte bara höna på engelska. Det är dessutom svenskans tredje personliga pronomen! Ett komplement till hon eller han. Det är så vi vill se det: som ytterligare en språklig möjlighet som underlättar i en könsstereotyp vardag. För språket spelar roll, särskilt när det handlar om att befästa eller förändra tankemönster och normer. Ord som hon och han bär med sig många föreställningar som ofta är stereotypa. Och i en bok som den här, där det viktiga är vem Kivi är och vad Kivi gör snarare än om Kivi är hon eller han, är hen ett utmärkt ord att använda. Hen är inkluderande och det läsande barnet står friare att själv identifiera sig med karaktären, oavsett om barnet kallas för hon eller han. Vi tror och hoppas att hen på ett lekfullt sägg kan bidra till att både synliggöra och utmana genusfällor som gömmer sig i språket. Kanske är hen det lilla ordet som kommer att uträtta stordåd? Ps. Men hen följer henom istället för henne eller honom. Och istället för att använda man så används en. Ds."

21. The word "*goraffen*" is a neologism—a combination of "gorilla" and "giraffe." So I made up a neologism in English. As for Lundqvist's comments, he states, "Ps. När Kivi & Monsterhund kom ut skapade den stor debatt och hundratals artiklar och blogginlägg har berört boken och hen finns nu i Nationalencyklopedin. I början var förvirringen stor mellan att använda ordet hen och att vara hen och frågan väcktes också om det verkligen fanns ett behov . . . I den här boken följer vi Språkrådets rekommendation, det vill säga hen/hen/hens (jämför men hon/henne/hennes—han/honom/hans" (Lundqvist, *Kivi och den gråtande goraffen*).

22. "Som illustratör gillar jag att skapa människor utifrån deras personlighet och egenskaper, inte enbart efter kön."

23. "Altfor heteronormativ, tradisjonell og konservativ."

24. "Poenget er ikke at han har to mammaer, men det er viktig at bøkene finnes der som en del av det naturlige utvalget."

25. This is not the space to analyze the link between vegetarianism/veganism and LGBTQ+ people, but one informal study suggests that over 65 percent of vegans/vegetarians identify as LGBTQ+ (Duke), and another study suggests that eating meat is viewed as masculine (Modlinska et al. 7), so perhaps it stands to reason that people who actively question gender norms and stereotypes might be less likely to feel tied into diets based on gender.

WORKS CITED

Books Surveyed

Fearon, Isak. *Prinsen och pojken* [The prince and the boy]. Illustrated by Roberth Fearon, Vombat, 2013.

Guettler, Kalle. *Jag vill ha baklava!* [I want baklava!] Illustrated by Pia Halse, OLIKA, 2010.

Halvorsen, Lone, and Maria Therese Olsen. *Wilma har to mammaer* [Wilma has two mothers]. Illustrated by Gina Snipp, LIV Förlag, 2015.

Jackson, Ida. *Brillebjørn* [Spectacled bear]. Illustrated by Jens A. Larsen Aas, Gyldendal, 2017.

Linderberg, Minna. *Allan och Udo* [Allan and Udo]. Illustrated by Linda Bondestam, Söderström, 2011.

Lundqvist, Jesper. *Kivi och den gråtande goraffen* [Kivi and the gorilaffe]. Illustrated by Bettina Johansson, OLIKA, 2012.

Lundqvist, Jesper. *Kivi och drakbrakaren* [Kivi and the dragon crasher]. Illustrated by Bettina Johansson, OLIKA, 2016.

Lundqvist, Jesper. *Kivi och monsterhund* [Kivi and the monster dog]. Illustrated by Bettina Johansson, OLIKA, 2012.

Schubert, Karolina. *Alice och papporna åker till USA* [Alice and her dads go to the USA]. Illustrated by Johanna Hermann Lundberg and Anneli Nygårds, Spegel, 2011.

Schubert, Karolina. *Astrid, mamma och pappa* [Astrid, mom and dad]. Illustrated by Johanna Hermann Lundberg and Anneli Nygårds, Spegel, 2012.

Schubert, Karolina. *Emil, mammorna och pappa åker på träningsläger* [Emil, his mothers and his father go to a training camp]. Illustrated by Johanna Hermann Lundberg and Anneli Nygårds, Spegel, 2012.

Schubert, Karolina. *Maja och mammorna åker till veterinären* [Maja and her mothers go to the vet]. Illustrated by Johanna Hermann Lundberg and Anneli Nygårds, Spegel, 2011.

Schubert, Karolina. *Max och Moa har två mammor, två pappor och ett alldeles eget hus* [Max and Moa have two mothers, two fathers and a house of their own]. Illustrated by Johanna Hermann Lundberg and Anneli Nygårds, Spegel, 2011.

Schubert, Karolina. *Noras pappor ska gifta sig—med varandra!* [Nora's dads are getting married—to each other!]. Illustrated by Johanna Hermann Lundberg and Anneli Nygårds, Spegel, 2012.

Schubert, Karolina. *Rufus härliga sommar* [Rufus's wonderful summer]. Illustrated by Johanna Hermann Lundberg and Anneli Nygårds, Spegel, 2012.

Skåhlberg, Anette. *Känn med hen* [Feel with them]. Illustrated by Katarina Dahlquist, Sagolikt, 2012.

Skåhlberg, Anette. *Prinsessan Kristalla* [Princess Kristalla]. Illustrated by Katarina Dahlquist, Sagolikt, 2008.

Susso, Eva. *Den magiska hajtanden* [The magical shark tooth]. Illustrated by Anna Höglund, Rabén och Sjögren, 2010.

Susso, Eva. *Den mystiska fyren* [The mysterious lighthouse]. Illustrated by Anna Höglund, Rabén och Sjögren, 2011.

Tidholm, Anna-Clara. *Min familj* [My family]. Illustrated by Tidholm, OLIKA, 2009.

Wirsén, Stina. *Vem är var?* [Who is where?]. Illustrated by Wirsén, Bonnier Carlsen, 2012.

Other

Andreassen, Trond. *Bok-Norge: En litteratur-sosiologisk oversikt* [Book-Norway: A literary-sociological overview]. 3rd edition, Universitetetsforlaget, 2006.

"Assisted Reproduction at a Clinic." *RFSL* (Riksförbundet för homosexuellas, bisexuellas, transpersoners, queeras och intersexpersoners rättigheter) [National Association for the Rights of Homosexual, Bisexual, Trans, Queer and Intersex People], 2021, https://www.rfsl.se/en/organisation/familj/att-bli-och-vara-foralder/assisted-reproduction-clinic/.

Audickas, Lukas, et al. "UK Election Statistics: 1918–2019; A Century of Elections." *UK Parliament*, 9 Aug. 2020, https://commonslibrary.parliament.uk/research-briefings/cbp-7529/.

DePalma, Renée. "Gay Penguins, Sissy Ducklings . . . and Beyond? Exploring Gender and Sexuality Diversity through Children's Literature." *Discourse: Studies in the Cultural Politics of Education*, vol. 37, no. 6, 2016, pp. 828–45.

Duke, Barry. "Is Avoiding Animal Produce a Gay Thing?" *Euro Weekly News*, 9 Jan. 2019, https://www.euroweeklynews.com/2019/01/09/is-avoiding-animal-produce-a-gay-thing/.

Epstein, B. J. *Are the Kids All Right? Representations of LGBTQ Characters in Children's and Young Adult Literature*. HammerOn Press, 2013.

Epstein, B. J. "Becoming versus Being: Nature, Nurture and Stereotypes in Swedish LGB Young Adults Novels." Epstein and Chapman, 2021, pp. 303–18.

Epstein, B. J. "The Case of the Missing Bisexuals: Bisexuality in Books for Young Readers." *Journal of Bisexuality*, vol. 14, no. 1, 2016, pp. 110–25.

Epstein, B. J. "Eradicalisation: Eradicating the Queer in Children's Literature." *Queer in Translation*, edited by B. J. Epstein and Robert Gillett, Routledge, 2017, pp. 118–28.

Epstein, B. J. "Heaven Forbid." *Norsk Barenboksinstitutt*, 2 July 2021, https://barnebokinstituttet.no/faglitteratur-om-barnelitteratur/heaven-forbid/.

Epstein, B. J., and Elizabeth L. Chapman, editors. *International LGBTQ+ Literature for Children and Young Adults*. Anthem, 2021.

Forni, Dalila. "LGBTQ Families and Picturebooks: New Perspectives in Italian Children's Literature." Epstein and Chapman, 2021, pp. 129–45.

FRI (Foreningen for kjønns- og seksualitetsmangfold) [Association for Gender and Sexual Diversity], 2021, https://www.foreningenfri.no/.

Fyhn-Pettersen, Ritva. *Cornelia flytter i fosterhjem* [Cornelia moves to a foster home]. Illustrated by Mette Fyhn, Norli, 2012.

Gelman, Andrew. "The Twentieth-Century Reversal: How Did the Republican States Switch to the Democrats and Vice Versa?" *Statistics and Public Policy*, vol. 1, no. 1, 2014, pp. 1–5. *Taylor and Francis Online*, https://www.tandfonline.com/doi/full/10.1080/2330443X.2013.856147.

"Hållbarhet & klimat" [Sustainability and climate]. *OLIKA*, https://olika.nu/pages/vart-klimatarbete. Accessed 28 Mar. 2024.

"Hem" [Home]. *Vombat Förlag*, https://www.vombatforlag.se/. Accessed 28 Mar. 2024.

"Hur många i Sverige är födda i ett annat land?" [How many in Sweden were born in another country?]. *MigrationsInfo*, 29 May 2020, https://www.migrationsinfo.se/fragor-och-svar/hur-manga-utrikes-fodda-sverige/.

"Legal Parenthood." *RFSL* (Riksförbundet för homosexuellas, bisexuellas, transpersoners, queeras och intersexpersoners rättigheter) [National Association for the Rights of Homosexual, Bisexual, Trans, Queer and Intersex People], 2021, https://www.rfsl.se/en/organisation/familj/att-bli-och-vara-foralder/legal-parenthood-assisted-fertilization/.

LIV Förlag. http://forlagshusetivestfold.no/nettbutikk/boker-sortert-pa-forlag/liv-forlag. Accessed 28 Mar. 2024.

Modlinska, Klaudia, et al. "Gender Differences in Attitudes to Vegans/Vegetarians and Their Food Preferences, and Their Implications for Promoting Sustainable Dietary Patterns—A Systematic Review." *Sustainability*, vol. 12, no. 16, 2020. *MDPI*, https://www.mdpi.com/2071-1050/12/16/6292.

Naidoo, Jamie Campbell, and Mercedes Zabawa. "Sameness and Difference in Visual Representations of Same-Sex Couples in International Children's Picturebooks." Epstein and Chapman, 2021, pp. 183–98.

Norberg, Johan. "Sweden's Lessons for America." *Cato Institute*, Jan./Feb. 2020, https://www.cato.org/policy-report/january/february-2020/swedens-lessons-america.

Nordseth, Linn Kristin. "'Brillebjørn' har to mammaer" ['Brillebjørn' has two mothers]. *Blikk*, 22 Mar. 2017, https://blikk.no/kulturgayden/brillebjorn-har-to-mammaer/138741.

Nylund, Bård. Foreword. *Wilma har to mammaer* [Wilma has two mothers], by Lone Halvorsen and Maria Therese Olsen, illustrated by Gina Snipp, LIV Förlag, 2015.

op de Beeck, Natalie. "Picture-Text Relationships in Picturebooks." *The Routledge Companion to Picturebooks*, edited by Bettina Kümmerling-Meibauer, Routledge, 2018, pp. 19–27.

Omsén, Elisabet. *Pappa sitter i fengsel* [Dad's in prison]. Illustrated by Eva Lindegren, Norli, 2015.

"Våra *Böcker" [Our books]. Sagolikt Bokförlag,* http://sagoliktbokforlag.se/vara-bocker/. Accessed 28 Mar. 2024.

RFSL (Riksförbundet för homosexuellas, bisexuellas, transpersoners, queeras och intersexpersoners rättigheter) [National Association for the Rights of Homosexual, Bisexual, Trans, Queer and Intersex People], 2021, https://www.rfsl.se/verksamhet/foralder/att-bli-och-vara-foralder/vanliga-fragor/.

Rydström, Jens. "Från fula fubbar till goda föräldrar—synen på sexualitet och genus I lagstiftning och debatt 1944–2004" [From ugly old men to good parents—the view of sexuality and gender in law and debate 1944–2004]. *I den akademiska garderoben* [In the academic closet], edited by Anna-Clara Olsson and Caroline Olsson, Atlas, 2004, pp. 37–65.

Sarles, Patricia. "Heather Has a Donor: 30 Years of International Lesbian-Themed Children's Picturebooks about Donor Insemination, 1989–2019." Epstein and Chapman, 2021, pp. 147–80.

Sayuno, Cheeno Marlo. "Of Fabulous Flowers and Powers: Queer Narratives of/for the Filipino Child in Philippine Contemporary Children's Literature." Epstein and Chapman, 2021, pp. 199–224.

Spegel Förlag. "Colors and other attributes that are often used to illustrate and describe what is manly/womanly or girlish/boyish." *Facebook*, 11 May 2011, https://www.facebook.com/spegel.forlag.

"Så jobbar OLIKA med normer" [This is how OLIKA challenges norms]. *OLIKA*, https://olika.nu/en/pages/sa-jobbar-vi-med-normer. Accessed 28 Mar. 2024.

"Välkommen" [Welcome]. *Sagolikt Bokförlag*, http://sagoliktbokforlag.se/. Accessed 28 Mar. 2024.

Warnqvist, Åsa. "'I'm Sure This Whole Boy Thing Is Just a Phase': Transgender Narratives in Contemporary Swedish Children's and Young Adult Literature." Epstein and Chapman, 2021, pp. 275–302.

CHAPTER 8

IL Y A PLEIN DE FAÇONS DE COMPOSER UNE FAMILLE
Some Recent French-Language LGBTQ+ Picture Books

Tim Morris

In any other year, surveying lesbian, gay, bisexual, trans, queer, plus (LGBTQ+) picture books in French could have meant spring break in Paris rummaging around the bookstores of Montmartre and Belleville, filling a suitcase with my finds, and feeling, with however little justification, that I had a cutting-edge sense of queer-themed books for Francophone children. In 2021, confined to Texas, it was a matter instead of scouring the internet and trusting the vagaries of online booksellers.

Thus, what follows is not definitive or even particularly thorough. I group, describe, and discuss French-language books that I have been able to access from at home in the United States. I sort them into provisional categories that parallel those in other languages. Translations from the texts are my own. And perhaps the more lost in translation, the more specifically French these books' treatment will be. The simpler books will seem very familiar to American readers; the more complex ones may offer a few culturally specific elements.

Queer picture books are an emerging phenomenon in France as in other countries. Francophone LGBTQ+ picture books track certain trends similar to their Anglophone counterparts. Those I've assembled here, for instance, match a pattern that Jennifer Miller observes in English-language titles: "The majority of LGBTQ+ children's picture books normalize accommodationist modes of relating to straight society. These texts most often position queers as similar to cisgender heterosexuals instead of constructing queerness as aspirational and transformative" (61). In so doing, Miller argues, these picture books "assume everyone desires the same things: a home, monogamous partner, children, and money" (58); all that's involved in making those dreams queer is a reversal of gender signs. Of course, a home, partner, children, and money are hardly bad things, but the cultural work of the books that extol them often seems primarily concerned with assuring us that queer aspirations in that direction measure up satisfactorily to a still-normative hetero model.

It strikes me that French titles readily available to a Texan reader and recommended on Francophone blogs or websites may simply be the ones that lie closest to the accommodationist end of the LGBTQ+ genre. If I chide these books at times for not going far enough, I may be speaking in ignorance of others that do but that have not yet filtered through to a broader audience. Literary history is always a work in progress, and each moment offers only a partial perspective to an observer—one that later observers may find quite blinkered once more innovative texts have entered wider circulation.

My corpus here is seven titles, ranging from a board book with minimal text to a picture book with almost as much text as images; the typical ones are illustration-heavy picture books and thus of the sort that are read to young children, at least until they memorize the text and can "read" it back. French books seem blissfully free of the hyperprecise developmental-level guidelines that come fused to American books, so all seven discussed here simply foster shared reading/looking experiences, without a lot of fuss over the exact age of the people who will share them.

Four of the books—*Jean a deux mamans* (2004) by Ophélie Texier; *Dis . . . mamans* (2011) by Muriel Douru; *Mes deux papas* (2013) by Juliette Parachini-Deny and Marjorie Béal; and *Les papas de Violette* (2017) by Émilie Chazerand and Gaëlle Souppart—feature kids with two same-sex parents. Two—*Philomène m'aime* (2011) by Jean-Christophe Mazurie; and *Je me marierai avec Anna* (1992) by Thierry Lenain and Mireille Vautier—are about children who feel same-sex love. The last, *Princesse Kevin* (2018) by Michaël Escoffier and Roland Garrigue, is about gender nonconformity.

This unscientific sample neatly sorts into three categories identified by Kenneth Kidd: (1) "books in which gay and lesbian families (not children) are affirmed and normalized," (2) "stories of same-sex romance," and (3) "picturebooks that shift focus to the gender-non-conforming child" (114–15). In this sense, my sample offers no surprises, yet within these provisionally established subgenres, there are some twists in the details.

I realize I have made nowhere near a useful survey of publication trends, let alone readerships. Yet it does seem, provisionally, that in France and Francophone markets, as in English-language publishing, the core of LGBTQ+ books for young kids are of the two-moms or two-dads variety.

Such books bracket the gender or sexuality of their protagonists and normalize monogamous two-parent households where the parents are the same sex.

The four same-sex-parents books range from the board book *Jean a deux mamans* to the relatively text-centric *Les papas de Violette*, the other two occupying steps on that scale. As the proportion of text increases, the books present more nuanced and problematic takes on their central situation.

Jean a deux mamans (Jean has two mothers) is part of a series of board books from the publisher L'école des loisirs and its imprint Loulou and Cie called Les petites familles (Little families). Each installment of Ophélie Texier's series features a different animal protagonist and addresses a nonstandard situation: *Camille a deux familles* (Camille has two families), *Lili vient d'un autre pays* (Lili comes from another country), *Petites familles malik est fils unique* (Malik is an only child), and *Jean a deux mamans* (Jean has two moms). And Texier's board book is so generalized that Jean isn't even human; he's a boldly drawn cartoon of an anthropomorphic wolf. His two moms are also wolves, and Jean is quick to note that they love each other "*comme un papa et une maman*" (like a dad and a mom) (Texier, *Jean*). The hetero couple is the frame of reference here, and Jean, the narrator, understands this and explains his own family to the readers. (He does so in about ninety words total, so I am explaining things at far greater length than Jean does.)

There's nothing genderqueer about Jean's parents. Both Jeanne and Marie wear dresses and—to the extent that the concept applies to cartoon wolves—they are both feminine in appearance, with a hint of lupine mascara. Yet their roles are distinctly sorted. Maman Jeanne, who gave birth to Jean, cooks and sews, while Maman Marie paints the house, teaches Jean to fish, and lets Jean ride on her back after he dons the Indian costume that Jeanne makes for him. (A reminder that queer-friendly books are not necessarily progressive with respect to Indigenous peoples.) Dichotomous as their domestic roles may be, however, Jeanne and Marie both come running when Jean is upset, and the three have "*un grôs calin*" (a group hug) (Texier, *Jean*).

Jean a deux mamans may be surprisingly conventional in terms of gender image and domestic division of labor, but it is an appealing and attractive book. Jean cries at one point, prompting the group hug, but the reasons are unspecified. We all cry, one supposes, and we all need comfort, and Jean's mothers are well up to the task.

"C'est Maman Jeanne qui m'a porté dans son ventre" (It was Mama Jeanne who carried me in her belly), says Jean (Texier, *Jean*), but Lilou, protagonist of *Mes deux papas* (My two dads), presents a more angst-ridden origin story. Lilou's parents are Tom and Enzo, stylized birds who wear hats and have torsos like tennis balls. Gendered only by their names, Tom and Enzo sleep together "*plumes contre plumes*" (feather to feather) in the same nest (Parachini-Deny and Béal). They wake up one morning to spot another nest nearby containing an abandoned egg.

Tom and Enzo are delighted; they have so wanted to have a baby. In the world built by authors Parachini-Deny and Béal, adoption services for same-sex bird couples are undersupported, so the mysterious-foundling approach is the most promising. Two of the book's twelve double-page spreads—the ones that bridge from the discovery of the egg to its hatching—center on anxiety over the whereabouts of the egg's parents: "Où sont sa maman et son papa?" (Where are its mama and its papa?), Enzo wonders (Parachini-Deny and Béal). Tom insists that they guard the egg until the parents return, but within a sentence or two, Enzo concludes, "Nous ne le saurons sûrement jamais" (We will never know why the parents have not returned). They promptly forget all about them.

The egg hatches; it is a girl they name Lilou. Tom and Enzo raise her. Their roles are not differentiated—an egalitarian arrangement made easier because Tom and Enzo are scarcely distinguishable except for the colors of their respective hats. The dads send her off to school. There, a boy named Oscar returns to the origin problem. In a scene we'll see repeated in *Dis . . . mamans*, the kids are assigned to draw pictures of their families. Oscar has a mother and father, and he asks why Lilou has two fathers. (That subplot goes nowhere; Oscar asks a simple question and does not use it as a springboard for teasing, and then he disappears.)

That night, Tom and Enzo explain that they love each other and they both love Lilou and they're a family—forever. This seems rather to sidestep Oscar's question, but the whole issue is drowned out by a final two-page spread of their extended family, amply provided with conventional grandparents and cousins and normative except that Lilou's two immediate parents are male.

Mes deux papas is interesting for raising problems that it then quickly obscures with flurries of energetic noise: Tom and Enzo's delight in their foundling and the well-populated group hug that ends the book. In *Mes deux papas*, the origin of male-male parenting is fabulous and seems dependent on the negligence and subsequent elision of Lilou's birth parents. Tom and Enzo want a child but do not seem to have chosen parenthood; it's thrust upon them, and they immediately make the best of it, but they are still substitute parents of a sort.

It may seem a bit odd to continually raise a problem one intends to gloss over, but perhaps that *Mes deux papas* dances away from Lilou's original parentage is healthy. Maybe it doesn't matter; all this is not needed to unveil our hatchling protagonist's primal scene. Maybe Tom and Enzo have it right: the kid is here, and the thing is to raise the kid in an atmosphere of love, not to fret about explanations for her existence.

More prosaic and more overtly rhetorical, the picture-heavy *Dis . . . mamans* (Say . . . moms) presents Théo, a human child who has human classmates. Like Lilou, Théo is called upon, in school, to draw his family tree. (The mise en abyme in these books is interesting, with school children expressing their family scenes in the same idiom as the surrounding narrative since both the child and the child's drawing are drawn by the book's illustrator.)

Théo draws two moms, one referred to as just Maman and the other as Maman Lili. The girl who shares his desk teases him. That can't be his family, brays little Pauline—"Dans une famille y'a un papa et une maman" (Families have a papa and a mama) (Douru). Their teacher quickly corrects her. You need a man and a woman to make a baby, she acknowledges, but a family can take many shapes. In a two-page spread that resembles the permutations for family composition that one sees when scrolling through a menu of emojis, the teacher ticks off six different possible family alignments, including single parents, same-sex couples, and a highly broad-minded *ménage à quatre*. The next two-page spread finds other children signing on to this analysis. One is adopted; two live with single parents (of each sex), another is being raised by his stepfather. "Il y a plein de façons de composer une famille" (There are lots of ways to make up a family).

You'd expect mean Pauline to experience a conversion, but the book simply jettisons her. The rest of *Dis . . . mamans* features Théo befriended by a girl named Camille, who asks to visit Théo's home and then opines, "Elle a tort de se moquer Pauline car elle est sympa ta famille" (Pauline was wrong to tease you because your family is nice) (Douru). On reflection, even if Théo's family were nasty, Pauline would still have been wrong to tease him, but they are nice anyway, and one doubts that Camille's approval was contingent on an interview.

Dis . . . mamans visually complicates the domestic arrangements in this nice family. Maman wears a dress and cooks, while "second mom," Maman Lili, wears jeans and bottle-feeds a younger child, baby Léa. Obviously, neither is the child's birth mother, and it's not really germane. The kitchen scene that presents them is intensely domestic, full of aprons, food bowls, pacifiers, teddy bears—and wineglasses; this is France, after all. "Moi je t'aime toujours autant" (I love you all the more), Camille exclaims to Théo at the end of the book (Douru). Having two *mamans* has its advantages, it seems.

In these three books, the parents present as highly confident in their lifestyles, less so in the more text-centered and problematic picture book *Les papas de Violette* (Violette's dads). "À l'école, j'ai zéro copine" (At school, I don't have any friends), starts Violette (Chazerand and Souppart). Violette is a bit older than Jean, Lilou, or Théo and more elaborately and realistically drawn. The book's first scene involves Violette's classmates teasing her at school for having two papas; same-sex love is a sickness, they say, and they twist the narrator's name into "*violettus*" on the analogy of "virus," running away so they don't catch it.

Violette bottles up her hurt, and we see her next in her fairly blissful home. Alone among the books we've looked at, *Les papas de Violette* never addresses how Violette was conceived and born. Papou is a bearded redhead; Papa is clean-shaven with brown hair. Their dress senses differ—Papou wears a sweater over a collared shirt, while Papa prefers T-shirts—and they take different roles in raising Violette, though they don't replicate the patterns of the stereotypical hetero household (as the mothers do in *Jean a deux mamans*). Papou cooks but also helps with arithmetic homework; Papa plays and tells stories. Both parents like to make over their daughter with "*coiffures bizarres*" (funny hairstyles), though only Papa is pictured doing it, laughing as he wields hairspray and blow dryer. Both are good consolers, and both like to take Violette for outdoor adventures.

But Violette's anxiety persists, even though her home life is so rich. She feigns the appetite her classmates' teasing dispelled and wonders about Papou: even while slicing onions, he doesn't have a runny nose, so how can his love for Papa be a "*maladie*"? Her fathers are terrifically supportive, but "Je suis quand même triste, parfois" (Sometimes I'm sad, all the same), says Violette (Chazerand and Souppart).

The parents in the other three picture books we've looked at have been marvelous, fun, and unapologetic. They're marvelous and fun here too, but Violette senses that her dads contribute to the shame she feels when she's teased. Papa and Papou stay in the car when they pick her up after school. They don't come to school events together for fear of embarrassing her; she says, "Ils se font toujours tout petits et ça, ça m'ennuie" (They always make themselves really small, and that bothers me) (Chazerand and Souppart).

As Violette explains her discontent, the illustrations shift to ones of hetero families, mom and dad happily together with kids. Violette is in one of the pictures too, but only with Papou; as she explains, wherever she goes, it's with one dad or the other, "*jamais ensemble tous les trois*" (never all three together)

(Chazerand and Souppart). Having two parents, Violette explains, is like having two feet or two ears—if one is lacking, it's just not the same.

Of course, even a child reader might anticipate the rejoinder—some kids don't have two parents. (And for that matter, some kids don't have two feet. Likening normative family status to abled status posits anything short of the norm as tragic. But there is no guarantee of normality, and difference need not mean disaster.)

Authors Chazerand and Souppart immediately explore this implication. The next day at school, Violette meets Cécile, the main teaser from the opening scene. Cécile's father has run off and isn't coming back. Having no father is worse than having no friends, Violette figures, but instead of taunting Cécile, she takes her hand, and Cécile accepts: "Peut-être qu'elle croyait qu'en attrapant le violettus, elle aurait un papa un plus" (Maybe she thought that by catching the *violettus*, she would get an extra father) (Chazerand and Souppart).

Les papas de Violette ends much as *Dis . . . mamans* does, with a new friend visiting the same-sex-parents household. Cécile, remarkably resilient, forgets her own scarpering father and basks in the friendship of Violette's two. At the same time, Violette has forgotten her own frustration at her fathers' quasicloseted behavior. In a two-page spread featuring Papa at the piano, a jump rope, ballet costumes, a cat, a cactus, and a cake baked by Papou, the three family members and their newly incorporated friend act out a new vision of harmony.

It's a nice ending but not altogether satisfying. As in *Mes deux papas*, a source of anxiety disappears in a general welter of fun. But the central dramatic problem of *Les papas de Violette*—the narrator's discomfort at her fathers' reticence to make their relationship fully public—is never resolved. One expects Violette to confront her parents and at least express her problem. Instead, she follows an implicit principle that if things are going well inside the boundaries of domestic space, the relation of that domestic unit to the larger social world shouldn't matter. The happy homosexual hearth needs to embrace straight visitors, even ones who have been homophobic until literally the page before. But the book does not depict public displays of queerness that might head off future homophobia.

Obviously, such a strategy might work in real life. Nobody is required to be an activist, privacy does not equate to cowardice, and how Papa and Papou choose to perform gay domesticity is their own business. But there's something unsettling in the idea that their daughter is bothered and that they need not talk about what's bothering her. Violette has made a friend who accepts her fathers, but she has also learned that it's best to keep her worries pent up—if she resists expressing them, they might go away.

None of these four books goes in much for public displays of affection between gay parents. Of course, they are books for very young children, and the depiction of adult romance is hardly a priority. But the books I've gathered seem to confirm a trend noted by Jamie Campbell Naidoo and Mercedes Zabawa in their survey of international LGBTQ+ picture books: "While it is acceptable to have a male-male or female-female couple in the same illustration or two-page spread as children, it is not acceptable for them to demonstrate that they are in a relationship or have more than a platonic bond" (190). Do these picture books really suppress representations of parental sexuality, especially as compared to books that represent heterosexual parents? I'm not sure the absence of such demonstrations is dispositive; all I can really remark, along with Naidoo and Zabawa, is that they are indeed absent.

Four books constitute a very small sample size, but even when you know that a corpus is fragmentary, it's hard to keep from generalizing on the basis of what you have in front of you. It is interesting to note, for instance, that all four of these same-sex-parent picture books show a protagonist whose gender contrasts to that of the parents. Tom and Enzo and Papa and Papou have daughters; Maman Jeanne and Maman Marie and Maman and Maman Lili have sons (though in the last example they also have an infant daughter). And the two sons with all-female parents seem more secure. It's the two father-daughter books that raise anxieties about the situation and then dispel them with a blast of fun. There's nothing terribly problematic here, but one can detect a slight sense that the two-father situation is less amenable to incorporation into larger social structures, and as long as it provides domestic reinforcement of the fathers' love for their daughter, the daughter is well advised to suppress her own anxiety in the face of social disapprobation.

Social and familial disapprobation surfaces in texts where a child of hetero parents begins to feel love for a same-sex friend. *Je me marierai avec Anna* (I'm going to marry Anna) is the earliest text in our group by over a decade and perhaps the most fraught. Narrator Cora's love for Anna flies in the face of her parents' wishes, and Lenain and Vautier's book has trouble finding a way to resolve the conflict; it provides only a stubborn reaffirmation of Cora's identity and intention.

Cora must inherit her stubbornness from her mother. "Elle voulait toujours savoir si j'avais un amoureux" (She [her mother] always wants to know if I have a boyfriend), Cora says (Lenain and Vautier). Her mother has one in mind: Bastien, son of her mother's best friend. Cora ascribes her mother's wish to her desire to stay best friends with Bastien's mom, not to express solicitude for her own happiness. And as for Cora, "Manque de chance. Je ne peux pas voir Bastien en peinture. C'est un nul. C'est un garçon" (No way. I can't stand Bastien. He's nothing. He's a boy) (9). The phrasing nicely reroutes Cora's aversion from Bastien personally. He may have his personal flaws too, but prime among them is simply his sex. Cora is not the kind of girl who falls in love with boys.

Cora, as we know from her book's title, loves Anna. She tells her mother forthrightly, "On est drôlement bien ensemble, on ne se quittera jamais de la vie" (We get along amazingly well, and we're never going to part as long as we live) (Lenain and Vautier 12). Their compatibility seems irrefutable. Cora's mother has to fall back on the topos of definition: "Ne sois pas idiote, une fille ne peut pas se marier avec une fille" (Don't be silly, a girl can't marry a girl) (12)—legally correct in France in 1992, of course, but one imagines that the mother is invoking a logical or cosmic impossibility. It just doesn't happen.

Papa is called in for a second opinion. He thinks Anna is nice. But he wonders how the couple will have babies. Each will have a baby of her own, Cora announces, whereupon her mother sends her to her room.

The next two passages in *Je me marierai avec Anna* comprise a sort of *Where the Wild Things Are* interlude (Sendak). Cora, locked in her bedroom and fortified with snacks, imagines the tables turned. Her parents will be taken to prison for imprisoning her. "J'imaginais papa et maman derrière les barreaux. Anna et moi, on leur apporterait des oranges, avec nos bébés dans les bras" (I picture papa and mama behind bars. Anna and I bring them oranges, with our babies in our arms) (Lenain and Vautier 23). The accompanying image is one of the sharper ones in the book, with the little girls both balancing orange-toting babies, each pair framed by the bars of the parents' cell.

Just as in Maurice Sendak's book, the confined child falls asleep, the mother relents, and supper is served. Cora's mother even goes as far as allowing that Cora and Anna, despite their lack of marriage rights, could live together some day. The conflict seems defused, but that night, Cora hears her parents talking once they believe she's asleep. Her father scoffs at Cora's intransigence. He tells the mother that she'll see, that someday, Cora will bring a nice-looking boy home—maybe even Bastien! Cora, beneath her covers, laughs and repeats the title's insistence: when she grows up, she's going to marry Anna (Lenain and Vautier).

Perhaps no better future could be imagined in 1992 than one of steely covert resistance to compulsory heterosexuality. But Cora is remarkable for her fidelity to both Anna and herself and for the grim humor she brings to her plight.

By 2011, Cora and Anna would still have to wait another two years to marry legally in France, but the title character of *Philomène m'aime* (Philomène loves me) could at least imagine a less proscribed childhood romance.

Despite its title, *Philomène m'aime* is not a first-person narrative. We don't know who the "me" of the title will be until the last two pages of this large-scale picture book, and even then, the girl that Philomène loves, Lili, is introduced in the third person. Philomène herself is the focus of the proceedings. As with Cora in *Je me marierai avec Anna*, a lot of other people assume that Philomène will find a boyfriend someday. But all of them are little boys—no adults appear in the book—and none of the boys try to tease or coerce her into loving them.

Philomène is a crush magnet. She rides her bike through a stylized countryside populated by lovelorn males. As she cycles along, she is at risk of running into a tree—or a boy; both are everywhere and "tous les garçons sont amoureux de Philomène" (all the boys are in love with Philomène) (Mazurie). Character after character goes weak in the knees and drops his usual occupation at the sight of Philomène on her bike: Jules Biclou, the backyard mechanic who can use a cooking spoon as a screwdriver; the maladroit anglers Guigui Ladi and Barnabé Lafé in their boat; Prosper Laguigne, the tubaist of the pastures; Raoul Poirier, who hides away because he can't even look at Philomène without blushing; and the Lasserre brothers, who punch each other all day long, but "mais lorsqu'ils aperçoivent la silhouette de Philomène glisser sur le chemin, ils décrètent une trêve" (when they spot Philomène's silhouette skimming along the road, they call a truce).

None of these swains interact with Philomène, let alone tease, harass, or try to win her over with rhetoric. She can stop a soccer match in its tracks just by riding by, but she herself is in constant motion—a two-page spread shows a flock of boys following in her wake, red cartoon hearts floating in the air above them, and Philomène herself headed off the right-hand margin— untouched and uncatchable, smiling all the while.

She is smiling not because of the attention she garners but because she is on her way to someone who has written the love note she clutches in her hand: "L [hearts] P" (Mazurie). The boys fall out of the picture, literally, and the suspense grows as P. arrives at L.'s place, and finally the mystery is revealed. L. is Lili, a little girl. "Ni bricoleuse, ni musicienne, ni bagarreuse, mais qui est juste Lili" (She doesn't repair things, or make music, or get into fistfights. She's just Lili), "ce qui la rend unique" (that's what makes her special).

Admittedly, this romance at the end, the heart of *Philomène m'aime*, occupies just one-twelfth of the book; the great bulk of it is taken up with establishing that Philomène is impervious to male admiration. Lili is special but at the cost of having no character development at all. Neither girl has a surname, and we learn more about each of the boys than we do about either of the title characters.

The rhetoric is somewhat hard to figure out. *Philomène m'aime* is a charming story and entirely pleasant. Despite the torrent of desire that Philomène releases, male desire proves more stupefying to boys than threatening to girls. On the one hand, these boys are defined by their skills at work and at play; on the other, they are in the thrall of their love object, and their occupations become discombobulated when she rides by. And on the one hand, Philomène and Lili are the only secure and confident characters in the book, but on the other, their love is locked away in a secret garden. They meet in Lili's yard, which is surrounded by a high wall, and their innocent romance is unobserved by anyone except a cat and two cows. For all the boys know, Philomène is racing off to meet Lucas or Louis; she does not bring Lili back into public view and assert their love.

I wouldn't call Philomène and Lili closeted—they are cartoon children who meet under the auspices of cartoon cows—but they are hardly young lesbian role models. We come away from the book happy that the two girls can spend time together unthreatened. But as they do so, the disappointed boys outside are presumably going back to their occupations. Philomène and Lili remain happy but at the cost of any public presence as lovers and women.

Cora, Anna, Philomène, and Lili are all girls. I didn't find a French book about boys who like boys, though they must exist. The one book about a boy who doesn't fit into prescribed roles, *Princesse Kevin*, is not about love but about gender roles and dress conventions. It is also, though the most recent, perhaps the least satisfying of the seven I survey here. Protagonist Kevin seems at first to be a "pink boy," in author-blogger Sarah Hoffman's terms, but as Miller notes, too often, such gender flexibility can get relegated to the realms of play and fantasy instead of constituting a challenge to gender norms (152). And after a brief fantasy, Kevin doesn't enjoy his play very much either.

"Kevin est une princesse, un point c'est tout" (Kevin is a princess, that's all there is to it) (Escoffier and Garrigue). But after that categorical assertion on its opening page, Escoffier and Garrigue's picture book backs away at several points and in several directions. On the second two-page spread, Kevin borrows a dress from his sister, along with high heels and jewelry; he borrows some makeup from his mother. (No adults appear in the book, so perhaps we are to infer the mother's acquiescence or even her support.) Resplendent in pink with a golden crown, Kevin, gazing at himself in a mirror with his sister's approbation, looks every inch a princess in the illustration.

But the text immediately starts backing off the idea that Kevin has discovered his true identity. Kevin sees nothing wrong with donning a princess costume, the book's free, indirect style says (it is told in third person). After all, a costume is a disguise: "*Quand on se déguise, c'est pour ne pas être reconnu. Sinon, ça ne sert à rien de se déguiser*" (When you disguise yourself, it's so that you won't be recognized. Otherwise, there would be no point in disguising yourself) (Escoffier and Garrigue). Girls might disguise themselves as cowboys or knights, Kevin reasons. What's that to him? They can do what they want, and they should let him do what he wants.

At once, then, we slip away from the flat claim that Kevin *is* a princess to the more theatrical and ephemeral contention that—like a girl in a suit of armor—he is adopting a temporary, if unconventional, disguise. He remains cisgender; his princessness is not so much a gender performance as a gender burlesque. The book proceeds to a playground, where a throng of children have adopted all kinds of costumes that contrast, presumably, to their inner identities: soldiers, superheroes, cowboys, and all kinds of animals.

Princesse Kevin verges on the theme of same-sex affection. If Kevin is a princess, he needs a knight, but all the knights are boys, and none of them wants to be his hero. "*Froussards*" (scaredy-cats), Kevin thinks, afraid perhaps that if he touches them, they will turn into princesses too (Escoffier and Garrigue). *Princesse Kevin* doesn't represent direct teasing; at worst, the costumed boys avoid Kevin rather than being actively mean toward him. But the rejection is a defeat. Kevin looks glum.

He resorts to a little teasing himself to lighten his mood. Chloé, one of the girls, is dressed like a big, green sock. No, wait—she's supposed to be a dragon—but her father—better at cooking than sewing—made the dragon costume and wasn't able to achieve much more than a socklike effect. Chloé and Kevin quickly bond over a development that undercuts the confident opening of the book. Her costume is inadequate, but so is his. The dress is hot; he's stifled in it. And how do girls put up with high heels? "*C'est un vraie torture*" (It's real torture), he thinks (Escoffier and Garrigue). The dress is too long; he keeps stumbling over the hem, and Chloé has to hold him upright. Kevin's eyes even start to water: Is he crying? No, he just put on too much makeup.

The kids assemble for a group photo, but we only see the image after the shutters have clicked and Kevin is already marching away. He can't wait to take off his dress, but even that proves a challenge—How do you get out of this thing? Chloé has to unzip him. "*Tu as encore des tas de choses à apprendre pour devinir une vraie princesse*" (You still have lots to learn in order to become a real princess), she tells him (Escoffier and Garrigue). Chloé's offer of tutelage might be the cue for Kevin to embrace his cross-dressing identity, but he's through with his princess phase. Next time, he says, he'll go as a mermaid.

We end with an uneasy feeling. Kevin imagines himself as a smiling, cavorting mermaid—a real mermaid in a real sea, not a boy in a crumby mermaid outfit—but the fact remains that his venture into adopting the dress of the other gender has been a failure. His absolute confidence that he was a princess has unraveled—and not because of teasing or lack of support or parental disapproval but because his intimate experience of feminine dress clashes with his bodily comfort and his self-image. Kevin resembles characters observed by B. J. Epstein in *Are the Kids All Right?*: "The very fact of their queerness is often depicted as being difficult; for example, a queer character might be represented as very stressed and unhappy due to being queer" (63). Kevin seems to be plucky enough, but his stress with his chosen physical gender markers leads one to wonder whether the very text that created him sees him as "creating inauthentic versions" of himself (Epstein 68).

We might be able to say that Kevin, in the end, rejects all sorts of conventional dress—some feminine attire may well be intrinsically uncomfortable, after all—and reimagines himself as organically female in the fantastic way that all mermaids are female. But he also rejects the project of crossing human gender lines or performing human femininity. Mermaids don't wear any clothes, but then again, they don't have any place in human society.

What can we conclude from this brief glimpse of queer-themed Francophone picture books? Most generally, perhaps, we can conclude that the genre was a new and growing phenomenon in the quarter century from the early 1990s to the late 2010s. Queer family situations, queer childhood romance, and perhaps even gender nonconformity gained increasing legitimacy as the pace of publication increased in the 2010s. This is certainly a great deal better than silence or disapproval.

Yet at the same time, none of the books in this survey seems to arise from a strongly queer perspective. Their rhetoric is addressed toward straight doubters; their solutions consist of assuring those doubters that a queer-inflected childhood is essentially the same as a normative straight one—that queerness is a matter of differently cast roles but, in other ways, normative. And to be sure, this is often really the case: queer families, queer attachments, can operate in functional respects exactly like straight ones. But some don't, and we don't see those alternative or truly unconventional attitudes much here.

In such a light, the uneasiness of Chazerand and Souppart's *Les papas de Violette* may make it the most engaged and socially nuanced of the seven texts.

Papa and Papou provide a happy domestic experience for Violette, but their reluctance to model their relationship for public consumption by the hetero couples around them may not be a simple failure on their part. They may be unwilling to assimilate their otherness to the conventions around them just to reassure straight society that they are only slightly different. Miller reminds us that "an affectively complex text likely to produce feelings of sadness, discomfort, even anger [can avoid] shame, replacing it with a story of queer resilience" (258). Perhaps these men enact their own resilience by refusing to measure up to straight parenting. If their recalcitrance comes at some psychic cost to Violette, perhaps that is better than raising her in denial of a difference that still operates in many social settings to exclude her parents.

Though on the other hand, she is fictional. The story of Violette, her two papas, and her lone straight-parented friend may be the only picture book some Francophone children ever read that depicts such family arrangements. For those readers, the demicloseted existence of Papa and Papou may suggest the inevitable condition of same-sex parents.

But as I said at the outset, the French LGBTQ+ picture book may be taking more radical directions even as I write, unknown to me. I have tried to offer a brief glimpse of where it's been—and where it's been since 1992 was, in turn, only a distant aspiration in the decades before the 1990s. The whole project remains a new, exciting, and welcome phenomenon.

WORKS CITED

Chazerand, Émilie, and Gaëlle Souppart. *Les papas de Violette*. Gautier-Languereau, 2017.
Douru, Muriel. *Dis . . . mamans*. Phare Blanc, 2011.
Epstein, B. J. *Are the Kids All Right? Representations of LGBTQ Characters in Children's and Young Adult Literature*. HammerOn Press, 2015.
Escoffier, Michaël, and Roland Garrigue. *Princesse Kevin*. Glénat, 2018.
Hoffman, Sarah. "My Son, the Pink Boy." *Salon*, 11 May 2012, www.salon.com/2011/02/22/son_looks_great_in_dress/.
Kidd, Kenneth. *Theory for Beginners: Children's Literature as Critical Thought*. Fordham UP, 2020.
Lenain, Thierry, and Mireille Vautier. *Je me marierai avec Anna*. Sorbier, 1992.
Mazurie, Jean-Christophe. *Philomène m'aime*. Glénat, 2011.
Miller, Jennifer. *The Transformative Potential of LGBTQ+ Children's Picture Books*. UP of Mississippi, 2021.
Naidoo, Jamie Campbell, and Mercedes Zabawa. "Sameness and Difference in Visual Representations of Same-Sex Couples in International Children's Picture Books." *International LGBTQ+ Literature for Children and Young Adults*, edited by B. J. Epstein and Elizabeth L. Chapman, Anthem Press, 2021, pp. 182–98. Parachini-Deny, Juliette, and Marjorie Béal. *Mes deux papas*. Des ronds dans l'O, 2013.
Sendak, Maurice. *Where the Wild Things Are*. Illustrated by Sendak, Harper and Row, 1963.

Texier, Ophélie. *Camille a deux familles*. L'école des loisirs, 2004.
Texier, Ophélie. *Jean a deux mamans*. L'école des loisirs, 2004.
Texier, Ophélie. *Lili vient d'un autre pays*. L'école des loisirs, 2004.
Texier, Ophélie. *Petites familles malik est fils unique*. L'école des loisirs, 2004.

PART 4
QUEER(ING) CULTURE

CHAPTER 9

MANY DANCES, MANY REGALIAS
Supporting the Two-Spirit Child in *47,000 Beads*

Kaylee Jangula Mootz

The picture book *47,000 Beads* (2017) by Angel Adeyoha and Koja Adeyoha represents the intersection of several underrepresented designations within children's literature: books with Native child protagonists, books written by Native authors, books with lesbian, gay, bisexual, trans, queer, plus (LGBTQ+) content, and books about Two-Spirit identity.[1] While the number of texts within each of these singular categories has grown in the last ten years, at the time of this writing, *47,000 Beads* is the only text that presents the story of a Two-Spirit Native child protagonist as written by Native authors.[2] A much needed addition to the field of children's literature, *47,000 Beads* is a beautifully illustrated text about a Lakota child named Peyton whose community comes together to support her journey on the Two-Spirit path. Written by two Lakota Two-Spirit sisters, this culturally grounded book not only offers a different view of gender from other queer children's texts by emphasizing gender as not tied to the body but rather to one's role in their community but also answers the call of so many Two-Spirit authors, artists, and activists to create Two-Spirit stories that act as a road map for young Native people to follow.[3] In this chapter, I consider how *47,000 Beads* is situated in the fields of children's literature and Native literature and examine the ways that Two-Spirit identity is celebrated in words and images throughout the text. Though I briefly discuss two potential problems within the text, I argue that *47,000 Beads* is a supremely important text for young Native readers in that it offers a path to embrace both gender identity and cultural/communal connection.

47,000 Beads is a story about a Native child named Peyton told from a third-person perspective. Peyton's aunt Eyota notices that she does not dance at the pow wow and seems unhappy. When Peyton explains that she does not want to wear her jingle dress and that there are no dances "for kids like me," Eyota understands that Peyton is likely Two-Spirit and needs someone to guide her (Adeyoha and Adeyoha 8). With the help of Eyota, a Two-Spirit elder named L, and the rest of her family and community, Peyton begins to understand that she can be true to herself and that she has a place in their community, regardless of what type of dance or what gender she feels fits her best. Peyton closes the book wearing new regalia handcrafted by members of her community, dancing and smiling as those around her look on with pride.

The first notable feature of *47,000 Beads* when situating it within children's literature broadly is that its characters are contemporary Native people. The characters of *47,000 Beads* are shown from the very first page as contemporary in the illustration of their clothing—T-shirts, jeans, and sneakers on Peyton and Auntie Eyota, as well as contemporary regalia on the other family members—and the Volkswagen van the family piles into. And if those visual details weren't enough to situate Peyton and her family within the twenty-first century, Auntie Eyota, who is pictured with white hair, suggesting advanced age, is shown using a cell phone and sends an email to the grandmother who taught her to bead (Adeyoha and Adeyoha 17, 19). These details might be unremarkable for children's books featuring other ethnic groups, but across children's literature as a whole, Native children and families are most often depicted as existing in the distant past. This problematic phenomenon is mostly due to the high percentage of children's books about Native peoples being written by non-Natives. These texts are often riddled with biases, stereotypes, and historical or cultural inaccuracies that lead non-Native readers to believe Native peoples no longer exist in the present (Reece; Chaudhri and Schau; Quigley; Roy). After years of intense criticism and the rise of the #ownvoices movement, this pattern is changing, and publishers are being more intentional about publishing Native-authored content.[4] Excitingly, Heartdrum, an imprint of HarperCollins children's publishing launched in November 2019, has emerged as a Native-only publisher with the intention of flooding the market with Native-authored children's books focusing on the present and future experiences of Native youth (Smith).[5] However, the problem remains that many "classic" and popular children's books are guilty of forwarding these stereotypes. As such, *47,000 Beads* contributes to the growing number of Native children's texts focusing on the experiences of contemporary Native children, offering Native readers more relatable reflections of themselves and non-Native readers culturally specific, nonstereotypical representations of Native peoples.

As the consideration of audience and authorial intention is a prominent practice in children's literature scholarship, it is worth noting that while anticipating a mixed readership, perhaps even a primarily non-Native (pro-LGBTQ+) readership, *47,000 Beads* is mainly concerned with reflecting a Two-Spirit experience to Native readers. Preferencing the Native child reader answers the famed call of Rudine Sims Bishop for authors of color to write children's texts that act as mirrors for children of color to see themselves in. The narrative and the illustrations found in *47,000 Beads* are filled with culturally specific content that remains unexplained within the body of the text. Terms like "pow wow," "regalia," "Two-Spirit," "*takoja*," and "*tiospaye*" and cultural practices like drumming, dancing, gift giving, and beading are not defined or commented upon until the glossary page at the very end of the text (if at all). The choice not to explain these cultural elements as they occur in the text suggests that the authors want to cultivate Native readers' sense of belonging rather than attend to the comfort of non-Native readers who may need additional guidance to understand some elements of the story.

The use of culture-specific insider knowledge replicates some of the community outcomes of oral narratives. As Diana Lopez Jones suggests, Indigenous oral narratives not only act as vehicles for cultural mores but also create a sense of shared identity and common understanding between members of the group (145). Because oral narratives are circulated within a closed group, overt explanation is not necessary for deep understanding of the narrative's intended message (146). This causes conflict when practices of oral narratives carry over into written narratives and brush up against readerly expectations of Euro-Americans, who often expect details to be thoroughly explained. In the case of *47,000 Beads*, the use of insider knowledge within the body of the narrative cultivates a feeling of belonging and shared identity for Native readers, particularly Lakota readers, who may have additional cultural insight into specific practices and symbols depicted throughout the text.

In addition to acting as a literary "mirror" for Native readers, *47,000 Beads* also acts as a "window" for children unfamiliar with the cultural experiences represented. Importantly, the inclusion of a glossary at the end of the text suggests an intention to educate non-Native readers and to cultivate respect and acceptance toward Lakota culture and Two-Spirit experience. The words featured in the glossary include "pow wow," "regalia," "jingle dress," "Grandparent/Grandmother/Grandfather," "Two-Spirit," "giveaway," "*takoja*," "*tiospaye*," and "honor song." The tone of the definitions is overtly instructional. For example, the final sentence of the definition to "pow wow" reads, "Bring some money for the blanket if you go to a pow wow and remember to listen to the MC!" (Adeyoha and Adeyoha 28). This statement aims to educate non-Native readers on appropriate cultural practice and ways to demonstrate respect while still participating in a cultural event that is not your own. Additionally, the definition of "Two-Spirit" reads, "A newer, English word used as a rough translation for older words in the languages of many Tribes and Nations. Two-Spirit describes someone whom non-Indigenous people might call gay, lesbian, bisexual, trans and gender-independent/nonbinary. The word Two-Spirit only describes Native/Indigenous/First Nations people and should not be used for others" (28). This definition not only is educational in that it describes "Two-Spirit" in a way that non-Native child readers can understand but also defines, for non-Native readers, both child and adult, the boundaries of what cultural knowledge can be shared with them. By refusing to give more specific examples of tribal names, roles, and customs and by emphasizing that "Two-Spirit" is for Indigenous persons only and not to be used by the general LGBTQ+ community, Adeyoha and Adeyoha delineate what is appropriate and respectful and what is not meant for general consumption.

While the glossary is overtly instructional in its tone and content, the narrative itself offers a different sort of education through modeling. This gentle mode of instruction may be missed by a reader who moves too quickly through the book. But for an attentive reader, *47,000 Beads* models the appropriate level of honor for Two-Spirit elders and also sets an example of how a community should embrace a Two-Spirit child. When Auntie Eyota approaches L, the Two-Spirit elder, for help in teaching Peyton, she honors L by calling them Grandparent, using "their" pronouns, and bringing L a gift of freshly baked bread (Adeyoha and Adeyoha 10, 13). Eyota is also depicted as looking downward and smiling when asking L for the additional favor of helping to create Peyton's new regalia (15). Her demeanor reflects the respect she feels for L and her humility in requesting something so significant and time consuming. In addition to the general respect and deference given to members of a community considered an elder, L is respected for their role in the community as a Two-Spirit person. This aligns with both historical documentation of Two-Spirit peoples during the 1800s–1900s, as well as the writings of Two-Spirit activists, authors, and artists of the late twentieth and twenty-first centuries. Documents from the past, such as journal logs, reports, and diaries, have provided significant historical documentation of Two-Spirit individuals being highly revered, both for their individual skills and in special spiritual roles (Roscoe 47, 48). Historical documents and oral histories confirm that many, possibly most, Native tribes have recognized gender fluidity and embraced Two-Spirit people in their communities (Cox 84; Roscoe

48). L's role throughout *47,000 Beads* suggests a continuance of, or perhaps a return to, the importance given to Two-Spirit people in their community.

I note "perhaps a return to" in the previous sentence in light of the history of colonization in what is currently known as the United States, Canada, and Latin America, which has done significant damage to the recognition of Two-Spirit identity. The movement to reclaim Two-Spirit roles within Indigenous communities is relatively new. In Alicia Cox's excellent review of the evolution of Two-Spirit identity formation, she writes, "Due to the violence inflicted on third-gender people, Native Americans were terrorized into discontinuing multiple-gender systems and conforming to the western sex/gender binary" (85). This terrorization lasted for decades at the hands of Bureau of Indian Affairs (BIA) agents, soldiers, white settlers, and, perhaps most heinously, priests, nuns, and schoolteachers at Indian boarding schools.[6] Qwo-Li Driskill (Cherokee) writes powerfully about the need to heal from the generational trauma resulting from Indian boarding schools, specifically through decolonizing their sexualities:

> The boarding school systems in the United States and Canada are one example of the ways our sexualities, genders, and spirits have been colonized by the invaders. Boarding schools continue to have severe repercussions on our communities, including colonized concepts of gender and sexuality. To decolonize our sexualities and move towards a Sovereign Erotic, we must unmask the specters of conquistadors, priests, and politicians that have invaded our spirits and psyches, insist they vacate, and begin tending the open wounds colonization leaves in our flesh. (54)

Driskill argues that Indigenous peoples must reject white culture's understanding of nonbinary genders and queer sexuality as sinful or shameful. Instead, Driskill, and others, argue for the necessity of naming and embracing Two-Spirit identity as outside of colonial definitions of sex and gender and dominant understandings of LGBTQ+ life and as a matter essential to Native sovereignty (52; see also Cox 86; Miranda 260).[7] In answer to these calls, *47,000 Beads* is doing the important and necessary work of celebrating Two-Spirit identities in adults and children and by depicting ways that Two-Spirit children can be embraced in their communities.

Peyton, as the Two-Spirit protagonist in this children's picture book, offers a particularly interesting site of discussion. Undoubtedly, Peyton, as a Two-Spirit child, is a literary reflection for Two-Spirit children who have not had a character that they can identify with in a picture book—perhaps ever.[8] Peyton

Figure 9.1. The first two pages of *47,000 Beads* depict Peyton's feelings about going with her family to a pow wow. On the left, she stands in plain clothes outside a van, looking away with a downturned mouth. On the right, Peyton looks forlornly out the window of the van and away from her family. *Source*: Adeyoha and Adeyoha 2–3.

is celebrated as "special" and "different" (Adeyoha and Adeyoha 13). Notably, Eyota remarks to L, "She feels alone but I know she isn't. I want to show her that she's not" (13). This moment of metanarrative seems to speak directly to the Two-Spirit reader: you feel alone, but you aren't; I want to show you that you aren't. Two-Spirit readers can see themselves in Peyton and use her journey as an example. They can be proud of who they are, as Peyton is proud of who she is at the end of the story, and feel secure that they have an important place in their community.

In addition to Peyton's importance as a mirror for Native child readers, the careful crafting of her journey to Two-Spirit identity by way of receiving new pow wow regalia is a brilliant way to educate those unfamiliar with Two-Spiritedness. At the beginning of the book, Peyton's feelings of being an outsider are made clear through captivating illustrations.

In the first two pages, there are no words, only illustrations, begging for the reader to stop and investigate the scene. The first illustration shows Peyton looking away from the family van, with her mouth in a slightly downturned line. The rest of her family is smiling, wearing regalia and waiting in the car, suggesting they are on their way to a pow wow. Peyton is the only family member not wearing regalia (Adeyoha and Adeyoha 2). Peyton's distress at attending the pow wow becomes clearer in the second illustration, which is a close-up image of Peyton with her head resting on her arm while she looks out the car window (3). Her eyes are partially closed and looking in the distance, her mouth downturned. After flipping the page, Peyton is shown in her bedroom alone, dancing and smiling (5). This suggests to the reader that it is not the act of dancing at the pow wow that has caused her distress.

Figure 9.2. This image depicts the interior of Peyton's bedroom, where she is seen dancing alone and smiling before her Auntie Eyota enters. *Source*: Adeyoha and Adeyoha 5.

Auntie Eyota's questioning gives readers more insight into Peyton's dilemma. When asked why she does not dance at the pow wow, Peyton responds, "I don't want to jingle dance, Auntie. I don't want to wear a dress" (Adeyoha and Adeyoha 7). The phrase "I don't want to wear a dress" may be enough to inform readers unfamiliar with Two-Spiritedness that Peyton does not feel comfortable being gendered as a girl (as patriarchal logic suggests that only girls can wear dresses). However, Eyota's response that "there are many dances . . . many regalias" begins to reveal the true struggle Peyton faces (7). Peyton feels like an outsider because she believes she does not have a place in the pow wow, meaning she does not have a role to fill in her community, at least not without putting on something that feels unlike herself. This feeling is shown again in later images of Peyton smiling while watching the grass dance (a dance typically done by dancers who are boys/men) and of Peyton curled up in a dark corner, frowning, while wearing her jingle dress (12, 13). In this way, *47,000 Beads* positions gender identity as not tied to the body but rather

as indicative of a role that a person plays in a community. And within the confines of Euro-American definitions of "gender," what role can a child that feels neither girl nor boy fill?

While I will discuss Peyton's "transition" from girl child to Two-Spirit child in an upcoming section,[9] I pause here to delve further into the crafting of Peyton's narrative journey toward Two-Spirit identity. The depiction of gender as tied to a particular role—or, in this case, a particular dance—begins to correct misconceptions about the nature of Two-Spiritedness. Though each tribe has their own culturally and historically grounded understanding of the Two-Spirit roles of their nation, what unifies each of these tribally specific identities is its focus on individuality and multiplicity as opposed to dichotomy, just as Eyota says, "there are many dances . . . many regalias." The "many dances, many regalias" approach to gender opens up new possibilities for readers beyond the limitations of the Euro-American gender binary. One does not necessarily have to reside on one side of the binary or the other or to choose a superior or inferior status. Within this conception of individualized and multiplicitous gender, children can be nurtured based on their particular interests and gifts and still valued for their contributions to the community without being locked into the boy-girl binary. This type of nurturance for children as they grow into who they are is reflected in Two-Spirit experiences of the past and present.

Before any reader of this chapter becomes too alarmed, I do not in any way endorse non-Native children taking on Two-Spirit as a self-identifier, nor do I endorse non-Native parents making that seem like an option for their children. Two-Spirit identities are cultivated through individual tribal histories, cultures, and stories. A non-Native person cannot ever be or fully understand what it means to be Two-Spirit. However, I do believe that the lives of countless individuals would be improved if we could all learn from our Two-Spirit brothers, sisters, aunties, uncles, and grandparents—if we could set aside colonial definitions of "gender" and "sexuality," which are tied up with ideologies of superiority/inferiority and purity/sinfulness—ideologies that assign value to some and refuse it to others. As L says to Eyota, "I'm happy to share teachings with her, and to guide while she learns which path is hers to walk" (Adeyoha and Adeyoha 14). L does not say they will show Peyton how to be Two-Spirit or how to follow in L's footsteps. Instead, L will act as a guide and a teacher while Peyton discovers her own way. Just like Peyton, children should be allowed to find their own place in their world with the support and guidance of their community.

The denial of binaries through the "many dances, many regalias" description of gender within *47,000 Beads* adds depth to Peyton's "transition." The pairing of Peyton's identity struggle with the change from one type of dance/regalia to another artfully affirms the self-determination of Two-Spirit identity outside the bounds of colonial gender expectations while still appeasing readerly desires for a change at the conclusion of the text.

The ceremonial elements of Peyton's "transition" reaffirms the cultural and communal importance of Two-Spirit individuals. Near the end of the narrative and directly before Peyton's "transition," Peyton prepares for the pow wow and the giveaway, choosing something she finds meaningful to give as a gift (Adeyoha and Adeyoha 23). At the giveaway, Peyton is surprised to find that she is receiving a very extraordinary gift—not only new regalia but also the support of her community and a new teacher to help her as she finds her way (26). Peyton's choosing of an abalone shell to give at the giveaway is an element that could have been left out of the story (23). However, choosing to include this scene suggests that Peyton must give before she can receive, honoring the

The next day, at the pow wow, in the arena with her auntie drumming an honor song, Peyton was finally dancing. Dancing as herself, not as a boy or as a girl, but as Peyton in her 47,000 beads.

Figure 9.3. In the final image of the text, Peyton is depicted wearing her new regalia and dancing while members of her community look on smiling. *Source*: Adeyoha and Adeyoha 27.

reciprocity and generosity central to Lakota culture. Furthermore, the acts of giving and receiving at the time of transition seal the relationship between Peyton and her community, again shifting the conversation about gender identity from a focus on individual self-identity (as in Western culture) to community-based identity.

The final page shows Peyton dancing in her new regalia (Adeyoha and Adeyoha 27). She is centered in the image, her eyes closed and her mouth open in glee. In the background stands L, Peyton's mother, a boy dancer (who may be her brother), an adult man dancer (who may be her father), and an unnamed woman who bore a rainbow US flag on a previous page. Auntie Eyota and an unnamed, gender-ambiguous elder sit around the drum. Each background character looks on smiling. The composition of this image further signifies the communal support of Peyton's transition from girl child to Two-Spirit child. Peyton's centrality in the final page, along with the final sentences, celebrates Peyton's uniqueness and importance in the community. The final two sentences of the text read, "The next day, at the pow wow, in the arena with her auntie drumming an honor song, Peyton was finally dancing. Dancing as herself, not as a boy or as a girl, but as Peyton in her 47,000 beads"

(27). The emphasis on Peyton's individuality, reiterated through the "not as a boy or as a girl," denies the Western gender binary *and* denies the gender transition from girl to boy that may be expected by those who assume Two-Spirit identity maps easily onto trans identity.[10]

However, Peyton *does* transition, she *does* change; though, it is not a transition from boy to girl or girl to boy.[11] In concluding the narrative this way, Adeyoha and Adeyoha play to the generic expectations of children's literature for characters to grow and change. A significant amount of children's literature scholarship contemplates this generic feature—the need for a clear solution to or character growth beyond a problem. Roberta Seelinger Trites, in her field-defining text *Disturbing the Universe: Power and Repression in Adolescent Literature*, terms the type of growth a protagonist experiences when they overcome the problem of their narrative as "entwicklungsroman" (14). Trites argues that entwicklungsromans, in addition to bildungsromans, serve a didactic function in that they depict adolescents struggling until they accept the power structures that define adulthood in an attempt to model appropriate behaviors and responses to life's problems. Similarly, Perry Nodelman argues that "because childhood is defined by change," children's literature "encourage[s] children to change in the proper way" (78). Of course, in both Trites's and Nodelman's assertions, the person(s) defining what constitutes appropriate and proper growth is the adult author and/or the adult who purchased the book for the child. Inevitably, this is damaging to child readers when the ideologies being espoused by the majority of adult authors are colonial and heterosexist. Derritt Mason and Joshua Whitehead (Oji-Nêhiyaw, Peguis First Nation Treaty 1) criticize these generic tendencies, describing them as "an ordering of childhood into a 'straight' trajectory of growth and development in tandem with the linearity of a heteronormative social order," and argue that queer children's literature has the potential to shatter futurist fantasies by refusing to conform to expectations of growth and hopeful endings. While I agree with Mason and Whitehead's compelling argument, I also think that the type of change and hopefulness found at the conclusion of *47,000 Beads* makes an important intervention in children's literature. Peyton's change and the community support of her changing open alternatives to the confines of colonial gender dichotomy and heteronormativity, prompting child readers to refuse these limitations themselves. By affirming and celebrating the Two-Spirit child, the Two-Spirit adult, and the whole of the community in relation to one another, *47,000 Beads* affirms and celebrates Native sovereignty.

Before I conclude this chapter, wherein I explicate the connection between *47,000 Beads* and sovereignty, I would like to address some potential problems with the text. The first of these potential problems is the limited voice given to Peyton as the protagonist of the story. Peyton speaks very little across the narrative as a whole; her thoughts and feelings are mostly conveyed through images. There are only three pages where Peyton speaks or shares her thoughts, as compared to thirteen pages where she is pictured without speaking (sixteen images of Peyton total). Of these sixteen images, ten depict Peyton feeling sad, two of which show her crying, and six feeling happy. When considering Peyton's role as the protagonist in this story, it seems strange that she speaks so infrequently. I acknowledge that I have no comprehensive data about the speech-to-image ratios for child protagonists in picture books at this time. However, when considering the problems of representation for Native characters in children's books, Peyton's lack of voice is worth commenting upon. Dawn Quigley (Turtle Mountain Ojibwe), in her critical review of children's literature used in the K–12 classroom to meet curricular requirements of including content about US Native peoples, finds that children's texts featuring Native characters written by non-Native authors most often include Native characters that do not speak. Quigley argues that "by silencing an American Indian character, non-Native authors in the past have seemingly made the decision to prevent the Indigenous voice from speaking, and in doing so, they were free to interpret and manufacture a contrived Native culture" (374). Quigley sees this use of manufactured Native identity as a type of theft, extending the long history of colonial theft of Native lands, resources, children, and lives (366). She questions what can be communicated through silenced characters and what can readers interpret from this silence (367). Certainly, the limited voice of Peyton in *47,000 Beads* is very different from the silencing that Quigley finds in the texts she surveyed—Native versus non-Native authors, twentieth century versus twenty-first century, nonqueer versus queer content—but I still wonder what may have been gained (or lost) from including more of Peyton's perspective in her story.

Another potential concern is that in *47,000 Beads*' pursuit of celebrating the Two-Spirit individual—which is part of Flamingo Rampant's mission to avoid "difficult stories of harassment or bullying" in favor of celebratory texts that are fun, beautiful, and full of love—the text does not identify any negative experiences or struggles that the Two-Spirit child may encounter ("About Flamingo Rampant"). While I admire the mission espoused by Flamingo Rampant, omitting the real problems of homophobia, sexism, transphobia, and violence that Two-Spirit persons face both within and outside of Native communities may paint a romanticized picture of Native cultures as purer and more idyllic than Western culture, positioning Native peoples as infallible and therefore unrealistic and inhuman. The tendency to romanticize Native cultures harms Native peoples by playing into stereotypes and inspiring non-Natives to "play Indian" while simultaneously holding Native peoples to unattainable standards. Furthermore, to deny that homophobia and sexism exist in Native communities not only sidesteps the real decolonial work that must be done but also denies the truth of many Two-Spirit individuals' experiences.

There are certainly hints that more may be going on with Peyton than what is verbalized in the text. Peyton is drawn repeatedly as sad and crying throughout the narrative, but there is limited explanation for her feelings aside from there being no dances or regalia for kids like her. As previously noted, this emphasizes Peyton's feelings of disconnection from her community but does not identify any other concerns or fears that a Two-Spirit child may have. Similarly, Peyton's mother is drawn with a concerned demeanor twice—once at the table with Eyota and once standing with Peyton at the pow wow—above her spoken question, "Should I be worried?" to which Eyota responds, "No, sister" (Adeyoha and Adeyoha 18). Again, the reader can perhaps infer that Peyton's mother is concerned about her and does not know how to help, but the details or depth of the mother's concern is not shared in the text. As such, *47,000 Beads* does not address issues like hate or discrimination, either within or outside of Native communities.

It is difficult to know where to draw the line when considering including examples of homophobia and transphobia in queer children's literature. The question I grapple with is, Is it more damaging to include examples of discrimination or to leave them out? This question is even more complicated when considering Two-Spirit texts for children. Driskill writes that "while homophobia, transphobia, and sexism are problems in Native communities, in many of our tribal realities these forms of oppression are the result of colonization and genocide. . . . As Native people, our erotic lives and identities have been colonized along with our homelands" (52). Similarly, Wilma Mankiller (Cherokee) writes, "Europeans brought with them the view that men were the absolute head of households, and women were to be submissive to them. It was then that the role of women in Cherokee society began to decline. . . . This was not a Cherokee concept. Sexism was borrowed from Europeans" (20). There are many, many more sources like these that document the ways Euro-American sexism, homophobia, and transphobia infected Native culture—most often through violent indoctrination. Unfortunately, these same sources often document the devastating damage done in Native communities by their own people because of the trauma they have endured. Recent decades have seen a significant push within Native communities to heal from these colonial wounds and return to traditional cultural values with regard to sex and gender. But even in Native communities where they have decolonized their gender/sex systems, non-Native culture is still deeply entrenched in heteropatriarchal and colonial hatred. All this is to say that regardless of whether or not homophobia and transphobia are prevalent within a particular Two-Spirit child's Native community, they are problems that contemporary Two-Spirit children will face from the dominant colonial culture. So the question remains, Is it more damaging to depict forms of oppression that are nontraditional to Native communities in books for Two-Spirit children than to leave them out?

Despite the potential problems I have identified, *47,000 Beads* is a supremely important contribution to the children's literature and Native literature landscape. Beyond its significance in terms of positive representation for Two-Spirit persons and Native children, and in addition to the ways that it offers alternative understandings of gender identity not bound by colonial gender binaries, *47,000 Beads* honors Native self-determination in individual and community. Peyton and L as individuals are examples of Native self-determination—or the sovereign right for Native peoples to choose for themselves how they will live based on their nation's teachings instead of based on colonial laws and ideologies. Additionally, Auntie Eyota provides an example of self-determination both as an individual and as a community. When speaking at the giveaway, Eyota says, "[Peyton,] you have heard how when I was a girl, how I wanted to drum, but all the drummers were men where I lived. Now, you know, I'm head singer on our drum here. My family believed in me and honored me, and today I am grateful to do the same for you" (Adeyoha and Adeyoha 24). This story, though brief, is another important celebration of Native self-determination. Eyota felt called to a particular role in her community, even though there were no women drummers/singers at the time. She was recognized for her special talent and spiritual strength, and as such, her community supported her and changed their customs to allow women to drum. Eyota and her community came together to change their customs in response to their strengths and needs and did not allow outside forces to influence them. The final example of self-determination can be found in the way that Peyton's family and community came together to create her new regalia. The large amount of community and family members[12] involved in the creation of Peyton's regalia is not merely pragmatic—in that beading and sewing of this type is very time consuming, difficult, and expensive; each contribution symbolizes another person's acceptance, support, and love for Peyton. Moreover, each contribution to the regalia symbolizes the communal decision to live in ways that honor Two-Spiritedness, another example of self-determination.

By way of conclusion, I make one final claim. *47,000 Beads* represents a beautifully crafted answer to the call of so many Two-Spirit authors, activists, and artists for others to write Two-Spirit stories. In another metanarrative phrase, *47,000 Beads* seems to speak itself into existence: "I have such stories to tell you. About people from all the nations who carry two spirits inside of them. I can't wait to tell them to you" (Adeyoha and Adeyoha 25). The stories L gives to Peyton are gifts, and so too is the story of *47,000 Beads* a gift to all Native and Two-Spirit children trying to find their way. Previous generations of Two-Spirit people were denied stories that reflected what they knew inside themselves to be true (Cox 85). But no longer. Two-Spirit writers, like Adeyoha and Adeyoha, are creating and publishing stories so that future generations of Two-Spirit individuals might learn how to live culturally relevant lives and begin to heal from historical traumas (88).

The importance of stories cannot be overstated. "Our stories as First Nations people," writes Driskill, "keep us alive in a world that routinely destroys and discards us" (55). It is through stories that Two-Spirit individuals can feel confident and assured in their communities and traditions (56). But perhaps more importantly, Driskill argues, "Two-Spirit people are creating literatures that reflect Sovereign Erotics, and in doing so participate in the process of radical, holistic decolonization" (58). Two-Spirit stories like *47,000 Beads* are so much more than simple books for children. *47,000 Beads* offers readers a path to a decolonial future, wherein gender is not tied to the body or defined by limiting ideologies that offer power and personhood to some and deny it to others—a future where children can be nurtured by their community and guided based on their individual gifts, a future where children can dance many dances and wear many regalias.

NOTES

1. I would like to begin this chapter by acknowledging that I am a settler scholar on the homelands of the Mohegan, Mashantucket Pequot, Eastern Pequot, Schagticoke, Nipmuc, and other Algonquin peoples. I see this chapter as an extension of my responsibilities as a settler scholar living and working on stolen Native land. Whenever possible, I preference the scholarship of Indigenous authors to inform my work. As such, the "big names" that I cite in this chapter may be different from the "big names" non-Native academics expect to see in a chapter of a book about queer children's literature.

Also, a note about terminology: there are several appropriate and several inappropriate terms that can be used to describe persons legally referred to as American Indians or Native Americans. The most appropriate identifier is always the person's individual nation—for example, Lakota or Cherokee—and I use these national names when possible. When speaking generally, I use either the terms Native or Indigenous. When referring to Indigenous individuals who do not ascribe to Eurocentric gender/sexual identities, I use "Two-Spirit." Some writers will alternatively use "two spirit" or "two-spirit" (differences of capitalization and hyphenation) or will use terms that are specific to their individual nations. While some Two-Spirit individuals may also describe themselves in Euro-American LGBTQ+ terms, white assumptions about trans or gay identity often do not align with Two-Spirit experience. A term that is no longer accepted is the term "berdache," which was used by explorers and missionaries to describe Two-Spirit persons. "Berdache" is offensive to most Native peoples in that its translation means "male concubine" or "kept boy." These definitions not only mischaracterize Two-Spirit peoples but also betray the colonial misogyny and patriarchal bias inherent in this term. For more on the development of "Two-Spirit" (and the discontinued use of "berdache"), see Driskill; Cox; Roscoe.

2. While there are a few children's picture books that address Two-Spirit identity, none of them represent this particular intersection of Two-Spirit children as written by Native authors. *Hoʻonani: Hula Warrior* (2019) by Heather Gale and illustrated by Mika Song is a narrative about an "in the middle" Native Hawaiian child and is said to be based on a true story, but neither author is Indigenous. *Families* (2017) by Kerry McCluskey and Jesse Unaapik Mike features Two-Spirit/LGBTQ+ content by way of exploring different family compositions. And while Mike is an Indigenous author of Inuit descent, neither the protagonist nor any of the other child characters identify as Two-Spirit. *The Eagle's Path* (2017) by Michelle Corneau (Mohawk and Haudenosaunee) includes Two-Spirit content and a Two-Spirit child, but the protagonist herself is not Two-Spirit. *The Eagle's Path* aligns most closely with the intersections I am invested in here, but I have chosen not to analyze it because the narrative is more concerned with the protagonist's acceptance of Two-Spirit as part of her Mohawk culture rather than exploring Two-Spirit identity specifically. *Families* and *The Eagle's Path* would both be excellent additions to any school or home library but are outside the purview of this particular chapter.

3. Koja Adeyoha describes herself as a Two-Spirit, mixed-blood Oglala Lakota and a Butch Dyke, activist socialist, feminist, atheist, skeptic, and native Californian ("Koja Adeyoha," *BUTCH Voices*; "Koja Adeyoha," *Strong Nations*). Angel Adeyoha is Two-Spirit, queer, gender defiant, and Indigenous and mixed-race, with a complex ability status, who also lives in California ("Zero Dads Club"). The illustrator, Holly McGillis, is not Indigenous, but the amount of collaboration between Adeyoha, Adeyoha, and McGillis is clear in the attention to detail and culturally relevant rendering of the characters in *47,000 Beads*. This is an example of what a respectful and productive collaboration between Native and non-Native people can look like.

4. The #ownvoices movement was a social media campaign, which began in 2015 after the Twitter hashtag "ownvoices" began to draw attention to authors who shared the same identity category as their protagonists. As the hashtag grew in popularity, the term began to be used by parents, librarians, authors, teachers, and readers to call for publishing companies to support authors who wrote from their own lived experience rather than writing about experiences that were outside of their racial, gender, sexual, ethnic, or ability categories. As I note in the body of this chapter, there is a long-standing trend in publishing books about underrepresented individuals written by authors in the majority (in this case, mostly white women), which often leads to bias and/or inaccurate and insensitive representations. And while the term "own voices" has fallen out of favor with some (see the statement by diversebooks.org), this descriptor is a useful generalization about the increased call for authors of diverse identities to tell their own stories.

5. As of this writing (October 2021), there are no LGBTQ+-themed texts under the Heartdrum imprint. However, there is an open call for Native-authored children's texts to be published by Heartdrum, so I expect that as the listings grow, there will be LGBTQ+ content included within the imprint.

6. BIA agents are federal agents. In the past, these agents were often violent, lawless, and not held accountable for any of their crimes against Native peoples. The BIA has shuffled between different government departments over the years but is currently housed under the Department of the Interior. This is worth noting because for the first time in its history, the BIA is being overseen by a Native person—namely, Secretary of the Interior Deb Haaland (Laguna Pueblo), who was appointed by the Biden administration.

7. For more information regarding the development of the term "Two-Spirit," see Cox; Driskill; Roscoe; Rifkin; Morgensen. This is not meant to be an exhaustive list as this area of study is growing rapidly.

8. Historical records containing interviews with Two-Spirit persons of the past confirm that Two-Spirit identity beginning in childhood was common. In his article "That Is My Road," Roscoe uncovers several such documents, which suggest that Native children follow the Two-Spirit path early in life based on their feelings, preferences, and proclivities toward different roles and activities within the tribe.

9. Later, I explain more fully why I am cautious about the word "transition" and mark it off with quotations. In brief, Peyton does transition in that her self-identification changes as the narrative progresses, but because a Two-Spirit child is not a trans child, Peyton does not "transition" in the way that trans individuals socially transition from one gender to another.

10. In searching *47,000 Beads* on GoodReads.com, there are a few reader/reviewers who express disappointment that Peyton is referred to with the pronoun "she" throughout the book even after she "transitions." There is no set way that a Two-Spirit individual may choose to use gendered or nongendered pronouns in English. This is up to the individual. Often Two-Spirit individuals will prefer the pronouns of their Native language, which may not have the same grammatical rules as English. Some Native languages have no gendered pronouns. Others have several.

11. For additional discussion of transitioning in queer picture books, see Austin's and Bittner's contributions in this collection.

12. There may be something to be said for the fact that those most prominently involved in welcoming and accepting Peyton are elders (either in title or in fact) rather than peers. In fact, there are no child-to-child interactions in the entire book. I do not have time to comment on this at length in this particular article but exploring this narrative choice may be of interest to others. For a somewhat outdated, but still interesting, source on the role of elders in Native children's literature, see Charles.

WORKS CITED

"About Flamingo Rampant." *Flamingo Rampant*, https://www.flamingorampant.com/about. Accessed 16 Feb. 2024.

Adeyoha, Angel, and Koja Adeyoha. *47,000 Beads*. Illustrated by Holly McGillis, Flamingo Rampant, 2017.

Bishop, Rudine Sims. "Mirrors, Windows, and Sliding Glass Doors." *Perspectives*, vol. 6, no. 3, summer 1990, pp. ix–xi.

Charles, Jim. "Elders as Teachers of Youth in American Indian Children's Literature." *Studies in American Indian Literatures*, ser. 2, vol. 12, no. 1, 2000, pp. 56–64.

Chaudhri, Amina, and Nicole Schau. "Imaginary Indians: Representations of Native Americans in Scholastic Reading Club." *Children's Literature in Education*, vol. 47, 2016, pp. 18–35.

Corneau, Michelle. *The Eagle's Path*. Strong Nations Publishing, 2017.

Cox, Alicia. "Recovering a Sovereign Erotic: Two-Spirit Writers 'Reclaim a Name for Ourselves.'" *The Routledge Companion to Native American Literature*, edited by Deborah L. Madsen, Routledge, 2015, pp. 84–94.

Driskill, Qwo-Li. "Stolen from Our Bodies: First Nations Two-Spirits/Queers and the Journey to a Sovereign Erotic." *Studies in American Indian Literatures*, ser. 2, vol. 16, no. 2, summer 2004, pp. 50–64.

Gale, Heather. *Ho'onani: Hula Warrior*. Illustrated by Mika Song, Tundra Books, 2019.

"HarperCollins Children's Books Launches Heartdrum, a New Native-Focused Imprint." *Cynthia Leitich Smith*, https://cynthialeitichsmith.com/2019/11/harpercollins-childrens-books-launches-heartdrum-a-new-native-focused-imprint/. Accessed 16 Feb. 2024.

"Koja Adeyoha." *BUTCH Voices*, https://web.archive.org/web/20210616150553/https://www.butchvoices.com/speakers/koja-adeyoha/. Accessed 16 June 2021.

"Koja Adeyoha." *Strong Nations*, https://www.strongnations.com/gs/show.php?gs=3&gsd=8504. Accessed 16 Feb. 2024.

Jones, Diana Lopez. "This Is Progress? Surveying a Century of Native American Stories about Hair." *The Lion and the Unicorn*, vol. 37, no. 2, April 2013, pp. 143–56.

Mankiller, Wilma. *Mankiller: A Chief and Her People*. St. Martin's, 1993.

Mason, Derritt, and Joshua Whitehead. "When Everything Feels like the Horror Movies: The Ghostliness of Queer Youth Futurity." *Research on Diversity in Youth Literature*, vol. 2, no. 1, 2019, http://sophia.stkate.edu/rdyl/vol2/iss1/3. Accessed 1 Mar. 2024.

McCluskey, Kerry, and Jesse Unaapik Mike. *Families*. Inhabit Media, 2017.

Miranda, Deborah. "Extermination of the *Joyas*: Gendercide in Spanish California." *GLQ: A Journal of Lesbian and Gay Studies*, vol. 16, no. 1–2, 2010, pp. 253–84.

Morgensen, Scott L. *Spaces between Us: Queer Settler Colonialism and Indigenous Decolonization*. U of Minnesota P, 2011.

Nodelman, Perry. *The Hidden Adult: Defining Children's Literature*. John Hopkins UP, 2008.

Quigley, Dawn. "Silenced: Voices Taken from American Indian Characters in Children's Literature." *American Indian Quarterly*, vol. 40, no. 4, 2016, pp. 364–78.

Reece, Debbie A. "Native Americans in Children's Books of the Twentieth Century." *Children's Literature Remembered: Issues, Trends, and Favorite Books*, edited by Linda Pavonetti, Libraries Unlimited, 2003, pp. 139–55.

Rifkin, Mark. *When Did Indians Become Straight? Kinship, the History of Sexuality, and Native Sovereignty*. Oxford UP, 2011.

Roscoe, Will. "'That Is My Road': The Life and Times of a Crow Berdache." *Montana: The Magazine of Western History*, vol. 40, no. 1, 1990, pp. 46–55.

Roy, Loriene. "Indigenous Children's Literature." *The Oxford Handbook of Indigenous American Literature*, edited by James H. Cox and Daniel Heath Justice, Oxford UP, 2014, pp. 333–43.

Steele, Katie, and Nicholson, Julie. *Radically Listening to Transgender Children: Creating Epistemic Justice through Critical Reflection and Resistant Imaginations*. Lexington Books, 2020.

Trites, Roberta Seelinger. *Disturbing the Universe: Power and Repression in Adolescent Literature*. U of Iowa P, 2000.

"The Zero Dads Club: About the Author." *Google Books*, 15 Oct. 2015, https://books.google.com/books/about/The_Zero_Dads_Club.html?id=l3ZmjwEACAAJ&source=kp_author_description.

CHAPTER 10

QUEERING CHRISTMAS

An Autoethnographic Author Interview about Publishing *The Christmas Truck*

J. Bradley Blankenship

When we talk about reading picture books, whether for fun or academic analysis, we generally talk about them as finished products. As readers, we are consumers experiencing the end product—an already finished narrative that has been brought to life through illustrations. By doing this, particularly as it relates to lesbian, gay, bisexual, trans, queer, plus (LGBTQ+) picture books, we risk taking the book's existence for granted.

In this chapter, I use autoethnography to not only reflect on the process of creating and publishing my book *The Christmas Truck* but also shed light on the specific mechanisms I used to narratively and illustratively "queer" Christmas. In sharing my journey, I highlight barriers LGBTQ+ authors face in bringing their picture books into existence and explain why publishing LGBTQ+ picture books is a political act of defiance that asserts existence and demands space in a market dominated by heteronormativity.

While I use autoethnography to reflect and analyze my personal experiences, I take a nontraditional approach of presenting my reflections in the format of an author interview. Acting as both the interviewer and the author, or interviewee, I present my reflections and analysis in an accessible and engaging format that invites the reader into the discussion. It is my hope that in addition to reading LGBTQ+ picture books as finished products, we can think critically about their journey to publication and appreciate how these books often forge new publishing and distribution paths.

Question: This edited volume, *Reading LGBTQ+ Children's Picture Books*, is a collection of academic essays meant to extend scholarly work about LGBTQ+ picture books. With that in mind, what should readers of this chapter know about you?

Answer: I think it's important for readers to know that I am both a storyteller and a scholar. I have a PhD in education, and my research interests center around gender, sexuality, and the role storytelling plays in identity development. I like stories. I like reading them, listening to them, and telling them. If I had to name a favorite type, I particularly enjoy subversive stories that inspire change and provide new perspectives. I have five children's books out, of which *The Christmas Truck* was the first.

From an identity and positionality perspective, I am a white gay cisgender man without disabilities and use he/him/his pronouns. I grew up lower working class in the mountains of Appalachia with heterosexual parents. I'm married to a first-generation Pakistani man. I think that's important to note because I wrote a book about Christmas. Half of my family identifies as Muslim, and there are cultural aspects of Islam that now structure my everyday life. We are a bicultural family, and while we currently do not have children, we hope that we will one day.

While my family is not particularly religious, I was baptized Methodist and, culturally, grew up adhering to Judeo-Christian norms. When I was a kid, my mother sold Christmas decorations year-round for a living. For years, our house was perpetually decorated for Christmas. I remember being six and sitting near a fully decorated Christmas tree in the living room while watching Fourth of July fireworks on television with my family. Christmas imagery was a large part of my childhood, yet I never saw any LGBTQ+ representations within this imagery. The lack of that representation was a key factor in my decision to write *The Christmas Truck*.

Q: The title of this chapter is "Queering Christmas." What do you mean by that?

A: In this context, I'm using the perspective of the academic framework of queer theory, wherein "queering" something means simply blurring boundaries between seemingly distinct categories, be it sexuality, gender, sex, race, and so on. In doing this intentionally, the assumption is that queering something disrupts the dominant order of things for the sake of exposing and challenging power structures. For me, "queering Christmas" is an act of challenging heteronormative (and cisnormative, sexist, and racist) iconic imagery and narratives of Christmas. I do this because Christmas is not politically neutral. It's not always positive. There is a long history of LGBTQ+ communities being targeted, hurt, and shunned by communities of faith. Yet even with a larger cultural narrative of Christmas that may include Santa and exclude Jesus, at the time I wrote *The Christmas Truck*, there still wasn't a picture book that allowed LGBTQ+ characters and Christmas to coexist in the same space.

I wrote a Christmas story and self-published it as a picture book—*The Christmas Truck*. As a picture book, obviously its illustrations are a defining part of my story. In addition to the choices that I made about words in the manuscript, when working with my illustrator, I made intentional decisions that would "queer" iconic Christmas imagery. This includes imagery like the Nativity scene, wherein the North Star shines in the night sky as Mary and Joseph kneel beside baby Jesus in the stable, and the iconic Santa driving his bright red sleigh across a full moon on a dark winter's night. In queering these images, it was my hope to create a picture book that allowed space for LGBTQ+ characters and Christmas to coexist. This chapter, specifically, allows academic space to discuss my intentionality in publishing a queer Christmas story.

Q: Besides queering Christmas, how would you describe your book? What is it about?

A: The short teaser description? When celebrating a special Christmas tradition, things go awry, and one family must work together to save Christmas for a child they have never met. I want to note that this is the official teaser language for the book, and it does not mention that it is a "gay" story. It was my intent to tell a unique Christmas story with a two-dad family that could stand on its own regardless of the parents' gender.

If you're asking about the narrative arc, then it's a story about a two-dad family with a kid and their Christmastime family traditions. This includes picking out and decorating a Christmas tree, driving around their neighborhood to look at decorations, family meals with extended family, and fulfilling a child's wish list from the town's wishing tree.

The conflict occurs when the family's Christmas tree falls over, breaks, and destroys the special present from the wish list—a toy firetruck. The unexpected heroine of the story is the grandmother. She is the town's retired fire chief and arranges to have a real firetruck help save the day. At its core, this is a story about family, traditions, teamwork, and the joy of giving. And yes, if you give it an analytic academic read, it is intentionally queer.

Q: Can you explain a little bit about the publishing process? How does it usually work, and how do you think that impacts LGBTQ+ picture books?

A: When I began this process, I was very naïve. I didn't understand how the publishing world worked. In the years since, I have a better grasp of the realities of publishing. When an author writes a manuscript, ideally, they sell the manuscript to a publisher, who then pays for the rights to publish and distribute it. In the picture-book market, there is sometimes an agent involved, sometimes not. In exchange for a percentage of the profit, an agent acts on behalf of the author and tries to get a publisher to buy the manuscript. The author is usually out of the picture once the publisher buys the rights. Generally, authors do not get a say in the illustrations, the layout, or when their book will come out. Some books are fast-tracked and published quickly; most take at least a year, usually more, before they are published.

When working with a publishing house, regardless of size, authors must contend with the reality that all publishers want to make money. This means that publishers try to choose manuscripts that will appeal to broad audiences and that will sell. The actual physical printing and marketing of a book is pricey, particularly a book with full-color illustrations. As a result, the profit margins for most books are very slim, which fuels publishers' pickiness about the books they decide to publish. When a publisher buys a manuscript, the author is given an advance (i.e., money). They only get royalties if the book earns out. Thus, their book must sell enough copies to make back all the printing costs, advertising costs, and so on, and any sales beyond that will result in royalty payments.

In addition to domestic sales, selling the foreign rights to a book is another source of revenue for the author. This means that the author receives another payment to give permission to a publisher overseas to translate, print, and sell the book. Often, the foreign rights are sold to individual countries. But sometimes, a large international publishing house will prefer to pay outright for worldwide distribution rights if they think the book will be a global success. This usually involves a significantly larger payment and is an ideal situation for the author—more money and a comprehensive contract.

Publishers are in this business to make money. This means that even with a renewed focus on diverse voices and stories from underrepresented communities, book publishers are still looking at their bottom lines. When considering whether to buy a manuscript, the publisher is asking themselves, Will this story make money? If they don't think enough people will buy it or that it won't earn out, then they are less likely to pick it up. This business model hurts LGBTQ+ representation. Publishers not only act as gatekeepers that decide whether LGBTQ+ content is allowed but also regulate which members of the wider LGBTQ+ community gain access based on who they think the public will respond to.

Q: Do you feel that was your experience with traditional publishers—that they didn't want to publish your story because they were afraid it wouldn't make money?

A: No, not exactly. There can be several reasons why agents or publishers reject stories. I sent queries to well over one hundred agents and any publisher I could find that allowed a direct author query. Most didn't respond (which I later learned is normal for rejections). A query is the sending of a manuscript or a pitch to a potential agent who would want to represent you to a publisher. Some publishers require an agent, while some allow the author to directly query without an agent. Of the twenty-six agents who responded, I received a range of feedback. Many liked the story but felt they wouldn't be able to successfully sell it to a publisher because of potential backlash about a two-dad family and Christmas. Another common critique I received was that early drafts of the manuscript were too long and that publishers don't want to publish rhyming books (*The Christmas Truck* is a rhyming story). I took the early feedback constructively and revised, shortened, and resubmitted to more agents, but the rejections kept coming.

In the years since I first began this process, I've frequently heard from other writers that publishing is a lot of "hurrying up and waiting." This just means that the process is long and tedious and that you are always waiting: waiting to hear back whether an agent likes your work; if they do, waiting to hear whether a publisher wants to buy it; then, it's waiting for the actual book to come out in print. For many authors, it takes years of patience and hundreds of rejections before their manuscript is picked up by a publishing house, if at all. The hurry up bit is wishful thinking on the author's part that the publisher will expedite the process.

But in 2014, I didn't know that. The concept of hurrying up and waiting was foreign to me. Even though I had only been querying for two and half years, I got tired of waiting. Two years felt too long. Sure, some people may say that I needed to pay my dues and wait for that coveted acceptance. In the picture-book writing community, there is an accepted assumption that the publishing process requires endurance: you pay your dues by amassing rejections until you finally get that acceptance.

But I think, as an author from a marginalized community and with a story that represents that community—and I can only speak for myself here—you get tired of waiting and wondering when it's going to be (y)our turn. Because all your life you've been told by mainstream culture that your experiences aren't valued and that your stories don't matter or that they are valued and matter, but dominant society isn't ready yet. I was getting frustrated. With each rejection, I felt as though agents and publishers were telling me that my story didn't matter because it wouldn't sell. At some point, I got tired of waiting for someone else to give me permission to tell my own story. So I decided to do it myself—to self-publish *The Christmas Truck*. This meant creating a business and figuring out how to produce my own book, get it illustrated, printed, marketed, and so on.

When I finally made the decision to self-publish, I felt a great responsibility on my shoulders. Having studied sexuality and gender within the context of identity and storytelling, I wanted to be very intentional about how this story was told and what images and messages were conveyed. These are decisions that would normally be passed off to a publisher, but since I decided to self-publish, I retained entire creative control of my book.

Q: Did it ever occur to you that maybe your story simply wasn't very good and that's why agents and publishers didn't want to pick it up?

A: Sure. I think every writer has a bit of imposter syndrome. I know I did and still do to an extent. I remember doing my research to see what other books were already on the market, and I didn't see any other Christmas books with same-gender parents. It was clearly a niche that needed to be filled, but I honestly didn't think a publisher would be willing to do that anytime soon. I had this moment when I thought to myself, "Wow, even if my book sucks, then at least it will be out there in the world; there will be a book with pictures of a two-dad family celebrating Christmas," which is more than I ever had growing up.

I had a clear vision of what illustrations I wanted to include. Even if my words and narrative arc were subpar, there were certain images—iconic Christmas images—that I wanted to see with a two-dad family. At that point, I didn't really care whether it made it into the mainstream. It became a personal project—a promise to my younger self that I would create the story I never had when I was growing up.

Q: That sounds very activist of you. Would you agree with that? That your decision to self-publish was a political act?

A: I would say so. I didn't think of it that way when I was going through the process. At that time, I was just trying to tell a story. But in the years since the book has come out and the more that I've become involved in the larger picture-book writing community and now that I understand how publishing works, I'd say absolutely, this was an act of activism. Not just my book but, I think, any LGBTQ+ picture book that is published, traditionally or self-published, is a political act. Publishing is funny because it can be both a site of power and oppression. When we let the gatekeepers decide which voices are heard, there is oppression. But when those voices find ways to make themselves seen and to make themselves heard, there is both power and liberation.

LGBTQ+ picture books is a genre that historically has not been represented. Our stories aren't easily found on mainstream bookshelves. The books that do exist are frequently challenged and banned from school libraries. LGBTQ+ voices have been excluded from picture-book conversations; only recently have we started taking them seriously. This textbook is a great example. It's the first time we're really looking at LGBTQ+ picture books with a scholarly lens. So yes, I think self-publishing my book was political, just as this edited anthology is a political act that asserts the validity, contributions, and impact of LGBTQ+ picture books within academia.

Q: Let's talk about the mechanics of queering Christmas. Can you discuss how you developed your characters and the ways you queered them?

A: There are a couple of layers to this. First, I want to take a moment to introduce the illustrator, Cassandre Bolan (she/her). When I decided to self-publish, I pitched the project to freelance illustrators. I was drawn to Cassandre not only because her work is beautiful and compelling but also because she describes herself as a feminist illustrator. Her motto is that she illustrates strong women in fantasy to inspire women in reality. To quote her website, "My brand is focused on providing artistic, academic, and firsthand acumen to the client looking for an illustration with a feminist conscience" (Bolan). Bringing Cassandre on board was instrumental because she not only understood what I was trying to do in creating a uniquely queer Christmas story but also was passionate about helping bring that project to life.

For me, one of the first steps in queering Christmas was to build a team who understood and embraced the diversity of gender and sexuality. Picture books are as much about their illustrators as they are their authors. The story and art directions may have been my ideas, but Cassandre is the one who translated these ideas into illustrations. It was my intention that, with her help, art and illustration would play a significant role in queering *The Christmas Truck*.

On a first read of the book, one of the most obvious ways we queered Christmas is seen in the characters themselves (figure 10.1). The story follows a family of two dads and their child. Instead of giving names, the fathers are referred to as Papa and Dad, while their child, the narrator of the story, is simply referenced as "me." The two-dad family disrupts the heteronormativity of Christmas narratives. Furthermore, the fathers comprise a mixed-race couple, with one dad being white and the other brown.

Illustratively, I wanted a racially ambiguous character that allowed readers to draw their own conclusions and stories about him. This is why I didn't use formal names, only the familial Papa, Dad, and "me." Names are racialized, and it's easy to make assumptions about them—assumptions like "Oh, that

Figure 10.1. The image depicts *The Christmas Truck*'s final character list—from left to right: Puppy, Dad, Papa, me, Grandma, Grandpa, Auntie, Uncle, Michael's mom, Michael Clay. *Source*: author's personal collection.

character isn't like me." I wanted LGBTQ+ families to see themselves in a story, and that meant trying to expand the reflections, not narrow them. The intention was to be inclusive while disrupting what is normative even within a marginalized community (in this case, LGBTQ+ people). I didn't want to tell a story about two white gay cis men. This theme can also be seen in the characters of the extended family. The child's/narrator's auntie and uncle are also a mixed-race couple, with one partner brown and the other Asian.

The kid, and protagonist, of the story is gender ambiguous. Throughout the story, there are no gender markers in the language to assign gender. Illustratively, I worked with Cassandre to create a child that allowed the reader to draw their own interpretations about the kid's gender. Again, I wanted to expand how many people saw themselves in the story. The gender ambiguity of the child is subtle. For me, it's always interesting to hear how readers describe this character. I've read reviews in which the reviewer assumed the kid was a little boy, others, a little girl, and a few astute reviews picked up on the absence of gender markers.

Since I'm talking about the characters, I want to talk about the grandmother. As I mentioned earlier, the grandmother is the heroine of the story and the town's retired fire chief. This was another chance to flip the normative gender scripts. The dominant narrative is that firefighters have traditionally been men (as referenced in the word "fire*man*"). I wanted to challenge that by not only creating a fire chief who was a woman but also noting that she was retired. Her retirement infers that she had been a firefighter for a long time and enjoyed a healthy career. This detail invites readers to imagine grandma in her early days as a confident young firefighter.

The final character-development aspect I want to acknowledge is the family structure of the wish-list recipient, Michael Clay. Both textually and

Figure 10.2. *The Christmas Truck* intentionally blurs boundaries, displayed on the book cover. *Source*: Blankenship.

illustratively, there is only reference to Michael and his mother. There is no evidence of a second parent. This was intentional because I wanted to continue to showcase the diversity of family structures—in this case, a single-parent family. In this context, the absence of a parent is just a fact, with the potential reasons left open for readers to draw their own interpretations from their own experiences.

Q: What are some other ways you intentionally queered this book?

A: While the characters are the most obvious way I queered Christmas, I want to also highlight some of the more subtle aspects of the book. If you look at the illustration style, there are few hard lines and defined edges. Instead, there is a softness around the edges that blurs the individual boundaries. An example of this is in the cover illustration (see figure 10.2). It's easiest to see this in the moon, but the firetruck and other elements all tend to

Figure 10.3. The illustration shows *The Christmas Truck*'s Christmas visions. *Source*: Blankenship, 10.

soften around the edges. You can also see this effect in the other illustrations I've included (see figures 10.3 and 10.4). I don't know if any readers picked up on this, but it was intentional, and it is a direct nod to the idea that queering something blurs boundaries.

Two more examples of how I used art as a queering device can be seen in the illustrations of the family driving around town looking at Christmas decorations (see figure 10.3) and the scene with the town Christmas tree (see figure 10.4). The inspiration for the composition of the illustration in figure 10.3 is directly inspired by *The Wizard of Oz* imagery. The city center in the distance was visually inspired by the Emerald City. The road winding to it is a reference to the yellow brick road, and the car with Dad, Papa, and their kid visually completes the illustration's composition by taking the place of Dorothy and her traveling companions. I know that the illustration sample in

Figure 10.4. This illustration shows the town square Christmas tree in *The Christmas Truck*. *Source*: Blankenship, 16.

this text is in black and white, but in the full-color illustration, I've inverted the colors. While the city center is glowing gold with the yellow hues reflected in the road, the family's car is an emerald green. Again, I don't know if any of my readers picked up on it, but it was a direct nod to the role Oz and Judy Garland played in queer history.

The illustration in figure 10.4 portrays the town square, where the family has just selected a wish to fill from the town's wishing tree. For context, I'll quote the relevant verses leading up to it:

> The tree is full of wishes with names of girls and boys.
> They come from different families who don't have many toys.
> Daddy lifts me up and Papa's voice rings clear,
> "It's time to pick our wish and spread some Christmas cheer!"

We find the perfect wish. The name is Michael Clay.
And written on the wish are things for Christmas Day.
"I would like a fire truck, a shirt and socks and shoes,
and Mama says that gloves are things that I can use."
When I finish reading, my Papa looks at me;
"Do you understand the meaning of this tree?"
My tummy starts to rumble. I feel for Michael Clay.
"Yes," I tell my parents, "it's the spirit of Christmas Day."
(Blankenship 11–15)

On the surface, this scene depicts the parents explaining to their child the importance of the wishing tree. Illustratively, this is a direct queering of the Christmas Nativity scene. The architecture of the town square was intentionally faded into the background to create the feeling of a stable. The silhouette of the family visually takes the space of Mary, Joseph, and baby Jesus, while the light shining from above and cascading over the tree references the North Star. In this illustration, I wanted to visually capture the religious origins of Christmas while also respecting the reality that many LGBTQ+ Christians have been ostracized and hurt by their faith communities. By having Papa and Dad ask their child, "Do you understand the meaning of this tree?" I attempted to create a safe space for all families to talk about their own values and beliefs about Christmas.

Finally, the last illustrative example I want to discuss involves the imagery of Santa and his sleigh against the full moon on a dark winter night. This one is a little more obvious, and it's the illustration I used for the book cover (figure 10.1). Instead of Santa, the fire chief grandma is driving her bright red firetruck through the night against the backdrop of a full moon to deliver Christmas gifts with her family of helpers. This was an attempt to flip Santa's normative Christmas script and put a woman in the driver's seat.

Q: You've spent some time discussing how you created the book. What happened once you published it?

A: The thing about self-publishing is that simply creating a book isn't enough. What good is a book if no one knows it exists? Because I funded everything myself, I was operating on a tight budget. I had to think about marketing on a grassroots level. This meant trying to get people to review the book and write about it—work that a publishing house usually does on behalf of an author.

My strategy involved trying to get my book into the hands of LGBTQ+ families. This included connecting with LGBTQ+ parenting groups on Facebook,

Figure 10.5. *The Christmas Truck* marketing files include, from left to right, the family in the Amazon rainforest, the family visiting Notre Dame, and the family visiting Castro District. *Source*: author's personal collection.

sending review copies to parenting blogs, and creating an Instagram account (@papadadandme) for the fictional family in my book.

Admittedly, initial responses were slow. Friends and family bought copies, and a few blogs agreed to do reviews, including Dana Rudolph's *Mombian* blog ("New Christmas Book"). In the beginning, I found the most success through Instagram. Using Photoshop, I was able to alter my illustrations and superimpose the characters onto my own travel photos. Whether visiting the Amazon rainforest, Notre Dame Cathedral in Paris, or exploring the Castro District in San Francisco, I was able to take my characters outside the boundaries of my book and explore their personalities in the real world (see figure 10.5). The Instagram posts captured people's imagination and helped direct attention to the book, ultimately resulting in sales. Even though I did not have the backing of a mainstream publisher, I was still able to use established social networks of LGBTQ+ families to slowly find an audience.

While the book came out in September 2014, it wasn't until the week of Christmas that year that I got my first hint that it was selling and resonating with people. The editor of the Barnes & Noble book blog cited *The Christmas Truck* as one of the top ten books to read on Christmas Eve (Villa). For any author, this is a big deal; a national book blog not only acknowledged the existence of my book but also highlighted it as a read for kids who can't sleep—a recommended Christmas book, not a recommended "gay" book. After working so hard to publish this story, I felt like I was finally being seen. My story, a Christmas story with two dads that couldn't land an agent or a traditional publisher, was finally taken seriously.

Word continued to spread among established social networks, and reviewers were taking note. I was grateful, but I also knew Christmas books usually only sell between Thanksgiving and the week of Christmas. The season was ending, and I wondered whether the interest in my book would carry into the next year.

Q: And did it? Was there still interest in the book?

A: The short answer is yes. In February 2015, I was informed that *The Christmas Truck* was one of eighteen national finalists in the picture-book category for *Foreword Reviews*' 2014 INDIES Book of the Year Awards. Only books published in small, independent, or university presses are eligible for the INDIES awards. Finalists are selected from a panel of over one hundred librarians and booksellers. All eighteen finalists received a bronze seal for their books and an invitation to the awards ceremony at the American Library Association's (ALA) 2015 national conference in San Francisco. The awards ceremony, serendipitously, was held on June 27, one day after the Supreme Court ruled on *Obvergefell v. Hodges*, making same-sex marriage the law of the land in the United States. The fates had aligned. I was in San Francisco during Pride at the ALA conference, and history had just been made. There was an excitement in the air that felt like Gay Christmas. This was clearly a sign that my self-published book was going to win the book of the year award.

Or so I thought . . .

The reality is that *The Christmas Truck* did not win. It lost out to *Classic Bedtime Stories*, a collection of classic fairytales with very traditional illustrations (Gustafson). In the quest to create a uniquely queer Christmas story, the irony was not lost on me that a collection of already-established, heteronormative fairytales took the spotlight. I did not get to put a gold seal on my cover, but I did get to keep the bronze, denoting it as a national finalist.

With the book officially declared a national finalist, interest continued to grow. During the fall of 2015, I was approached by Women & Children First, an independently owned feminist bookstore in Chicago, Illinois, to collaborate on a wishing tree like the one in my story. The project would include an author reading of *The Christmas Truck* to launch a wishing tree that would collect diverse books to be disseminated to Chicago Public School elementary students. The turnout for the reading included a crowd of fifteen people, including many LGBTQ+ families. The wishing tree stayed up through New Year's Day, 2016, and collected over 150 diverse books for local students.

With the success of the wishing tree, Women & Children First invited me back the following year for what would become an annual reading of *The Christmas Truck* to launch their wishing tree. Each year, not only did the crowd grow, but also I saw some of the same families return from the year before. By 2017, Women & Children First had implemented Drag Story Hour as part of their children's program. While I enjoy giving author readings of my book, having it read by a Christmastime drag queen to launch the wishing tree seemed too perfect. A very queer Christmas story read by a drag queen in the feminist bookstore to solicit diverse book donations—that's a queer picture book in and of itself waiting to be written!

The audience continued to grow, and again, families from the first reading returned. By 2019, the annual drag queen reading of *The Christmas Truck* had grown to standing room only. All kinds of families now filled the aisles of the bookstore while drag queens adorned with ornaments read my story. With each reading, *The Christmas Truck* was celebrated for its queerness.

Q: *The Christmas Truck* is in five different languages. Can you talk about the foreign editions? How did that happen?

A: Like everything else, the process of translating the book was a grassroots effort that would traditionally have been handled by a publisher. The foreign editions came about because international members of the LGBTQ+ community wanted to share the story with their non-English-speaking friends and family members. Individuals reached out to me directly for translations, and when I told them they didn't exist, they asked permission to translate. Each translation came into existence because a native-language speaker felt passionately that this story needed to be shared. Volunteers translated the manuscript to ensure the story would be accessible in their native language. This was quite an undertaking on the translators' parts. Translating the book required capturing not only the story but also its rhythms in a different language. That's not an easy task.

If you remember from my overview of book publishing, foreign rights are usually sold to international publishers for translation and distribution. Doing this by myself meant I had to figure not only out supply-chain and distribution channels but also marketing strategies in different languages. The editions are currently available in the United States, across most of the European Union, and Australia. At this point, marketing is predominantly word-of-mouth as I simply don't have the resources to launch a global marketing campaign.

The challenges to a global market aren't only linguistic but also cultural; not every country is as progressive as the United States when it comes to talking about LGBTQ+ issues, so finding positive exposure can be challenging. Some countries embraced the translations. For example, the Netherlands' division of Gay & School (a government organization, now known as Gendi, that develops inclusive curriculum) included the Dutch edition as part of its primary school curriculum ("De Kerstmistruck"). What's important to me is that the foreign editions weren't created to make money. This takes me back to why I made the choice to self-publish: even if the foreign editions don't sell a lot of copies, at least the story and its illustrations exist and can be found by those actively seeking this representation.

Q: I have a final question: What are your thoughts on the power of *The Christmas Truck* to transcend uniquely queer spaces and enter the mainstream?

A: A lot has changed since I first published *The Christmas Truck* in 2014. There are now other Christmas picture books representing LGBTQ+ characters.[1] Because of the COVID-19 pandemic, many holiday book readings in 2020 that would normally be in person were recorded. For the first time, I got a sense of how diverse my book's audience had become. In addition to LGBTQ+ community groups, Christian churches of different denominations, including the First United Methodist Church in Colorado Springs, posted online public readings of the book for their congregations (FUMC-CS). There was even an official read by NFL Football player Dalton Risener as part of the Denver Broncos' Holiday Community Outreach (@BroncosOffField).

I don't know if these churches or professional sports organizations were reading *The Christmas Truck* before the pandemic because these kinds of readings generally take place in person and in much smaller, intimate settings. They also don't usually get a lot of press, if any. As readings moved online, people started finding them and then forwarding links to let me know they existed.

Until 2020, I spent the majority of time thinking of this as a queer Christmas story, a book that blurs boundaries and redefines what we think of as traditionally Christmas. I think back to how I had to fight to bring this book into existence. It wasn't the marketing department of a large publishing house that created demand; it was a gradual grassroots word-of-mouth phenomenon. It has been a very interesting experience to watch this book—which, to my knowledge, has predominantly only existed in queer spaces—suddenly not only exist but now be embraced in spaces that have historically been hostile to LGBTQ+ individuals: the church and professional football. For me, it validates, on a visceral level, the importance, the power, and the impact LGBTQ+ picture books have in our world.

NOTE

1. These include Daniel Kibblesmith's *Santa's Husband* (2015), Sophie Labelle's *Rachel's Christmas Boat* (2017), and Tobias Mile's *Two Dads under the Christmas Tree* (2020).

WORKS CITED

Blankenship, J. B. *The Christmas Truck*. Illustrated by Cassandre Bolan, NarraGarden, 2014.
Bolan, Cassandre. "The Art of Cassandre Bolan." *Cassandre Bolan's Portfolio and Blog*, www.cassandrebolan.com. Accessed 1 July 2021.
@BroncosOffField. "If you're surprised that he picked '*The Christmas Truck*' by J B Blankenship as this holiday book of choice, you just don't know @Dalton_Risner66." *Twitter*, 25 Dec. 2020, 12:57 p.m., https://twitter.com/broncosofffield/status/1342544892103254017.
"De Kerstmistruck." *Gay & School*, 2015, www.gayandschool.nl/kennisbank/de-kerstmistruck/. Accessed 30 June 2021.
FUMC-CS [First United Methodist Church, Colorado Springs]. "Day 9: The Christmas Truck." *YouTube*, 9 Dec. 2020, www.youtube.com/watch?v=Y46YQh1fr7w.
Gustafson, Scott, illustrator. *Classic Bedtime Stories*. Greenwich Workshop, 2014.
Kibblesmith, Daniel. *Santa's Husband*. Illustrated by A. P. Quach, Harper Design, 2017.
Labelle, Sophie. *Rachel's Christmas Boat*. Illustrated by Labelle, Orca Book, 2017.
Mile, Tobias. *Two Dads under the Christmas Tree*. Illustrated by Milan Samadder, True Colors Lab, 2020.
"New Christmas Book Features Child with Two Dads." *Mombian*, 24 Nov. 2014, mombian.com/2014/11/24/new-christmas-book-features-child-two-dads/.
Villa, Dell. "10 Books for Kids Who Can't Sleep on Christmas Eve." *Barnes & Noble Reads*, 19 Dec. 2014, www.barnesandnoble.com/blog/10-books-for-kids-who-cant-sleep-on-christmas-eve/.

CHAPTER 11

THE HIPS ON THE DRAG QUEEN GO SWISH, SWISH, SWISH

Playing Around with Gender and Celebrating Difference

J. River Vooris

Years ago, I attended DC's Pride Parade with my friend and her two kids, who were finally old enough to handle the crowds and thick summer heat. Jack, age eight, was mostly interested in catching the beaded necklaces, candy, stickers, and fans that were thrown from the various floats. Josie, age five, was fascinated by the pageantry of it all: the brightly colored floats, the marching bands, the costumes, the flags. My favorite memory from that day was when she suddenly gasped in excitement and shouted, "Look! Princesses!!" And as the float of drag divas passed by, including someone in a brilliant-red ball gown, she clasped her hands and said, in absolute awe, "And there is the queen!"[1]

I often think about this moment when people express concern about children at Pride or argue that introducing children to drag queens is akin to child abuse (Hamilton; Casey) or when legislators introduce bills to ban drag performances under the guise of protecting children (Burga; Cochrane).[2] The drag queens we saw dancing on that float that June day fit perfectly into a world of Disney princesses, fairy tales, and magic that Josie was already familiar with. Jack was curious about why everything was rainbow, but neither kid was confused or scared about what they saw. It was like any other parade to them, albeit with more color.

This chapter delves into the topic of children and drag queens. I first explain a short history of drag in the United States and the ways that drag is being introduced to children through *RuPaul's Drag Race* and Drag Queen Story Hour. I then delve into a close reading and analysis of six recently published picture books that feature drag queens: *The Hips on the*

Drag Queen Go Swish, Swish, Swish (2020) by Lil Miss Hot Mess; *Auntie Uncle: Drag Queen Hero* (2020) by Ellie Royce; *Be Amazing: A History of Pride* (2020) by Desmond Is Amazing; *RuPaul Charles* (2020) by Little Bee Books; *Tabitha and Magoo Dress Up Too* (2020) by Michelle Tea; and *RuPaul* (2021) by Maria Isabel Sánchez Vegara. These books introduce children to the world of drag through song, biographical stories about RuPaul and other famous drag queens, and stories of adventure at Pride parades and at Drag Queen Story Hour at the library. Although drag has historically been associated with adult gay men, these books define drag as a fabulous art form, an act of play and self-expression that is available to everyone. Overall, the books teach children about breaking free of the gender binary and the importance of self-love and self-expression. However, the representations of drag in many of these books are disconnected from the lesbian, gay, bisexual, trans, queer, plus (LGBTQ+) community and do not address the historical connections between drag and the LGBTQ+ rights movement. This ultimately means that children are only taught a partial view of what drag is, which limits the work that these texts are able to do in terms of challenging heteronormative ideas and providing queer kids with a sense of identity and community.

FROM TELEVISION TO LIBRARIES: CONNECTING DRAG PERFORMANCE AND CHILDREN

There is a long history of drag—theatrical and gender bending—in many cultures. From Shakespeare to Japanese theater, characters have often been played by people of a different gender (Heller), and in the nineteenth century, "cross-dressing" was a part of burlesque, vaudeville, and theater shows (Schacht and Underwood). In the late nineteenth century to the twentieth century, drag was a key part of LGBTQ+ subcultures, and drag performers have played an important role in the LGBTQ+ rights movement. From William Dorsey Swann, "the Queen" who organized drag balls in DC in the 1880s (Joseph), to the Chicago drag queens featured in Esther Newton's classic ethnography *Mother Camp* (1979) to Marsha P. Johnson and Sylvia Rivera, who participated in the Stonewall riots (Stryker), to Willi Ninja and Pepper LaBeija, who shaped ballroom culture in New York City (*Paris Is Burning*), drag queens have been a key part of LGBTQ+ community spaces and have redefined the ways that feminist and queer studies scholars think about gender and sexuality (Rupp and Taylor; Bailey).

Historically, drag queens and children have been placed in opposition to each other, particularly in a culture that presumes that gay identities are adult identities (Stockton) and that adult sexualities are dangerous to children (Rivers; Halberstam; Talburt). Drag has also often been performed in adult spaces, like bars and nightclubs, which are not accessible to children. However, over the last decade, children have been gaining access to drag culture through *RuPaul's Drag Race* and Drag Queen Story Hour.

RuPaul's Drag Race is a competition show hosted by RuPaul Charles that premiered in 2009 on Logo, a LGBTQ+-focused television channel. By season 9, it had moved to VH1, and today, it can be found on numerous streaming platforms. It has introduced a mainstream audience to the techniques of drag and has shaped drag culture around the world (Brennan and Gudelunas). The influence of RuPaul himself is evident in the collection of books that I am analyzing for this chapter: two of the six books are RuPaul biographies, and two more include RuPaul quotes or biographical information about him in explanations of the history of drag.

RuPaul's Drag Race has also introduced drag to a younger audience and contributed to the increase in the number of children performing in drag. Two of the more famous drag kids, Queen Lactacia and Desmond Is Amazing, began performing in drag for a public audience before the age of ten, and both of them have noted that *RuPaul's Drag Race* introduced them to the art of drag (Desmond Is Amazing; ELLE). They are now both young drag stars in their early teens with large numbers of followers on social media sites, like Instagram.

Another way that children are introduced to drag is through events like Drag Story Hour. Writer and queer activist Michelle Tea founded Drag Story Hour (DSH) because she wanted to introduce her kid to more queer culture after attending a local story hour at a library that was very heteronormative.[3] DSH is a national organization that hosts events in schools, libraries, and bookstores, where drag queens read books to kids. On their website, they explain that "DSH captures the imagination and play of the gender fluidity of childhood and gives kids glamorous, positive, and unabashedly queer role models. In spaces like this, kids are able to see people who defy rigid gender restrictions and imagine a world where everyone can be their authentic selves!" ("About"). Since its founding, DSH has experienced a lot of media attention, with opponents stressing the danger to kids being exposed to drag queens and sexuality and proponents pointing out that this event is not about sex and sexuality but rather about dressing up, celebrating difference, and breaking gender norms (Hajela; Hamilton; Goldberg; Iqbal; Casey).[4]

THE VALUE OF TEACHING CHILDREN ABOUT LGBTQ+ CULTURE AND DRAG

Drag Story Hour challenges the strict gender binary, but it is not a sexual space, despite the fears of many conservative critics. In fact, the assumption that gay men performing in drag will sexualize children is based on homophobic ideas that gay men are pedophiles or that images of queer people are inherently sexual and inappropriate for kids. Keeping drag queens and children in separate realms also presumes that all children are heterosexual and cisgender, and yet an increasing number of children and youth are coming out as LGBTQ+ (Jones; Brill and Pepper; Ehrensaft). Furthermore, while Western society has often framed children as "innocent" and asexual, in need of protection from sexuality, studies show that children from a young age are already learning about and reflecting back narratives of sexuality (Ryan). If they are not taught in queer-inclusive ways, their stories, jokes, and games will reflect heteronormative ideas where queer sexuality is disparaged and where heterosexuality is upheld as the norm (Ryan).

Events like Drag Story Hour, Pride parades, and LGBTQ+-inclusive children's books are ways that LGBTQ+ children can be introduced to queer culture and LGBTQ+ communities, which is especially important if we consider the number of LGBTQ+ youth who grow up in heterosexual families. Youth studies scholars Lauren B. McInroy and Shelley L. Craig write about how LGBTQ+ media representation validates LGBTQ+ young people's identities, and Caitlin L. Ryan et al.'s research shows that even for kids who are not gay or trans, introducing children to gender-inclusive and LGBTQ+-inclusive texts is important in reducing bullying and spreading understanding of social differences.

Teaching about drag specifically can be a positive thing, especially in terms of what drag can teach kids about playing with gender, creatively expressing themselves, and resisting oppressive norms (Keenan and Lil Miss Hot Mess). Drag also provides a way to introduce children to queer culture and queer world making (Keenan and Lil Miss Hot Mess). In an Associated Press article about a Brooklyn Drag Queen Story Hour event, Christia Spears Brown, a professor of developmental psychology at the University of Kentucky, points out that DQSH "ultimately provides children with a really flexible model of gender. And that mental flexibility about gender will benefit all kids, regardless of how gender-typical they themselves are" (Hajela).

CHILDREN'S BOOKS ABOUT DRAG

It was only in 2020 that children's picture books about drag were first published, which is somewhat surprising given how important drag queens have been in LGBTQ+ history and community building and yet not surprising when we consider the ways that drag queens have been considered deviant and potentially damaging to children, as discussed above. Two of the books that came out in the last several years are authored by folks who are connected to Drag Story Hour. *The Hips on the Drag Queen Go Swish, Swish, Swish* is a colorful book by Lil Miss Hot Mess, a drag queen academic, who is a frequent host of Drag Story Hour in New York City. The book is based on a song that Lil Miss Hot Mess performs for kids attending DSH, a parody of "The Wheels on the Bus." In the book, each verse follows a diverse group of drag queens marching, dancing, and swaying through the streets of a city. *Tabitha and Magoo Dress Up Too* is written by the founder of Drag Story Hour, Michelle Tea. It follows a brother-and-sister duo who like to dress up but are nervous to go out in public in their finery. They are visited by Drag Queen Morgana, a sort of fairy godmother in drag, who invites them out to a Drag Queen Story Hour at the library and teaches them about the gender binary and the idea that all clothing is drag.

Two other books that were published in 2020 include *Be Amazing: A History of Pride* and *Auntie Uncle: Drag Queen Hero*. *Be Amazing*, by Desmond Is Amazing, is both an autobiography and history book. Desmond connects their own story of discovering drag as a kid to the history of the Stonewall riots and the stories of Marsha P. Johnson, Sylvia Rivera, and RuPaul.[5] Desmond credits their LGBTQ+ forebearers for their current ability to express themself and urges readers to "pay the haters no mind" (5). *Auntie Uncle* is a book about a kid and their Uncle Leo, who is an accountant who also performs as a drag queen, known as Auntie Lotta.[6] Auntie Lotta saves a dog at Pride and is awarded a medal, which means that her drag queen friends and Uncle Leo's accountant friends meet each other at the award ceremony.

And finally, there were two biographies of RuPaul published in 2020 and 2021. One is a board book that is from the People of Pride series by Little Bee Books. There is no named author, but it is illustrated by Vincent Chen. The book introduces RuPaul's gender-bending childhood and her experiences as a drag queen supermodel and talk show host. The second biography of RuPaul, published in June 2021, has more details about RuPaul's family and experiences in New York as a young person (Vegara). It is a part of the Little People, Big Dreams series and is illustrated by nonbinary artist Wednesday Holmes.[7]

In the sections that follow, I will describe the ways that these texts provide children with a model for breaking gender rules and playing with gender. They also spread a message of self-love and the importance of self-expression. While these are valuable messages for all children—and LGBTQ+ children in particular—I also point to the ways that several of the texts do not explicitly connect with the LGBTQ+ community and LGBTQ+ activism.

GENDER PERFORMANCE AND BREAKING GENDER RULES: HOW THESE BOOKS DEFINE "DRAG"

In the preface to *The Drag Queen Anthology* (2008), edited by Lisa Underwood and Steven P. Schacht, Judith Lorber writes, "Drag's core elements are *performance* and *parody*." This parody, she notes, is about exaggerated gender, and "the joke is that a man can be a woman or a woman a man convincingly enough that the 'unmasking' or 'unwigging' at the end of the performance gives a pleasurable *frisson* and evokes laughter, even though the audience has been in on the joke from the beginning" (Lorber xv). This definition of "drag" as gender parody is a fairly widespread one, although many drag artists and scholars argue that contemporary drag is not necessarily about men playing women or women playing men. Meredith Heller writes that we should move away from binary understandings of drag that are bound in binary-sexed ideas of the body to think about drag as a queer practice of gender bending. In their article about drag pedagogy, Harper Keenan and Lil Miss Hot Mess define "drag" as follows:

> [Drag is] not merely ... gender reversal, but through the expansive description provided by both gay liberation activist Tede Matthews and contemporary drag superstar RuPaul (2014): "we're all born naked and the rest is drag." This simple but profound statement suggests that no performance of gender or other cultural signifiers is ever natural (Butler, 1990), whether on stage or in everyday life, and that drag serves as an intentional way of rewriting these scripts. (446–47)

Overall, these children's books explore drag as a broad performance of gender or as gender play. Desmond Is Amazing writes, "When I am not Desmond, I like to dress up as characters of a different gender. This is called drag" (2), and in the People of Pride biography of RuPaul, the reader is told, "Drag is when a person dresses as a gender that is different than their own" (Little Bee

Books). This book continues, "as RuPaul would say, 'You're born naked and the rest is drag,'" a quote that Michelle Tea also uses in *Tabitha and Magoo Dress Up Too*. Fairy godmother Drag Queen Morgana says, "Like Mama Ru said, we are all born nude. / All our clothing is drag—every dress, tie, and snood" (Tea 13). As Harper Keenan and Lil Miss Hot Mess explain above, this points to the performativity of all types of gendered expression, not just performances of drag.

The Hips on the Drag Queen Go Swish, Swish, Swish does not offer a specific definition of "drag," but the text shows that being a drag queen includes big hair, stompy boots, shimmying shoulders, and lots of bling. The book jacket invites readers to "shimmy, bling, and twirl your way through the fabulous world of drag . . . join a multitude of drag queens in a show-stopping performance as you celebrate what makes you *you* along with some of these fun and playful divas" (Lil Miss Hot Mess). This text introduces children to very different types of drag queens, who have a multitude of different gender expressions. Some of the queens have beards or are dressed primarily in a dress of blue hair, along with a blue mustache. Most of them have on long eyelashes and lots of makeup, but some have short hair and boots, and not all of them are wearing dresses.

The Little People, Big Dreams biography of RuPaul, by Maria Isabel Sánchez Vegara, is another text that does not offer a specific definition of "drag." However, the text notes that "drag was not only about having fun and dressing up. For Ru, it was a way to express himself as an artist. He mixed a spoonful of everything he loved and admired, and put his heart into becoming the woman of his dreams" (Vegara 13–14).

The book *Auntie Uncle* does not include a definition of "drag" in the main text, and initially, the character of Uncle Leo / Auntie Lotta fits into the masculine-feminine binary that is representative of the traditional definition of "drag." However, the character ultimately creates a new drag look that is more androgynous and becomes Auntie Uncle, thus showing the complexity and flexibility of gender. Furthermore, the book includes a definition of drag in the introduction, by Marti Gould Cummings, a drag artist who has been performing in New York City for decades and who recently became a viral sensation when a video of them singing "Baby Shark" to a toddler at a drag brunch was posted online (Wong). Cummings writes that "drag is an art form rooted in activism and protest; a way to show the world that being different is beautiful. Drag is anything you want it to be. . . . Drag is a way to bring people together in times of joy and triumph, and a way to bring people together in community."

This definition connects drag to a history of activism, protest, and community. Likewise, in *Tabitha and Magoo Dress Up Too*, when the kids and Morgana head to Drag Queen Story Hour, they offer an expansive view of what a drag queen is with several definitions that move beyond gender: "A unicorn without a horn! / True to themselves since the day they were born!" (Tea 25); "A teacher! A mentor! A role model! A Leader! A stitcher! A Painter! Hot-gluer and beader! An artist! A diva who gives us Drag Fever!" (26). Thus, readers learn about the theatrical elements of drag, as well as the way that drag queens have often been community leaders and mentors. However, this connection to community and leadership is not present in all the texts.

FREEDOM OF EXPRESSION AND SELF-LOVE

Linked to the many definitions of "drag" is the theme of being yourself and the value of breaking free of gender norms. In *Tabitha and Magoo Dress Up Too*, the text notes that pink is usually thought of as a girl color and that Magoo is "nervous to wear it because he's a boy" (Tea 10). This is the text that is the most explicit about teaching about gender, in terms of not only gender expression but also gender identity. The drag queen notes, "All these 'boy' rules and 'girl' rules just simply aren't true!" and some "girl-kids inside feel like boys" and some kids have "both boy *and* girl in their heart" and "some kids have neither, a *new* gender they'll start" (15). While the text does not use the term "transgender," these few lines teach kids that it is possible to have a gender that is different than the one assigned at birth. Ultimately, the message is that when you are able to freely create your own gender expression, "it leads to a playful rainbow liberation!" (17). This type of information validates trans and nonbinary children's experiences of their gender and provides cisgender children with information about trans and nonbinary identities, which is important for creating safer spaces for trans kids.

While Michelle Tea's book is the most explicit in regard to teaching about LGBTQ+ identities, the majority of the other texts provides a more general message about loving oneself. The People of Pride biography of RuPaul notes that he "spoke about caring for yourself, being true to yourself, and most importantly, loving yourself" and that, ultimately, "RuPaul's message to love yourself has helped make the world a more fun and accepting place to live" (Little Bee Books). Similarly, Vegara's biography of RuPaul notes that he broke rules that girls and boys are supposed to follow and inspired many kids to feel less lonely and to love themselves.

In *Auntie Uncle*, the message of self-acceptance isn't explicit, but rather implicit, through the actions of Auntie Uncle's friends, who all celebrate his award (Royce). And in the introduction, Marti Gould Cummings notes, "For me, drag is about spreading love and kindness." When you are a member of a marginalized community, loving oneself and others can be an act of revolution. Black feminist writers Audre Lorde and Mia McKenzie have both written about how it is an act of resistance to love oneself in a system that does not want to see Black and queer folks survive. Activist and actress Laverne Cox notes that love is revolutionary for trans folks, who are often told that they are not worthy of love (National LGBTQ+ Task Force). Indeed, the idea of self-love and pride in one's identity has been a key part of the LGBTQ+ movement in the United States, where queer and trans identities have historically been seen as shameful or sinful.

Desmond Is Amazing's book explicitly connects the text to antibullying measures with a reader's note about self-expression and the importance of not teasing others for being different, and the main text ends with the idea that everyone should be free to do what they love and to "feel amazing, always" (26). Thus, these books contribute to a growing number of children's picture books that advocate the importance of breaking gender norms and celebrate differences between people.

LGBTQ+ ACTIVISM

I appreciate that these texts offer an expansive definition of "drag" and emphasize the importance of celebrating different gender expressions, as well as the value of self-love. However, I found that the texts do not specifically connect drag queens with LGBTQ+ identities, activism, or communities, and I find this to be a limitation of the books. Queer and trans folks have had to fight for the right to express themselves publicly and love openly, and these books are about the fight for self-expression, yet only one of the books uses the word "gay" to describe a character, and only a couple of them use the term "LGBTQ."

People of Pride's biography of RuPaul uses the word "gay" to describe RuPaul and explains that this word is used for someone who loves someone who is the same gender (Little Bee Books). *Be Amazing* uses the term "Gay-In" to describe the original Pride parade after the Stonewall riots (Desmond Is Amazing 14). These two books also include a glossary at the end of the book and use the term "LGBTQ+" to describe people in the books. The Little People, Big Dreams biography of RuPaul also uses the term "LGBTQ+" in the longer biography at the end of the book to describe RuPaul, although it is not a part of the main text (Vegara).

The other books do not include explicit mentions of the LGBTQ+ community, although there are images of Pride parades and Pride flags and references to actions that take "courage" (Tea 29). There is also a page in *Tabitha and Magoo Dress Up Too* where a drag queen is reading a book that includes an image of folks protesting outside the town hall, and one of them is holding a sign that says, "human rights" (27).

I think this points to ways that it is becoming more acceptable to talk with children about gender and gender nonconformity, but overall, our society is uncomfortable talking with children about sexuality, queerness, or gay identities. While drag is not inherently about sexuality, it is grounded within queer culture and LGBTQ+ history. And while there are a number of children's books that include gay characters, these are often adult characters. As Kathryn Bond Stockton points out in *The Queer Child* (2009), in the early 2000s, there was more and more attention given to trans children in the media, but the idea of gay children was still taboo. And yet we know that children are coming out at younger and younger ages, and it's important for them to have examples of gay and queer people (McInroy and Craig).

While removing sexuality from these books might make them more palatable to adults who are worried about children learning about sexuality while also emphasizing that drag is about gender and not sexuality, the representations in these children's books untethers drag from its history within the LGBTQ+ community. This means readers are given an incomplete view of drag and the way that drag queens have been instrumental in the fight for LGBTQ+ rights over the last century.

There are many who argue that even without being a part of political organization, drag queens are engaging in political activism just through their performances (Rupp and Taylor), and thus, perhaps, it is not necessary for all these texts to explicitly link drag queens with LGBTQ+ activism. Harper Keenan and Lil Miss Hot Mess argue that Drag Queen Story Hour teaches children about queerness and gender creativity in a way that does not rely on pedantic lessons about LGBTQ+ vocabulary and that this is a valuable way to teach children. The mere visibility of LGBTQ+ people in picture books, even without explicit messages about LGBTQ+ history and/or queerness, has a transformative potential in shaping culture and children's understanding of difference (Miller). However, as John H. Bickford III argues in his analysis of LGBTQ+ picture books, showing only the positive elements of LGBTQ+ identity and disconnecting stories from larger histories and communities mean that children are not being taught the full realities of LGBTQ+ lives.

Be Amazing is one of the texts that does include a discussion of LGBTQ+ rights and the fight for equality. This text not only is an autobiography but also includes LGBTQ+ history. Desmond Is Amazing writes that LGBTQ+ people have been "punished, humiliated, and discriminated against. They could lose their jobs, be forced into hospitals, or even get arrested, just for being who they were" and then explains how LGBTQ+ folks have fought back, for example, by participating in the Stonewall riots, marching in Pride parades, and creating organizations like STAR (7–9).

The People of Pride biography of RuPaul also explains a short history of the fight for equality, providing context for the experiences that RuPaul had and the importance of drag queens within LGBTQ+ activism: "At that time, LGBTQ people did not have equal rights. They could not get married, and service members could be discharged from the military if they were openly gay. . . . But drag queens have a long history of changing society. From actors to activists, Shakespeare to Stonewall, drag has played an important part in making the world a more accepting place" (Little Bee Books). This text also references the AIDS epidemic and RuPaul's role in raising awareness and money to stop the virus.

I think that these texts that explicitly show children how LGBTQ+ folks have fought back against discrimination are valuable because many LGBTQ+ youth will experience discrimination in their lives. While self-love is a political act in a homophobic and transphobic world, I believe that it is not enough to only teach children about self-love. I also think that it is important to include people's identities in their biographies—too often, historical figures have their sexuality erased (Crisp et al.), and this limits queer kids' ability to see themselves reflected in history. Only one of the RuPaul books names him as gay, even though this is a significant part of his identity.

I am most frustrated with the *Auntie Uncle* text because unlike *The Hips on the Drag Queen* or *Tabitha and Magoo*, which are about having fun with gender, Ellie Royce's book is about an act of heroism at a Pride celebration and public recognition of that moment. Royce's story had the potential to show readers the importance of standing up for the LGBTQ+ community, and yet the storyline revolves around saving a dog. For this, *Auntie Uncle* is awarded a medal of bravery, and headlines in the paper declare that she "Saves Pride" (Royce 12). And yet this action is not directly related to LGBTQ+ rights or even related to LGBTQ+ people and identities. Overall, the story feels like a watering down of the meaning of Pride, which started in response to the

Stonewall riots; Pride parades have historically been a way to march in support for LGBTQ+ rights. The text does touch on the way that LGBTQ+ folks can be scared to come out or reveal parts of their lives—as Auntie Uncle navigates her drag queen friends meeting his accountant friends, and an astute reader or parent reading to a child could explain those nuances; however, it is not explicit in the text.

LGBTQ+ COMMUNITY

One of the other aspects of drag that several scholars have written about is the presence of drag families and drag houses (Bailey; Rupp and Taylor; Newton). Marlon Bailey argues that we should think about drag not only as a performance of gender but as a cultural practice imbedded within queer-family kinship networks. Traditionally, drag queens were introduced to drag by other queens and became a part of family structures and mentoring relationships. However, this may be changing for new generations as more queens learn about drag from *RuPaul's Drag Race* and from social media accounts (Alexander).

Just as these texts engage with LGBTQ+ activism to varying degrees, the texts differ in regard to how they engage with the LGBTQ+ community. Some of them, like *Be Amazing* and *Tabitha and Magoo*, explicitly connect their protagonists to historical and contemporary figures in LGBTQ+ history. Desmond Is Amazing writes, "I can freely be the character Desmond Is Amazing because of the hard work of generations of people in the LGBTQ community," and then there is a page that shows illustrations of various famous people next to their names: Pepper LaBeija, James Baldwin, Laverne Cox, Miss Major, Stormé DeLarverie, and Willi Ninja (23–24). Similarly, Michelle Tea's book gives a shout out to some of the key folks who have contributed to drag history: "To RuPaul, Hot Mess, or Flawless Sabrina / To Pepper or Marsha, Divine or Heklina / Their dazzling chutzpah did pave the way / For Drag Queen Story Hour to happen today" (35). In contrast, while Auntie Uncle has drag queen friends, we do not meet them by name, and the LGBTQ+ community is not named directly. The main character goes to a parade, which is clearly a Pride parade due to all the rainbows, different Pride flags, and presence of drag queens but isn't named as such. Again, this may reflect a positive shift in terms of the mainstreaming of queer culture and drag culture; however, it does not provide children with clear information about the history of Pride or explain what it means to be a part of the LGBTQ+ community.

These drag books match the findings of Bickford's study of LGBTQ+-based elementary trade books, which showed the majority of them did not mention the LGBTQ+ community or an LGBTQ+ social network (414). He writes, "Most LGBTQ characters had meager connections with the LGBTQ community. The surprisingly scant connection to the LGBTQ community, though, appears in comparable research on different topics. Children's and young adult literature about the civil rights movement often celebrates the individual and disregards the collective" (417). And yet the civil rights movement and the LGBTQ+ rights movement succeeded not because of the actions of a few stars but because of collective resistance. Furthermore, given the ways that LGBTQ+ youth often feel isolated, I think books that emphasize that there is an entire LGBTQ+ community can be helpful for their well-being and sense of identity.

CONCLUSION

A screenshot that I have seen circulating around on Facebook every few months is a response to the question, "What is your opinion about drag queens and children?" William Salyers writes, "I am against drag queens being exposed to children. A lot could go wrong. Nails could be broken, wigs pulled off, someone could get knocked off her heels. Children are wild, irrational, and unpredictable, and their characters are still in formative stages. Someone fabulous could get hurt" (Have a Gay Day).

This tongue-and-cheek response to the question of drag queens and children flips the script about who might be dangerous to whom. And yet it affirms the idea that drag queens and children are opposed to each other. However, many parents and children who have attended DQSH can attest that drag queens and children can actually get along fabulously. Drag queens' pageantry, love of color, big hair, elegant gowns, and wacky sense of humor can fit well into children's worlds of make-believe.

In April 2023, I cohosted a celebration of the LGBTQ+ Children's Book Collection at the Wells College Long Library and was interviewed by the local newspaper about the event (Wilcox). Campus security had to attend due to the number of calls the library received that day accusing the librarians of being "groomers" and "pedophiles." It was a sobering reminder about the consequences of the current political rhetoric about LGBTQ+ people. A week later, I hosted a group of school children at the Wells College Long Library for a reading hour with the LGBTQ+ Children's Book Collection. One boy, about eight years old, declared that *The Hips on the Drag Queen Go Swish*,

Swish, Swish was the best book in the collection because it was "funny," and he proceeded to read it three times in a row! I wish the people who are scared of these books and think that they are corrupting children could have seen the joy and delight on his face.

In this chapter, I have explored the narratives within the first books about drag for children and how they provide examples of ways that people can express their gender creatively, move their bodies in joy, and make a difference in the world. The books engage with LGBTQ+ history and activism to differing degrees, and I argue that we need more books about drag that engage more fully with the LGBTQ+ community.

NOTES

1. Story shared with generous permission of Jack, Josie, and their mom, Jeannette.
2. In the start of 2023, fourteen states had introduced bills banning drag in public spaces (Burga). Several states including Montana, Kentucky, and Tennessee passed bills restricting drag, although all of these were ultimately struck down by federal court judges under First Amendment protections (Lenora).
3. "Heteronormative" refers to something that upholds heterosexuality as normal, typical, and preferred and which either ignores the presence of queer/LGBTQ+ identities or indicates that they are lesser sexualities than heterosexuality.
4. While there are plenty of adult drag shows that are sexual and raunchy, drag shows are *not* inherently sexual.
5. Sylvia Rivera and Marsha P. Johnson are two important figures in LGBTQ+ history. They were both at the Stonewall riots and founded Street Transvestite Action Revolutionaries (STAR), an organization that helped LGBTQ+ homeless youth. "Transvestite" is a word that is no longer used today but is one that Rivera and Johnson identified with at the time, along with the term "drag queen." They also both identified as women and are considered trans activists and pioneers. Johnson says that the *P* in her name stood for "Pay It No Mind." For a children's book about Rivera and Johnson, see *Sylvia and Marsha Start a Revolution* (2020) by Joy Michael Ellison.
6. For more about books with representations of gay uncles, see Miller.
7. This series, created by Maria Isabel Sánchez Vegara, highlights the accomplishments of "outstanding people, from designers and artists to scientists and activists" (https://littlepeople-bigdreams.com/).

WORKS CITED

"About." *Drag Story Hour*, 21 Mar. 2024, https://www.dragstoryhour.org/about.

Alexander, Claire. "What Can Drag Do for Me? The Multifaceted Influences of *RuPaul's Drag Race* on the Perth Drag Scene." *"RuPaul's Drag Race" and the Shifting Visibility of Drag Culture: The Boundaries of Reality TV*, edited by Niall Brennan and David Gudelunas, Palgrave Macmillan, 2017, pp. 245–69. *Springer Link*, https://doi.org/10.1007/978-3-319-50618-0_17.

Bailey, Marlon M. *Butch Queens up in Pumps: Gender, Performance, and Ballroom Culture in Detroit*. U of Michigan P, 2013.

Bickford, John H., III. "Examining LGBTQ-Based Literature Intended for Primary and Intermediate Elementary Students." *Elementary School Journal*, vol. 118, no. 3, 2018, pp. 409–25.

Brennan, Niall, and David Gudelunas. *"RuPaul's Drag Race" and the Shifting Visibility of Drag Culture: The Boundaries of Reality TV*. Springer International, 2017.

Brill, Stephanie, and Rachel Pepper. *The Transgender Child: A Handbook for Parents and Professionals Supporting Transgender and Nonbinary Children*. Cleis Press, 2022.

Burga, Solcyré. "Tennessee Passed the Nation's First Law Limiting Drag Shows: Here's the Status of Anti-drag Bills across the U.S." *Time*, 5 Mar. 2023, https://time.com/6260421/tennessee-limiting-drag-shows-status-of-anti-drag-bills-u-s/.

Casey, John. "Exposing Kids to Drag Isn't Abuse." *The Advocate*, 17 Sept. 2019, https://www.advocate.com/commentary/2019/9/17/exposing-kids-drag-isnt-abuse.

Cochrane, Emily. "Judge Finds Tennessee Law Aimed at Restricting Drag Shows Unconstitutional." *New York Times*, 3 June 2023, https://www.nytimes.com/2023/06/03/us/politics/tennessee-drag-ruling.html.

Crisp, Thomas, et al. "The All-Heterosexual World of Children's Nonfiction: A Critical Content Analysis of LGBTQ Identities in Orbis Pictus Award Books, 1990–2017." *Children's Literature in Education*, vol. 49, 2018, pp. 246–63. *PALNI*, https://doi.org/10.1007/s10583-017-9319-5.

Cummings, Marti Gould. Introduction. *Auntie Uncle: Drag Queen Hero*, by Ellie Royce, illustrated by Hannah Chambers, POW!, 2020, p. 1.

Desmond Is Amazing. *Be Amazing: A History of Pride*. Illustrated by Dylan Glynn, Farrar, Straus and Giroux, 2020.

Ehrensaft, Diane. "Listening and Learning From Gender-Nonconforming Children." *The Psychoanalytic Study of the Child*, vol. 68, no. 1, 2014, pp. 28–56.

ELLE. "Meet the 8-Year-Old Boy Who Transforms into a Drag Queen Named Lactatia." *YouTube*, 19 Oct. 2017, https://www.youtube.com/watch?v=bdCXxUxI-WE.

Ellison, Joy Michael. *Sylvia and Marsha Start a Revolution! The Story of the Trans Women of Color Who Made LGBTQ+ History*. Illustrated by Teshika Silver, Jessica Kingsley Press, 2020.

Goldberg, Michelle. "Leave Drag Queen Story Hour Alone!" *New York Times*, 7 June 2019, https://www.nytimes.com/2019/06/07/opinion/conservatives-culture-trump.html.

Hajela, Deepti. "Library Brings Drag Queens, Kids Together for Story Hour." Associated Press, 16 May 2017, https://apnews.com/article/6b9a9e0574794ec9974364bd7ae023af.

Halberstam, Jack. *The Queer Art of Failure*. Duke UP, 2011.

Hamilton, Amelia. "Tax Dollars Are Paying for Drag Queens to Read Stories to Children." *National Review*, 30 May 2017, https://www.nationalreview.com/2017/05/drag-queen-stories-libraries-use-tax-money-promote-gender-fluidity/.

Have a Gay Day. "A Screenshot from the Website Quora." *Facebook*, 22 May 2023, https://m.facebook.com/photo.php?fbid=543632137798305&set=a.408385401322980&type=3.

Heller, Meredith. *Queering Drag: Redefining the Discourse of Gender-Bending*. Indiana UP, 2020.

Iqbal, Zainab. "It's 2019 and Some People Don't Want Drag Queens Reading to Kids." *Bklyner*, 7 June 2019, https://bklyner.com/drag-queen-protest/.

Jones, Jeffrey. "LGBT Identification Rises to 5.6% in Latest U.S. Estimate." *Gallup*, 24 Feb. 2011, https://news.gallup.com/poll/329708/lgbt-identification-rises-latest-estimate.aspx.

Joseph, Channing Gerard. "The First Drag Queen Was a Former Slave: Who Fought for Queer Freedom a Century Before Stonewall." *The Nation*, 31 Jan. 2020, https://www.thenation.com/article/society/drag-queen-slave-ball/.

Keenan, Harper, and Lil Miss Hot Mess. "Drag Pedagogy: The Playful Practice of Queer Imagination in Early Childhood." *Curriculum Inquiry*, vol. 55, no. 5, 2020, pp. 440–61. *Taylor and Francis Online*, https://doi.org/10.1080/03626784.2020.1864621.

Lil Miss Hot Mess. *The Hips on the Drag Queen Go Swish, Swish, Swish*. Illustrated by Olga de Dios, Running Press Kids, 2020.

Little Bee Books. *RuPaul Charles*. Illustrated by Vincent Chen, Little Bee Books, 2020. People of Pride.

Lorber, Judith. Preface. *The Drag Queen Anthology: The Absolutely Fabulous but Flawlessly Customary World of Female Impersonators*, edited by Lisa Underwood and Steven P. Schacht, Taylor and Francis, 2004, pp. xv–xvi.

Lorde, Audre. *A Burst of Light: Essays*. Firebrand Books, 1988.

McInroy, Lauren B, and Shelley L. Craig. "Perspectives of LGBTQ Emerging Adults on the Depiction and Impact of LGBTQ Media Representation." *Journal of Youth Studies*, vol. 20, no. 1, 2017, pp. 32–46.

McKenzie, Mia. *Black Girl Dangerous: On Race, Queerness, Class and Gender*. BGD Press, 2014.

Miller, Jennifer. *The Transformative Potential of LGBTQ+ Children's Picture Books*. UP of Mississippi, 2022.

National LGBTQ Task Force. "Laverne Cox at Creating Change 2014 (E)." *YouTube*, 5 Feb. 2014, https://www.youtube.com/watch?v=6cytcop4Jwg.

Newton, Esther. *Mother Camp: Female Impersonators in America*. U of Chicago P, 1979.

Paris Is Burning. Directed by Jennie Livingston, Kanopy Streaming, 2021.

Rivers, Daniel. "'In the Best Interests of the Child': Lesbian and Gay Parenting Custody Cases, 1967–1985." *Journal of Social History*, vol. 43, no. 4, 2010, pp. 917–43.

Royce, Ellie. *Auntie Uncle: Drag Queen Hero*. Illustrated by Hannah Chambers, POW!, 2020.

Rupp, Leila J., and Verta Taylor. *Drag Queens at the 801 Cabaret*. U of Chicago P, 2003.

Ryan, Caitlin L. "Kissing Brides and Loving Hot Vampires: Children's Construction and Perpetuation of Heteronormativity in Elementary School Classrooms." *Sex Education*, vol. 16, no. 1, 2016, pp. 77–90. *EBSCOhost*, https://doi.org/10.1080/14681811.2015.1052874.

Ryan, Caitlin L., et al. "Discussing Princess Boys and Pregnant Men: Teaching about Gender Diversity and Transgender Experiences within an Elementary School Curriculum." *Journal of LGBT Youth*, vol. 10, no. 1–2, 2013, pp. 83–105.

Schacht, Steven P., and Lisa Underwood, editors. *The Drag Queen Anthology: The Absolutely Fabulous but Flawlessly Customary World of Female Impersonators*. Taylor and Francis Group, 2004. *ProQuest Ebook Central*, https://ebookcentral.proquest.com/lib/depauw-ebooks/detail.action?docID=1111319.

Stockton, Kathryn Bond. *The Queer Child, or Growing Sideways in the Twentieth Century*. Duke UP, 2009.

Stryker, Susan. *Transgender History*. Seal Press, 2008.

Talburt, Susan. "Introduction: Transforming Discourses of Queer Youth and Educational Practices Surrounding Gender, Sexuality, and Youth." *Youth and Sexualities*, edited by Eric Rofes and Mary Louise Rasmussen, Palgrave Macmillan, 2004, pp. 1–13.

Tea, Michelle. *Tabitha and Magoo Dress Up Too*. Illustrated by Ellis van der Does, Feminist Press, 2020.

Vegara, Maria Isabel Sánchez. *RuPaul*. Illustrated by Wednesday Holmes, Frances Lincoln Children's Books, 2021. Little People, Big Dreams 61.

Wilcox, David. "'Visibility and Knowledge': Wells College Launches Trans, LGBQ+ Children's Library." *Auburn Citizen*, 7 Apr. 2023, https://auburnpub.com/lifestyles/visibility-and-knowledge-wells-college-launches-trans-lgbq-childrens-library/article_db51fabb-c3f8-5555-8bc8-8b7fb2260d96.html.

Wong, Curtis M. "Drag Queen Performs 'Baby Shark' at 2-Year-Old's Request, and It's Delightful." *Huffington Post*, 19 Mar. 2019, https://www.huffpost.com/entry/baby-shark-drag-queen-brunch_n_5c893c7ee4b038892f49caa9.

PART 5

WORLD MAKING IN LGBTQ+ CHILDREN'S PICTURE BOOKS

CHAPTER 12

APPLES BEGONE

Queer and Trans of Color Aesthetics of Joy in ABC Books

Isabel Millán

Contemporary alphabet books are artistic subversions of the notion that alphabetic literacy can only survive at the expense of the image. Today's alphabet books openly acknowledge that language is or becomes part of the reality it describes.
—KAREN COATS, "P Is for Patriarchy" (96)

Deceivingly nuanced, alphabet, or ABC, books are often dismissed as merely teaching children the alphabet. Though, as scholars of alphabet books have argued, they accomplish a great deal more and are by no means "innocent" children's literature.[1] Intertwined within each letter are the political ideologies of their creators. Across time and space, ABC books have been utilized for the purpose of religious indoctrination, colonization, empire building, and promoting national ideologies (Norcia; O'Sullivan). Is it possible to strategically utilize the ABC children's literary genre to imagine an alternative or utopic world order? How do authors mobilize queer and trans of color ABC books to reimagine their own communities—both within and off the page?

Two alphabet books that lend themselves to a queer and trans of color analysis are *M Is for Mustache: A Pride ABC Book* (2015) and *They, She, He: Easy as ABC* (2019). The first was written by author and playwright Catherine Hernandez, who describes herself as "a proud queer woman" of "Filipino, Spanish, Chinese, and Indian descent and married into the Navajo Nation" ("About"). Its vibrantly colorful illustrations were created by Marisa Firebaugh, a "proud mixed race Chinese-American" illustrator known for her creative brand Sketches by the Sea (see also *Sketches by the Sea*). Published by Flamingo Rampant Press (Canada), it debuted alongside five other picture books funded through the publisher's Kickstarter campaign. Four years later, Maya C. Gonzalez and Matthew Smith-Gonzalez cocreated *They, She, He*, publishing it under their independent press, Reflection Press (United States). Together, their identities encompass queer, trans, Chicanx, and white, describing their press as "a POC queer and trans owned independent publisher of radical and revolutionary children's books" ("Our Mission and Values"). Each alphabet book provides a queer and trans of color textual and visual political framework imbued with an aesthetic of joy. This is accomplished through their creators' idealized or utopic vision of what may be possible, representing these as visual and textual affirmations of queer and trans of color communities not only surviving but thriving, loving, and rejoicing.

THE ABCS OF ALPHABET BOOKS

As a subgenre of children's literature, ABC, or alphabet, books rarely follow a typical narrative arc and often lack a plot. Like individual episodes of a television series, each page or letter has the potential to present its own world within the wider book. As David L. Russell observes, "It is unlikely that a single alphabet book will accommodate all the eccentricities of the English language. On the bright side, this simply gives us an excuse to read several different alphabet books to our children" (112). Scholars such as Mary Agnes Taylor have attempted to classify alphabet books into categories based on each letter's relationship to illustrations or the book's overall narrative (173). Despite their seemingly formulaic structure, ABC books encompass a range of textual and visual strategies.

Because of their often-segmented alphabetical format, not all ABC books include people or characters, instead relying on objects or animals for each letter of the alphabet. Yet even these can entail their own biases or have ideological implications. For example, when it comes to gender there are, not surprisingly, extremely gender-normative or stereotypical examples, like Michael Kracht's *ABC's for Boys* (2015) and *ABC's for Girls* (2017), where the first depicts "all of boys' favorite things" ("ABC's for Boys), like airplanes and dump trucks in dark primary colors, while the latter includes "all of girls' favorite things" ("ABC's for Girls"), like butterflies and castles in pastels. Karen Coats correctly asserts, "When A is for apple, then, it would seem that P is for patriarchy" (96).

In an attempt to counter these binary narratives, feminist, queer, and social justice examples of ABC books emerged—with many of these now appearing on lists of challenged or banned books.[2] Examples include *C Is for Consent*

(2018) by Eleanor Morrison and illustrated by Faye Orlove; *A Is for Activist* (2013) by Innosanto Nagara; and *An ABC of Equality* (2019) by Chana Ginelle Ewing and illustrated by Paulina Morgan. While some queer or white authors include characters of color within their ABC books—for example, *ABC: A Family Alphabet Book* (2000) by Bobbie Combs and illustrated by Brian Rappa and Desiree Rappa; and *The GayBCs* (2019) by M. L. Webb—the goal of this chapter is to highlight ABC books that explicitly center queer and trans of color communities in order to examine the idealized world each creator imagines for themselves, their children, and their audiences.[3]

M IS FOR MUSTACHE: A PRIDE ABC BOOK AND *THEY, SHE, HE: EASY AS ABC*

Unrestrained by the limitations of normative plot structures, ABC books may forego conflict and resolution narrative strategies altogether, allowing for a unique opportunity to only display iterations of joy. Even in her critical assessment of "happiness" in *The Promise of Happiness*, Sara Ahmed argues, "There are of course good reasons for telling stories about queer happiness, in response to and as a response to the very presumption that a queer life is necessarily and inevitably an unhappy life" (94).[4] All marginalized people and marginalized communities, including marginalized children, deserve joy and joyous depictions of themselves in children's literature—and ABC books. While *M Is for Mustache* introduces each letter of the alphabet with phrases such as "A is for" (Hernandez 2), *They, She, He* uses children's first names to read out the alphabet, such as "Zahara zooms in and out" (Gonzalez and Smith-Gonzalez 29). They both, in their uniquely ludic style, portray joyous queer, trans, nonbinary, and gender-nonconforming experiences among loving communities of color.

Happy, fearless children grace each cover. The child on *M Is for Mustache*'s cover joyfully displays their rainbow pride in a ruffled rainbow dress. Dark brown hair flies about, loosely pulled back with a bouncing-stars headband, while a brown, drawn-on mustache frames the smiling child. They hold a rainbow pinwheel and banner in one hand and appear to be holding someone else's hand just off the page (see figure 12.1). In contrast, the cover of *They, She, He* features four rambunctious children of color dancing about, their black and brown complexions dressed in various shades of purple set against the white backdrop. At least one of them appears visibly disabled, depicted through their arm braces. Another child shakes a maraca (see figure 12.2). Both picture books tell us they are alphabet books, using "ABC" within each title.

Figure 12.1. The cover of *M Is for Mustache: A Pride ABC Book* depicts a child in rainbow flair with a drawn-on mustache. *Source*: Hernandez, M.

Although the titles and covers inform readers that *M Is for Mustache* will focus on lesbian, gay, bisexual, trans, queer, plus (LGBTQ+) pride and *They, She, He,* on pronouns and gender identity, each does so from a queer and trans of color political framework that prioritizes coalitional politics. Here, I mean the praxis of identifying with and working alongside others who may or may not share all your experiences or identities but still fall under the umbrella of "queer and trans of color." Or, as José Esteban Muñoz theorizes, "This desire to be with, and to be alongside in the face of the various enclosures that consume us, is all part of why the language of commonness takes shape" (*Sense of Brown* 140). Applying this to our two ABC books, they each visually and textually create a world of "color"—in this case, communities of color, brought together through their shared experiences and identities, while still appreciating that each character is uniquely distinct, just like each letter of the alphabet is different but a letter, nonetheless. Simultaneously, as Sara Ahmed notes, "While sharing is often described as participation in something (we share this or that thing, or we have this or that thing in common), and even as the joy of taking part, sharing also involves division, or the ownership of parts. To have a share in something is to be invested in the value of that thing" (*Queer*

Figure 12.2. The cover of *They, She, He: Easy as ABC* depicts four rambunctious children dancing. One is depicted with glasses and arm braces, and another shakes a maraca. *Source*: Gonzalez and Smith-Gonzalez.

Phenomenology 123). In this manner, each letter, like individuals within a community, makes up and becomes invested in the whole alphabet. Thus, all the letters—and, by extension, characters—of each picture book function alongside each other, intertwined and invested in the coalitional, communal, or collective well-being of one another.

The shared space occupied by the letters, characters, and communities looks strikingly different within each ABC book. Not only is the color palate different—one emphasizes rainbows, while the other emphasizes purple—but also *M Is for Mustache* is firmly located within Toronto, Canada, whereas there is no sense of time or place in *They, She, He*. Each letter in *M Is for Mustache* pertains to a detail from a specific day and event—Toronto Pride—introduced through a child and their mother. We are told that "A is for Ally, which me and mama try to be every day by speaking up for people who need someone to be on their side" (Hernandez, *M* 2). To the right, the letter *B* informs readers it is "Pride Day" (3). Other clues throughout the book, such as "C is for colours" and "Y is for Yonge Street" (4, 26), position the book in Toronto. Notably, Steven M. Kates and Russell W. Belk's ethnography of Toronto's Pride parade tells us that "the parade does not travel on Church Street in the heart of the gay ghetto. Rather, it leaves the community and takes over a main Toronto street outside of the ghetto (Yonge Street).... This route symbolically takes gay pride out of the ghetto and flaunts it in front of a wildly cheering crowd of straights and gays alike" (397–98). By including Yonge Street, Hernandez is identifying a specific place and, with it, invoking its historical significance for local LGBTQ+ communities. Within the book, the child narrator functions as both participant and spectator. The illustration depicts the child propped up on the street sign that reads "Yonge St." with three rainbow flags draped alongside nearby windows (Hernandez, *M* 26). However, the child also participates in the march in prior pages and even within the text of this one, noting how they too are cheered on.

In contrast, *They, She, He*'s characters exist or can exist at all times, in all places, marked only by their use of English. Gonzalez and Smith-Gonzalez open with a two-page spread that emphasizes their focus on pronouns. A character waves a banner with the words "They! they! They! they! New friends are everywhere waiting to play!" (Gonzalez and Smith-Gonzalez, *They, She, He* 2–3). This child is joined by three more who dance about the page encircling the following:

> Out on the dance floor **we** love to sing **they**.
> **They** is a way to let everyone be.
> No one left out and everyone free.
> Then when **we**'re friends, **we** sing **they, she, he, ze**.
> Making it easy as a-b-c-d. (2; emphasis original)

The words in bold above are visually set aside on the page or enhanced through color; whereas the text is predominantly black, these are in purple. In subsequent pages, they mark the first initial of each child's name along with their chosen pronouns. Aside from the children and the letters of the alphabet, all the backdrops are white or blank space. Here whiteness functions not as overbearing or symbolic of white privilege or normativity but as an opportunity for readers to situate the characters within their own lives and environments—as in space that is yet to be filled in or completed.

Within both ABC books, the chosen families function as anchors for specific letters of the alphabet. Within *M Is for Mustache*, the protagonist's chosen family includes a group of Titas, which Hernandez described as "Tita, our Filipino word for Auntie, which is a kind of chosen family I am lucky to have so many of" (21). They include Titas Gein, Audrey, Lisa, Charm, Jazz, Fay, and Kim. In an interview, Hernandez shares that each character was based on a real person within her own chosen family at the time of the book's publication (personal interview). These individuals represent many local and international community leaders and performers. Tita Fay, for example, was modeled after JP, or Fay Slift, a Toronto drag queen who is part of the Drag Story Time duo Fay and Fluffy and "an educator with the TDSB," or Toronto District School Board ("About Us"; see also Hernandez, personal interview). Another, Tita Audrey, was based on writer, actor, and director Audrey Dwyer, whose play *Calpurnia* won the Cayle Chernin Award, while Tita Kim was inspired by Kim Katrin, an educator, writer, artist, and cofounder of the People Project, "an initiative to bring forth local and international community development for queer and trans folks of color and their allies through alternative education, art-activism and collaboration" ("Kim Katrin Milan").[5] These contemporary figures gesture not only to chosen family but also to community leaders and role models impacting current queer and trans of color movements. Hernandez also incorporates the legendary Black trans and nonbinary activist Marsha P. Johnson as a way to honor intergenerational legacies and communities. Through the child protagonist, we learn: "F is for the Flowers that Tita Audrey puts in my hair. She tells me stories of a very important person named Marsha P. Johnson, who wore them just like this" (Hernandez, *M* 7). Johnson is depicted within a gold frame atop a rainbow table, resembling an altar in her honor.

Chosen family and gender identity also overlap within *They, She, He*. Whereas "they" or "ze" are usually used as an additive to "he or she," Gonzalez and Smith-Gonzalez topple this by not only including but beginning with and centering nonbinary children and their pronouns. For example, "they" is not only the first word in the title, but also the first word one reads (e.g., in the previously mentioned banner) and the first pronoun used by a child within the alphabet. Under the letter *A*, the text reads: "**Ari** loves to arabesque. / **They** hold **their** pose with ease" (Gonzalez and Smith-Gonzalez, *They, She, He* 4; emphasis original). Like "they," "ze" has also become an easily recognizable gender-neutral pronoun. Within *They, She, He*, at least three children use the pronoun, beginning with the letter *I* and the character named Indigo. Other children who might identify with "ze" include Zahara and Sky, the latter of whom is open to numerous pronouns, noting "**All** the pronouns are right" (22; emphasis original).

In addition to "they" or "ze," however, the coauthors incorporate "tree" as a lesser-known but equally viable pronoun. At least two children use "tree" as their pronoun. The first wears a beanie with hair parted into two long braids, drumming with one hand while the other flares upward. We are told that "**Diego** drums and dances. / **Tree** has all the sounds" (Gonzalez and Smith-Gonzalez, *They, She, He* 7; emphasis original). The second child, whose name is Ocean, has equally long hair and wears a dress. Gonzalez first established "tree" as a pronoun in her earlier works for children, such as *Call Me Tree* (2014), as well as in *They, She, He, Me: Free to Be!* (2017), cowritten with Smith-Gonzalez.[6] Their ABC book (and second coauthored collaboration) further solidifies "tree" as a possible pronoun option for readers.

Gonzalez and Smith-Gonzalez's gender philosophy also allows children to use more than one pronoun. For example, Jorge, who "jams to jazzy tunes" uses "he" and "they," whereas Marley, who "is a star mermaid," prefers "he" and "she" (Gonzalez and Smith-Gonzalez, *They, She, He* 13, 16). Names can also be used as pronouns (e.g., Brody), whereas other letters serve to challenge the gender commonly associated with names or play with gender-neutral names, such as Rene or Kelly. As evidenced above, each letter of the alphabet is linked to a uniquely gendered child, most of whom might fall under the larger categories of genderqueer, gender fluid, pangender, nonbinary, or transgender. In doing so, Gonzalez and Smith-Gonzalez provide a text where "inclusive pronouns are learned alongside the alphabet in this joyously illustrated take on the classic ABC book," as stated on the copyright page. Learning pronouns alongside the alphabet suggests they are both equally important for children. Adults are also a target audience. And while they may be likely to already know the alphabet, their greatest feat will be unlearning what they have previously learned about pronouns.

Authors and illustrators worked in tandem to incorporate disability within their respective ABC books. Within *M Is for Mustache*, accessibility at Pride is most evident with the letter *H*, which the child protagonist shares is "for Hands, which we use to sign our happiness in sign language when our Deaf friends march past" (Hernandez 9). The illustration includes three characters, each one signing (the protagonist, "Happy"; mom, "Pride"; and Tita Fay, "applause")—collectively wishing everyone a "Happy Pride!" Characters are also visually disabled within *They, She, He*, such as Yoli, who uses arm braces, and Viola, shown in a wheelchair. Also on the cover, we are told that "**Yoli** yells

YES! Joyously. / **Their** voice becomes the song," whereas "Viola's a volcano. / **Her** power's in **her** ground" (28, 25; emphasis original). As Leah Lakshmi Piepzna-Samarasinha writes, "Because of the work of disability justice, more and more people are coming out as disabled earlier.... This joyful, self-determined claiming of disabled cultures changes how many of us we think we are." Within each ABC book, disabilities are presented as strengths. Moreover, just because these are the only characters who might "appear" visibly disabled does not mean others are not.

Both *They, She, He* and *M Is for Mustache* end with scenes of community, reiterating the importance of chosen family. The final page of *M Is for Mustache* has no text—only an illustration of the protagonist being propped up by their chosen family (Hernandez 28). This illustration is a replica of the one on page 21, which celebrates *T* for "Tita." Meanwhile, *They, She, He* culminates in all the children—all twenty-six of them—coming together for a dance party (Gonzalez and Smith-Gonzalez 30–31). They fill most of the two-page spread, except for the center of the right page, where readers are invited to join: "Now's your chance. We need your moves. Join the dance. There's always room" (30–31). This invitation suggests that the characters and, by extension, the authors have made room—blank, empty space on the page—for the reader to literally draw or color themselves "into existence" alongside the other characters.

LGBTQ+ studies—specifically, nonbinary and transgender children's literature—has expanded considerably since Jody Norton's "Transchildren and the Discipline of Children's Literature" (1999).[7] While many contemporary picture books include a coming-out point of reference, "in which the transgender character is socially transitioning" (Capuzza 329), transgender, nonbinary, and gender-nonconforming characters are present across *M Is for Mustache* and *They, She, He* without having their gender identity be a source of conflict within the narrative. Instead, layered within each letter of the alphabet are blissful moments of sheer joy and celebration.

QUEER AND TRANS OF COLOR POLITICS OFF THE PAGE

The authors' ideal readers include not only children and adults but also the authors' own children and the child versions of themselves. Gonzalez and Smith-Gonzalez dedicate the text to their children: "For Sky and Zai, may you always be free! —M+M" (*They, She, He*). They also reimagine their own childhoods, noting,

> Maya makes the art and words. She sings the song to life.
> Matthew dreams and tinkers. He makes the work tight.
> Together they make books for the kids they used to be.
> And for their own two kids so all kids can grow free! (33)

Although Hernandez does not name the protagonist or mother within the picture book's text, she does provide textual and visual clues within the book. For example, her dedication reads, "To Arden: For you, I march. Beside you, I will always be proud" (Hernandez, *M*). Moreover, within the illustration on the page for the letter *N* for "Names," a brown hand writes "Arden" alongside the names of Titas mentioned throughout. Additionally, in interviews and public talks, she identifies herself and her daughter as the main characters: "I think often of how easy it was for my daughter to be proud during our marches, with Stetson hat and bicycle riding down Yonge street," Hernandez reminisced ("My Queer Children's Book").[8] "If only it were that easy for us adults," she wished, "to be free of oppressive thinking, to be truly accepting of others."

Since potential censorship battles are always a possibility, Hernandez was forced to contend with this as well. For Hernandez, this occurred at her own daughter's school. She recalls,

> I was excited as heck when the book was finally published and printed, in my hands and ready to show the world. Only—not everyone in the world wanted to see it, and most certainly not the school within my district. Marlie Delicieux, Vice Principal at Charlottetown Junior Public School said "not now" citing that the timing would likely create a backlash due to the introduction of Ontario's new progressive sex education curriculum. (Hernandez, "My Queer Children's Book")

Instead of welcoming the author, school administrators were more concerned with their desires to not be perceived as too queer friendly. This case demonstrates the limitations of an "ally"—or, at least, the rhetoric of allyship—rather than the actual efforts of political accomplices.[9] Noting the administrators' contradictions, Hernandez continued,

> My heart was heavy. I just wanted to scream from the top of a mountain "Holy jeez, it's about a girl on a bicycle celebrating her family!" I was incredulous. In the midst of Pride season, I thought how ridiculous it was that we were given the brief privilege to march and be who we are, but god forbid we sit in a classroom and read a book to children in hetero-normative families. I thought

of how ridiculous it is to have such a courageous and progressive sex education curriculum and have administrative staff reveal their own phobias while attempting to implement it.

The outrage and trauma caused by this experience should not be taken lightly. Hernandez was forced to contend with not only disappointment but a reevaluation of her trust in her own daughter's school. However, experiences such as these have not stopped her from sharing the book with receptive audiences.

Meanwhile, *They, She, He* has gained national attention as a banned book in states such as Texas and Pennsylvania ("PEN America Index"; "Banned in the USA"). It was also incorporated into the Human Rights Campaign Foundation's "Welcoming Schools" curriculum. It is featured within a PDF lesson plan titled "*They, She, He, Easy as ABC*: Understanding Names, Pronouns and Gender Expression," designated for children in grades kindergarten through second, which was then featured at the 2021 National Association for Media Literacy Education conference. Its inclusion also caught the attention of at least one person from the Right who opposed its content.[10] Similarly, while most of the comments embedded within the reviews on Amazon are favorable, a couple use the excuse of "poor grammar" to justify a one-star rating. While reviews are often biased and should not be taken too seriously, what is interesting is how these two reviews justify their bias through the guise of grammar: "Absolute rubbish. The Grammar is incorrect. Very confusing" and "Poor grammar, confusing" (Dembovsky; Mike). The confusion occurs not because the book is confusing but rather because it contradicts the reviewer's own gender bias. In this manner, the book has been effective in challenging the gender binary and society's limited view on gender. In an interview for *Raising Luminaries: Books for Littles*, Gonzalez states: "When you're claiming your power instead of upholding the status quo, the stress is real. Your heart and body are on the line. . . . The stronger we are in ourselves, the more we pass that on to our kids. Use these books as seeds—something small and potent that can take root and grow deep within" (Ray). Pronouns beyond "he" or "she" continue to remain controversial, which is why it should also not surprise us that it made national headlines when *Merriam-Webster* added "they" as a pronoun to their dictionary in 2019.[11] Perhaps, in the near future, we might also see "tree" as another pronoun option included within the dictionary.

Taken together, both *M Is for Mustache* and *They, She, He* provide models for engaging queer and trans of color aesthetics of joy within alphabet picture books. Their focus on representing overly joyful queer and trans of color children does not constitute, nor should it be understood as, a denial of the injustices or prejudices that exist and that children no doubt will encounter if they have not already. Certainly, picture books that directly address and depict social inequalities exist and are absolutely necessary. Instead, what I am advocating for is a balance between learning about our world and imagining another possible world—one without prejudices or injustices. Through these utopic representations of joy, we might be able to not only imagine but actually create these in our near future. And like Muñoz cautions, once we get "there," it will no longer be utopic since our concerns would have changed and other things will be necessary then (*Cruising Utopia* 29). Most urgently, what matters is that *M Is for Mustache: A Pride ABC Book* and *They, She, He: Easy as ABC* provide possible paths for the "here and now" of alphabet books.

NOTES

1. For a brief history of ABC books, see Hahn 1–2. For the pedagogical use of ABC books, see Nodelman. For a general history of children's literature, including ABC books or alphabets and primers, see Hunt.

2. The American Library Association, which compiles data on book challenges, notes, "Overwhelmingly, we're seeing these challenges come from organized censorship groups," whose aim is to "suppress the voices of those traditionally excluded from our nation's conversations, such as people in the LGBTQIA+ community or people of color" ("American Library Association Reports").

3. Although numbers are gradually improving, the majority of LGBTQ+-themed children's picture books are overwhelmingly white and cisgender (Lester; Crawley 36; Capuzza 327).

4. For an extensive discussion of happiness as a discursive and political field, see Ahmed, *Promise of Happiness*. Ahmed begins to develop some of her arguments on affect within her earlier works; see *Cultural Politics of Emotion*.

5. Visit each of their personal websites for more details. Additionally, Tita Charm is modeled after Charm Torres, an astrologer; Tita Jazz, after Jazz Kamal, a martial artist and trainer; Tita Gein, after Gein Wong, an artist and performer; and Tita Lisa, after Lisa Morrison, whose drag name is Lizzy Strange.

6. I discuss *Call Me Tree* and Reflection Press's gender philosophies in greater detail within my book *Coloring into Existence: Queer of Color Worldmaking in Children's Literature* (2023); see Millán 66–154. I also mention both ABC books within these pages.

7. E.g., see Miller, "Little Queers"; Miller "Little Queer."

8. Hernandez documented her experiences in a personal essay published online; see Hernandez, "My Queer Children's Book."

9. For the differences between being an accomplice as opposed to an ally, see the zine created by IndigenousAction.org "Accomplices Not Allies." See also Clemens, who has applied the differences to educational settings.

10. E.g., see Sailer, who is a member of the National Association of Scholars.

11. The news appeared throughout TV and print media, such as NBC and the *New York Times*, among many others; headlines included "*Merriam-Webster* Adds Nonbinary 'They' Pronoun to Dictionary" (2019) and "'They' Is the Word of the Year, *Merriam-Webster* Says, Noting Its Singular Rise" (2019).

WORKS CITED

"ABC's for Boys (Alphabet Book, Baby Book, Children's Book, Toddler Book) Hardcover – Illustrated, December 30, 2015." *Amazon*, https://a.co/d/7wfC9SZ. Accessed 28 Mar. 2024.
"ABC's for Girls (Alphabet Book, Baby Book, Children's Book, Toddler Book) Hardcover – December 30, 2016." *Amazon*, https://a.co/d/7zG07Bj. Accessed 28 Mar. 2024.
"About." *Catherine Hernandez*, https://www.catherinehernandezcreates.com/. Accessed 19 Feb. 2024.
"About Us." *Fay and Fluffy's Storytime*, https://fayandfluffy.com/about/. Accessed 19 Feb. 2024.
"Accomplices Not Allies: Abolishing the Ally Industrial Complex." *Indigenous Action*, 4 May 2014, https://www.indigenousaction.org/accomplices-not-allies-abolishing-the-ally-industrial-complex/comment-page-1/.
Ahmed, Sara. *The Cultural Politics of Emotion*. Routledge, 2004.
Ahmed, Sara. *The Promise of Happiness*. Duke UP, 2010.
Ahmed, Sara. *Queer Phenomenology: Orientations, Objects, Others*. Duke UP, 2006.
"American Library Association Reports Record Number of Demands to Censor Library Books and Materials in 2022." *American Library Association*, 22. Mar. 2023, http://www.ala.org/news/press-releases/2023/03/record-book-bans-2022.
"Banned in the USA: Rising School Book Bans Threaten Free Expression and Students' First Amendment Rights." *PEN America*, April 2022, https://pen.org/banned-in-the-usa/#what.
Capuzza, Jamie C. "'T' Is for 'Transgender': An Analysis of Children's Picture Books Featuring Transgender Protagonists and Narrators." *Journal of Children and Media*, vol. 14, no. 3, 2020, pp. 324–42.
Clemens, Colleen. "Ally or Accomplice? The Language of Activism." *Teaching Tolerance*, 5 June 2017, https://www.tolerance.org/magazine/ally-or-accomplice-the-language-of-activism.
Coats, Karen. "P Is for Patriarchy: Re-imaging the Alphabet." *Children's Literature Association Quarterly*, vol. 25, no. 2, 2000, pp. 88–97.
Combs, Bobbie. *ABC: A Family Alphabet Book*. Illustrated by Brian Rappa and Desiree Rappa, Tow Lives, 2000.
Crawley, Stephen Adam. "Be Who You Are: Exploring Representations of Transgender Children in Picturebooks." *Journal of Children's Literature*, vol. 43, no. 2, 2017, pp. 28–41.
Dembovsky, Tanya. Review of *They, She, He: Easy as ABC*, by Maya Christina Gonzalez and Matthew Smith-Gonzalez. *Amazon*, 21 Aug. 2019, https://www.amazon.com/product-reviews/1945289171/ref=acr_dp_hist_1?ie=UTF8&filterByStar=one_star&reviewerType=all_reviews#reviews-filter-bar.
Ewing, Chana Ginelle. *An ABC of Equality*. Illustrated by Paulina Morgan, Frances Lincoln Children's Books, 2019.
Firebaugh, Marisa. "Posts." *Instagram*, 2024, https://www.instagram.com/sketchesbythesea/?hl=en.
Gonzalez, Maya C. *Call Me Tree/Llámame árbol*. Illustrated by Gonzalez, Children's Book Press, 2014.
Gonzalez, Maya C., and Matthew Smith-Gonzalez. *They, She, He: Easy as ABC*. Illustrated by Gonzalez, Reflection Press, 2019.
Gonzalez, Maya C., and Matthew Smith-Gonzalez. *They, She, He, Me: Free to Be!* Illustrated by Gonzalez, Reflection Press, 2017.
Hahn, Daniel. *The Oxford Companion to Children's Literature*. 2nd ed., Oxford UP, 2015.
Harmon, Amy. "'They' Is the Word of the Year, *Merriam-Webster* Says, Noting Its Singular Rise." *New York Times*, 10 Dec. 2019, updated 3 Nov. 2021, https://www.nytimes.com/2019/12/10/us/merriam-webster-they-word-year.html.

Hernandez, Catherine. *M Is for Mustache: A Pride ABC Book*. Illustrated by Marisa Firebaugh, Flamingo Rampant Press, 2015.

Hernandez, Catherine. Personal interview. September 9, 2023.

Hernandez, Catherine. "Why Was My Queer Children's Book Too Radical for Kindergarteners?" *Huffington Post*, 23 June 2015, updated 24 June 2016, https://www.huffpost.com/archive/ca/entry/why-was-my-queer-childrens-book-too-radical-for-kindergarteners_b_7640328.

Hunt, Peter, editor. *Children's Literature: An Illustrated History*. Oxford UP, 1995.

Kates, Steven M., and Russell W. Belk. "The Meanings of Lesbian and Gay Pride Day: Resistance through Consumption and Resistance to Consumption." *Journal of Contemporary Ethnography*, vol. 30, no. 4, 2001, pp. 392–429.

"Kim Katrin Milan." *TED*, https://www.ted.com/speakers/kim_katrin_milan. Accessed 15 Mar. 2024.

Kracht, Michael. *ABC's for Boys*. Illustrated by Kracht, Majella Publishing, 2015.

Kracht, Michael. *ABC's for Girls*. Illustrated by Kracht, Majella Publishing, 2017.

Lester, Jasmine Z. "Homonormativity in Children's Literature: An Intersectional Analysis of Queer-Themed Picture Books." *Journal of LGBT Youth*, vol. 11, no. 3, 2014, pp. 244–75.

Mike. Review of *They, She, He: Easy as ABC*, by Maya Christina Gonzalez and Matthew Smith-Gonzalez. *Amazon*, 4 Aug. 2019, https://www.amazon.com/product-reviews/1945289171/ref=acr_dp_hist_1?ie=UTF8&filterByStar=one_star&reviewerType=all_reviews#reviews-filter-bar.

Millán, Isabel. *Coloring into Existence: Queer of Color Worldmaking in Children's Literature*. New York UP, 2023.

Miller, Jennifer. "For the Little Queers: Imagining Queerness in 'New' Queer Children's Literature. *Journal of Homosexuality*, vol. 66, no. 12, 2019, pp. 1645–70.

Miller, Jennifer. "A Little Queer: Ambivalence and the Work of Gender Play in Children's Literature." *Heroes, Heroines, and Everything in Between: Challenging Gender and Sexuality Stereotypes in Children's Entertainment Media*, edited by CarrieLynn D. Reinhard and Christopher J. Olson, Lexington Books, 2017, pp. 35–50.

Morrison, Eleanor. *C Is for Consent*. Illustrated by Faye Orlove, Phonics with Finn, 2018.

Muñoz, José Esteban. *Cruising Utopia: The Then and There of Queer Futurity*. New York UP, 2009.

Muñoz, José Esteban. *The Sense of Brown*. Edited by Joshua Chambers-Letson and Tavia Nyong'o, Duke UP, 2020.

Nagara, Innosanto. *A Is for Activist*. Illustrated by Nagara, Seven Stories Press, 2013.

Nodelman, Perry. "A Is for . . . What? The Function of Alphabet Books." *Journal of Early Childhood Literacy*, vol. 1, no. 3, 2001, pp. 235–53.

Norcia, Megan A. "'E' Is for Empire? Challenging the Imperial Legacy of *An ABC for Baby Patriots* (1899)." *Children's Literature Association Quarterly*, vol. 42, no. 2, 2017, pp. 125–48.

Norton, Jody. "Transchildren and the Discipline of Children's Literature." *The Lion and the Unicorn*, vol. 23, no. 3, 1999, pp. 415–36.

O'Sullivan, Emer. "S Is for Spaniard: The Representation of Foreign Nations in ABCs and Picturebooks." *European Journal of English Studies*, vol. 13, no. 3, 2009, pp. 333–49.

"Our Mission and Values." *Reflection Press*, https://reflectionpress.com/about-us/mission-values/. Accessed 19 Feb. 2024.

"PEN America Index of School Book Bans – 2021–2022." *PEN America*, https://pen.org/banned-book-list-2021-2022/#:~:text=From%20July%202021%20to%20June,affecting%201%2C648%20unique%20book%20titles. Accessed 19 Feb. 2024.

Piepzna-Samarasinha, Leah Lakshmi. *The Future Is Disabled: Prophecies, Love Notes and Mourning Songs*. E-book ed., Arsenal Pulp Press, 2022.

Ray, Ashia. "Dismantling Cissexism in Kidlit: Maker Spotlight with Maya and Matthew of Reflection Press." *Raising Luminaries: Books for Littles*, 28 Mar. 2019, updated 2 Oct. 2021, https://booksforlittles.com/reflection-press/.

Russell, David L. *Literature for Children: A Short Introduction*. 5th ed., Pearson Education, 2005.

Sailer, John D. "Media Literacy's False Promise: Another Social-Justice-Steeped Pedagogy Is Gaining Ground—and Like the Others, It Won't Help Students Understand the World" *City Journal*, 16 Aug. 2021, https://www.city-journal.org/article/media-literacys-false-promise.

Sketches by the Sea. https://www.sketchesbythesea.com. Accessed 19 Feb. 2024.

Taylor, Mary Agnes. "From Apples to Abstraction in Alphabet Books." *Children's Literature in Education*, vol. 9, no. 4, 1978, pp. 173–81.

Trammell, Kendall. "Merriam-Webster Adds the Nonbinary Pronoun 'They' to its Dictionary." *CNN* 18 Sept. 2019, https://www.cnn.com/2019/09/17/us/merriam-webster-nonbinary-pronoun-they-trnd/index.html.

Webb, M. L. *The GayBCs*. Illustrated by Webb, Quirk Books, 2019.

CHAPTER 13

CHILDREN'S IMAGINATION AND THE DESIRE FOR SOMETHING DIFFERENT
Nonhuman Subjects in LGBTQ+ Children's Literature and the Possibility of More Just Futures

Caitlin Howlett

INTRODUCTION

Nonhuman characters have long been a staple of children's literature, as has been the use of animals or other natural objects and beings to help children (and sometimes adults) make sense of the world. It has only been more recently, however, that nonhuman characters have been called upon to support exploration of the nuances of identity difference and politics in contemporary culture, especially around lesbian, gay, bisexual, trans, queer, plus (LGBTQ+) representation, equity, and dignity. Indeed, this small but ever-growing body of LGBTQ+ children's literature is, according to the authors of such books, a valuable way of engaging children and students in the quest to "help other parents, adults and educators to start conversations with their kids about diversity, gender identity, and the importance of being yourself and a good friend" (Walton, "Teachers Guide"). Nonetheless, the use of nonhuman subjects for such purposes is complicated by histories of dehumanizing accounts of queer life.[1] In this piece, I explore these complications and offer a framework for navigating picture books' nonhuman subjects with children in a way that resists the possibility of further dehumanization while also helping to expand children's imagination about who they can be(come). At stake is sustaining the political value of such books, particularly in a society wherein the political nature of education—and the legitimacy of the extant hierarchies of being and knowing upon which such politics rest—is hotly contested. This chapter therefore asserts the potential for such literature to create openings into new and different future worlds—an act that is essential to any social justice project.

I will begin by offering a brief and generalized history of the idea of the "human" in queer history, focusing mainly on the United States, and the centrality of dehumanization to that history to contextualize the use of nonhuman subjects in LGBTQ+ children's picture books. Then, I analyze three examples of LGBTQ+-related children's picture books: *Introducing Teddy* by Jessica Walton, *The Prince and the Frog* by Olly Pike, and *Neither* by Airlie Anderson. These three books were chosen because they stand out from other LGBTQ+ children's picture books in using nonhuman—yet still living—beings rather than animate objects. This matters because it means we can discuss interspecies relationships without reifying a false distinction between human and nonhuman as a difference *between living and nonliving beings* (e.g., *Red* [2015], by Michael Hall, features a main character that is an animate crayon).

My intent here is to query about the ambiguity of the idea of the "human" within histories of queer life by discussing its vulnerability to appropriation for political purposes that are arguably aligned with politics that aim to suppress, exclude, and even eradicate queer lives. This includes addressing an important tension about the idea of difference: one's difference can be used to affirm their humanity or to articulate a lack or failure to adhere to the constructed and malleable standards ascribed to the category of "human." Using insights from queer and queer of color theories and critiques, which offer different ways of challenging political and normative assumptions made about sex, gender, and sexuality, I argue that using a *speculative* framework to contextualize the discussions about sex, gender, and sexuality may help in foregrounding the political implications of such texts. More specifically, I humbly offer a suggestion as to how readers might approach such books as the political artifacts that they are, utilizing a speculative framework to cultivate curiosity, questioning, and imagination of a radical kind.

DEVIANCE AND DEHUMANIZATION: HUMAN PROBLEMS

Be it animals, toys, or any other mobile or immobile being or object, children's picture books regularly use nonhuman subjects to facilitate discussions about topics like sex, gender, and sexuality with children. However, there is a long history of equating queerness in any form with the less than human, if not inhuman altogether. This is a two-pronged concern, then: to ask about the meaning and significance of the use of nonhuman subjects here is to ask about *both* the potential for further dehumanization *and* the potential for creating an altogether less violent world. The following brief and generalized history of queer lives in the United States and beyond demonstrates the necessity of attending to the status of the human in these children's books.

There are many ways to talk about queer history as well as how these histories are shaped by debates about what it means to be a "human" or, more specifically, what constitutes "normal" "human" sexuality, sex, and gender. For many scholars, European colonization across various continents transformed the idea of the "human" into a mechanism for enforcing violence against those determined by colonialist logics to be less than human. Sylvia Wynter's work on the "human" shows how the very distinction upon which Western concepts of "human" rest is also where the "human" resides: in the ability to think "rationally." Under colonization, a perceived lack of rationality justified inhuman treatment; failure to adhere to such norms justified abuse, enslavement, and murder. One mark of a lack of rationality was a failure to perform and practice kinship or family relations in the way that colonizers practiced. Any deviation from the traditional Victorian model of the heterosexual nuclear family structured by stereotypical gender norms was sufficient for justifying inhumane treatment against queer people and groups.

Similarly, determinations of one's "civility" were often based on the establishment of a sturdy link between norms about intelligence and behavioral norms, such that to be civil was to be rational and to be deserving of a full life, whereas to be deemed uncivilized was enough to justify oppression, exemplified in the treatment of Indigenous groups around the world by colonial powers and actors. Further, strictly limiting access to the category of "human" helped to normalize and justify among those in power the institution of slavery, including the theft and sale of African people to slave traders and owners, as well as sexual- and gender-based violence. As Saidiya V. Hartman argues, one of the ways that colonization and slavery were justified by colonizers and enslavers was by reducing them to less than human in an effort to minimize, if not condone, the violence they enacted. The label "human" was therefore *not* simply extended to include presently or formerly enslaved people but instead was used to "tether, bind, and oppress" through exclusion (Hartman 5). Importantly, most any sexual behavior of colonized and enslaved groups was regularly used as evidence for their lack of humanity.

The emergence of modern medicine and science in the mid to late 1800s coincided with the "end" of slavery, but this mostly served to bolster the legitimacy of defining what it means to be "human" through an obsession with defining "deviance" and "perversity," including and especially anything related to gender, sex, sexuality (Foucault). It is also well documented that the study of human sexuality was founded upon and continues to be implicated in and by the construction of racial categories and the maintenance of racism (D'emilio and Freedman; Terry; Somerville; Kunzel). The *erasure* of queer and nonwhite people from the dominant histories of the United States is one of the most important examples of how the selective use of the "human" continues to shape queer politics today. As Ladelle McWhorter writes, "Historically, those positioned to manage human populations and human evolution were the ones to define key terms —such as 'human' and 'species'—and they did so in ways many queer activists would likely find objectionable" (75).

This thinking has had many pathologizing and stigmatizing effects on queer life. For example, as Roderick A. Ferguson details, the very concept of the "American citizen" was derived through the assumption of sexual normativity and, more specifically, the privileging of marriage and traditional nuclear-family formations as signals of one's access to the benefit of citizenship. This is evidenced in the use of marriage as the vehicle for determining property ownership, wealth distribution, and, eventually, access to health care, as well as reproductive rights and tax benefits. Similarly, Susan Stryker argues that gatekeeping around what constitutes "health" was and is used to pathologize trans* people as deviating from sex and gender binaries were explained away as signs of a lack of health and well-being (162). Indeed, scientists, medical specialists, politicians, and other public figures even went so far as to suggest that these deviations were indicative of a kind of disability or feeblemindedness. And the word "queer" was itself used as a euphemism for deviancy in the 1900s precisely because it signaled a deviation from the standard definition of "human" (Kunzel 1564).

These histories show how "human" was defined and used to maintain violence and reveal the necessity of engaging with the history of the idea of the "human" in discussing gender, sex, and sexual identity today. Without this contextualization, the politics can be so easily *neglected* that the possibility of achieving any authors' intended goals related to social justice is undermined.

THREE BOOKS, THREE TENSIONS

In order to demonstrate the impact of these histories on children's literature, this section will explore the way that they come into play in three different children's books released in the decade prior to the time of this writing. The first book I want to discuss is *Introducing Teddy* (2016) by Jessica Walton. Written as "a simple, positive story with a transgender character that she could read to her young son" (Walton, "Teachers Guide"), *Introducing Teddy* is the story of a teddy bear, first named Thomas, and the teddy bear's companion, Errol, a male-identifying human child. The book begins with an account of the usually playful and happy duo having an uncharacteristically bad day: suddenly, Thomas "doesn't feel like playing" with Errol (Walton, *Introducing Teddy* 9). Errol tries to find ways to cheer Thomas up, including by doing some of their favorite things, but Errol can't help but notice that Thomas remains "sad" nonetheless (10). Finally, after receiving reassurance that Errol will be his friend no matter what, Thomas tells Errol, "I need to be myself, Errol. In my heart, I've always known that I'm a girl teddy, not a boy teddy. I wish my name was Tilly, not Thomas" (15). Much to the teddy's relief, Errol is quick to respond by saying, "I don't care if you're a girl teddy or a boy teddy! What matters is that you are my friend" (17).

With the duo now feeling better, Errol calls his (human) friend, Ava, to ask her if she'd like to play with him and his teddy, and she soon arrives accompanied by her own friend, a robot. Ava's arrival leads to the reintroduction of the teddy as Tilly. We also learn about the other changes Tilly desires and that these changes are both important yet uncompromising of her value and dignity. For example, Tilly decides to turn her bowtie into a bow for her hair, a significant act that is further emphasized by Ava's support of Tilly *and* Ava's residual decision to ditch her *own* bow altogether. The group resumes their usual activities, and the book ends with a reiteration of the moral of this story: an image of the teddy labeled with her new name, Tilly.

The Prince and the Frog (2018) is a twist on the classic tale "The Frog Prince." Princess Caroline and Prince Oskar are siblings *and* great friends, and both are invested in ensuring that the other finds love. Oskar, however, is the one who is most eager to find "someone whom he could share his life with," an eagerness explicitly born of his own love of fairy tales (Pike 8). Soon enough, the duo comes across a frog who turns out to be a human trying to become human again, which, in true fairytale fashion, can only be secured by a kiss from his true love. They all quickly assume that it will be Caroline's kiss that breaks the spell. However, after initially rejecting this idea, stating that "I'm not even sure I like kissing humans, let alone frogs," she kisses the frog's head, but no transformation ensues (15). Oskar reacts by insisting on helping his sister fall in love with the frog despite Caroline asking, "Oskar, you do realise you can't *make* people fall in love?" (18). They learn in time, though, that Oskar has more in common with the frog, whose name is finally revealed as Alex, than does Caroline. Upon noticing this, Caroline becomes more aware of "how they both looked very happy, and how they were both very good at listening to each other" (26). While they do not have *everything* in common, what they do share grows.

Nonetheless, Oskar still encourages Caroline to try to kiss the frog now that they know each other better, but again, it fails to return Alex to human form. And again, Caroline reminds Oskar that love cannot be forced. The turning point comes when, after expressing how bad Oskar feels that Alex is still a frog, Alex tells Oskar, "You have made me feel very special, and cared for and ... loved" (Pike 35). Caroline gasps and declares, "Oskar ... did you hear that? It's you! You are Alex's true love!" (36). Oskar then kisses Alex, and this time, it works: Alex is human again. In the final pages, a discussion of how the love between Alex and Oskar came to be ensues: they talk about how Oskar "saw Alex for who he really was and not just a little green frog," how they made each other "feel special," and that their love grew because "you were kind and thoughtful, selfless and caring, good at listening and both brought joy to each other's lives" (39). Not to be dismissed is Caroline's own "love story." When asked about it, Caroline tells Oskar and Alex, "I am overjoyed for you both, but we are very different and what is right for you isn't necessarily right for me. Besides, I am already in love ... I love my life ... just the way it is" (42).

The third book is fully inhuman. Set in the "Land of This and That," *Neither* (2018) opens with a depiction of a world of binaries where every being is only ever "this" or "that," "one" or "the other" (Anderson 1–9). More specifically, this land is inhabited by birds and bunnies. However, suddenly, Neither is born; a creature that looks like a mix of rabbit and bird, Neither is told they cannot be both, and because they are neither, they are told they do not fit in. Neither is judged by the others as "not rabbity enough" and "not birdy enough" (13–14). Neither thus embarks on a quest to find "Somewhere Else to fit in" (20). Neither eventually finds a "Somewhere Else": "The Land of All" (20–22). In this land, there are "so many different kinds," Neither exclaims (21). Neither is invited to play with those in this land, but Neither is confused because of their previous experiences, which have taught Neither that their differences are bad. However, Neither is praised by these others as belonging *because* they are different. Then, other creatures from the Land of This and That appear and ask to join the Land of All. Neither reminds them that he had been excluded by them but then says, "Well, this isn't Somewhere Else. This is the Land of All. And everyone fits in here" (30). The story begins again at this point but very differently: "Once upon a time, there were many kinds: this and that, somewhat and whatnot, either, very, sort of, just, rather, a little, neither and both" (31). This time, "all are welcome" (33–34).

Each book presents a somewhat distinct but substantially overlapping view of an imaginary world that does not abide by the rules of identity, by which many of us are still so restricted and confined. This commonality might be due to the authors' similar understandings of what motivated them to write their respective books: a wish to represent identity differences as good, valuable, and desirable in order to create a better, more accepting world. For example, according to the accompanying "Teacher's Notes," written by Walton herself, the intent in writing *Introducing Teddy* was that it "may help other parents, adults and educators to start conversations with their kids about diversity, gender identity, and the importance of being yourself and being a good friend" (1). Likewise, on Olly Pike's website, the children's book author says this about *The Prince and the Frog*: "This brightly illustrated take on a classic fairytale teaches children about same-sex relationships and attraction. Exploring what it means to be in a healthy, loving relationship, it encourages children to listen to others, be kind, and embrace diversity and equality" ("Prince and the Frog"). Further, Pike's general aim across each book they have published is described as "usualising" "different types of people, particularly those who may be LGBTQ+, and ultimately aims to combat homo-, bi- and transphobia before it can even begin" ("Pop'n'Olly"). And though Anderson acknowledges that her book *Neither* has been interpreted by readers as speaking to many identify differences, she writes that she was inspired by an experience with a middle school student in one of her art classes: "One of them had been identifying as female, and over the course of the next year, transitioned to identifying as male. The idea of questioning something as ingrained in our society as gender made me think of my characters and story in a new light" (Adler). She later adds that the one thing that all her readers agree upon, even if they do not associate the story directly with gender identity, is that "it's about inclusion and acceptance." Being yourself, being a good friend, valuing healthy relationships, listening, practicing kindness, embracing diversity, equality, inclusion, acceptance—these encouraged qualities coalesce into a shared, generalizable aim: to improve the conditions under which we live together and make our world more accepting and equitable.

Despite this shared aim, though, there are reasons to be skeptical about whether or not the books necessarily lead to their enactment. First, I question the processes of othering at play in these books. On the one hand, there is the depiction of queer subjects as other than human (exhibited in each book), and on the other hand, there is the divide between human and the nonhuman itself (though not in *Neither*, where there are no humans at all). Certainly not all depictions of difference enact a kind of othering that is inherently concerning, but using them to navigate a conversation with children about difference without asking about difference itself does not necessarily address the politics of power at stake. Even further, why *not* use humans? I think this question is especially important in the context of creating a more representative and/or inclusive body of children's books about gender, sex, and sexual differences. Might the turn to nonhuman subjects to discuss with children topics that have historically been deeply contentious be a way of avoiding such contention? Does this practice move us *too* far away from the human? I am worried that without using an explicitly political approach, the potential of these books to impact social relations is negated.

Finally, how do we ensure we are still talking about the issues of equity and acceptance that are claimed to be at stake when not speaking of people at all? If equity and acceptance are at stake, then these books are explicitly political in nature, but each book, read without context, reads as apolitical and almost purposefully so. It would be quite easy to engage with each of these books without engaging in these politics. In *Introducing Teddy*, the change in name and shifts in gender performance that Tilly desires are processed by Ava as an opportunity to play with her own gender signaling. The lesson for the *humans* in the story could be boiled down to acknowledgment that girls can like boy things and boys can like girl things. Any lesson Tilly's own experience might offer children can therefore easily be explained away as a difference in style. *The Prince and the Frog* is arguably more resistant to this reduction particularly because there is no getting around the fact that the story is about two boys falling in love. Here too, though, love is idealized in a way that is similarly depoliticized. Here, love is love, but as with the idiom itself, this logic erases the fact that, in lived experience, queer forms of loving and kinship building are typically understood through a *heteronormative* lens, perhaps best evidenced by the centering of marriage equality in media representations of queer politics. So what makes a difference in maintaining the centrality of the politics of sexuality and gender differences that implicitly motivated these texts in the first place? Underlying each of these concerns is, I think, a larger one—one about histories of queer lives and the status of the "human" within them.

SPECULATIVE FRAMING

The proposal I want to make, then, is that the issue of the "human" and "nonhuman" and "inhuman(e)" might be better addressed through a framework that explicitly *centers* the historical and political context out of which these children's books emerged *and* actively *resists* the possibility of their being appropriated for contradictory purposes by those invested in maintaining the status quo. What I am calling "speculative framing" is, I believe, one promising way of holding both of these intentions in place for anyone—adult and child alike—interested in using these books for the purposes for which they are intended to serve. Here, then, I will briefly describe this framework as an *imaginative* one and highlight five distinct elements of this imaginative lens, or five sites of possibility, that are particularly valuable in engaging in conversations about LGBTQ+ experiences with young people. These are absorption, transportation, estrangement, opening, and multispecies responsibilities.

The word "speculate" carries with it many meanings, but the meaning I am invoking is one that has been developed within scholarship at the intersection of literature and creative writing, philosophy, and Black studies—and especially Black feminist and/or queer studies. In the first category, which is likely to be more familiar to the reader, "speculative" signals a certain kind of futuristic fiction writing, often related to science fiction, in which authors play with images of the future to challenge and reinterpret the present political, cultural, economic, and social world. These authors are speculating about the future, imagining what the consequences of our current political and economic arrangements might be, unrestrained by what those arrangements might otherwise suggest will come about. Philosophically speaking, the idea of speculative practices is distinguished from other forms of thinking by virtue of its power in "drawing readers emotionally into a story," creating a sense of *absorption* into a different world that ideally leads one to experience "a reduced focus on the self" (De Smedt and De Cruz 62). To speculate in general, and to engage with speculative fiction in particular, is to allow oneself to become absorbed by a different world. Doing this can ignite contemplation and deliberation about the status of the world in which we live more so than general imaginative practices or thought experiments.

This difference is grounded in a *transportation* of the reader/thinker into a different world, but one that is neither restricted by the logics of the present nor so unfamiliar that transportation is impossible (De Smedt and De Cruz 59). That is, speculative engagement is not a complete dismissal of the present or an attempt to escape "reality" (68). Instead, it is a framework that puts both what is and what could be in conversation with each other in a way that emotionally and imaginatively transports one into a space that is so moving that what is begins to look strange, problematic, or even evil. Transportation is also enhanced or made possible by the *estrangement* that speculative imagination can cause. Reading these books as speculative fiction may be fruitful in maintaining political and critical conversations precisely because doing so renders common and dominant stories unfamiliar—or creates an experience of estrangement—rather than perpetuates these common and dominant stories by assimilating new stories into the narratives about queer life that might otherwise be challenged.

That the experience of engaging in speculative writing, thinking, and deliberating is inherently political is part of its value here. There is no apolitical way of experiencing this kind of emotional and mental transportation precisely because speculating always has political implications. This is, at least, the nuance that Black intellectual, scholarly, artistic, and literary works bring to the idea. These traditions are deeply rooted in both critique and imagination and add complexity to thinking about a speculative framework by embedding it in larger political movements. They ask us to consider the labor of addressing and dismantling racism and white supremacy, of undermining the almost all-consuming power of capitalism in determining how we live our lives, and, of course, the way the sex, gender, and sexuality, as identities and concepts, are implicated in both (Kelley).

Importantly, then, speculative thinking is also about *openings* or about insisting on openings that might move us out of what is into something that *might* be. Whereas general imaginings or mere thought experiments typically operate to support a kind of sensemaking that is focused on forming certainties, coming to concrete conclusions, or arriving at stable solutions to problems, speculative thinking helps us revel in the never-ending possible futures that we might begin to wish for and labor toward. Johan De Smedt and Helen De Cruz describe this concern as one about "cognitive enclosures," which fulfill the need for "immediate resolution or action" that so many of us seek in working toward more equitable futures (66). One of the most profound impacts that the speculative can have is in making what is common look strange, though, or making what we are used to uncomfortable. It is always about creating "another way of seeing that remains stably anchored, due to its ambiguity and dynamism, in the here and now" (Thaler, "Hope" 690). It also asks of us to see the other—whatever or whomever that other is—differently. A speculative framework therefore invokes curiosity, play, experimentation, and criticality through its capacity to reorient—or, at least, to create—a space within which to begin the world of reorienting. This is its core political value: it can open us up to new forms of resistance that might then inspire us to act and exist in new ways.

Finally, because of these openings, speculative work grants us the opportunity to rethink the meaning of "responsibility" for the politics implicated in that work. It is *not* speculative if it is *not* politicized (including if it is treated as an apolitical practice), and as such, invocation of the speculative requires evoking critical consideration of what makes humans distinct from all other life forms—the issue that guided my choice of picture books for this project. In each story, we see life in nonhuman forms; in each story, we see *moralizing* about life in nonhuman forms. This is a space of further potential for politicization as speculative frameworks offer a politicized way of seeing the blurring of the line between human and nonhuman. Speculative fiction almost always refuses these distinctions—or, at least, the traditional significance of them—and offers a space and place within which we can play with the way we draw distinctions in the world. To borrow a phrase from Karen Barad, we (humans) are always making "cuts" in the world, dividing it up according to our needs, desires, and hopes and making determination about what "matters" in the process (see, e.g., 175–79, 217, 348). In speculative fiction, new and different cuts are made; different ways of producing knowledge are explored; our interactions with the world are reimagined. Mathias Thaler, in his work on utopias, speculative fiction, and political theory, adds that the imaginative power of speculative-like thinking can also foster a sense of "multispecies justice," or an opportunity to radically rethink "what sort of relationships ought to obtain between human and non-human actors," and the imaginative power of utopian thought ("Multispecies Justice" 3). A speculative framework therefore provides a way of maintaining the political implications of such thinking by emphasizing discussions about the responsibilities we have to being able to account for those differences that we decide make a difference in how we operate individually and collectively. This is also an intervention that could carry with it the potential to critically address the processes of othering that are at stake in this conversation.

REIMAGINING READING

In conclusion, I offer a reimagined reading of these texts guided by what I have described as a speculative framework, focusing on what it might look like to read these texts through a foregrounding of absorption, transportation, estrangement, and openings, especially in terms of rethinking responsibility and justice. In *Introducing Teddy*, the story of Tilly offers a unique opportunity to be pulled into a world where gender identity is fluid and definitions of identity come more from an individual's own sense of self than from societal expectations. Becoming absorbed into this world might also mean that the reader and listener take breaks to imagine how they might think of themselves differently if there was more acceptance and encouragement of this kind of self-definition than in the worlds in which they currently live.

In my own imagination, I can see all kinds of new questions bubbling to the surface for children and adults alike, especially those about where these societal expectations come from in the first place. Asking such questions of children intentionally could potentially bring the history of queer life into play in such moments of absorption, making such absorption a space for political considerations. Because *Introducing Teddy* highlights friendship, the reader could also engage the listener in an explicit discussion of what friendship means and how identity matters—and in how many ways identity matters—in friendship. And because there is not just Tilly but also Ava's robot friend Max, there are more questions to be asked about how our relationships with other valued subjects that are not themselves fully human are shaped by the world as it is and, perhaps most importantly, the extent to which we might desire different relations to and between those for whom we care, regardless of what form they take. This is an ethical conversation itself, of course, and it might mean asking children about what they imagine to be most important to them, why, and what role they might play—realistically or not—in nurturing those relationships. It might even make space for encouraging younger people to develop a sense of curiosity in general, to practice contemplation and questioning, and to reflect upon the feelings that come with such practices.

While most of these examples from *Introducing Teddy* could easily be applied to readings of *The Prince and the Frog* and *Neither*, each of the latter also hold their own unique possibilities. In *The Prince and the Frog*, for example, we could consider the evolving *romantic* relationship between the frog and Oskar. The language that is used in this story is particularly rich and full of possibilities for igniting conversations about politics, justice, and responsibility largely because it directly takes on the question of what it means to love another and what happiness might look like, too. Oskar, Caroline, and the frog certainly develop friendships that could be explored through a speculative framework as demonstrated above; however, a speculative lens also opens up possibilities for reveling in the disorientation that is evoked in Caroline's "failed" kiss.

Like a mathematical equation that just can't be worked out, this moment of failure could be framed as a moment of possibility by encouraging both absorption into a new world and estrangement with the world as it is. Again, encouraging this might also make possible more politicized discussions of why there was a sense of failure in the first place and why it was frustrating for Oskar that he could not seem to make Caroline and the frog fall into *true* love. These are affective, emotional experiences that can be reveled in and reflected upon if absorption is allowed and encouraged. And what I think is one of the most powerful potentialities in this book is Caroline's own expression of joy for the love between her brother and Alex as well as of love for her *life*. What might Caroline mean when she says she is in love with her life? And how does that love compare to and contrast with the way that Oskar and Alex feel each other's love? Once again, we have the opportunity, by evoking the speculative, to be absorbed into the emotional world of others and to explore the possibilities that these different relations between people and animals and entire ways of being in the world make available for contemplation.

Lastly, *Neither* and its story about an entirely inhuman world might be framed, through a speculative posture, as an opportunity to directly consider what we humans have to learn from the relations between other parts of our world and environments. In this case, absorption means positioning oneself as a nonhuman being—or, at least, destabilizing one's sense of certainty about the superiority of their human status—and its potential to bring political histories to life in conversation with children might lie in the fact that it poses a simple yet essential question about difference. Whereas *Introducing Teddy* could be a vehicle for having conversations about the politics of friendship and identity and *The Prince and the Frog*, a vehicle for considering the politics of love, *Neither*—despite it being arguably the more simple story—offers an opportunity to foster engagement in a different political discussion: Why is identity important to us, and why is it that it's importance so often makes it a matter of inclusion, exclusion, and belonging?

In other words, reading *Neither* through speculation might mean familiarizing one's own self with the history of queer life itself, or it may mean actively exploring that history with others, over time, and not just in one sitting. It might mean being direct about the way that some differences come to matter more than other differences, or maybe it means ruminating together over the ambiguity around the lines between species that are presented to us regularly as certain. In fact, one form that a speculative framework might take in this space is encouraging ambiguity itself in welcoming children to identify confusions, ask questions—in *not* requiring or settling with something that allows for "cognitive enclosure." I think it is also important to approach ambiguity and uncertainty as launching pads for critique, too. If something seems strange, we might prod the child to say more about that: Why is it strange? *Should* it be strange? What if the *normal* is what is strange?

Grounding the reading of these books in speculation as a means of maintaining the political import of these texts can generate experiences for children that make the exploration—the transportation, the emotional movement, the practice of opening oneself up to new possibilities—the most important thing itself. The speculative therefore might be a way of cultivating a sense of such experiences as *essential* to wishing for a better world and not—as neoliberalism tells us to think and feel—tangential, impossible, unimportant, or wasteful. The radical imagining and the openings made possible by the speculative is, instead, what just might be the most educational and politicizing experiences that we can have in reading LGBTQIA+ picture books to and with children.

NOTE

1. For the sake of clarity and consistency, I use the phrase "queer life" in this chapter to refer to the lives, experiences, and political desires of people who identify themselves as lesbian, gay, bisexual, transgender, queer/questioning, intersex, asexual/aromantic/agender, plus (LGBTQIA+). This is *not* to say that this is a homogenous group, however, as there exists as much tension, contradiction, difference, and disagreement across this group as there is within any other category of identity. There is much nuance missing here, then, but I use this term nonetheless because those differences matter less to the purpose of this chapter—though they do, of course, matter greatly for other reasons—which is to explore the link between queer political aims in general and children's picture books.

WORKS CITED

Adler, Dahlia. "*Neither* Author-Illustrator Airlie Anderson on Creating a Genderfluid Picture Book: Guest Post." *LGBTQreads*, https://lgbtqreads.com/2018/06/18/neither-author-illustrator-airlie-anderson-on-creating-a-genderfluid-picture-book-a-guest-post/. Accessed 12 Mar. 2024.
Anderson, Airlie. *Neither*. Little, Brown Books for Young Readers, 2018.
Barad, Karen. *Meeting the Universe Halfway: Quantum Physics and the Entanglement of Matter and Meaning*. Duke UP, 2007.
D'Emilio, John, and Estelle B. Freedman. *Intimate Matters: A History of Sexuality in America*. U of Chicago P, 1997.
De Smedt, Johan, and De Cruz, Helen. "The Epistemic Value of Speculative Fiction." *Midwest Studies in Philosophy*, vol. 39, no. 1, 2015, pp. 58–77.
Ferguson, Roderick A. *Aberrations in Black: Toward a Queer of Color Critique*. U of Minnesota P, 2004.
Foucault, Michel. *The History of Sexuality: An Introduction*. Translated by Robert Hurley, vol. 1, Vintage, 1990.
Hall, Michael. *Red: A Crayon's Story*. Greenwillow Books, 2015.
Hartman, Saidiya V. *Scenes of Subjection: Terror, Slavery, and Self-Making in Nineteenth-Century America*. Oxford UP, 1997.
Kelley, Robin D. G. *Freedom Dreams: The Black Radical Imagination*. Beacon Press, 2002.
Kunzel, Regina. "The Power of Queer History." *American Historical Review*, vol. 123, no. 5, 2018, pp. 1560–82.
McWhorter, Ladelle. "Enemy of the Species." *Queer Ecologies: Sex, Nature, Politics, Desire*, edited by Catriona Mortimer-Sandilands and Bruce Erickson, Indiana UP, 2010, pp. 73–101.
Pike, Olly. *The Prince and the Frog: A Story to Help Children Learn about Same-Sex Relationships*. Jessica Kingsley, 2018.

"Pop'n'Olly." *Crediblemind*, wellscreenmonterey.crediblemind.com/organizations/https-www-popnolly-com. Accessed 1 Apr. 2024.

"The Prince and the Frog." *Pop'n'Olly*, www.popnolly.com/product-page/the-prince-and-the-frog. Accessed 1 Apr. 2024.

Somerville, Siobhan B. *Queering the Color Line*. Duke UP, 2000.

Stryker, Susan. "Trans Health Is Queer (and Queer Health Isn't Normal)." *Lambda Nordica*, vol. 18, no. 3–4, 2013, pp. 147–65.

Terry, Jennifer. *An American Obsession: Science, Medicine, and Homosexuality in Modern Society*. U of Chicago P, 1999.

Thaler, Mathias. "Hope Abjuring Hope: On the Place of Utopia in Realist Political Theory." *Political Theory*, vol. 46, no. 5, 2018, pp. 671–97.

Thaler, Mathias. "What If: Multispecies Justice as the Expression of Utopian Desire." *Environmental Politics*, vol. 31, no. 2, 2021, pp. 258–76.

Walton, Jessica. *Introducing Teddy: A Gentle Story about Gender and Friendship*. Bloomsbury, 2016.

Walton, Jessica. "Teachers Guide *Introducing Teddy*." *Bloomsbury*, https://www.bloomsbury.com/media/jayfuenk/introducing-teddy-teachers-guide-final.pdf. Accessed 12 Mar. 2024.

Wynter, Sylvia. "Afterword: Beyond Miranda's Meanings; Un/silencing the 'Demonic Ground' of Caliban's 'Woman.'" *Out of the Kumbla: Caribbean Women and Literature*, edited by Carole Boyce Davies and Elaine Savory Fido, Africa World Press, 1990, pp. 355–72.

PART 6

LGBTQ+ NONFICTION CHILDREN'S PICTURE BOOKS

CHAPTER 14

AIDS AND THE ANTISOCIAL SUBJECT IN QUEER BIOGRAPHICAL PICTURE BOOKS
A Case Study on Keith Haring

Gabriel Duckels

The American children's biography is an expanding genre, whose subjects constitute a pantheon of notable people deemed worthy of admiration by the adult creators and gatekeepers of children's literature. Hence to map the historical development of the children's biography, including the recent emergence of the lesbian, gay, bisexual, trans, queer, plus (LGBTQ+) subject therein, is to illustrate how some lives, communities, and histories get reconstituted into accessible narratives for children while some remain beyond the scope of cultural production. By examining three recent biographical picture books about the queer American artist Keith Haring as a case study, this chapter asks: How can the life stories of queer historical figures who are at once deeply political and highly sexual be constructed in texts for children? How do these representational practices change or challenge the meanings of "queerness" that young people are permitted to access within a dramatically expanded scene of youth-oriented queer visibility?

HOMONORMATIVE HEROES AND QUEER LIFE STORIES

While it is inspiring to see an increase in the number of picture books that celebrate the lives of noteworthy LGBTQ+ people in the historical and recent past (see Miller's contribution to this collection for an overview of the field), their representational task remains charged—such are the stakes of joining the pantheon of all-American heroes that the children's biography has stereotypically constituted. Jon M. Wargo and James Joshua Coleman recently argue, for example, that this emerging market, for all its gains, tends to work toward a homonormative and homonationalist subject—a whitewashed view of LGBTQ+ people focused on gay men and inequitable mythologies of American supremacy. Wargo and Coleman's critique of these queer biographical picture books corresponds with perspectives on children's biographies in general. Leonard S. Marcus, writing in 1980, argues that "some biographers, intent on their moral, have reduced their subject's life to an implausible ideal, an image of ghostly perfection quite literally too good to be true" (17). More recently, Peter C. Kunze notes that "children's biographies . . . presume an innocent child reader" by offering "quaint moral lessons and easily digestible characterizations of often complicated, even scandalous historical figures" (315). As such, the "goodness" of the biographical subject can be presented as prepolitical, universal, and disarticulated from structural oppression and inequity. This depoliticization speaks to who gets figured as good and who belongs to the social and therefore representable world.

In general, scholarship on LGBTQ+ representation in children's picture books has focused on its relation to the production of homonormativity, a concept introduced by Lisa Duggan to describe this depoliticization of gay politics toward an absorption into neoliberal, heteronormative ideals. This relationship between children's picture books and the process of homonormativity is logical because the success of queer representation in texts intended for young people is often contingent upon mainstream publishers and booksellers; queer associations with the cultural industry of childhood are ideologically weighty. Writing in the early 2010s, Nathan Taylor argues that several queer picture books published in the first decade of the twenty-first century focus on "monogamous relationships, family, consumerism, middle-class, and White values" (149). In exchange for supporting conservative practices, "lesbian and gay adults are granted recognition of their existence by different institutions including courts and schools" (150). Writing a few years later, Jazmine Lester analyzes sixty queer picture books within an intersectional critical paradigm and finds that narratives that might seek to challenge heteronormativity in fact fail to interrogate the systems of oppression that enforce it. Lester argues that queer picture books implicitly "exclude and silence problems facing queer people who are not able-bodied, White, upper middle class, cisgender males" (262). It is precisely this sort of homonormative politics that Keith Haring's life story stands against because of his association with Black gay culture, public sex, and HIV/AIDS—making the analysis of his identity in multiple picture books a compelling object of study for the issues that underpin my argument.

Writing in 2019, Jennifer Miller locates a sea change in the availability of queer narratives in children's picture books. To Miller, many recent titles break away from the representational logic of homonormativity to instead constitute what she calls "a new queer children's literature" that involves "queer-affirming shifts . . . that are not inevitably bound to normativity" but "which permit young people to envision new queer worlds" ("Little Queers" 1667). Expanding interest in queer subjects and histories in children's literature (demonstrative of changes in popular culture more widely) can interrupt the politics of assimilation and normalization that first shaped LGBTQ+ representation in mainstream children's picture books. If queer representation has grown exponentially in children's literature, then LGBTQ+ identities are increasingly coherent within mainstream conceptualizations of childhood. At the same time, if LGBTQ+ biographical picture books have the potential to render their queer subjects properly patriotic, validating their life stories as pedagogically worthy, then the burden of expectation upon them points to the unstable relation between the life stories of notable queer people and the marketized or real child that they address. In other words, how can the children's biographical picture book celebrate the lives of queer subjects whose lives retain an association with the unrepresentable?

KEITH HARING, QUEER SEXUALITY, AND THE ANTISOCIAL SUBJECT

We might say, then, that queer themes emerged in texts for young people in a paradigm of absence, outrage, and impossibility, which the logic of homonormativity hoped to solve and which the expansion of queer representation now challenges further. The elevation of the LGBTQ+ subject in children's literature is always potentially radical, and yet its legitimization in texts for young people creates new representational tensions. A conspicuous element of the children's biography is to what extent these historically queer lives are in conflict—today or at the time—with prevailing ideologies of childhood. In this regard, the question of what is "normal" becomes obfuscated into what is "suitable for children." In this context, then, the "heroification" (Kunze 312) effect of the children's biography yields a reparative alchemy, able to transform implicit or explicit attitudes of deviance and pathology about LGBTQ+ cultures and communities into expressions of virtue and relevance to all children's lives.[1] What was *unrepresentable* for young people in earlier decades becomes *representable* today.

These texts thus map the changing parameters of the social and the antisocial—to draw upon queer theory's antisocial thesis, it is an "arena of interpretive battle" (Wiegman 220) among scholars such as Lee Edelman in the context of the AIDS crisis in the United States. The concept is connected to the subsequent uneven assimilation of some LGBTQ+ people into the dominant culture at the end of the twentieth century. Recently, Benjamin Kahan summarizes the antisocial thesis as the argument that "all social life and sociality—encompassing the good life, happiness, and citizenship—is organized by heterosexuality and reproductive futurism (emblematized by the figure of the child) and constitutively excludes queerness" (811).

The origins of the antisocial thesis describe an oppositional relation between queerness and the social construction of childhood. The recent expansion of queer children's literature seemingly undermines this premise because it suggests a queering of childhood itself. To Edelman, queerness "names the side of those not 'fighting for the children'" (3) when "fighting for the children" describes the disruptive relation between LGBTQ+ people and the status quo. Edelman is interested less in real children than in the hetero-patriarchal future that the ever-produced images of "the child" prop up, around which the mainstream realizes its borders. As José Esteban Muñoz notes in his critique of Edelman's polemic, this phantasmic child is bound up in racialized, nationalized ideologies of childhood, which are produced as the badge of (hetero)normativity.

Children's literature for the most part exists *within* rather than *against* the social and so demarcates the limits of mainstream representational possibility. In this chapter, I invoke the antisocial subject within the social field to foreground the oppositional and historical rather than assimilatory and contemporaneous relationship between queer culture and the status quo. This focus means acknowledging the importance of the erotic to queer culture (even problematizing its self-explanatory absence in texts intended for children) and the connection between the erotic and the racialized and socioeconomic contexts of queerness that Taylor sees as absent within the traditionally homonormative associations of the LGBTQ+ children's picture book. The queer antisocial subject, as I understand it, thus involves considering the sexual politics of queer culture within a larger conceptualization of the "social death" (see, e.g., Patterson) of minoritized subjects and their invisibility in homonormative, white-coded industries of children's textual production. My point is not to demand that texts for young people display the erotic but to judge the ways in which the elision of queer sexuality is handled and how this contributes to the erasure of connected examples of structural oppression, including HIV/AIDS.

The inclusion of sexually/socially transgressive queer subjects in children's biographies works to construct a juvenilized queer history within a field of production in which LGBTQ+ lives are by definition no longer excluded but upon which the politics of homonormativity are still instrumental. This queer movement from antisocial to prosocial is indicative of larger questions regarding the centrifugal/centripetal relation between queer themes and the prescribed, unstable, but deeply residual heteronormativity of texts for young people. I invoke this oppositional relation to acknowledge the epistemological violence of childhood as a protected, innocent class—a class not open to many nonwhite, poor, or queer young people, as Muñoz's critique of Edelman makes clear. Muñoz argues for queerness as a utopian project rather than accepting Edelman's focus on queerness's negation of the social so that queerness might create new worlds rather than the negation of one. The antisocial thesis is crucial to consider in children's literature because the panicked question of how to address sexual contexts of queer history for young people quickly draws attention to broader histories and geographies of oppression—which is to say sexuality is discursive and demands the discussion of race, prejudice, and queer world making. Protecting children from insensitive exposure to sexual themes is rightly fundamental to what children's literature is and does, but such themes are often central to "queer history" as an overall project.

If the simplification of LGBTQ+ lives begets a problematic normalization that sanitizes those lives to the point of misrepresentation, then it is useful to consider the construction of especially transgressive individuals. Keith Haring is an example of this dilemma. Haring is associated with children's rights and popular culture, but at the same time, his life story speaks to the queer history of AIDS and the urban gay male sexual cultures that AIDS impacted, including Haring's participation in—and arguable fetishization of—Black gay culture. These simultaneous resonances challenge an oversimplistic binary between child-friendly and adults-only aspects. In a heteronormative, white-supremacist-dominant culture, Haring hence constitutes an antisocial subject, but his immense popularity with children signifies him as *with* rather than *against* the social insofar as the social here stands for the child.

To examine these representational politics, it is compelling to consider the construction of his life story in three recent biographical picture books: *Keith Haring: The Boy Who Just Kept Drawing* (2017) by Kay A. Haring; *Drawing on Walls: A Story of Keith Haring* (2020) by Matthew Burgess; and *Art Is Life:*

The Life of Artist Keith Haring (2021) by Tami Lewis Brown. Their emergence within five years of each other provides three expressions of the same queer life story in the same context of children's cultural production—a rarity. All three titles are child-focused variations of what Ricardo Montez calls the "standardized narrative" of Haring's life (19). They chronicle his early life as a creative, free-spirited child in Pennsylvania, his wunderkind years at art school, and his arrival in the gritty New York City art scene in the late 1970s. This narrative culminates in Haring's ascent to fame, followed by his AIDS-related death, which hangs at the end of each life story, either implicitly or explicitly addressed. All three titles foreground his artistic brilliance and affirm his artwork as a social good: *Art Is Life* acknowledges that Haring "wanted everyone to see and feel art all around them" (Brown 31), while *Keith Haring* foregrounds Haring's artistic and philanthropic work with children, including urban children of color. All three picture books acknowledge Haring's AIDS diagnosis and death in the endpapers, although none provide any information about HIV/AIDS as though passing that demand to other people in the reader's life, which arguably implies that these picture books see HIV/AIDS as no longer being a risk or reality in children's lives other than as history.

I assume that these picture books have a duty to explicitly name Haring's sexual identity and his relationship to queer history, including his relationship to HIV/AIDS. Only *Drawing on Walls*, however, incorporates AIDS and Haring's sexuality in the main narrative, thereby affirming both as essential to a child's view of his life story. This includes his relationship with Juan Dubose, a Black gay DJ. Today, Dubose is recognizable in the photographs of him and Haring taken by Andy Warhol, which depict the two men in a shirtless embrace.[2] Crucially, *Art Is Life* does not represent Haring's sexuality anywhere, either in the main text or paratext, such that Haring's relation to queer cultural history is arguably withheld. *Keith Haring* only acknowledges Haring's sexuality briefly in a discussion of his cause of death in the afterword. Essentially, only *Drawing on Walls* represents Haring's life story as a queer biographical narrative with broader queer world-making implications. *Keith Haring* and *Art Is Life* dodge these contexts, eliding the queer intersections of Haring's life story to instead position it less controversially as a juvenilized artist-genius narrative.

Keith Haring, *Drawing on Walls*, and *Art Is Life* join a fraught scene of Haring-related cultural production. Montez notes acerbically that posthumous representations of Haring tend to encase his legacy "in a moral structure" shadowed by AIDS: the assertion of his "investment in children becomes a way to maintain a sense of legacy despite his aberrant sexual behaviour and his lack of biological progeny" (24). Haring's creative and financial investments in children—urban children, economically disadvantaged children, children affected by HIV/AIDS, children of color—make him an obvious candidate for memorialization in children's literature (a moral structure of sorts). But his association with queer sexuality challenges the child-centered associations upon which these picture books find their space in the market. Haring's participation in the pre-AIDS and pregentrified culture of public sex in New York City is an explicit inspiration (so to speak) in his work, which features cartoon phalluses and anuses and orgiastic patterns of fellating and fucking bodies.[3] But Haring has two bodies of work: these signifiers of an adult outsider Eros, which reflect his life in the nightclubs and bathhouses of queer New York and then playful mass-culture work, which often draws upon childhood and childishness.

Indeed, Robert Farris Thompson notes that "the counter-trope to sex in Haring's life and art is innocence," emerging "out of his respect for infants and for children" (xxv). I would modify Thompson's distinction, understanding Haring's style as unifying the conflicting queer, erotic, and child-focused themes, which his biography so clearly speaks to. It is not so much that sex and children's innocence oppose each other in his work but that his aesthetic—his iconic simple-line drawing—constitutes a field of production in which queer sexuality is rendered as innocent and childhood is rendered as queer. In other words, adult sexuality and the joy of childhood are distinct from one another as direct themes but emerge through the same palette of vibrant pleasure, even jouissance. Haring's work portrays queer sexual worlds without the usual hue of shame not despite his aesthetic proximity to childhood but because of it, and this is a proximity that he cultivated proactively. Haring was self-aware about his responsibility toward his younger audiences: as Thompson notes, he self-censored his public art to ensure it could not (in his own view) cause harm to the innocence of onlooking children.

Haring's artwork is bound up in his problematic, libidinal investment in Black gay subjectivity—a subjectivity which Haring saw as an idealized, eroticized means of self-realization. Only *Drawing on Walls* represents Haring's sexuality through his relationship to Dubose, and so only this picture book acknowledges that the majority of his lovers—many of whom also died from AIDS complications—were men of color. Writing against the homonormative connotations of a romanticized view of Haring's relationship with Dubose, Montez sees Dubose as Haring's "site of becoming," the "origin" of the pattern of "ever-present dark-skinned boys who occupied his life" (14). Indeed, Montez uses Haring's line drawings to theorize this proximity to

Blackness—Montez sees his artwork as "neo-primitive inscriptions within a modernist tradition of primitivist fantasy" (5). Especially considering Haring's rapid ascension in the American art world, this fantasy signifies a "Western desire for other bodies" (5), in which Haring's identification with and sexualisation of the Black gay male body amounts to what bell hooks would call "eating the other" (39). To hooks, an effect of popular interest in the mediation of race and racism in mass culture in the late twentieth century is the objectification of otherness, in which the Black subject gets "eaten, consumed, and forgotten" (39). It is important to acknowledge these tensions within the representational politics of Haring's life because his relationship to Dubose is either totally absent in these picture books, as in *Keith Haring* and *Art Is Life*, or couched in radically romantic but comparatively uncritical terms, as in *Drawing on Walls*.

The New York subway system features prominently in the mediation of Haring's life in these three titles, which all conceptualize his early chalk murals as much-needed decorations of the "decayed, dank and dreary" stations (Brown 15), reflecting the deprivation of early 1980s New York. Not represented, however, is the subway system's role as an erotic zone in Haring's life story, which is in turn connected to socioeconomic factors. The subway was a "scene of debauchery" (Montez 48), as John Giorno describes in his biographical account of meeting Haring in a subway toilet, which was then a cruising ground. John Giorno luridly recalls Haring's "thick gooey" semen (74), a noxious objectification of Haring's then-unknown HIV status. This description of anonymous public sex signifies the subway as a part of a queer social world of cruising, drug use, and sex work, which all contribute to the mise-en-scène of queer history in the United States (see Delaney; Berlant and Warner) but which, for obvious reasons, contradict the conventional homonormative landscape of queer picture books. Whether through his affiliation with a Black gay culture that the mainstream would struggle to name or his participation in public sex, Haring constitutes a "bad sexual citizen" (Seidman 3)—the wrong sort of gay man according to the terms of homonormativity: licentious, not monogamous; HIV positive, not HIV negative; and, as a white man, a "race traitor" (Ignatiev and Garvey), who self-consciously sought out the company of Black men. These components of Haring's life story challenge the task of juvenilization by foregrounding controversial and inherently political contexts of queer history—contexts which emerge sexually but which therefore conflict with the erotophobic terms of children's textual production.

I refer to this posthumous account of public sex to emphasize that the "antisocial" in queer culture is bound up in accessible versions of queer history. Unsurprisingly, the sexual dimensions of Haring's life are at odds with his child-friendly audience. Indeed, the official children's website for Haring prominently declares itself a *"fun and safe* space for children" (*Haring Kids*; emphasis added), tacitly acknowledging the need for caution when navigating resources about Haring while at the same time making clear his legitimacy as a children's heroic figure. The precarious context of Haring's legacy sets the stage for the appearance of *Keith Haring, Art Is Life*, and *Drawing on Walls* as picture books that offer a child-friendly space to introduce his life and work, but which therefore draw attention to the challenges of constructing his life story without addressing the enormous and immediate sexual-political dimensions therein.

SILENCE, QUEER PEDAGOGY, AND THE AESTHETICS OF REPRESSION

I should reiterate that I am not critiquing these picture books simply for failing to construct Haring's sexual experiences; such moments are often necessarily absent. Rather, I am interested in the implication of these moments, in how the erotophobic limits of the children's picture book as a cultural form deal with this absence. I follow Perry Nodelman in understanding children's literature as a field of representation symbolically and narratively formed around that which it represses. In other words, texts for young people are structured not only by what is on the page but by what lurks beneath it. This repressive model of children's literature is useful because it provides a language to recognize the omission of sexual-political contexts in these picture books—an aesthetics of repression—while acknowledging how these contexts nevertheless remain inextricable to the effect and coherence of Haring's life story in these expressions. This model provides an alternative to merely questioning how far taboo themes can or should be represented in picture books, which is not my purpose in this chapter because I begin with the assumption that on some subtextual level they always already are.

The peritextual elements of these picture books can be as pedagogically viable as the main multimodal visual narrative because they can contain information that is withheld or concealed within the main text.[4] In a survey of LGBTQ+ picture books, S. Adam Crawley argues that this extratextual content is especially salient for queer representation because publishers "may fear censorship and thus require that such information—if included—occur in the backmatter where it may be less likely to be noticed" (31). Indeed, Crawley's survey includes the afterword of *Keith Haring*, which Crawley argues provides relevant contextual information about Haring's gay identity and AIDS-related death and activism, compensating for the absence of both in the main text. I would add, however, that the somewhat awkward phrasing of this paratext ("Haring, who was gay, died from AIDS complications" [Haring]) illuminates the larger instability of such themes within children's picture books. This discreet reference to the queer context of Haring's life story in the final paragraph of the afterword manages to both bury his sexuality and conflate it with AIDS. *Art Is Life* contains no reference at all to sexuality in the main text and refers to Haring's death without referring directly to AIDS. The paratext does not address his sexuality at all, although it acknowledges his AIDS-related death and activism: "Even as his health grew worse, Keith continued to make art for everybody all over the world and worked hard to spread the word about AIDS prevention" (Brown). The publisher's blurb that promotes the book online makes no connections between Haring's life story and its importance within queer cultural history, marketing it instead as a biography of a "modern art icon" ("Art Is Life").

The invisibility of AIDS and queer identity in *Art Is Life* is incongruous because this invisibility feels pronounced. The main text acknowledges Haring's political activism by describing his "pictures against racism and drug abuse, pictures supporting unity and love" (Brown 34). This reference draws attention to the absence of AIDS especially because racism and drug use are implicated in the spread of HIV, while the phrasing "unity and love" denotes an insubstantially implicit nod to LGBTQ+ rights. The absence of Haring's sexuality across the picture book whether in the main text or in the two afterwords means his relationship to queer history is not attached to the picture book, even though the main text nods to the "vibrant, edgy neighborhood" that he called home (see the afterwords). The incongruity here is that if this picture book is read from a stance of "compulsory heterosexuality" (Rich 631) (still the dominant strategy in children's educational and parent-led reading environments), Haring's sexuality disappears, even putting him back into the closet. This invisibility misrepresents not only his life story but his artistic, political, and cultural legacy. One could say, without trying to be paranoid, that the picture book cashes in on the queer cultures that Haring lived within, without acknowledging them as such.

Art Is Life and *Keith Haring* deemphasize Haring's sexuality and his connection to AIDS to the extent that the queer pedagogical potential of each picture book is unrealized—certainly next to *Drawing on Walls*. Indeed, HIV/AIDS pandemic and LGBTQ+ issues are so bound up in silence that representing them explicitly in books for children is radical, and so their omission amounts to suppression. But this makes it too easy to condemn the picture books outright when the repressive representational strategy of *Keith Haring* has reparative as well as suppressive effects. I say this drawing upon Miller's concept of "critical optimism" to describe a reading lens that "assumes LGBTQ+ children's picturebooks can be productively read multiple ways and that the reading strategies one employs is political" (*Transformative Potential* 27). For example, the motif of drawing runs throughout *Keith Haring*, taking on iterative dimensions as a symbol of Haring's transgressive tendency and its world-building potential. Kay Haring describes teachers' condemnation of her brother's artistic experimentation at school and college: "Why are you drawing pictures that look like scrambled bodies?" The narratorial voice rebuts the teacher with the riposte that Haring "just wanted to draw in different ways," resonant of *sexual* as well as creative difference insofar as his transgression of the classroom is inseparable from his transgression of other institutional hierarchies and norms (Haring 13). Later on, the drawing motif takes on another resonance. Haring is represented moving to New York City to 'draw with other artists' and proceeds to 'draw all over the city'" (14). The moment encapsulates Haring's spontaneous output and implies a sort of ejaculatory progeny of line drawings, which underhandedly evoke the erotic freedoms he found in the city and their social, world-making potential. The act of drawing comes to stand for the life drive itself in the final illustration alongside his implied but unstated death: his line traces across a wall, everything but his hand out of sight in the space beyond the right of the page. By hiding Haring, the implication of this final use of the drawing motif is that soon his productivity will cease, and the pen will fall to the floor, withholding the starkness of his AIDS-related death for readers who are unaware of it (e.g., the implied child reader) but still soberly alluding to it for those who are. This analysis of *Keith Haring* may seem somewhat fruity, but my point is this: the story is so tightly plotted around the act of drawing and the questioning of norms that Haring's drawing provokes that one might struggle *not* to read it as a sublimation for alternative examples of transgression, covertly including Haring's sexual associations.

Finally, I want to point out the gallery scene in the center of the visual narrative, which includes representations of other notable figures from Haring's art scene and life story, including celebrities such as Grace Jones, Andy Warhol, and Lou Reed. The crowd includes cult figures like Nomi Klaus and John Sex, whose idiosyncratic hairstyles stand out as niche but instantly recognizable—to those already in the know. Both figures lived with HIV and died from AIDS complications. Although not explicitly identified, their inclusion demonstrates an investment in the political and emotional politics of AIDS in Haring's life story and New York City—an implicit investment meant to go over the heads of younger readers rather than an attempt to foreground this history in that youth context.

The famous faces in the crowd make the absence of Haring's romantic partners more conspicuous, and with this in mind, the representation of Haring's relationship to Dubose in *Drawing on Walls* becomes more revealing. The publisher's blurb for *Drawing on Walls* is the only one of the three picture books to identify Haring's relationship to HIV/AIDS and LGBTQ+ people, noting that Haring was "a member of the LGBTQ community" who "died tragically at the age of thirty-one from AIDS-related complications" ("Drawing on Walls"). The prominence of these themes demonstrates the picture book's investment in Haring's life story as a queer pedagogical narrative rather than as a desexualized art hero. Unlike *Art Is Life*, *Drawing on Walls* does not prioritize the conventional workings of the conservative, pedestal-gazing children's biography; rather, it evokes what Elizabeth Marshall calls "graphic life writing" to describe multimodal visual children's narratives "by and/or about traditionally marginalized groups," which allow "previously unheard stories as well as alternative images that counter the status quo" (80). In other words, while *Keith Haring* and *Art Is Life* incorporate Haring's life into the existing story of children's literature without directly challenging it, *Drawing on Walls* explicitly subverts that story through its inclusion of Haring and Dubose's relationship.

Drawing on Walls constitutes a queer counterstory because it explicitly addresses gay identity, queer community, and HIV/AIDS in the main text rather than relying on the paratext as an adjacent educational space. Haring does not come out per se, but the picture book lingers on his adolescence, emphasizing his "restless" youth in suburban Pennsylvania and his decision to move to New York City "to find the intensity and freedom that he desired" (Burgess 11, 19), calling upon the arc of the young queer person who leaves behind the suburbs to find acceptance in the big city. The lush panorama of Manhattan obviously does not acknowledge the "subterranean world of public sex" (Halberstam 33), which Haring found, but does allude to the city's scope for queer world making. Haring's relationship with the Juan Dubose is represented on the next page: a gentle embrace shared between the two men on a subway train represents Haring's queerness as an embodied, social fact. Their eyes are closed in the illustration as though cordoning off the adult sexual knowledge that their embrace signifies while still affirming their public, unproblematic romantic connection. Importantly, *Drawing on Walls* depicts Haring's AIDS-related death without positioning him as a victim. At the end of the picture book, bare white text sits across a black empty page and tells the reader that even after Haring discovered he had "a serious illness called AIDS, [he] didn't stop making art and sharing his gifts with the world" (Burgess 42). Haring's life after his diagnosis is represented in the following pages through his trip to Pisa to paint a mural in a church. By showing Haring's life *beyond* and *after* his HIV/AIDS diagnosis, *Drawing on Walls* signals a commitment to the Denver Principles, a manifesto for AIDS representation made by people living with HIV/AIDS at the start of the pandemic, which calls for people living with AIDS "to die—and to LIVE—in dignity" ("Denver Principles").

If *Drawing on Walls* provides a queer historical narrative rather than a more conventionally depoliticized and pedestal-gazing biography, then it should be measured by its success as such rather than simply lauded for the perspective it takes. The author does not depict their breakup or Haring's other relationships or Dubose's AIDS-related death. If the representation of Haring and Dubose is rightly radical within the form of the children's picture book, it still does not dispel the assumption that the couple were monogamous and stayed together until Haring's death. While it is unsurprising that the picture book does not address these dimensions of the relationship, it is also true that their absence might shore up what Brett Krutzsch calls "the narrow confines of coupled monogamy as necessary for American citizenship" (162). Furthermore, Haring and Dubose's relationship appears once more in the main text, with the couple next to each other in a mass of people on the dancefloor at Paradise Garage. The name of the nightclub is prominent across the top of the page in stencils to draw attention to its historical significance; the nightclub is listed by the NYC LGBT Historic Sites Project, and Haring writes in his journals of his interest in the nightclub as a transcendent space. The euphoric depiction of this iconic venue in the West Village stands in as a significant allusion to the queer sexual and social lifeworlds of 1980s New York in the form of the children's picture book. Its representation of the racial makeup of the clientele, however, points to a decision by the creators to disengage from Haring's participation in Black gay culture, his professional identification with Black and Latinx men, and even his disavowal of his own whiteness, which he writes about at length in his journals. The sexual-political contexts of queer history may be obscured in children's texts to cover up the erotic, but this covering up is bound up in sexuality's intersections with race, racism, and power.

CONCLUSIONS

Analyzed here, these picture books about Haring demonstrate an ambivalent relation between his artistic genius and his countercultural queerness, with only *Drawing on Walls* explicitly recognizing that one cannot be separated from the other. Marcus argues that the images in biographical picture books "traffic to some degree in unnameable objects, states and feelings" due to the complex adult knowledge they contain and work around (17). Certainly, that is the case here, and it would surely be impossible for the ideological and material parameters of the children's picture book to ever fully convey the complexity of Haring's signification. The dilemma of the queer antisocial adds an integral, perhaps irresolvable, layer that intersects with other political dimensions of queer experience in the status quo. The tension between the visibility of queerness in mainstream conventions of childhood can also be identified in the furor about "drag queen story times" and the place of children and families at Pride marches. The avoidance of sexual or sexual-seeming contexts of queer representation in texts for young people can be closeting. Ironically, the style and form of the children's picture book is already well suited to the allusion to queerness and transgression; there are different silences at work, and not all are harmful. At the same time, these processes of representation cannot replace the radical political fact of explicitly naming gay identity and queer experiences of HIV/AIDS in texts intended for children, and for that reason, *Drawing on Walls* is the most path-breaking expression of Haring's life story. Regardless, children's literature's association with allegory, euphemism, and sublimation can be at once concealing and revealing from a queer pedagogical stance.

NOTES

1. A recent picture book about trans activists Sylvia Riviera and Marsha P. Johnson, Joy Michael Ellison's *Sylvia and Marsha Start a Revolution!* is a comparable object of analysis. Although these two figures have been rightly foregrounded in recent years as crucial to the early LGBTQ+ rights movement, the antisocial connotations of their life stories are challenging to juvenilize in the mainstream. The pair were sporadic sex workers, often unhoused, and associated with HIV/AIDS. Johnson was brutally murdered. In the picture book, Ellison acknowledges their homelessness but avoids the topic of sex work or murder.

2. Montez notes Warhol's objectification of Dubose, who is referred to only as Haring's "black boyfriend." Montez writes, "To research Juan Dubose in the readily available sources on Haring's life is to witness the production of a brown and black sign that is an amalgamation of projections. A direct citation of Dubose's voice appears to be absent from the record.... The absence of his voice and the difficulty in locating alternative representations of him generates a productive resistance to the fantasy of a complete and correct narrative" (17).

3. To be clear, this culture of public sex may have a particular stake in queer history but is not inherently queer; rather, the visibility of sex in New York in the 1970s and 1980s demonstrated an alternative social consensus than that of the present with pros and cons that go beyond the scope of this chapter.

4. Gerald Genette defines "paratext" as the endpapers of a book, while "peritext" includes additional materials related to the text, such as advertisements, reviews, and even word of mouth.

WORKS CITED

"Art Is Life." *Macmillan*, https://us.macmillan.com/books/9780374304249. Accessed 21 Feb. 2024.

Berlant, Lauren, and Michael Warner. "Sex in Public." *Critical Inquiry*, vol. 24, no. 2, 1998, pp. 547–66.

Brown, Tami Lewis. *Art Is Life: The Life of Artist Keith Haring*. Farrar, Straus and Giroux, 2021.

Burgess, Matthew. *Drawing on Walls: A Story of Keith Haring*. Illustrated by Josh Cochran, Enchanted Lion, 2020.

Crawley, S. Adam. "Peritext as Windows, Mirrors, and Maps: LGB+ Representation in the Backmatter." *Voices from the Middle*, vol. 18, no. 2, 2020, pp. 29–32.

Delaney, Samuel R. *Times Square Red, Times Square Blue*. New York UP, 1999.

"The Denver Principles (1983)." *UNAIDS*, https://data.unaids.org/pub/externaldocument/2007/gipa1983denverprinciples_en.pdf. Accessed 21 Feb. 2024.

"Drawing on Walls: A Story of Keith Haring." *Enchanted Lion*, https://enchantedlion.com/all-books/drawing-on-walls-a-story-of-keith-haring. Accessed 21 Feb. 2024.

Duggan, Lisa. "The New Homonormativity." *Materializing Democracy: Toward a Revitalized Cultural Politics*, edited by Russ Castronovo and Dana D. Nelson, Duke UP, 2002, pp. 175–94.

Edelman, Lee. *No Future: Queer Theory and the Death Drive*. Duke UP, 2004.

Ellison, Joy Michael. *Sylvia and Marsha Start a Revolution! The Story of the Trans Women of Color Who Made LGBTQ+ History*. Illustrated by Teshika Silver, Jessica Kingsley, 2020.

Genette, Gerard. *Paratexts: Thresholds of Interpretation*. Translated by Jane E. Lewin, Cambridge UP, 1997.

Giorno, John. *You Got to Burn to Shine: New and Selected Writings*. High Risk Books, 1994.

Halberstam, Jack. *In a Queer Time and Place: Transgender Bodies, Subcultural Lives*. New York UP, 2005.

Haring, Kay A. *Keith Haring: The Boy Who Just Kept Drawing*. Illustrated by Robert Neubecker, Dial Books, 2017.

Haring Kids. https://haringkids.com/. Accessed 25 Feb. 2024.

hooks, bell. *Black Looks: Race and Representation*. Routledge, 2014.

Ignatiev, Noel, and John Garvey. *Race Traitor*. Routledge, 1996.

Kahan, Benjamin. "Queer Sociality after the Antisocial Thesis." *American Literary History*, vol. 30, no. 4, 2018, pp. 811–19.

Krutzsch, Brett. *Dying to Be Normal: Gay Martyrs and the Transformation of American Sexual Politics*. Oxford UP, 2019.

Kunze, Peter C. "What We Talk about When We Talk about Helen Keller: Disabilities in Children's Biographies." *Children's Literature Association Quarterly*, vol. 38, no. 3, 2013, pp. 304–18.

Lester, Jazmine. "Homonormativity in Children's Literature: An Intersectional Analysis of Queer-Themed Picture Books." *Journal of LGBT Youth*, vol. 11, no. 3, 2014, pp. 244–75.

Marcus, Leonard S. "Life Drawings: Some Notes on Children's Picture Book Biographies." *The Lion and the Unicorn*, vol. 4, no. 1, 1980, pp. 15–31.

Marshall, Elizabeth. "Counter-Storytelling through Graphic Life Writing." *Language Arts*, vol. 94, no. 2, 2016, pp. 79–93.

Miller, Jennifer. "For the Little Queers: Imagining Queerness in 'New' Queer Children's Literature." *Journal of Homosexuality*, vol. 66, no. 12, 2018, pp. 1645–70.

Miller, Jennifer. *The Transformative Potential of LGBTQ+ Children's Picture Books*. UP of Mississippi, 2022.

Montez, Ricardo. *Keith Haring's Line: Race and the Performance of Desire*. Duke UP, 2020.

Muñoz, José Esteban. *Cruising Utopia: The Then and There of Queer Futurity*. New York UP, 2009.

Nodelman, Perry. *The Hidden Adult*. John Hopkins UP, 2008.

Patterson, Orlando. *Slavery and Social Death: A Comparative Study*. Harvard UP, 2018.

Rich, Adrienne. "Compulsory Heterosexuality and Lesbian Existence." *Signs*, vol. 5, no. 4, 1980, pp. 631–60.

Seidman, Steven. "From Identity to Queer Politics: Shifts in the Social Logic of Normative Heterosexuality in Contemporary America." *Social Thought and Research*, vol. 24, no. 1–2, 2001, pp. 1–12.

Taylor, Nathan. "U.S. Children's Picture Books and the Homonormative Subject." *Journal of LGBT Youth*, vol. 9, no. 2, 2012, pp. 136–52.

Thompson, Robert Farris. Introduction. *Keith Haring Journals*, by Keith Haring, Penguin Books, 2010, pp. xv–xlii.

Wargo, Jon M., and James Joshua Coleman. "Pinkwashing Picturebooks: Reading Homonational Heroes through Contemporary US LGBTQ+ Biographies." *Children's Literature in Education*, 2022, pp. 1–23.

Wiegman, Robyn. "Sex and Negativity; or What Queer Theory Has for You." *Cultural Critique*, vol. 95, winter 2017, pp. 219–43.

CHAPTER 15

NOW VS. THEN, HERE VS. THERE
Queer Identity and Community in Picture-Book Biographies

Jennifer Miller

The year of 2015 was a significant one for lesbian, gay, bisexual, trans, queer, plus (LGBTQ+) picture books; many contributors to this collection identify it as the year the number of LGBTQ+ picture books available and the diversity of content represented within them both grew substantially. It is also the year that LGBTQ+ picture-book biographies became available to young audiences. In my recent publication *The Transformative Potential of LGBTQ+ Children's Picture Books*, which surveys the LGBTQ+ picture book scene through 2019, I consider the transformative work that nonfiction can do. I write,

> Building a rich bookshelf of nonfiction LGBTQ+ children's picture books can play a significant role in helping young people develop queer consciousness. I think it is possible to imagine becoming queer as a project in empathy and understanding that forces us to rethink attachments to oppressive ideas, identities, and institutions that reproduce oppression, indignity, and injustice for a newly conceptualized all of us. History can be a resource, but the scant histories children are currently inheriting is not. (Jennifer Miller 204)

Since 2019, many more picture-book biographies have been published. However, quantity doesn't correlate with quality. Although visibility itself is an achievement, when what comes into focus reproduces a problematic construct of liberal individualism at the cost of queer community, the victory is hardly an unmitigated success.

My previous research archive ended in 2019 when only a handful of picture-book biographies existed. Most of these titles were created by Rob Sanders and Gail E. Pitman. At the time, Sanders had authored a book about Harvey Milk, and Pitman had created one about Gilbert Baker and another about Phyllis Lyon and Del Martin. It's a short chapter. When I was revising, however, I was able to briefly acknowledge several texts that came out in 2020. These include Joy Michael Ellison's biography of Marsha Johnson and Sylvia Rivera, Lisa Robinson's biography of Dr. James Barry, and Rob Sanders biography of Albert D. J. Cashier. Since then, several more titles have emerged (see table 15.1). In this chapter, I map the 2020–21 growth of the nonfiction LGBTQ+ picture-book field in order to understand what access to our queer past and present picture-book audiences were given in that brief but significant period. In addition, this chapter analyzes existing picture-book biographies to better understand the imaginative constraints liberal ideologies and dominant tropes have on the archive. Throughout my book project, I use the phrase "critical optimism" to "highlight the field's transformative potential as a queer worldmaking project while accounting for, perhaps inevitable, attachments to regimes of normativity and social hierarchy so frequently present" (Miller 26–27). I apply this reading lens to my analysis of more recent picture-book biographies to consider the difference between representing queers and representing queerness.

My hope for nonfiction LGBTQ+ children's picture books mirrors my hope for LGBTQ+ children's picture books generally. It is not that representations will normalize difference but instead that representations of queerness will prompt critiques of heteronormative institutions that reproduce inequality—not toward the inclusion of queer subjects into existing social institutions but toward new visions of what we mean by "the good life," how we understand and evaluate success, and how we relate to each other. To that end, I'm particularly critical of representations and representational strategies in LGBTQ+ picture books that foreground the individual without paying significant attention to context or community because these texts foreclose imaginative possibilities. Even more, focusing on individuals instead of communities, particularly community action, reproduces problematic liberal investments in the individual as an agent of free will, free thought, and free action. Finally, I observe that the existing archive problematically relegates homophobia and transphobia to the past while enclosing it in the country, so the city, specifically New York City and San Francisco, becomes a space free of homophobia and transphobia—places where queerness can thrive.

AUTHOR	ILLUSTRATOR	PUBLISHER	TITLE	YEAR
Joy Michael Ellison	Teshika Silver	Jessica Kingsley	*Sylvia and Marsha Start a Revolution!*	2021
J. P. Miller	Markia Jenai	Discovery Library	*Bayard Rustin*	2021
Lisa Robinson	Lauren Simkin Berke	Schwartz and Wade	*Were I Not a Girl: The Inspiring and True Story of Dr. James Barry*	2020
Rachel Rose		Bearcub Books	*Megan Rapinoe: Soccer Superstar*	2020
Rob Sanders	Nabi H. Ali	Little Bee Books	*The Fighting Infantryman: The Story of Albert D. J. Cashier, Transgender Civil War Soldier*	2020
Rob Sanders	Levi Hastings	Henry Holt	*Mayor Pete: The Story of Pete Buttigieg*	2020
Rob Sanders	Jamey Christoph	Magination Press	*Stitch by Stitch: Cleve Jones and the AIDS Memorial Quilt*	2021
Maria Isabel Sánchez Vegara	Wednesday Holmes	Frances Lincoln Children's Books	*RuPaul*	2021

Table 15.1. LGBTQ+ picture-book biographies available as of May 31, 2022. This is not an exhaustive list.

CRITICAL OPTIMISM AND QUEER BIOGRAPHIES

Activist and scholar Charlene Carruthers's *Unapologetic: A Black, Queer, and Feminist Mandate for Radical Movements* (2018) explores the importance of passing on radical histories to encourage the transformative thinking and action necessary for collective liberation. This text, more than any other, has influenced my feelings about the potential of nonfiction to inspire critical queer consciousness. Carruthers's book is one of several texts by queer scholars of color to politicize and mobilize hope as a strategy for social change (Muñoz; Chambers-Letson). Privileging hope over skepticism prompts several queer theorists of color to identify and strategize alternatives to present and historical social injustices, similar to much recent work in the field of transgender studies. For Carruthers and others taking this approach, there is an understanding that the world can change because it must. Hope for these scholars isn't that of liberal-progress narratives that assume the inevitability of positive social change while ignoring the role of collective action in creating it. Instead, a demand is placed on social agents acting in the present to make change happen, and the past is a resource.

Carruthers introduces the idea of a Black queer feminist (BQF) lens as a model to perceive unjust realities and enact justice-oriented change. She describes the BQF lens as "a political praxis (practice and theory) based in Black feminist and LGBTQ traditions and knowledge, through which people and groups seek to bring their full selves into the process of dismantling all systems of oppression" (Carruthers 10). According to Carruthers, if we think and act through the intersectional model offered by the BQF lens, we can "effectively prioritize problems and methods that center historically marginalized people in our communities" (10). Centering the lived experience of marginalized people, perhaps marginalized "others," demands an acknowledgment of various modes of difference and a reckoning with complex systems of privilege, power, and oppression. My readings of the handful of nonfiction LGBTQ+ children's picture books that currently exist suggest that material histories of struggle and the internal diversity of the LGBTQ+ community are both obscured, which constrains readers' ability to understand the past in ways that could meaningfully contribute to imagining and enacting change in the present, thereby leading to a transformed future.

Carruthers gestures toward the political possibilities of expanded cultural archives when discussing the significance of including Black queer voices in the canon of Black radical literature to weave "a more complete story" about Black liberation (49). Although she is not considering children's literature specifically, the logic and significance of her claim is applicable to an argument for expanding queer representations in children's picture books. Carruthers suggests that studying Audre Lorde, Joseph Beam, and Lorraine Hansberry could change the contours of the thinkable (59). According to Carruthers, omitting Black queer people, or obscuring queer specificity, prevents an intersectional understanding of historical struggles and allows scholars and activists to refuse to acknowledge the complex organization and manifestation of power within and outside of collectives. Even more, it fails to account for how gender and sexuality affect Black people and limits the ability to identify injustice as well as to imagine and enact solutions. Carruthers connects expanding the Black radical tradition to developing the Black imagination, specifically the ability to imagine "alternative economics, alternative family structures, or something else entirely" (39). Carruthers passionately argues that envisioning and enacting a just future needs to account for the most vulnerable among us. In other words, we need to envision a world in which justice is justice for all.

FROM SMALL TOWN BOYS TO BIG CITY QUEERS

There's always a too-small town and a white boy with big dreams and unknown potential. Or at least that appears to be how the small but steadily growing field of LGBTQ+ nonfiction picture books is developing.

Pitman's 2018 *Sewing the Rainbow: A Story about Gilbert Baker*, which is beautifully illustrated by Holly Clifton-Brown, introduces Baker as a child, and many young readers will likely identify with him as a result of this strategy. At the start of the book, a young protogay Gilbert Baker negotiates "gray and dull and flat" Kansas (Pitman, *Sewing the Rainbow*). Kansas is represented as boring and uninspiring, a decidedly unqueer geographical site for such a creative child to call home. However, even in the seemingly straightest of states, Baker finds creative inspiration. His grandmother's love of fashion encourages his own, and he creates "beautiful gowns and costumes." Baker's father doesn't approve of his predilection for design and is depicted angrily tearing up Baker's sketchbook. Pitman describes young Baker's reaction to his father's outburst, suggesting that without his art, Baker's "colorful, sparkly glittery personality started to fade." Young Baker "became gray and dull and flat, just like the Kansas landscape." Pitman suggests that Baker cannot be himself in Kansas, where he is instead stifled by the state's provincialism and his father's toxic masculinity. In fact, Baker's geographic location is emphasized throughout the text, eventually producing a binary between the "there" of Kansas that young Baker suffers through and the "here" of San Francisco that adult Baker flourishes in. The spatial opposition between Kansas and San Francisco can be mapped onto a temporal opposition between the "then" of childhood as well as the "then" of the "bad gay past" and the "now" of adulthood, with movement across time and space represented as progress à la the It Gets Better Project (*It Gets Better*).

Within the text's reality, young Baker lacks agency and mobility. He envisions adulthood as a threshold he will cross into freedom. Ironically, although Baker imagines choice and control as features of adulthood, when he turned eighteen, he "received a letter that knocked every last bit of sparkle out of him" (Pitman, *Sewing the Rainbow*). Details of the letter are not revealed, but the next page depicts Baker in a military uniform doing push-ups. The reader with historical competency can contextualize Baker's personal life within a larger national framework, identifying this as the Vietnam War and understanding that Baker was drafted. Of course, this troubles the idea of agency as a feature of adulthood since Baker's movements and actions are circumscribed by the state when he turns eighteen years old.

Baker's time in the military appears to be short-lived. Because of his inaction, specifically his refusal to shoot a gun, "they sent him to San Francisco, where he would never have to pick up a gun again" (Pitman, *Sewing the Rainbow*). Adult Baker is again positioned in a passive role. He ends up in San Francisco not by choice but because "they" sent him there. Even more, Baker appears to be transformed by San Francisco. He experiences a rebirth that is a reversion to the person he was before his father tore up his sketchpad, before the United States drafted him to fight in a war. Pitman writes, "He could be his colorful, sparkly, glittery self," which implies an essentialism that Pitman doesn't fully commit to since the possibility of queer identity and identification are attached to the city, which is emphasized via an image of Baker standing near the Golden Gate Bridge, smiling widely, as confetti rains down on him—a queer baptism.

Although Kansas represents a time and place Baker dreamed of escaping, traces of his time there inspire him once he is in San Francisco. Pitman writes, "He thought about his grandmother's clothing store. He thought about the drawings his father tore up. And he realized he wanted all of that back" (Pitman, *Sewing the Rainbow*). Baker put his skill as a designer and tailor to use creating fashions for queer cultural figures as well as by participating in community building and political projects in San Francisco. For instance, he created banners for political protests and "was making the city more and more colorful by the day." Gilbert is finally represented as putting things into the world, although the community he helped create isn't present in the text. In fact, most illustrations depict Baker by himself, visually emphasizing the individual.

Of course, as the title suggests, this is a book not only about Gilbert Baker but also about queer history, specifically the creation of the rainbow flag. Details surrounding the creation of the flag are not given full expression. Instead, a two-page spread depicts Baker sitting comfortably in a chair across from a man referred to as "his friend" (Pitman, *Sewing the Rainbow*). The man is shown smiling as Baker holds up a vertical rectangle with eight striped color blocks—a prototype of the Pride flag. Text on the facing page identifies Baker's friend as a man named Harvey, who a reader with queer background knowledge will identify as Harvey Milk. Harvey suggests the need for a symbol to unite the gay and lesbian community under a sign of Pride, which gestures toward queer collaboration while maintaining the focus on Baker found throughout the text.

After the two friends' brief exchange, Baker is portrayed creating what becomes the rainbow flag. Although the narrative states that a group of friends helped Baker create the flag, this is not depicted in illustrations, which continue to show Gilbert alone cutting, dyeing, and sewing two flags. This is a missed opportunity to visually represent the community discussed throughout the biography. In fact, when community is present in *Sewing the Rainbow: A Story about Gilbert Baker*, it is described as a "crowd" that stands in opposition to and judgment of the text's protagonist. After Gilbert completes his project, he prepares to display the flags. Pitman writes, "The big day arrived. A crowd gathered around City Hall. Gilbert held his breath. Would people understand his flags?" (*Sewing the Rainbow*). The use of the singular possessive pronoun "his" depicts the flag less as a community project and community symbol and more as a personal creation, as does the visual focus on Gilbert. The "community" is a crowd of people that Gilbert literally and figuratively stands apart from. The accompanying image is of a white building with a dome shaped roof. A group is shown with their heads turned toward the building on which the flags are displayed. The image on the next page zooms in on a small, racially diverse "crowd" of eight people standing under the flags as they blow in the breeze.

The text concludes with a two-page spread of Gilbert wearing a paper crown underneath the rainbow flag. Pitman writes, "Today, the rainbow flag is everywhere. Even in the small town in Kansas where Gilbert grew up. Whenever you see a rainbow flag, you'll know that it's okay to be your colorful, sparkly, glittery self" (*Sewing the Rainbow*). Community is not represented by the symbol; it is subsumed under the symbol. Even more, the past and present are represented as oppositional, disallowing a sense of continuity and collectivity.

Instead of complementing each other, image and text often appear to be telling different stories. Furthermore, queer community is thematized but never presented within the text. Instead, it is an idea that is gestured toward. Pitman's picture books don't encourage young readers to imagine themselves as part of a collective. Nor do they encourage queer-subjectivity formation, identification with shared or similar experiences and desires. Instead of showing and sharing the community building that Gilbert Baker participated in, a homophobic "before" and queer-affirming "after" are represented with the collective struggle and action that occurred in between largely left out.

Rob Sanders's *Pride: The Story of Harvey Milk and the Rainbow Flag* (2018), published the same year as Pitman's biography of Gilbert Baker, tells the story of the Pride flag through Harvey Milk's role in its creation. The relationship between image and text works to produce a story that reads as both personal and community history. Steven Salerno illustrates the book with a touch of whimsy. It begins with a barefoot Harvey Milk lying on a green paisley background that's reminiscent of grass but clearly artificial. The world is visually positioned at his feet. The text reads, "Harvey Milk was an ordinary man, but he had an extraordinary dream. That dream would change history" (Sander, *Pride*). Milk's dream, that "he and his friends would be treated like everyone else," is visually represented through an image of two white men with wavy brown hair sharing a two-seater bike with a Just Married banner floating behind them. Representing being "treated like everyone else" through access to marriage seems like an anachronistic choice since it was decades before white middle-class gays and lesbians galvanized behind the single issue. Just as the focus on marriage gestures toward the future, characterizing Milk as a dreamer conjures associations with Martin Luther King Jr. and gestures toward the past while bringing gay rights activism into conversation with civil rights activism. This is a generative slippage that doesn't so much collapse time and identity-based differences as subtly bring to light their affinities.

Throughout the book, Sanders emphasizes that Milk sought to change laws by going into politics and motivating his community to demand change. He is a leader, not a loner. Even more, the homophobia experienced and challenged is visually present in Salerno's illustrations, which depict signs with phrases including "Gays must go" and "God says no" (Sander, *Pride*). By presenting homophobia, a reality impossible to avoid in a biography of Milk, Sanders thematizes stigma without introducing feelings of shame. In fact, although Sanders creates an affectively complex text likely to produce feelings of sadness, discomfort, or even anger, he avoids depictions of shame, replacing shame with a story of queer resilience.

It is in his role as an activist and community builder that Milk begins to consider the need for a symbol that will unite the queer community during future marches. A pensive Milk is depicted standing alone in a sea of symbols that include peace signs and recycling signs. The next two-page spread introduces Milk's friend Gilbert Baker, who is depicted at a sewing machine working on a rainbow flag. Unlike in Pitman's version, three people are shown in the background cutting and dyeing cloth. It is a subtle but significant difference from the focus on individual actors and actions foregrounded in Pitman's biography of Gilbert Baker.

The next two-page spread shows the finished project flowing across a cityscape. Milk is illustrated in the left corner, hands raised, smiling in front of street signs that locate him at the intersection of Castro and Market Streets. The text reads, "On June 25, 1978, when it was time for the march, a breeze stirred in San Francisco" (Sander, *Pride*). Small details like marking time and space provide a sense of history, which is lacking in Pitman's version of the text. Also, Sanders represents the unveiling of the Pride flag as part of a larger community event, whereas Pitman describes it as one man's moment to shine. Here, the flag unites a community; there, the flag was an individual achievement to be judged by a crowd.

The representation of the march as a community event continues in the next two-page spread, which shows a community of queers marching behind Harvey as he leads them through the streets of San Francisco under the unifying banner of the rainbow flag. Although Harvey is leading, the collective is present in word and image. Sanders writes, "Harvey and the people asked for equality. They asked to be treated like everyone else. They asked to live and love as they pleased. They hoped the march would make a difference" (*Pride*). Words like "the people" and "they" remind the reader that social action must be collective action to be successful action.

The tone of the text soon changes from one of celebration to one of sorrow. A newspaper with the headline "Moscone, Milk Killed" leaps from a two-page spread (Sander, *Pride*). The dates and text of the paper are illegible, but the image still serves as a reminder that this is nonfiction, historical fact, a point reiterated by the corresponding text, which reads, "Five months later—on the morning of November 27, 1978—Harvey and the mayor of San Francisco, George Moscone, were assassinated. Their lives were taken by a man who did not think like Harvey, or feel like him, or love like him." Sanders is not reticent in his representation of homophobic violence. The reality that people have been and can be murdered for challenging gender and sexual norms, as well as for demanding social change, is a painful one. Sanders's depiction allows readers to feel a sense of loss, which effectively collapses time, encouraging "backward feelings."

The subsequent two-page spread depicts a community in mourning walking through the streets of San Francisco while carrying candles to honor Milk. The mood is contemplative. Although a grieving community is depicted, the collective feeling of loss emphasizes the gains made by Milk as a community builder. The queer collective is his legacy. This is reiterated on the next two-page spread, which depicts rainbow flags spelling the word "hope." Complementary text reads, "More rainbow flags were created. . . . More and more people began to think of the flag as their flag. And they began to feel pride. They began to feel hope" (Sander, *Pride*). Several other depictions of the Pride flag are shown, demonstrating that Milk's legacy of community building and community activism lives on, at least symbolically.

Gilbert Baker is reintroduced as the story flashes forward to 1994, the year he redesigned the Pride flag with six instead of eight stripes. Other images depict the spatial and temporal reach of Milk's legacy. For instance, one image shows the rainbow flag's global reach; another depicts the White House lit up in the colors of the rainbow flag on June 26, 2015, again subtly linking liberation and marriage. The book ends with Milk, sporting a rainbow tie and waving a rainbow flag, dressed up, megaphone at his hip, against a paisley green background like the one in the book's opening image. However, unlike the opening image, which depicts Milk as a dreamer with his eyes closed, here, his eyes are wide open. The text reads, "Equality. Pride. Hope. Love. Harvey's dream became a flag for all of us" (Sander, *Pride*). Harvey, the individual, the dreamer, the leader, frames the story, but his isn't the whole story.

THEN VS. NOW: QUEERING THE CITY

Published in 2017, Gayle E. Pitman's *When You Look out the Window: How Phyllis Lyon and Del Martin Built a Community*, illustrated by Christopher Lyles, unfolds in the first-person plural, producing a sense of intimacy as protagonist-narrators Phyllis Lyon and Del Martin reflect on San Francisco's transformation into a LGBTQ+-affirming community. To track the city's transformation in time, Pitman takes readers on a queer tour of San Francisco's landmarks that can be seen from the couple's home. This technique could allow the narrative to develop as both an intimate personal story and a community history, but the text does not live up to this potential. Instead, by constructing the text as a reflection on progressive change, Pitman creates a binary between the "then" of a homophobic past and the "now" of a transformed present that problematically excludes the work of community building and community struggle required for the social transformation it celebrates. Moreover, by focusing on a couple in the private sphere of the home, queer community and public culture are downplayed.

The book opens with an image of a young Lyon and Martin, arms around each other, with the Golden Gate Bridge in the background. The image locates them in love and in San Francisco. On the next page, the young couple are seen in their newly purchased home as they peer out their window while holding hands. They critique the imperative that lesbian love must remain private and lament the lack of community they experience in San Francisco. Pitman writes, "We saw, quiet streets. Doors tightly shut. So many women who didn't have rights" (*When You*). The critique reads as ironic since the queer utopia the text presents is centered on the home and the lesbian couple.

The next page further develops a critique of "old" San Francisco, focusing on the couple's social isolation and introducing their experience of homophobia. The couple recall what they saw when they left the privacy and security of their home: "People who were afraid of us. People who didn't think we should love each other. No feeling of community" (Pitman, *When You*). The associated illustration depicts five people whose expressions include horror, disgust, and anger at the sight of a lesbian couple. The use of past tense to describe homophobia and lack of community frames time as oppositional, a then and a now to be traversed in the turn of a page.

In fact, the next illustration does just that. The two-page spread offers readers a bird's-eye view of the city that provides a sense of expansiveness in contradistinction to the busy San Francisco street that greeted the lesbian couple in the previous illustration. Although the spread portrays space, it represents a temporal crossing between San Francisco's homophobic past and its queer-affirming present. The sentence "So we worked to change that" accompanies the image (Pitman, *When You*), gesturing toward a history of collective struggle and activism that isn't visually represented or described in the text. Instead, progress appears to be something that occurs naturally as time passes. Image and text contradict each other—as confused as the representational slippage between space and time.

The book ends with images of "new" San Francisco—a city decorated with rainbows, a church that welcomes everyone, and shopping queer couples. Pitman closes the text: "We see a big rainbow community" (*When You*). Again, image and text tell different stories as the spectacle of rainbow objects stand in for the actual community. Queerness appears to be commodified, packaged, and sold. Rainbows identify spaces that welcome queers without depicting queer cultural specificity or community. Instead, queer couples have been accepted into society and can shop and attend church alone or in pairs.

Young readers asked to explain who Lyon and Martin are and what important contributions they made to society—in other words, why they were significant enough figures to warrant a quasibiography—would be hard pressed to think of anything to say. There is, however, detailed back matter. In contrast to the picture book, Pitman's "Reading Guide" is rich with historical detail and specific references to time. The purchase date of the couple's home is referenced as 1953, and their participation in the 1955 founding of Daughters of Bilitis (DOB) as well as the 1966 founding of the National Organization for Women (NOW) are discussed. In this case, the text's back matter does not supplement the historical tale; it is the only place history makes an appearance. In Pitman's "Note to Parents, Caregivers, and Educators," she writes, "Children from historically marginalized groups don't always see positive and empowering images of themselves in books or other forms of media, and their histories aren't always well represented in school materials" (*When You*). Although Pitman has created a positive image of lesbians and introduced children to homophobia, the text doesn't provide readers with access points to identify with the narrators or encourage them to develop an understanding of homophobia, community, or transformative action.

Rob Sanders and Gayle E. Pitman have long dominated the LGBTQ+ nonfiction book market. Well, they're the authors behind the handful of biographies published since 2018 anyway. However, some recent publications are authored by newcomers to the field. One such example is the 2020 biography *Were I Not a Girl: The Inspiring and True Story of Dr. James Barry*, written by Lisa Robinson and illustrated by Lauren Simkin Berke. The cover of the book depicts a white person with long auburn hair wearing a green dress while holding two books. They stare into a golden mirror that depicts an image of a person with much shorter hair wearing a red and gold military uniform. In picture books, this visual trope is often used to depict transgender experience of self. The clothing depicted in the cover image as well as the mirror and other simple decorations lend an old-fashioned feel to the text. This inspiring true story will be about someone, Dr. James Barry, who lived a long time ago.

The text opens by requesting the reader to muse on what it would be like to live in the past. Robinson writes, "Imagine living at a time when you couldn't be the person you felt you were inside. You couldn't be your true self." Robinson continues, "This is a story about someone who refused to let that happen: Dr. James Barry." The story creates a deliberate distance between the present and past. It's suggested that the reader will need to imagine a time when it was difficult, even impossible, to be yourself. Even more, it is alleged that a strong and committed individual has the power to refuse to be constrained by society.

The story then focuses on James Barry, who was born in Ireland around 1789. Robinson explains that James Barry was given the name Margaret Ann Bulkley at birth but used the name James Barry for over fifty years. Robinson then describes James Barry's childhood, which he lived as a girl, with the attendant constraints girls experienced at the time, including lack of education. The author attributes abstract "big dreams" to the child but notes that because girls had a limited number of possibilities, the child's "future looked small" (Robinson). Robinson quotes Barry's own writing in text that reads, "Were I not a girl, I would be a Soldier!" The text laments the limited opportunities experienced by girls in the late 1700s.

When Barry was sixteen, his father abandoned the family. Barry and his mother traveled to England for more opportunities. This is when Barry's namesake, an uncle named James Barry, is introduced into the story. The uncle died, leaving the family some money, and one of his friends agreed to tutor Barry, still living as a young woman, so she might work as a governess.

At this time, Barry discovered an interest in medicine. Robinson reemphasizes that although Barry had an interest in medicine, "women could not become doctors."

The next two-page spread depicts Margaret cutting her hair. The text reads, "So Margaret, who wanted to be a soldier and a doctor, took charge" (Robinson). There doesn't seem to be transgender subjectivity but instead a rejection of gender roles. At this point, Margaret takes on the name of her uncle James Barry, travels to Scotland, and enrolls in medical school. James Barry eventually joins the military and travels the world. One image shows James Barry and a man embracing. The accompanying text explicates that he fell in love, presumably with the man he is embracing. The text ends with the author conceding that much is unknown about James Barry's life but reinforces that he was living his truth. Back matter reaffirms the general ambiguity characterizing James Barry's life. It's noted that he did indeed fall in love with a man, Lord Somerset. Additionally, in an author's note, Robinson suggests that Barry "likely identified as a man." I agree that James Barry was likely what would now be referred to as transgender. Yet I am a bit bothered by how his story is represented. It is implied throughout that James Barry didn't want to be constrained by gender roles, not that he didn't want to be contained by gender. There are nuanced differences.

Many of these issues are avoided in *The Fighting Infantryman: The Story of Albert D. J. Cashier, Transgender Civil War Soldier*, written by Rob Sanders and illustrated by Nabi H. Ali, which provides young audiences access to a fascinating queer historical figure. Like most picture-book biographies, this one begins when the protagonist is a child. As a result, instead of meeting Albert D. J. Cashier on the first page of the book, readers are first introduced to him through his deadname and presenting as a young girl. In subsequent pages, the child grows into a teen. As a child, Cashier often wears boy clothes. Sanders suggests this is because wearing pants is easier when tending sheep and, later, while sailing to America because it is "more practical—and safer— that way" (Sanders, *Fighting Infantryman*).

Once in the United States, the teen begins using the name Albert D. J. Cashier. Sanders doesn't speculate as to why this is. When the Civil War begins, Albert decides to enlist. He passes his physical and begins training. Several pages of the book depict Albert working alongside other soldiers. After the war, Albert continues to live as a man. He collects a military pension and supports himself through farming. Throughout the text, Sanders describes Albert as a true patriot who grows into his identity alongside a country struggling to grow into its identity. Albert lives peacefully after the war until suffering an injury when he is in his sixties. At this point, his doctor and employer learn that Albert "wasn't born a man" (Sanders, *Fighting Infantryman*). However, they agreed not to tell anyone.

Sadly, as Albert's health worsens and more medical professionals examine him, Albert is increasingly vulnerable. Eventually, a nurse tells a reporter that he is not a man, which eventually leads to his participation in the Civil War being questioned as well as his military pension being compromised. At one hospital, Albert is even forced to wear dresses. However, even as he experiences this awful abuse by the medical institution, the soldiers he fought with work to have his military pension continued and his gender identity respected. The government finally agrees.

Upon his death, the men Albert served with ensure he has a full military funeral.

In back matter, Sanders acknowledges the difficulty of identifying Albert's motivations, desires, and identifications. He writes, "We don't know for certain why Albert D. J. Cashier lived his life as a man. Maybe doing so was more comfortable, more convenient, or safer. Maybe Albert lived as a man because it provided him with more opportunities and choices in life. But it's likely that Albert was transgender and identified as a man" (Sanders, *Fighting Infantryman*). Importantly, although Sanders notes that we do not have access to Albert's motivations, throughout the text, he tends to attribute practical motives to Albert's early decision to wear masculine attire. These representations move beyond statements of fact to interpreting and implying motive. My critique is meant to elucidate the real challenges of representing transgender identity in picture-book biographies, especially those of historical characters whose language to describe gender was very limited and whose nuanced motivations and personal identifications are likely inaccessible to contemporary biographers.

ADDITIVE QUEERNESS AND THE STRUGGLE TO DEPICT INTERSECTING MODES OF OPPRESSION

Bayard Rustin (2021), written by J. P. Miller and illustrated by Markia Jenai, is a Rourke Education Media publication. The press creates texts that align with curriculum standards and primarily promotes to libraries and schools. *Bayard Rustin* is part of their Leaders Like Us series, which includes biographies of other Black leaders, including Henry Louis Gates Jr., Shirley Chisholm, and Rebecca Lee Crumpier. Bayard Rustin is portrayed throughout as a Black man with a strong sense of justice. The story begins with the march on Washington in August 1963. The march is described as supporting jobs and freedom, presumably for Black Americans. The story then moves backward in time, depicting the roots of Rustin's activism in his family life. His parents were activists who often entertained civil rights leaders like W. E. B. Du Bois.

Throughout the story, injustices African Americans experienced, including segregation, are discussed to contextualize Rustin's activism as a response to inequality and injustice. Rustin's behind-the-scenes role in the civil rights movement is also noted. Rustin's sexuality is mentioned in an awkward aside. The author writes, "Some people treated Bayard unfairly because he was gay" (J. P. Miller). Whereas the ways Rustin was treated unfairly as an African American are discussed, his arrest for so-called lewd conduct because of the criminalization of homosexuality is not mentioned. Indeed, his posthumous receipt of the Presidential Medal of Freedom, which was awarded by President Barack Obama, was only stated in the back matter, not the story proper. The award was accepted by Rustin's partner, and Obama noted that Rustin would have received it sooner if he wasn't gay.

This picture book depicts Rustin as a Black man, not a Black gay man. Although the authors have a strong sense of how to depict and why they are depicting racism, they are less confident in their depiction of homophobia. This is significant because it represents a struggle to depict intersecting modes of oppression that is found in multiple picture books.

Written by Brad Meltzer and illustrated by Christopher Eliopoulos, *I Am Billie Jean King* is a biography of activist and athlete Billie Jean King. Billie Jean King was confronted with gender inequality in sports as a young girl when she realized that professional sports teams were comprised of men. A friend introduced her to tennis, and with the support of her parents and a coach willing to work with children for free on public courts, Billie Jean King's love for the game grew exponentially. Along with her knowledge of the game, King's awareness of the race and class dimensions of tennis increased. She was uncomfortable with the whiteness and the wealth of her peers and vowed to make the game more accessible when she became a tennis star.

King practiced and practiced. She competed at Wimbledon at the age of seventeen and was ranked number three in the country when she started college. Since women athletes were so undervalued, King did not receive a scholarship, although her future husband—by all accounts, a lesser player—did. Inequities mounted as King continued to play competitively, winning tournaments but getting paid far less for victories than men.

Eventually, Billie Jean King and several other women tennis players, called the Original Nine, created their own tournament to compete with and protest the pay inequalities they experienced. Fans paid to see the women's impromptu tournament. Even though women tennis players had the support of a strong fan base, men continued to harass and bully women players. Bobby Riggs, onetime number one tennis player in the world, challenged Billie Jean King to a match. She refused, but another woman player, Margaret Court, accepted the challenge. She lost. This served as "evidence" of men's superiority. After Riggs's victory against Court, King agreed to play against him. The match, called the Battle of the Sexes, took place in Texas for a $100,000 payday in 1973. King understood that she wasn't just playing for money, she was playing for women and girl athletes everywhere. Billie Jean King won.

Although King's tennis career is centered throughout the text, it clearly intersects with her personal life and her advocacy work. Meltzer explains that around the same time King was preparing for her match with Riggs, she was coming to terms with her sexual identity. She divorced her husband and fell in love with a woman named Ilana. Meltzer writes, "Being gay means that if you're a girl, you love and have romantic feelings for other girls—and if you're a boy, you love and have romantic feelings for other boys." Although children are expected to be able to understand complex descriptions of sexism as well as race and class inequality, they are provided a simplistic, depoliticized, and truncated discussion of sexuality.

Additionally, in word bubbles, readers are provided access to King's thoughts. She explains her love for Ilana, with Eliopoulos illustrating King holding a picture of the two women staring into each other's eyes while clasping hands. The picture book also references King's advocacy work, including testifying before Congress about Title IX and working with her ex-partner Larry to establish World Team Tennis to provide women and men the opportunity to play together as equals. Meltzer mixes comic-like panels linked by narrative text to move the story forward. This allows him to pack in the facts without making the book too text heavy for young readers.

My one, minor issue is the depiction of Billie Jean King. She is represented as the size of a child throughout the text. This includes when she is testifying in front of Congress and playing against Bobby Riggs. Although a feature of the Ordinary People Series that the book is part of, this representation runs the risk of infantilizing a woman in a story about gender equality. Although both books explicitly identify their characters as gay, in neither is sexuality explored as a category of analysis essential to an intersectional depiction of the character's life. I find this problematic as both books explore the character as an activist affected by social identifiers. This is particularly true in Billie Jean King's biography as multiple intersecting identities, particularly class and gender, are considered in tandem.

Rachel Rose's *Megan Rapinoe: Soccer Superstar* portrays Rapinoe's sexuality much like King's is represented. Both characters' coming-out moments are noted, as is their relationship. I find this less problematic in Rose's text as the author doesn't highlight Rapinoe's activism, although her choice to come out is represented as a political act. An image of a smiling Rapinoe holding a Pride Leadership Service Award faces text reading, "In 2012, Megan told the world she is **gay**. She wants to stand up for people. She wants what is fair for everyone" (Rose; emphasis original). Although "gay" is not defined in the text, it does appear in bold and can be found in the glossary. In the following two-page spread, the text-facing image depicts Megan with her girlfriend.

QUEER THERE AND HERE, THEN AND NOW: RUPAUL

After reading many, although certainly not all, currently available LGBTQ+ picture-book biographies, it seems that the way stories of queer pasts are passed down to children employ containment strategies that relegate homophobia and transphobia to history. This limits their usefulness as resources for helping young audiences understand the persistence of regimes of gender and sexual normativity and hierarchy across time and space. Even more concerningly, they appear to assume there is no more work to be done because the heroes of the past have successfully changed the world. As a result, young audiences who do experience homophobia and transphobia may read these as personal instead of collective, social, and political experiences that they share with others—now *and* then, here *and* there.

As noted throughout my analysis, most of the texts discussed focus on individuals not as embedded within communities and not as navigating space and time but as isolated social actors moving through space and time to make change. Little People, Big Dreams' recent picture-book biography simply called *RuPaul* is written by Maria Isabel Sánchez Vegara and illustrated by Wednesday Holmes. The cover features a visual trope often found in picture books about transgender characters. A young Ru with short hair wears masculine, albeit flamboyant, clothes. The child holds up a mirror. It reflects a pink-cheeked Ru with wavy blond hair and pretty earrings. In picture books about transgender girls and boys, women and men, this type of image provides readers access to how transgender characters perceive themselves versus how they are perceived by others.

Within the text, Ru is portrayed as a child who is confident and bold enough to project his unique take on fashion and gender into the world. For instance, in the book's opening image, a young Ru is depicted sitting inside a wardrobe wearing earrings, blue pants, and a green shirt decorated with a rainbow. Text on the facing page provides biographical information about where he grew up (San Diego) as well as who he grew up with (his mother and three sisters). His family is depicted in an image looking at the queerly dressed Ru; hearts surround them demonstrating their love for the child.

Ru is depicted wearing a mix of feminine and masculine clothes in all subsequent images. This appears to demonstrate that Ru was comfortable with his gender expression and the clothes used to construct his unique sense of fashion—even at a young age. However, similar to the cover, a trope often found in books about transgender and nonbinary youth is awkwardly plopped into the text. Two facing pages—one featuring Ru "playing dress-up," the other representing Ru "in real-life"—are juxtaposed (Vegara). Transgender and nonbinary youth as well as effeminate boys are often described as "playing dress-up" to contain their nonnormative gender expression within the realm of make-believe. However, in this book, Ru is wearing feminine attire and has a smile on his face in both images. The difference between "play" and "real-life" is the presence of gawking children in the "real-life scenario." Ru seems unaware and undaunted by the children, uncompromisingly true to himself. Within the text, this self-confidence and queer resilience are related to familial support. For example, the following two-page spread shows Ru's mother lovingly standing behind him, arms wrapped around her child, solidifying a message of love as the author notes that Ru's mom taught him to love himself and do what made him happy. Later images show an older Ru dressed in clothes that defy binary gender expectations while singing in a punk band and attending parties in New York City.

A subtly revised replica of the cover image appears around midway through the text. It is the first of a two-page spread, which depicts a dreamy bedroom with pale-green walls and a bubble-gum-pink floor. This time, it is an adult Ru who looks into the mirror he is holding. He wears a yellow suit with large flowers and pink heels as the young Ru did on the front cover. The image in the mirror is of a woman with blond hair, earrings, and elaborate makeup. The room contains a table scattered with makeup and a table with several wigs. The accompanying text explains that drag was a way for Ru to express himself as an artist. Vegara writes, "He mixed a spoonful of everything he loved and admired, and put his heart into becoming the woman of his dreams." Subsequent images depict Ru in both feminine and masculine attire, and the author notes he is just as comfortable in each.

The book goes on to represent Ru's many career successes from singing to modeling. The popular television show *RuPaul's Drag Race* is also represented. The author notes that "thousands of lonely kids . . . felt that they had finally found their people" (Vegara). This is my favorite two-page spread. It depicts a living room with several children watching *RuPaul's Drag Race*, showing how the television program brought drag into American households, introduced it to children, provided a sense of community, and affirmed identity for queer youth.

IMAGING AND ENACTING A TRANSFORMED WORLD: MARSHA JOHNSON AND SYLVIA RIVERA

Written by Joy Michael Ellison and colorfully illustrated by Teshika Silver, *Sylvia and Marsha Start a Revolution!* (2021) is a fantastic snapshot of queer activist history. In the picture book, Marsha and Sylvia are often represented walking down a city street, arms linked, a golden halo surrounding them. Marsha has dark-brown skin and flowing honey-colored hair. Sylvia's skin is light brown; her wavy hair is both darker and shorter than Marsha's. The women are fierce friends who help each other but also support the queer youth who hang out on New York City's Christopher Street.

Image and text provide brief insights into what motivates the women's community involvement. For instance, early in the text, an image of Sylvia as a child provides readers a glimpse into her past. Sylvia is shown wearing a dress over jeans, head down, as if ashamed. An older woman is seen towering over her. The image is explained in the text: "She remembered what her grandma said when Sylvia wore a dress the first time" (Ellison). Sylvia's grandmother told her that she was a boy and needed to act like it. Ellison immediately challenges this, noting that both Sylvia and Marsha are transgender girls. The experience of vulnerability and pain that Sylvia and Marsha share with each other and with transgender people generally encourages them to imagine a more just future while acting in the present to support the trans community.

Some battles are more easily won than others. For example, in one image, an older cisgender woman is shown pointing at Marsha and proclaiming that she is a man in a dress. Marsha quickly rejoins that she is a woman, and she rejoices in her queer gender expression. This scene is followed by transphobia that is far more difficult to challenge—that of police violence. An image of a feminine person centers the text. Police, framed in gray, are depicted on one side of the centered image; Marsha and Sylvia, framed in bright green, can be seen on the other. The person at the center yells, "Here comes Alice in the blue dress" (Ellison). Below the image, text explains that the phrase is a code used to warn others that the police are coming. Readers are informed that police can arrest transgender women for wearing dresses. Although Martha can laugh at an older woman mocking her dress, she and Sylvia are forced to run when confronted with institutionalized transphobia.

Sylvia and Marsha both desired a transformed world where they would be respected and where their basic human needs would be met. They worked together to create that world. The first focus of their collective action is the Stonewall rebellion of 1969. The two women are shown celebrating Marsha's birthday at the inn. Then, it is raided by police who begin to arrest patrons. Marsha and Sylvia are depicted helping their friends resist arrest. The following day, they joyfully walk down the street only to experience more police harassment. They lament the constant injustice while watching transgender youth run from the police. The women decide to help transgender young people by getting a house they can live in safely. The next image is of a cozy living room. Several people sit around talking comfortably. The accompanying text reads, "Young transgender girls came from miles around to live with Sylvia and Marsha" (Ellison).

The book ends by proclaiming that Marsha and Sylvia "spent their lives fighting for the survival and rights of transgender people" (Ellison). Much of the back matter addresses children. Young readers learn about how Marsha and Sylvia met and that Sylvia was homeless from the age of eleven. There's also a very accessible glossary of terms about gender. Other details are provided to contextualize Sylvia and Marsha's story, including a brief history of the Stonewall rebellion as well as a description of Street Transvestite Action Revolutionaries (STAR). Additional back matter is addressed to parents and teachers. This includes discussion questions, further resources, and extension activities. These features add to the teachability of an already strong text that will make a wonderful addition to libraries.

QUEER COLLECTIVITY: CLEVE JONES

I'm particularly critical of representations and representational strategies in LGBTQ+ picture-book strategies that foreground the individual without paying significant attention to context or community. Rob Sanders newest picture-book biography (as of this writing), *Stitch by Stitch: Cleve Jones and the AIDS Memorial Quilt* (2021), offers a new model for picture-book biographies by placing Cleve Jones within a vibrant activist community to demonstrate the radical relationality that inspires and buttresses activism.

Even the cover of Sanders's latest biography, illustrated by Jamey Christoph, implies that the book will be less about one individual than a collective. It depicts quilt squares placed across the National Mall with the Capitol building centered in the distance. The first two-page spread introduces readers to Cleve as a baby wrapped in a quilt made for him by his great-grandmother. Far less time is spent on Cleve's youth than in most biographies of children. The next two-page spread shows a teenage Cleve sitting on his bed, hand covering his face. The text explains that he was bullied often. The facing page notes that he told his disapproving parents he was gay when he was eighteen. The accompanying image is of Cleve hitchhiking with a sign for San Francisco in his hands. San Francisco is described as "a place where he *might* fit in" (Sanders, *Stitch by Stitch*). Although this does represent the spatial movement from country to city that I have been critical of throughout this essay, Sanders makes it clear that Cleve didn't need to leave his hometown to find himself but instead to be himself within a community of queers.

Cleve finds the community he desires in San Francisco. A two-page spread depicts him walking down the street in San Francisco's Castro District. The text explains that the new friends were "held together by a common thread" (Sanders, *Stitch by Stitch*). The common thread referred to is their collective status "on the fringes" or "outside" straight society.

Cleve's political consciousness and activism is discussed. Cleve enrolled in college, worked for Harvey Milk, and began to advocate for equal rights. Cleve's life and personal experiences are juxtaposed with shifts in the social world around him, including Milk's assassination and the waxing and waning of homophobia. AIDS becomes an intrinsic part of his story, and Sanders brings the uncertainty and urgency of AIDS into the picture book with sensitivity. He doesn't shy away from noting that homophobia influenced the lackluster response to AIDS by the medical field and US government. He writes, "Many people looked down on those with AIDS. Some said they deserved it" (Sanders, *Stitch by Stitch*).

I am critical of picture books that create an opposition between past and present and here and there because this paints an incorrect picture of queer realities. Even more, as Heather Love writes in *Feeling Backward: Loss and the Politics of Queer History*, "Backward feelings serve as an index of the ruined state of the social world; they indicate continuities between the bad gay past and the present; and they show up the inadequacy of queer narratives of progress. Most important, they teach us that we do not know what is good for politics" (27). As my chapter demonstrates, the small but growing archive of nonfiction LGBTQ+ children's picture books often creates a binary between "the bad gay past and the present." Although many substantial changes have indeed been made, these texts too often contain struggle. There is no sense of continuity but instead an awkward rupture between "then" and "now" and a too-simplistic binary between "here" and "there" that fails to account for the persistence of queer shame and the power of the sex-gender-sexuality system to oppress in the biggest of cities.

WORKS CITED

Carruthers, Charlene. *Unapologetic: A Black, Queer, and Feminist Mandate for Radical Movements*. Beacon Press, 2018.

Chambers-Letson, Joshua. *After the Party*. New York UP, 2018.

Ellison, Joy Michael. *Sylvia and Marsha Start a Revolution! The Story of the Trans Women of Color Who Made LGBTQ+ History*. Illustrated by Teshika Silver, Jessica Kingsley, 2021.

It Gets Better. https://itgetsbetter.org/. Accessed 21 Feb. 2024.

Love, Heather. *Feeling Backward: Loss and the Politics of Queer History*. Harvard UP, 2009.

Meltzer, Brad. *I Am Billie Jean King*. Illustrated by Christopher Eliopoulos, Rocky Pond Books, 2019.

Miller, Jennifer. *The Transformative Potential of LGBTQ+ Children's Picture Books*. UP of Mississippi, 2022.

Miller, J. P. *Bayard Rustin*. Illustrated by Markia Jenai, Rourke Educational Media, 2021.

Muñoz, José Esteban. *Cruising Utopia*. New York UP, 2019.

Pitman, Gayle E. *Sewing the Rainbow: A Story about Gilbert Baker*. Illustrated by Holly Clifton-Brown, Magination Press, 2018.

Pitman, Gayle E. *When You Look out the Window: How Phyllis Lyon and Del Martin Built a Community*. Illustrated by Christopher Lyles, Magination Press, 2017.

Robinson, Lisa. *Were I Not a Girl: The Inspiring and True Story of Dr. James Barry*. Illustrated by Lauren Simkin Berke, Schwartz and Wade Books, 2020.

Rose, Rachel. *Megan Rapinoe: Soccer Superstar*. Bearport, 2021.

Sanders, Rob. *Pride: The Story of Harvey Milk and the Rainbow Flag*. Illustrated by Steven Salerno, Random House, 2018.

Sanders, Rob. *Mayor Pete: The Story of Pete Buttigieg*. Illustrated by Levi Hastings, Henry Holt, 2020.

Sanders, Rob. *The Fighting Infantryman: The Story of Albert D. J. Cashier, Transgender Civil War Soldier*. Illustrated by Nabi H. Ali, Little Bee Books, 2020.

Sanders, Rob. *Stitch by Stitch: Cleve Jones and the Aids Memorial Quilt*. Illustrated by Jamey Christoph, Magination Press, 2021.

Vegara, Maria Isabel Sánchez. *RuPaul*. Illustrated by Wednesday Holmes, Frances Lincoln Children's Books, 2021. Little People, Big Dreams 61.

ACKNOWLEDGMENTS

The editors of this volume would like to thank all the contributors, as well as the broader community of queer scholars and activists, who make such work possible.

Jennifer Miller was awarded a Children's Literature Association faculty research grant during the summer of 2021, which allowed her to complete essential research for her chapter. She would like to thank Sara Austin for accepting the invitation to serve as a coeditor. Without her dedication to the project, it would not have been completed.

Rob Bittner's research was funded by the Social Sciences and Humanities Research Council of Canada.

B. J. Woodstein would like to thank her wife, Fi, and their children, Esther and Tovah, for all their support and love. She would also like to extend thanks to Jennifer Miller for inviting her to participate in this important and exciting book.

ABOUT THE CONTRIBUTORS

Sara Austin is an assistant professor of English at Kentucky Wesleyan College. Her interest in race, gender, and childhood identity has yielded articles in *Transformative Works and Cultures*, *The Lion and the Unicorn*, *The Looking Glass: New Perspectives in Children's Literature*, *Journal of the Fantastic in the Arts*, *International Research in Children's Literature*, *Research on Diversity in Youth Literature*, *Adaptation*, and the *Journal of Graphic Novels and Comics*. Her book *Monstrous Youth* (Ohio State UP, 2022) explores monstrosity as a cultural metaphor for child identity.

Rob Bittner has a PhD in gender, sexuality, and women's studies (Simon Fraser University) and is also a graduate of the MA in children's literature program at the University of British Columbia's (UBC) iSchool in Vancouver, BC. He studies and writes about a wide range of literature but particularly enjoys stories with diverse and intersectional depictions of gender and sexuality. Email: rob_bittner@sfu.ca.

J. Bradley Blankenship completed his PhD in education from Indiana University. He is the author of multiple diverse picture books and early readers, including *The Christmas Truck* (NarraGarden, 2014), a Christmas story that features two dads, a nonbinary kid, and a fire-chief grandmother. He currently works as a curriculum consultant in Chicago, Illinois, where he lives with his husband and two dogs.

Gabriel Duckels is an Early Career Research Fellow at Fitzwilliam College, University of Cambridge. His research has been published in various places, including the *Children's Literature Association Quarterly* and the *Journal of European Cultural Studies*.

Caitlin Howlett is an assistant professor of Education Studies at DePauw University and thinks, talks, and writes about critical sexual pedagogies, anti-capitalist sex education, and the role of speculative imagination in education. She is the author of *Against Sex Education: Pedagogy, Sex Work, and State Violence* (Bloomsbury, 2021) and has authored articles that have been published in *Educational Theory*, *Philosophical Studies in Education*, and *Issues in Teacher Education*.

Isabel Millán is an assistant professor in the Department of Women's, Gender, and Sexuality Studies at the University of Oregon. Her book *Coloring into Existence: Queer of Color Worldmaking in Children's Literature* (New York UP, 2023) analyzes queer and trans of color children's picture books across Canada, the United States, and Mexico. She is also the author and illustrator of the award-winning queer, bilingual children's picture book *Chabelita's Heart / El corazón de Chabelita* (Reflection Press, 2022). Her other publications include articles in *Signs* and *Aztlán* as well as chapters in *Graphic Borders: Latino Comics Past, Present, and Future*, *The Routledge Companion to Latina/o Popular Culture*, and *Keywords for Comic Studies*. Millán specializes in critical ethnic studies, transnational feminist and queer theories, children's literature and media, comics, and science fiction. Website: IsabelMillan.com.

Jennifer Miller is a high school teacher in Arlington, Texas. She has published scholarship about children's literature, LGBTQ+ identity and culture, and digital culture in many journals and edited collections. Her first book, *The Transformative Potential of LGBTQ+ Children's Picture Books* (UP of Mississippi, 2022), identifies and analyzes over 150 US-based picture books with explicit LGBTQ+ representation. Jennifer is invested in public-facing scholarship and open-access scholarship. She coedited and contributed to *Introduction to LGBTQ+ Studies: A Cross-Disciplinary Approach* (State U of New York P, 2022), the first open-access LGBTQ+ studies textbook of its kind. Additionally, she managed a book-review blog, *Raise Them Righteous* (RaiseThemRighteous.com), from 2018 to 2022. The blog features over one hundred reviews of LGBTQ+ picture books. Email: jlmiller1@gmail.com.

Kaylee Jangula Mootz recently received her PhD in the Department of English at the University of Connecticut. Her dissertation explores the ways that Native and Black kinship relations shape temporality in Native and African American fiction. Kaylee's work has been published in the *Journal of* *the Fantastic in the Arts* and in the collection *Beyond the Blockbuster: Themes and Trends in Contemporary Young Adult Fiction*.

Tim Morris is professor of English at the University of Texas at Arlington and has written about children's books in *Making the Team* (U of Illinois P, 1997) and *You're Only Young Twice* (U of Illinois P, 2000), as well as in essays with topics ranging from the Hardy Boys to bullfighting fiction for children.

Dana Rudolph is the founder and publisher of the two-time GLAAD Media Award–winning blog *Mombian*. She also writes one of the longest-running newspaper columns for and about LGBTQ+ parents, which runs in several LGBTQ+ papers around the United States. She was honored in 2018 with the Hostetter-Habib Family Award from Family Equality for her commitment to their core values. One of her special areas of focus is LGBTQ+-inclusive children's literature, and her Mombian Database of LGBTQ Family Books contains her reviews of most titles for ages zero to twelve. She has a BA (summa cum laude) from Wellesley College in medieval/renaissance studies and astronomy and an MPhil from Oxford University in history.

j wallace skelton is a PhD candidate in curriculum teaching and learning at the Ontario Institute for Studies in Education. j's project is coresearching with Two-Spirit, lesbian, gay, bisexual, transgender, queer (2SLGBTQ) children and children from 2SLGBTQ+ families what school and learning could be like if it was designed by children. j uses qualitative arts-based methods. j's worked in public education for fifteen years, looking to make more room and possibilities for children of diverse sexual orientations and gender identities. j's master's work looked at trans representations in picture books, and what j found led to them launching Flamingo Rampant, a feminist, queer, diverse micro press. j's writing has appeared in *Trans Studies Quarterly*, numerous book chapters, the Canada Broadcasting Corporation, TVOntario, the *Globe and Mail*, and *Xtra!* j is currently editing a trans anthology for young readers (https://www.annickpress.com/News/2020/Call-for-submissions!-Trans-Anthology-for-Young-Readers) and writing a book about teaching and parenting toward justice for Book*hug. Both books are anticipated for 2025. Website: jwallaceskelton.com.

Jason Vanfosson works as an associate professor of youth literature and cultures at West Chester University of Pennsylvania and received the 2023–24 Wilma Dykeman Faces of "Appalachia" Post-Doctoral Research Fellowship from the Appalachian Studies Association for his work on queer Appalachian youth literature. His research has been published or is forthcoming in *Beyond the Blockbusters: Themes and Trends in Contemporary Young Adult Fiction*, *Reading LGBTQ+ Children's Picture Books*, *Research on Diversity in Youth Literature*, and *Pennsylvania Reads*.

J. River Vooris is an LGBTQ Studies scholar whose work focuses on children's gender and sexuality. They were an assistant professor of women's, transgender, and queer studies at Wells College in Aurora, New York until it closed in June 2024. They previously taught at DePauw University, Amherst College, Dickinson College, and the University of Maryland. Vooris is currently working on a project about LGBTQ+ summer camps, and writing blog posts for their website: *The Spaces in Between*, riverhuntervooris.com.

B. J. Woodstein (formerly B. J. Epstein) is Honorary Professor in Literature and Translation at the University of East Anglia in England. She's also a doula, lactation consultant, writer, editor, and Swedish-to-English translator. Her most recent book is *Translation Theory for the Practicing Translator* (Anthem Press, 2024), and she is also the author of *Translation and Genre* (Cambridge UP, 2022), *We're Here! A Practical Guide to Becoming an LGBTQ+ Parent* (Praeclarus Press, 2022), *The Portrayal of Breastfeeding in Literature* (Anthem Press, 2021), *Are the Kids All Right? The Representation of LGBTQ Characters in Children's and Young Adult Literature* (Intellect Books, 2013), *Translating Expressive Language in Children's Literature* (Peter Lang, 2012), and *Ready, Set, Teach!* (Studentlitteratur, 2005), a textbook for usage in English as a foreign-language course. Additionally, she is the editor of two books on translation in the Nordic countries and coeditor of both *International LGBTQ+ Literature for Children and Young Adults* (Anthem Press, 2021) and *Queer in Translation* (Routledge, 2017). She has also translated many works from Swedish, including children's books such as *The Book That Did Not Want to Be Read* (Puffin, 2021) and *The Summer of Diving* (Triangle Square, 2022). B. J. lives with her wife and their children. Email: bjwoodstein@gmail.com.

INDEX

ABC book. *See* alphabet book
absorption, 12, 230, 232–34, 240
abuse, 68, 107, 108, 122, 189, 224, 248, 269
activism, 8, 20, 57, 61–62, 83, 96, 169n3, 177, 194–202, 202n5, 248, 252n1, 262–63, 265, 269, 271, 275. *See also* Stonewall
Adeyoha, Angel, 10, 46, 53, 59, 84, 91, 153–54, 156, 158–60, 162–64, 166–68, 169n3
adoption, 34, 119, 123, 138
aesthetic of joy, 208
Ahmed, Sara, 209, 210
AIDS, 12, 20, 110, 199, 239–52, 252n1, 257, 275
Alam, Rumaan, 52
ally, 6, 99, 212, 213, 216, 218n9
alphabet book, 11, 207–21, 218
American Sign Language (ASL), 214
Anderson, Airlie, 223, 227–28
animals, 11, 26, 30, 32–33, 48, 82–83, 118, 121–23, 127, 129, 137, 146, 208, 222–23, 234. *See also* multispecies justice; nonhuman
antisocial thesis, 242–43
Antonio's Card/La Tarjeta de Antonio, 44, 47
Ariès, Philippe, 111n3
art, 44, 104–5, 178, 181, 190–91, 195, 216, 228, 243–50
Asha's Mums, 41, 43
Austrian, J. J., 27–28
awards, 81, 185, 193, 197, 199, 213, 269, 271

backmatter, 98, 247
Bailey, Marlon M., 190, 200
Baker, Gilbert, 256, 259–63
Barad, Karen, 232
Barry, James, 256–57, 266–67
bildungsroman, 164

biography(ies), 8, 12, 96–101, 106, 110, 190–99, 239–52, 255–75
BIPOC (Black, Indigenous, and people of color), 82–83, 90
bisexual, 3, 11, 19, 34, 39, 52n1, 57, 73n2, 73n4, 82, 97, 127, 129n1, 135, 153, 156, 172, 190, 210, 222, 235n1, 238, 255
Bishop, Rudine Sims, 72, 88, 155
Bittner, Robert, 7, 13, 56, 58, 102, 170n11
Black/African American, 48–49, 82–83, 89, 111n3, 197, 213, 230–31, 240, 243–46, 251, 252n2, 257–58, 269–70
Blankenship, J. B., 5, 10, 14, 183
Boenke, Mary, 58, 60, 62, 64–65, 69–70
Brannen, Sarah, 21, 23–24, 26, 33–34
bride, 27–28, 31
Brown, Tami Lewis, 244, 246, 248
Burgess, Matthew, 243, 250, 251
Buttigieg, Pete, 257

Canada, 71, 89, 157, 207, 211
Carr, Jennifer, 100, 106, 109
Carruthers, Charlene, 257–58
Cashier, Albert D. J., 257, 267–68
censorship, 216, 218n2, 245, 247
Chambers-Letson, Joshua, 257
Charles, RuPaul, 189–200, 257, 271–73
Chin-Lee, Cynthia, 21, 24–25, 26
cisgender, 11, 98, 99, 101–3, 106–7, 117, 122–23, 135, 146, 192, 218n3, 240, 274
classroom, 14, 63, 71, 87, 89, 103, 165, 216, 249
Coats, Karen, 208
collective liberation, 257
colonize/colonization/colonizing, 157, 162, 164–68, 169n1, 207, 224. *See also* decolonize/decolonization/decolonizing

283

Combs, Bobbie, 209
Conan, Neal, 47
Corneau, Michelle, 169n2
Cox, Laverne, 8, 80, 197, 200. *See also* activism
critical optimism, 249, 256, 257
Cullen, Myles, 30
Cummings, Marti Gould, 195, 197

Daughters of Bilitis (DOB), 265
deadname, 104, 112n4, 267
death, 85, 244, 248, 249, 251. *See also* violence
decolonize/decolonization/decolonizing, 157, 168
Delaney, Samuel R., 246
dePaola, Tomie, 57, 85, 88
Desmond Is Amazing, 190, 191, 193, 194, 197, 199, 200
disability, 8, 71, 82–84, 90, 173, 209, 214–15, 225
Doherty, Carroll, 47
Doshi, Payal, 52
Dubose, Juan, 244–46, 250–51, 252n2
dysphoria, 107, 110

Edelman, Lee, 242–43
elders, 10, 154, 156, 165, 170n12
Ellison, Joy Michael, 83, 202n5, 252n1, 256, 257, 274–75
Elwin, Rosamund, 41–42
empathy, 110, 255
Epstein, B. J., 3–4, 14111, 22, 81, 103, 117, 118, 119, 120, 123, 124, 128, 129, 147
equity, 57, 58, 79, 222, 229, 240
estrangement, 12
Ewert, Marcus, 57, 96
Ewing, Chana Ginelle, 209

fairy tales, 31–33, 189, 226. *See also* mermaids; princesses
Farr, Rachel, 37–38
Ferguson, Roderick, 225
Firebaugh, Marisa, 207
Flamingo Rampant Press, 5, 14, 53, 58, 59, 71, 74, 91, 92, 94, 165, 170, 207
Ford, Elizabeth, 4
Foucault, Michel, 224

Gabriel, Dani, 96, 100, 105
Gale, Heather, 169n2
Garden, Nancy, 42–43, 52

Gartrell, Nanette, 37–38
Garvey, John, 246
Gates, Gary, 49
gender: binary, 11, 28, 80, 87, 122, 157, 161, 164, 190, 192, 193, 217; identity, 10, 37, 62, 79, 84, 99–110, 153, 160, 163, 167, 198, 210, 213, 215, 228, 232, 268; presentation, 27, 99, 108, 109, 112n4. *See also* nonbinary
Genette, Gerard, 253n4
Genhart, Michael, 47–48
Gianino, Mark, 52
Giorno, John, 246
Gipson, Cynthia Kay, 49
GLAAD, 33. *See also* activism; heteronormativity
Goldberg, Abbie E., 38, 49, 52
Gonzalez, Maya, 208–10, 212–17
González, Rigoberto, 44
Goodridge v. Department of Public Health, 19, 38
Gould, Lois, 57, 96
Green, Bernadette, 51
groom, 21, 27–28
Gubar, Marah, 99, 110

Haack, Daniel, 31–33, 35n3
Hahn, Daniel, 218n1
Halberstam, Jack, 11, 191, 250
Hall, Gae, 73n2
Haring, Kay A., 249
Hartman, Saidiya, 224
healthcare, 20, 34, 107
Heather Has Two Mommies, 21, 40, 43, 71, 97
Hernandez, Catherine, 207, 209–10, 212–17, 218n8
Herthel, Jessica, 57, 89, 96
heteronormativity, 6, 20–21, 23, 25–29, 33–34, 57–58, 80, 87, 126, 131n23, 164, 172–73, 178, 190–92, 202n3, 229, 240, 243, 256. *See also* homonormativity; homophobia
Higonnet, Anne, 111n3
HIV, 20, 246, 249. *See also* AIDS
homonormativity, 4, 124, 239–43, 246. *See also* heteronormativity; homophobia
homophobia, 12, 23, 24, 47, 141, 165–67, 199, 256, 261–62, 263, 264–66, 269, 271, 275. *See also* heteronormativity; homonormativity
hooks, bell, 246

Hull, Kathleen, 19–20, 25, 26
human rights, 198, 217
Hunt, Peter, 218n1
Huskey, Melynda, 4, 97, 98

ideology, 29
Ignatiev, Noel, 246
imagination, 11–12, 84, 184, 191, 222–23, 233, 258, 282
immigration, 20, 82
Indian. *See* Indigenous
Indigenous, 82, 89, 137, 155–57, 165, 168n1, 169nn2–3, 207, 218n9, 224
injustice, 8, 11, 82, 89, 218, 255, 258, 269, 274
innocence, 98–99, 110, 111n3, 145, 192, 207, 240, 243, 245
InterACT, 45, 73n5. *See also* activism; heteronormativity
intersex, 65, 69, 73n5, 235n1. *See also* gender; sex
IVF, 119

Jennings, Jazz, 57, 89, 96, 100–102, 109
Johnson, Marsha P., 190, 193, 202n5, 213, 252n1, 256, 274. *See also* Rivera, Sylvia; Stonewall
Jones, Cleve, 257, 274–75
justice, 7, 11–13, 24, 39, 58, 89, 90, 171, 208, 215, 223, 225, 232, 233, 257, 258, 269. *See also* activism; human rights

Katz, Robert, 29
Kelley, Robin D. G., 231
Kibblesmith, Daniel, 187n1
Kidd, Kenneth, 3, 5, 136
kinship, 224, 229
King, Billie Jean, 269–71
Kirst, Seamus, 50–51
Kracht, Michael, 208
Krutzsch, Brett, 251

Labelle, Sophie, 58, 68, 187n1
Lakota, 153, 155, 163, 169n1, 169n3. *See also* Indigenous
Langhout, Regina Day, 37, 42
Lester, Jasmine, 4
library, 13, 57, 60, 63, 69, 70–71, 81, 109, 112n6, 169n2, 185, 190, 191, 193, 201, 218n2, 219, 257
Lil Miss Hot Mess, 190, 192–95, 198
Litovich, Marianna, 37, 42

Little People, Big Dreams (book series), 193, 197, 271
Lorde, Audre, 197, 258
Lots of Mommies, 40–43, 50
Love, Jessica, 23
Love Is Love, 43, 47–49, 51
Lukoff, Kyle, 57, 111n1
Lyon, Phyllis, 256, 264–65

Mankiller, Wilma, 166. *See also* Indigenous
Martin, Del, 264–65
Martinez, Jason, 58, 66–67
Mason, Derritt, 164
McKenzie, Mia, 197
McRuer, Robert, 4
McWhorter, Ladelle, 225
Meadow, Tey, 105, 112n7
mermaids, 68, 100, 147, 214. *See also* fairy tales
Meltzer, Brad, 269–70
microaggressions, 7, 37–52. *See also* heteronormativity; violence
Mile, Tobias, 187n1
Millán, Isabel, 5, 11, 218n6
Miller, Jennifer, 5, 13–14, 67, 107, 135, 145, 198, 202n6, 218n7, 239, 241, 249, 255, 256
Miller, J. P., 257, 268–69
Milk, Harvey, 260–64, 275
M Is for Mustache: A Pride ABC Book, 11, 207, 209–11, 213–18
Molly's Family, 42, 43, 49, 50
Montez, Ricardo, 244, 245–46, 252n2
Morrison, Eleanor, 209
Mossiano, Lilly, 58, 67
multispecies justice, 232. *See also* animals
Muñoz, José Esteban, 210, 218, 242–43, 257
My Footprints, 48, 49

Nagara, Innosanto, 209
Naidoo, Jamie, 3–4, 81, 103, 122, 142
Native/Native American. *See* Indigenous
Newman, Lesléa, 4, 21, 25–26, 40–41, 45, 52, 59, 71, 73n6
Newton, Esther, 190, 200
New York, 24, 190, 193, 195, 244–46, 249–51, 253n3, 256, 272, 273
Nodelman, Perry, 164, 218n1, 247
nonbinary, 7, 8, 56, 59, 60, 64–65, 67, 80, 125, 129n1, 156, 157, 193, 196, 209, 213, 215, 218n11, 272. *See also* gender

nonhuman, 11–12, 23, 122, 222–23, 228–29, 232, 234. *See also* animal
norm-critical, 118, 129
Norton, Jody, 4, 70, 108, 215
Norway, 117, 119–20, 129, 130n2

Obergefell v. Hodges, 19, 21, 26, 29, 31, 39
op de Beeck, Natalie, 129n1

Papa, Daddy, and Riley, 50
Paulse, Michele, 41–42
Peck, Richard, 59
pedagogy/pedagogical, 8, 13, 61, 64, 102–3, 117–18, 121–29, 130n9, 130n13, 194, 218n1, 241, 247, 248, 250, 252
pedophiles, 57, 192, 201
Pence, Charlotte, 29–31
Pence, Mike, 29–31
peritextual, 247
PFLAG, 58, 65, 73n3, 106, 112n10
Pleck, Elizabeth, 23
Phi, Bao, 48
Pike, Olly, 223, 226–28
Pitman, Gail E., 58, 69–70, 256, 259–62, 264–66
POC (people of color), 49, 82, 83, 90, 208, 218n
Pollit, Amanda, 20
pow wow, 153–56, 158–63, 166. *See also* Indigenous; Lakota
pride, 41, 49, 154, 197, 209–10, 212, 263, 264. *See also* heteronormativity
Pride (event), 49–50, 185, 189–90, 192–93, 197–200, 211–12, 214, 216, 252, 260. *See also* heteronormativity
Pride/rainbow flag, 163, 198, 200, 212, 260–64, 271
princesses, 31–32, 35n3, 100, 109, 132, 136, 145–48, 189, 226. *See also* fairy tales
pronouns, 61, 63–64, 66–67, 71, 104–5, 109, 112n4, 125, 131n19, 156, 170n10, 173, 210, 212–14, 217
protest, 46, 195–96, 198, 260

queer and trans of color, 11, 207–10, 213, 215, 217
queer history, 182, 223–24, 243–44, 246, 248, 251, 253n3, 260, 275. *See also* Johnson, Marsha P.; Rivera, Silvia; Stonewall
queer pedagogy, 247

rainbow, 3, 47, 52, 58, 59, 73n2, 106, 121, 130n1, 163, 189, 196, 200, 209–10, 259–66, 272, 277
Rapinoe, Megan, 257, 271
Reflection Press, 5, 208, 218n6
resilience, 6–8, 37–49, 52, 98, 101, 148, 262, 272
responsibility, 12, 79, 82, 85, 86, 103, 168n1, 177, 230–33, 245
Rifkin, Mark, 170n7
Rivera, Sylvia, 190, 193, 202n5, 256, 274. *See also* Johnson, Marsha P.; Stonewall
Rivers, Daniel, 11, 191
Robinson, Lisa, 256, 257, 266–67
Rose, Rachel, 257
Ross, Eric, 21
Royce, Ellie, 190, 197, 199
Rubin, Henry, 8, 80
RuPaul. *See* Charles, RuPaul
RuPaul's Drag Race, 189, 191, 200, 273
Russell, David L., 208
Rustin, Bayard, 257, 268–69

same-sex parents, 7, 37–40, 43, 45, 47, 49–50, 52, 52n1, 136, 148
Sanders, Rob, 256, 257, 261–69, 275
San Francisco, 184–85, 256, 259–63, 264–65, 275
Scandinavia, 9, 117–19, 125, 127–28, 130n2
Schiffer, Miriam B., 45–46
Sendak, Maurice, 143
Severance, Jane, 40
sexuality, 12, 20, 56, 57, 72, 99, 111, 137, 142, 157, 173, 177, 178, 190–92, 198, 199, 223–25, 229, 231, 241, 243–45, 248, 251, 258, 269–71
silence, 83, 147, 165, 240, 247, 248, 252
Smith, Cynthia Leitich, 52, 154
Smith-Gonzalez, Matthew, 208–15
social justice, 7, 24, 58, 90, 208, 223, 225. *See also* human rights
Somerville, Siobhan B., 225
sovereignty, 157, 164, 167, 168
Spade, Dean, 107
Stella Brings the Family, 45
Stockton, Kathryn Bond, 11, 191, 198
Stonewall, 190, 193, 197, 199, 200, 202n5, 274. *See also* Johnson, Marsha P.; queer history; Rivera, Sylvia
straight (heteronormativity), 88, 135, 141, 147–48, 164, 212, 259, 275
Stryker, Susan, 190, 225
Sweden, 117–20, 123, 128–29, 130n2

Talburt, Susan, 11, 191
Taylor, Nathan, 4, 240, 242
Texier, Ophélie, 136–37
Thaler, Mathias, 231, 232
They, She, He: Easy as ABC, 11, 207, 209, 211, 218
Toronto, 211–13
toys, 57, 68, 100–101, 174, 182, 223
transformation, 13, 107, 226, 264
transition: medical, 60, 107, 111; social, 67–71, 98–101, 104–11. *See also* gender; nonbinary
transphobia, 165–67, 228, 256, 271, 273–74. *See also* gender; homophobia; nonbinary
Travers, Ann, 97, 106, 107, 112n9
tree (as pronoun), 214, 218n6
Trites, Roberta Seelinger, 164
tropes, 26, 88, 89, 118, 256
Trump, Donald J., 29
Twiss, Jill, 29–30

unicorn, 72, 196
United States v. Windsor, 39
US Supreme Court, 19, 26–27, 39, 59, 185

Vegara, Maria Isabel Sánchez, 190, 193, 195–98, 202n7, 257, 271, 272
violence, 20, 72, 87, 89, 157, 165, 224, 225, 243, 263, 274. *See also* death

Walton, Jessica, 222, 223, 225–26, 228
Warner, Michael, 20, 30
Webb, M. L., 209
West, Candace, 100
Who's Your Real Mum?, 51
Willhoite, Michael, 21–23, 26
Woodstein, B. J. *See* Epstein, B. J.

ze (as pronoun), 212
Zero Dads Club, The, 46–47, 59, 62, 84
Zimmerman, Don, 100
Zolotow, Charlotte, 57, 87

www.ingramcontent.com/pod-product-compliance
Lightning Source LLC
Chambersburg PA
CBHW022000220426
43663CB00007B/898